What it Means to Write About Art

What it Means to

Write About Art

Interviews with art critics
by Jarrett Earnest

David Zwirner Books

For Betsy Baker

Jarrett Earnest
Some Ways of Writing about Art in the Twenty-First Century   6

Hilton Als   16
John Ashbery   28
Bill Berkson   38
Yve-Alain Bois   48
Huey Copeland   68
Holland Cotter   84
Douglas Crimp   102
Darby English   120
Hal Foster   144
Michael Fried   160
Thyrza Nichols Goodeve   186
Dave Hickey   206
Siri Hustvedt   230
Kellie Jones   244
Chris Kraus   258
Rosalind Krauss   272
Lucy Lippard   284
Fred Moten   304
Eileen Myles   322
Molly Nesbit   338
Jed Perl   354
Barbara Rose   374
Jerry Saltz   390
Peter Schjeldahl   408
Barry Schwabsky   428
Paul Chaat Smith   442
Roberta Smith   460
Lynne Tillman   478
Michele Wallace   492
John Yau   510

Acknowledgments   527
Further Reading   531
Index   547

Some Ways of Writing about Art in the Twenty-First Century

Jarrett Earnest

The one duty we owe to history is to re-write it. That is not the least of the tasks in store for the critical spirit.

—Oscar Wilde, "The Critic as Artist" (1891)

Art criticism is really a kind of speculative fiction—*The World According to Rosalind Krauss*, or *Dave Hickey's Fantastic Planet*, or *The Moons of Lynne Tillman*. Flora and fauna, weights and measures—not to mention who lives there and what they enjoy—vary wildly from one writer's body of work to the next. Contrasting Krauss's with Hickey's writing on Ed Ruscha—an artist they both admire—is like slipping between alternate universes. That both of their very different arguments are anchored in the artwork, materially and historically, illustrates the inherent multiplicity of form, the ability to generate manifold meanings that makes something "art" in the first place. These disparate takes coexist in a multiverse we call art criticism. Every value judgment and distinction in "quality"—the usual expectations of criticism—manifests a particular worldview, formed by highly contingent emotional, intellectual, and aesthetic predispositions, making it all the more surprising how little attention is paid to understanding critics' perspectives. I always want to know, *Who is this person and what do they want from art?* Which is another way of asking, *What do they want from life?*

This collection aims to show that these thirty critics, theorists, historians, and thinkers are each unique in their approach and underlying motivations, while all engaging in essentially the same activity— finding words for visual art. It's worth pointing out that this unifying gesture will horrify many of them. (Participants in a 2001 *October* roundtable on criticism that included Hal Foster and Rosalind Krauss made a special point of beating the "belletristic" criticism of Hickey and Peter Schjeldahl like a piñata, declaring it devoid of "critical rigor." And that's but one of many antagonisms.) Frank O'Hara's line, supposedly quoting Franz Kline, that "to be right is the most terrific personal state that nobody is interested in" sums up my approach to the history and the future of criticism. I aim to move away from tedious cries of "crisis" and tiresome brawls over "good" or "bad" to instead understand what is striking about any given critic's work—the nuances of how they approach writing and the way these styles and tactics become meaningful across a body of work and, perhaps more importantly for the purposes of this collection, over the course of a life.

The cultural context for every polemic or appreciation is always in motion, shifting kaleidoscopically through time. Objects don't change, but social and historical forces do, continually. Art and criticism are both *highly relational*, and one ambition of this book is to sketch how each critic sees the particular formations of their work. My hope is that putting these often contradictory perspectives together will let them inflect each other, creating a holographic sense of a past that shapes our present and future discussions. Thus my deliberately anachronistic use of the word "means" in the book's title, *What it Means to Write About Art*—meaning itself is the slippery byproduct of human intention and attention.

Two books have been vital to shaping the one you're now holding: Linda Montano's *Performance Artists Talking in the Eighties* (2000) and Amy Newman's *Challenging Art: Artforum 1962-1974* (2000). Montano is herself an artist, and *Performance Artists Talking* was a decade-long "talking performance." She interviewed a hundred artists about how "Sex," "Food," "Money/Fame," and "Ritual/Death" related to their work. What struck me most was her willingness to push the conversation into uncomfortable places. For instance, the book opens confrontationally with Vito Acconci. Montano begins, "I would like to ask you about sex because your work reflects that theme, even though you indicated that you didn't want to be identified that way. Can we talk about it just the same?" Acconci pushes back, the way anyone might. They continue talking, largely about how language constructs and constricts both art and identity, using their exchange in real time as a case study. Montano sticks with him, step for step, until eventually Acconci is comfortable enough to loop back: "Now that we've gotten an atmosphere of talking, we can go back to that first question. As a child, sex had the same kind of mystification that religion had . . . "

In contrast to the generic questions I knew from journalistic interviews, Montano showed me what it would be like to highlight tussling intersubjectivity. Foregrounding the interviewer, who brings his or her own weird desires, curiosities, and eccentricities into the exchange, could illuminate an artist's work in more complex ways, expanding

8

the understanding of "discourse" itself.

Similarly, in *Challenging Art*, Amy Newman conducted individual interviews with the original participants of *Artforum*, including Philip Leider, John Coplans, Rosalind Krauss, Michael Fried, Barbara Rose, Max Kozloff, Annette Michelson, Sidney Tillim, Robert Pincus-Witten, and Peter Plagens. She then chopped the transcripts up, shaping each flamboyant proclamation into a perfectly faceted jewel within the larger setting of the book. Her own voice is removed, but you sense her presence and intelligence in the structure and montage, like that of a filmmaker. The resulting polyphony conveys the *human, all too human* dynamics that drive culture and constitute intellectual history.

*　*　*

After graduating from the San Francisco Art Institute in 2009, I moved to New York City, intent on having an adventure and figuring out how to write in the process. As an artist myself, I felt I knew how to talk about art and that doing interviews would be a kind of back door into becoming a writer. Through my late teacher, the poet and critic Bill Berkson (who is also interviewed here), I met Phong Bui, publisher of the monthly arts newspaper *The Brooklyn Rail*, which features four or five long interviews in every issue. As I read through its eclectic assortment of "artists' artists," I began to see it as an alternative oral history of the last few decades of art in New York. (In 2017, I was lucky enough to coedit sixty of these into the volume *Tell Me Something Good: Artist Interviews from The Brooklyn Rail*, also published by David Zwirner Books.) The *Rail* gave me a free hand to interview whomever I wanted and to experiment with different forms—including an often incomprehensible "epistolary glossary" with Richard Tuttle that spread over three issues and a prolonged analysis of Nina Simone's devastating performance of "Feelings" (1976) in a discussion of Giovanni Bellini's San Zaccaria altarpiece (1505) with Lisa Yuskavage. In the *Rail* I published idiosyncratic conversations with artists including

Nayland Blake, Christo, Robert Gober, Barbara Hammer, Roni Horn, Lorraine O'Grady, Genesis Breyer P-Orridge, Luc Tuymans, Dana Schutz, Jack Whitten, and Martha Wilson, among many others. This openness helped me find my own voice in ways that would have been impossible at a mainstream magazine. That voice, in turn, helped clarify my larger project as a writer in the art world.

When preparing to conduct an interview, I gather everything that's been written on or by the subject—all the reviews, interviews, catalogues, and books—and read them sequentially, in chronological order. Through this process, you see that the language around some-one's work gets set very quickly and continues to be recycled for decades. Reading the complete body of critical writing on a specific artist is like tracing the rings of a tree—a cross section of growth in time. You begin to sense the underlying shape of their thought, and how the artist is in a dynamic exchange with their critics, attempting to steer conversations in certain directions in response to what is being written. I also focus on the art itself, attending as closely as possible to how it looks and the way it was made. Often, I'm trying to identify the things an artist strategically avoids speaking about, which their work nonetheless suggests. Artists are always trying to understand new aspects of what they've done—being paradoxically and essentially both inside and outside of it—and these conversations become forms of collaboration, ways of inventing new language that fits their work more precisely.

Over a few years of interviewing artists every month, a couple of writers slipped into the mix, beginning with Dave Hickey, while we were both residents at the Robert Rauschenberg Foundation in Captiva, Florida, in 2014. Aside from being really fun, that discussion directly addressed some of my actual questions about the mechanics of writing. At the end of 2016, in dialogue with the *Rail*'s then managing editor Laila Pedro, I framed the idea of publishing a year of conversations with different writers on art in *The Brooklyn Rail*, under the title "Close Encounters." Around the same time, through ongoing talks about literature, criticism, poetry, and philosophy with Lucas Zwirner, Lucas and I conceived of bringing these and additional interviews together as a book (about half being published previously, often in altered form, with the rest appearing here for the first time). Taken together, they argue for approaching and evaluating criticism as itself essentially creative—that writing criticism is a craft that contributes palpably to our shared world. In each conversation, the goal is to provide enough space to experience that complexity, showing that critics have more in common with artists themselves than with the reactionary hacks of popular imagination. This vital dialogue between artists and critics is a major way art stays relevant and connected to its culture.

In the most foundational sense, this book insists that art criticism isn't any *one thing*, even while presenting all the critics foremost as writers. Throughout the process of writing, every critic develops their own idiosyncratic framework for understanding what a work of art is, how they relate to an artist and an audience, and what their specific goals are. They create their own, often unstated rules. Roberta Smith, for example, sees herself on the readers' side and doesn't write about artists she's friends with. Lucy Lippard, on the other hand, considers herself an artists' advocate, and the people she champions are often enmeshed in her personal life. Neither of these positions is right or wrong, better or worse; each represents a negotiation between individual talent and cultural necessity. As Michele Wallace puts it in her interview, talking about Lippard as her role model: "The only person who wanted Lucy Lippard to be 'Lucy Lippard' was Lucy Lippard"— the art world didn't have a job description waiting for her to fill, so she invented one. The same is true of all of these writers, to varying degrees. Every critic is in some essential way self-made.

There are a number of overlapping constellations scattered throughout, of people knowingly and unknowingly in conversation with one another. Some are directly illustrated within the book—Eileen Myles on her early friendships with Chris Kraus and Peter Schjeldahl, or John Yau on his enduring closeness with the late John Ashbery. It's touching to realize how much talking about ourselves is actually talking about others—for instance, Kellie Jones recalling bits of Robert Farris

Thompson's biography, or Fred Moten of Amiri Baraka's, or Michael Fried of Kenneth Noland's, showing how other people's stories become woven into the fabric of our own. Taken as a collection, these accounts emphasize that artists and critics are never performing monologues in a vacuum, but always partaking in a multitiered discussion that at any given moment veers off beyond their control.

Across these thirty interviews, there are references to more than three hundred artists, ranging from Édouard Manet to Kerry James Marshall, Edgar Heap of Birds to Eva Hesse, Elizabeth Catlett to Caravaggio. They span the traditional art historical canon and the quirky personal influences that make up each critic's specific universe. Often there are overlapping encounters that reveal new aspects, as when Jerry Saltz and Thyrza Nichols Goodeve both talk about their experience of Matthew Barney's *Cremaster 4* (1995) in the early nineties, or when Darby English and Huey Copeland describe the impact of seeing Glenn Ligon's work as college students.

A similarly sprawling array of writers are mentioned in the conversations, including poets, critics, novelists, essayists, and historians from Richard Crashaw to Robert Creeley, Mohammed Mrabet to Toni Morrison, James Baldwin to Roland Barthes. Because of the sheer range of these references, spanning several centuries and many subjects, there is no elegant way to provide adequate scholarly or contextual information for everything. Their proper names sparkle in every conversation, letting them catch you as they may. An index gathers these references at the end of the volume, opening new ways of moving through it— tracking the multiple appearances of Clement Greenberg or Jeff Koons or Simone Weil, for instance. Additionally, an expanded "Further Reading" list is included, providing all relevant citations, as well as additional titles on the topic of art writing.

Every book of interviews is in its way both partial and arbitrary, especially when seeking to expand rather than circumscribe a territory. I limited mine to US critics, with a heavy emphasis on New York City. There are "historians" here, but I focused on those who have also written substantially about the art of their own time. While several have curated important exhibitions, I excluded "curators." Despite the fact that many of my favorite critics are themselves artists, I chose to omit such authors from this project, feeling that the impulses and pitfalls of an artist writing about their peers are necessarily different from those of a critic. Even with these limitations in place, I could rattle off the names of thirty more critics I'm interested in and admire whom I wasn't able to include for various reasons, time and space chief among them. But if there are hard feelings, give me a call—*let's talk about it*.

*   *   *

Over a hundred years ago, in "The Critic as Artist" (1891), Oscar Wilde argued for approaching criticism as an aesthetic attitude toward being—"the influence of the critic will be the mere fact of his own existence." The essay is staged as a dialogue between two characters named Ernest and Gilbert. Near the end of their meandering night of talk, Ernest asks: "You have explained to me that criticism is a creative art. What future has it?" To which Gilbert begins his reply, "It is to criticism that the future belongs." In that sense, I see this book as both *bouquet* and *gauntlet*: a gesture of affection, given in thanks to those who've spent their lives making and talking about art, and a challenge to future artists, writers, and thinkers to imagine new worlds— keeping open channels for possible futures to flow through, for our conversations to continue.

You have to learn to write about
love in order to write. It's the most
fundamental thing, and if you don't
write about it, then you are missing
something that is so profound—
how could you even carry on?

Hilton Als (b. 1960) is an essayist and critic, best
known for lyrical meditations that weave together art,
literature, theater, pop culture, and autobiography.
His books include *The Women* (1996) and *White Girls*
(2014) and the edited volume *Drawing Us In: How We
Experience Visual Art* (2001). He's published frequently
in *The Village Voice*, *The New York Review of Books*,
The Believer, and *Vibe*. He has contributed to many
exhibition catalogues, including those for Robert
Gober's retrospective *The Heart Is Not a Metaphor*,
at The Museum of Modern Art (2014), and *Alice
Neel, Uptown*, at David Zwirner (2017), which he
also curated. He has been a staff writer at *The New
Yorker* since 1994, becoming the theater critic in 2002,
and is an associate professor of writing at Columbia
University's School of the Arts. In 2017, he received
the Pulitzer Prize for Criticism.

Before we start, I have something else to ask you about: walking over here, I was listening to those Dionne Warwick and Burt Bacharach recordings from the sixties—I can't figure out what exactly makes them so incredible, but I'm *obsessed* with them.

Actually, this is how you are going to start your piece, because whenever I listen to her, I feel like a plagiarist. Particularly "Trains and Boats and Planes" [1965]—it feels like my complete rhythm as a writer, the strongest influence on me in terms of tone and syncopation—Dionne Warwick and Burt Bacharach.

Her phrasing seems almost too slow, but it never is, it's just she's unhurried about delivering it. I can't figure out the stresses, what makes that particular sound.

It's because she's not singing in black vernacular. She's singing in a pop vernacular but with soul phrasing—it's not something you would identify as R&B. She is obviously a black woman, but her syntax and phrasing, while rooted in the black church, are not a black style of singing. Dionne Warwick was really unique in that way, being soulful without being a soul singer. Then, of course, she had to deal with *all those words*.

Her diction is so precise.

She's one of the clearest singers.

I guess that also produces a rhythm.

Well, breathing—you have to be really mindful of your breathing if you're singing a lot of language. If you're singing a Sondheim song, you have to deal with your breath on some intense level.

I keep listening to "Are You There (With Another Girl)" [1965] and trying to figure out the emotional register of it, because it's kind of an upbeat song but it's also sad—layered, not self-pitying.

She's not sentimental *in the least*. All those great singers, like her or Billie Holiday, were able to transcend what a song was supposed to be about by making it bigger. Dionne Warwick works in miniature and gets expansive—a beautiful example of what syncopation can do. I think she had a huge effect on me as a kid. I had all these 45s of her singing, and I would listen to them over and over again. They really transported me, not into a dream world so much as feeding my dreams about what life would be like, eventually.

They're a fantasy about being a "grown-up"—a dream of emotional sophistication.

It was like I knew I was going to wake up and be that grown-up in those songs.

To shift slightly: What else would you say was an early important aesthetic experience?

What I remember were family photographs and my obsession with cataloguing them properly—finding out the names of people. I think that that was the way that I became obsessed with looking, as a way of not forgetting someone. Photographs, snapshots—the first art that really interested me.

The second significant event was that I used to cut high school all the time—I was one of those kids who cut high school and went to the library. My school was at Forty-Sixth Street, and one day I went to The Museum of Modern Art while they had an exhibition of Robert Rauschenberg—it was a retrospective, 1977 or something. *Monogram* [1955–1959], with the goat, was there when you went in, and I didn't know what it meant at all. I went back and the docent was giving a tour, and I asked if I could follow along. *Sure.* As she talked and explained it, it was like the top of my head flew off—that I could understand this coded language was so profound to me. I think those were the two really significant early events in my life of looking.

18

When did you start engaging with criticism or writing about art?

I dropped out of school at SUNY Purchase, and then I was taking a class at The New School in Chinese art. The professor said, *You know, you're very good at this; you should think about studying art history.*

Oh, there used to be a door guy named Drew at Club 57, who was this kind of aesthete. He was always reading Roland Barthes. Because of that I went to the bookstore and got one of his books. I remember *A Lover's Discourse* [1977] being very significant, and me not finishing it even, but being fixated on the language part of it, not the theory as much. Kenneth Silver was a huge influence as a teacher, because he really gave us a narrative context for art—that it was attached to someplace else, that there was a shimmer of the past around things. He was significant in not letting me veer out into theory writing, but to keep writing as clearly as possible about stuff.

The other thing that strikes me about Kenneth Silver's writing is that it's such a cinematic form of social art history—you're really told stories through the objects. What did you study with him?

It was a course called Art of the Sixties, and I wrote my first piece of art writing, about Warhol's *Ethel Scull 36 Times* [1963] and his 1966 portrait of Holly Solomon. It was so gorgeous, the way he loved that piece of writing and showed me, in his enthusiasm, that I could do it. And that is all you need, one person. And he really was that one person.

And you worked as a student in the art history department at Barnard?

Yes—I was a terrible assistant because first of all, I lived in Brooklyn, so I was always late, and I was also interested in my own writing, so not answering the phones, not dealing with the tasks at hand. It was a way for me to be close to my best friend Kevin, who worked across the street in the art history department at Columbia. Of course he was always on time, and impeccable. The thing that really stopped me from pursuing art history was connoisseurship—it was a requirement then, and it was so politically repugnant to me as an ideal that I just couldn't go forward.

You were also making art installations at the time?

Yes, I was close to a guy named Darryl Turner, and we did installations together, and they got a lot of attention. The first one we did was at Feature Gallery in 1990, called *I Only Want You to Love Me*, after the Fassbinder film. It was about my mother, who had died a year before. She had been a hairdresser, and I hung hair up all over. A woman we knew at the time did a body print of herself and left the gallery. It was a beautiful show. Then we were able to go to Simon Watson Gallery and propose another show, *Life Is Beautiful Now* [1990]. That was really the first kind of "slacker" show, about photography and the image. I remember that Darryl blew up this great Bette Davis photo of her falling on a cactus, and I had Edward Steichen's text from *The Family of Man* [1955] up on the wall—that was the introduction to the show. Then we did a window at the New Museum. Then we stopped, I think because he wanted to be known as an artist on his own.

Were you contributing texts?

There's a New Museum book called *The Interrupted Life* [1991] that has little bits of writing. And I was reviewing for *Artforum* at that time too. I also did some art criticism for *The City Sun*, the Brooklyn paper. But I think whenever my writing started to become circumscribed by anything I'd just stop doing that. So if I was becoming an art critic, I didn't like that. I just always had jobs, so I could do the writing that I wanted to do.

How did you articulate that to yourself, about what the writing you wanted to do was like?

Through *feeling*. At the *Voice* I would write sometimes about art things like Adrian Piper, but they were almost always more about ideas than profiles or interviews. I felt really fortunate that it was such a particular time in publishing where people could take way more chances. It's funny; I was thinking about, *Where do all those fragments go?* I used to like very much the conceptual aspect of all these little bits of work disappearing. I don't think I like that so much anymore. It's like I'm trying to understand the value now of permanence—like books.

You talked about the writing in *A Lover's Discourse*—when you were figuring out ways to write, what were some of the models that showed you a way to do it?

20

An essay by Proust called "On Reading" [1906] had a huge effect on me. It's one of the great essays. Proust showed that you could talk about a sensation and then go twenty or thirty pages before you got to the ostensible idea, and that was so refreshing to me. Or Machado de Assis, where you could do little stories and ideas together. Plays were also very important, Tennessee Williams especially, because you could again talk about your *difference*. These are the people I felt very close to.

Why did you not include the dates of publication anywhere in the book for the different essays that make up *White Girls*?

I was reluctant to make it have the appearance of a traditional book of essays. I wanted it to be emotionally—not factually—chronological.

In putting the book together, did you find yourself relating to the earlier pieces differently than you did the more recent writing?

To commit to making a book, you have to confront a despair about whatever you've done in the previous years it took to get there. I think I felt a lot of despair about the book, because you always expect to accomplish more than you have. I don't think I am being disingenuous in saying that. It felt like the best I could do when, in fact, I wanted somehow to do better. I don't mean to sound ungrateful or immodest, but I feel that I'm just developing. Books fix you in a way that makes me very nervous.

I wondered about that aspect of it. As I was reading *The Women*, I was thinking that it embodies such a specific moment of thinking and feeling. How do you relate emotionally or stylistically to that book twenty years later?

I haven't reread it. I feel that I didn't read it because I didn't want to get fixed there. In the period of time between those two books I was trying to understand myself and also deal with the ramifications of having written about my family, which I think traumatized me.

How?

My sisters weren't thrilled by it. And it took me many years to realize that they would have found fault with anything because of competitiveness. I didn't understand that at the time. So to avoid competing, I stopped writing books. *White Girls* is almost a testament to having worked through those issues.

It seems to me that your writing is at its most stylistically adventurous when the subject is directly autobiographical, or a very clear surrogate for you. Both *The Women* and the opening long essay in *White Girls*, "Tristes Tropiques," are almost pure autobiography, and have a different quality as writing than the more conventional essays or profiles.

Elaine Pagels prefers the more conventional pieces—the examinations of other people's lives. A big model for me was Faulkner's *Go Down, Moses* [1942]; he called it a novel, but it is a group of stories. It's amazing to realize that you can just call it whatever you want, and that's it. Let's call *The Women* a novel. I've noticed younger people prefer the raw autobiographical fantasia and the older prefer more considered, traditional things. Everybody has a thing that they're drawn to, and I don't think anything is worse or better, just different.

I didn't think of that distinction as a judgment, but wondered if, as the person who wrote them, you have different relationships to these different modes, or is it just like, *I love all my children the same*?

If you look at the long piece that opens *White Girls*, everybody that comes later in the book is mentioned in it. The point is: you cannot have one of those people without the others. I don't love one more than the other, but I think I have more fun with one than the other. I also think that they each demanded their own form. I couldn't have written about Flannery O'Connor the way I wrote a fiction piece about Richard Pryor's sister—O'Connor's biography doesn't allow for that kind of intimacy, or for making up.

I guess the difference between Flannery O'Connor and Richard Pryor's sister is that Flannery authored the things about herself that she wants you to know—a public self—and Richard Pryor's sister didn't.

Right, I made her up—Richard Pryor's sister wasn't known to the public, so when she's talking to that journalist, it's her big shot to talk about herself.

A lot of your writing has to do with that relationship—not just of self to other, but of private self to public self.

If you have a job that is being a public self, what interests me is how much authenticity can be left once you make that decision. It's a real decision. Richard Pryor is famous, in part, because he wanted to be. Richard Pryor's sister was not famous, in part, because she couldn't be. One of the great calamities in American life is celebrity. I've seen it make people different. So what interests me is getting underneath the mechanism of public regard, and self-regard, and really seeing what human behavior is and how attention reshapes a certain kind of body —does it fuck them up endlessly? Or not? Where is the innocence out of which most people initially create? Does that get dissipated? It's almost like the perfect metaphor for the self, for interiority: How authentic can we remain once we are seen, or once we want to be seen?

Thinking about talking with you today, I immediately had very personal questions, and then I stopped myself and wondered why I felt entitled to ask you very personal questions—

Well, you can.

But that impulse relates to the nature of your work: you disclose, or seem to disclose, a lot of personal information about who you are. I wonder how your relationship to being a public self has evolved, or how it has influenced your writing.

I don't think it's changed my writing because I'm really careful about it. It's a choice—like what I said about Richard Pryor wanting to be famous. The desire for that kind of mass love generally suggests a very insecure person, or a person who feels unseen. I don't feel unseen as a writer, because I'm writing. When you're writing, you're being seen by your words, by yourself. I don't have a real desire vis-à-vis becoming known. What I feel desirous of is becoming a better writer. It doesn't have to do with an audience; it has to do with not cheating yourself as an artist.

I am interested in the emotional aspects of art, and in my responses to it. The way you deal with that is one of the things I really like about _The Women_. There is a moment when you say, "Time has not changed my point of view, nor has the knowledge that what divide people are not the dreary marginal issues of race, or class, or gender but this: those who believe friendship and love dispel our basic aloneness, and those who do not."

I still believe that. When I started going out in the gay world, I had a romantic idea that gay people were united. But they were still men, and because they were still men, there was an aspect of territory and conquest, and also of isolation—and I don't think I've ever recovered. I always believed in my Dionne Warwick child self that one of the things that would greet me would be this beautiful community of love, and I was shocked to find that people are people everywhere, and that they are mostly self-interested.

You put that beautifully in a part of *White Girls*, and I was grateful to read it. I had a similar experience, thinking that as a faggot artist I had a "queer art scene" to join, and when I met them all I thought was—

These are not my people! Isn't that a shock! And what are you supposed to do with that knowledge? It's not something that makes you bitter as much as something that makes you think about isolation in a profound way. It makes you revisit the isolation you had as a kid, but as an adult. That is the weird, harmful part of all of it: you return to the place of hoping, but now knowing the hope won't be met. I find it difficult still.

What is that beautiful line Marilyn Monroe has in the *The Misfits* [1961]: *But we're dying all the time, all the people, everywhere.* Facing the fact that we are terminal doesn't so much make you grow up as make you acknowledge the sadness.

For instance, there is sadness being here now: this moment won't be repeated. Theater interests me for that reason—if I see it twice, it's different. As humans, no matter how much we try to relegate ourselves to sameness in any group, we are different, all the time. We are different no matter how much we cleave to the quotidian, to the status quo, to ideals of identity—whether it's gay, bi, trans, whatever.

I want to talk about the book that you did on Alice Neel, *Alice Neel, Uptown*, because I was really moved by it. You spend a lot of time writing from the perspective of the people Neel painted and imagining the feelings of Neel herself. How did you get to that?

It goes back to childhood: I want to find out who the people are in the photographs and I want to save them by naming them. I feel that book is about ventriloquism in a certain way, imagining how some-

body felt. Also imagining my own mother, a single mother on welfare—
that experience. The love that I felt for my mother I used to try and
understand Alice Neel as an artist. It takes a lot of will to have kids
and pursue being an artist. I think Neel must have been an incredibly
willful person to make all that work and send her kids to good schools
and have this kind of insane erotic S&M shit going on at the same time.
It was very important to get the tone right to honor what she would
have said. And venting some of the characters in the paintings was an
act of empathy.

**How do you regard the difference between fiction and nonfiction in
your writing?**

Now, I am just treating everything as fiction, because I'm distrustful
of the imagination, which is what memory is. I prefer to move forward
treating the books as novels—let's say, novels about memory. Or a poem,
in that no one ever asks a poet if what they've written is true or not.
I'm a stickler for accuracy, but that doesn't mean everything I write is a
hundred percent true. There is a great emotional truth there, and I'm
trying to honor that.

My mother had a sister; I left that out of *The Women* because it would
have been very painful to her memory to talk about that. So I changed
certain things to leave out that fact. Now, that makes it "not accurate,"
because I left out a character from the story, but I did it to preserve
something of my mother's privacy.

When you're writing about real people it is important, in order to
get through it, to treat them as characters—but there is also such a
thing as honoring the copyright someone has on their own life. That
part of the book took me five years because I wanted to honor the copyright on my mother's life while being honest to myself. Even though
there was a distance of seven or eight years from the time she died until
the book was published, it was still a very complicated relationship for
me. I adored her, and I never wanted to see her hurt. I'm beginning to
understand more that my protecting my mother might not have been
the best thing for my writing, but it was the best thing for my relationship to her.

I'm very interested in how we navigate the biography of an artist as relevant or not to the work they make. Most of the pieces that you've written about artists situate their work within the narrative of their life.

More than anything else, I use a bit of the life to talk about things chronologically. If I'm interviewing them I think I go more on observation. I've found that words are suspect in some way, and the thing that is most helpful to me is the language of bodies—what they are doing and how they are responding to me, as opposed to what they are saying. I think I go much more with behavior now than with the standard "telling quote."

I thought it was beautiful in *The Women* when you said you were fascinated by your mother as "a kind of living literature."

I think I'm just so much a part of her story, and yet I haven't really told her whole story. Which means I haven't told the story of myself, which I guess is the work of the writer—you keep going. I'm very shy about the "I" character—

How has the "I" character evolved in your writing?

I think I've been incredibly withdrawn about the "I" because the story is really about an experience: you go to the theater and have an experience and you're telling people about it; it's not a time to say "I."

Often I feel like your writing is about the displacement of your "I" onto the subject. Like "The Only One" [1994], your profile on André Leon Talley—

That was the first one I wrote for *The New Yorker*. Well, I loved him, in a way. I actually had a love for him, so it would be displaced in that way. The complications of "he and I" or "me and him" in retrospect get played out there. But the psychic energy of it is not something you can manufacture. I think he's a great person in a crummy field. He's better than the fashion industry.

I think of your writing as extremely stylish, almost to the point of opacity. When did using language flamboyantly enter into your mind— how did you realize you could do it?

I think the act of writing is having the tiniest bit of belief in yourself, that you can do it.

26

What's the rest of it?

Blind faith, and hope that you can't really explain.

One of the things I like about your writing's worldview is that you don't give anyone an easy out.

I hope myself more than anyone.

Well, that is where it begins and ends, isn't it?

I don't want anybody to feel judged harder than I judge myself. Do you think I condemn people?

No, but sometimes I'm surprised at how hard you are on certain writers. But I wonder if it's about trying to be unsentimental.

I think you are right in terms of indirection and what that means: ultimately it's about being hard on one's self.

One thing you said about Flannery O'Connor: "What was lacking in O'Connor's life—and in her art—was the spontaneous experience of intimate love, with its attendant joys and tedium and security." It made me think of an offhand observation you made about Owen Dodson in *The Women*: "I found out the sin in his work: the inability to convey intimacy." I'm curious about the ways intimacy is made manifest in art.

You have to learn to write about love in order to write. It's the most fundamental thing, and if you don't write about it, then you are missing something that is so profound—how could you even carry on? It is a very profound thing to touch another human being. I haven't had the best luck with it, but it seems to me that staying vulnerable to experience is why we're here. That means all sorts of weird things, like being responsible for someone else's soul, which is what it comes down to. So if you're an artist, and intimacy is the most profound thing, then you have to deal with it, with what it means to love someone. It doesn't get any deeper than that. If your job as a writer is to convey human emotion and interactions, you can't skip the intimacy part.

How did you learn to write about it?

I didn't know how to write any other way. I'm not a master of the classic essay form; I don't know how to do it unless I *feel* it. Not to be all Janis Joplin about it, but something has to connect with me personally in order for me to write about it.

I'm sort of notorious for my use of
the pronoun "it" without explaining
what it means, which somehow
never seemed a problem to me.
We all sort of feel the presence of
"it" without necessarily knowing
what we're thinking about.

John Ashbery (b. 1927; d. 2017) was widely considered the greatest American poet of the second half of the twentieth century. For much of that time he also wrote art criticism, first for *ARTnews*, and later for the Paris edition of the *New York Herald Tribune*, *New York*, and *Newsweek*. He provided a crucial link between French and American ideas and aesthetics, publishing lyrical and authoritative translations of the French avant-garde, including Stéphane Mallarmé, Arthur Rimbaud, and Raymond Roussel. Ashbery wrote over twenty books of poetry, including his early masterpieces *Some Trees* (1956); *The Tennis Court Oath* (1962); *Rivers and Mountains* (1966); *The Double Dream of Spring* (1970); *Three Poems* (1972); and *Self-Portrait in a Convex Mirror* (1976). His collected criticism was published as *Reported Sightings: Art Chronicles 1957–1987* (1989); *Other Traditions* (2000); and *Selected Prose 1953–2003* (2004).

John Ashbery

Instead of asking you a lot of specific questions about poems, which is what people usually do and which I find quite tedious, I'm going to ask you more human-being-type questions, if that's okay.

Okay.

One thing that struck me in the chronology in the Library of America's *Ashbery: Collected Poems 1956–1987* [2008]: "1936—Reads about landmark Surrealism exhibition at The Museum of Modern Art in New York in *Life* magazine; decides to become a surrealist painter." You would have been about nine. It's interesting to note that you were first introduced to surrealism through visual art, rather than poetry.

Yes—actually through that article. At the time I read *Life* every week, like everybody else in the country. I don't think I decided to become a surrealist painter when I read it. I used to take art classes at the art museum in Rochester, near where I grew up. I told the teacher about this and she said, *Why don't you try something surrealist,* so I did these rather crude pictures. It just seemed like a great idea. Every day, I'd do a lot of drawings, usually of women in beautiful gowns—maybe I thought I'd be a dress designer, which I would have been quite good at. The art department closed in the little school I went to, so they allowed me to go to Rochester to take the art class there. That was in the late thirties. Aside from a few childhood ventures, I didn't start writing poetry seriously until the early 1940s. When I started writing poetry, I carried it over into that.

Do you have any recollection of when you first thought that you wanted to be an artist or a poet, or what that might have meant?

I think I always did.

In several places you've downplayed or disparaged your work as an art critic. I wonder why you feel the need to do that?

First of all, I felt that I was never really qualified to be an art critic. The only reason I did it was because I needed to earn some money. It wasn't the best way of making rent by any means.

You started writing for *ARTnews*. When you first met with Thomas B. Hess, the legendary editor there, to get a job writing art criticism, what did he say?

I was living in New York after spending two years in France as a Fulbright student and I didn't have any job, and I was taking graduate courses in French at NYU, thinking I would get a PhD and become a professor of French. I was sharing an apartment with James Schuyler, and although it was only fifty-eight dollars a month, it was hard coming up with half of the rent, so Jimmy, who was already writing for *ARTnews*, said, *Why don't you write criticism?* I said, *I don't know how to do that.* He said, *Sure, it's easy, and Tom Hess prefers to have poets writing art criticism because they have a fresh approach without unnecessary knowledge about the subject.* Also, I think he could pay poets slave wages. I went to see Tom, and he was a little forbidding, and I felt of course very unqualified to be there. He assigned me an article, which was the first thing I ever wrote about art, a review of a show by Bradley Walker Tomlin—did you ever hear of him?

Yes, a terrific artist, but hidden—I've seen very few in person. He was gay, wasn't he?

Yes! I often wonder if that wasn't why Tom assigned it to me.

So he immediately knew you were gay?

Oh, probably. I don't know, we never talked about it; not then, at least. So I did that and he liked it, and then he had me writing monthly reviews of gallery shows. They claimed to cover every show in New York. The really forgettable ones were the ones in the back of the book, which were very short and paid five dollars, which was nice to have.

Well, they were just a couple lines, right? Sounds like good money to me.

Yeah, subway fare.

Was there art that was easier or harder for you to write about?

That is an interesting question, which I don't think I can answer. It was obviously pretty easy to write about abstract expressionist painting, since it was brand new and nobody knew anything about it, so what you had to say would be as valid as what anyone else might. Also, it's not unlike the poetic process in its being a record of its own coming into being, so I guess that might have been easier. I can't think of any that were difficult, unless they were historical and required a lot of research, but I don't remember that I wrote very many of those.

In a conversation you did with Kenneth Koch in the midsixties, there is a wonderful exchange: Koch says, "Have you ever been physically attacked because of your art criticism?" You say, "No, because I always say I like everything." Then he says, "Would you say that is the main function of criticism?" To which you answer, "If it isn't it should be."

Well, I suppose there is a grain of truth in that!

In the introduction to one of the volumes of your translations from French, there is an aside that says you'd keep parts of your childhood diaries in French so that no one could read them.

Yes!

What kind of feelings were you writing in French?

Crushes on boys.

I also read that before you went to college, your mother read your letter to a boy revealing you were gay, and I wanted to know more about that: When did you know you were gay?

Well, first of all, the word "gay" didn't really exist then. The concept might have been more nebulous than it is now, but I knew I was attracted to boys. I spent two years at Deerfield Academy. My senior year they decided I was too young to go to college, having skipped a year in grade school, so I ended up spending two years there. At the end of the second year I got accepted to Harvard, where I went in the summer of 1945. I graduated Deerfield in June and went to Harvard in July.

I had had this good friend the first year at Deerfield who had already graduated, who was gay, and I wrote him a letter bringing him up-to-date on all the gossip that had happened in the last year—not much had—and that was the letter that my mother found. I left it out without sealing it and went away for the night, and of course my mother naturally read it and was very upset. She somehow forced herself to forget about it, because it was never referred to after that. She said she never told my father, though I'm sure she did. In any case, he never mentioned it to me.

Did your mom commonly go through your things as a child?

Oh, sure; that's why I wrote in French in my diary. I believe one of my techniques was to use the word "*garçon*," but I figured she might very well know what that means, so I used the slang word "*gar*" instead.

In an interview from the midsixties you say, "In my poetry, the pronouns can never be trusted to refer to any one person for any length of time. I believe in a kind of polyphonic effect, which I try to get," which interests me immensely.

I'm sort of notorious for my use of the pronoun "it" without explaining what it means, which somehow never seemed a problem to me. We all sort of feel the presence of "it" without necessarily knowing what we're thinking about. It is an important force just for that reason, it's there and we don't know what it is, and that is natural. So I don't apologize for that, though I've been expected to on many occasions.

How does that relate to writing criticism, where the job is to describe the "it"?

Writing criticism is a completely different procedure. Your task is pretty well defined by what you're writing about. There are pictures or sculptures, which are concrete and present, and the presence of "it" is not a problem, I think, though I've never thought about that before.

You've made both collaged poems and collaged pictures—how does it work differently to collage words instead of images?

I don't know, though undoubtedly it does. It's much more difficult to control the meaning of language, but if you're using an image cut from a picture, which is just *there*, it may reflect on the other elements of the collage, but not in the vast way that language allows or uses.

Have you always made collages?

I think I started when I was in college. My roommate and I used to make them. I still have a couple from that period, one of which was in my first show, at Tibor de Nagy Gallery in 2008. A bunch of others unfortunately got thrown out when our house was sold—I wasn't around when it happened—not that they were works of great importance, but it would be nice to have them. One of those I still have is really good; in fact, I think it may be one of the best I've done.

What makes it the best?

It's just complete. It was taken from a nineteenth-century children's book illustration. The top half shows a little boy running off to school with his little sister waving. In the bottom half he is coming back from school. In the top one I put a large head of a bird looking through the gate that the boy is about to come through. In the bottom one, coming back, he has the bird's head replacing his head, and the girls are looking apprehensive, as well they might. There is a black figure in a loincloth behind the girls, approaching the scene. It's pretty creepy.

Mysterious, suggestive of some undefined narrative. It reminds me of your translations of Giorgio de Chirico's novel *Hebdomeros* [1929].

I felt tremendous love for that text. It's so precious. Especially when you consider it was written by de Chirico, who was known as a painter and not as a writer, but who invented a literary style that no one had ever used before. He was also an old grouch. I actually met him once in New York. He had a show at the museum in Columbus Circle, and I wanted to get permission to translate all of *Hebdomeros*—he had sent me a letter once, in response to my letter, saying I could translate a section, but I wanted to do the whole thing, even though it had already been translated by somebody else. I was passed along by these two Americans who were apparently his dealers in Rome, who I had to meet first; then by his wife; then, finally, I got to meet the great man himself, and I said how much I admired *Hebdomeros* and how much I'd like to translate it, and he just waved his hand—*Eh!*—and that was the extent of our conversation. So I never did the rest of it because the rights situation seemed unclear.

Dante supposedly knew all of the *Aeneid* by heart, which must entail a certain kind of knowing. While translation is not memorizing, it seems that the act of translation would give you a special relation to the text, some similar kind of internalization. Or is that just my fantasy as a nontranslator?

Maybe it's true. I certainly feel on an intimate level with Rimbaud and other things I've translated. I also may feel that this will add some dimension to my own writing, having done this exercise, but I'm not sure that I really feel that.

What did you learn about Rimbaud from translating all of *Illuminations* [1886], which you published in 2011?

I felt more at ease in reading him having translated him. It's something I could walk around in and observe once I had translated it. I'm always waiting for possible repercussions in my own writing from translating him, which are probably there, but I'm not sure what they are.

A lot of people resort to poetry when they are in love, or are upset. I wonder how falling in love affected your poetry, or your relationship to language?

Actually, my first love was the summer I was sixteen, with a boy a year older, from Massachusetts, who was working on a farm nearby. He was the one who first told me about Rimbaud.

Really!

He had read him. And he showed me the short poem "*Ô saisons, ô châteaux*" [1872]—which I thought was the most beautiful thing I'd ever read. I think I had already begun to write poetry when I first met him, but that opened a more intriguing way of poetry. My early poems are really embarrassing now, and he was very kind about them, but obviously he didn't think they were worth much, offering genial criticism. And he also knew the poet Robert Francis, who was sort of like Robert Frost—younger and lesser known—and who lived in Amherst near my friend.

Did you have a dramatic parting?

34

He went home to Amherst, and I was going to Deerfield that September for my first year, and after he left I felt very guilty about having done all this, and I stopped replying to his letters. He was very upset.

That must have cemented your relationship to both French and poetry. I think about you writing your *private* feelings in French, and then having this intense romance featuring Rimbaud! *Fabulous*. When you finally ended up in France, what about it agreed with you?

What's not to like, as they say. Just about everything, except the uncomfortable quarters I was obliged to live in, squalid rooms.

It's striking that you left New York for Paris when you did, especially in an art context. French art was being eclipsed by American art at exactly the moment you found yourself in Paris.

I didn't really mind about that. I wasn't really a part of what was happening in New York—I didn't know the artists really, not the way Frank O'Hara got to know them. They couldn't have cared less about me; I was an unknown poet. That was the visual arts anyway, which was something I liked along with poetry, but poetry was what I was mainly interested in. For a long time, I wasn't really able to read French well enough to tell if they were producing great poetry or not—turned out they weren't. Just the life of the place was what attracted me. I didn't feel deprived by not being in the hot artistic center.

Why did you decide not to finish your PhD on Raymond Roussel?

What I really wanted to do was just go back and live in Paris. I went back and did research on Roussel, and after a while I realized I didn't want to go back to New York. I was living with a French friend whom I met when I had first arrived, and I just wanted to stay with him, so little by little I managed to scrounge out a living while I got a job writing reviews for the *Herald Tribune* —which paid miserably, fifteen dollars an article—but with that I was able to get assigned reviews at other publications. None of this enabled me to live very comfortably, but, on the brink of poverty, I was able to stay in Paris, which was what I wanted.

You have said in the past that most of your early writing, when you were an "unknown poet," was done without the expectation of an

audience or even of publication. But by the midseventies you became so lauded. How did that affect the way you approached writing?

When I first started writing poetry, I thought, *This is great, people will love this, I'll become a celebrated poet*, and that turned out not to be the case at all. My first book, *Some Trees*, published in an edition of eight hundred copies, took eight years to sell out. And the next book, *The Tennis Court Oath*, was even less successful. So then I thought, *Well, people aren't going to think I'm a great poet. So what do I do? Do I go on writing because this is what I like to do, or should I give it up and take up something else, like macramé?* I decided, *I'm going to go on doing it—I like doing it and the hell with them.* Then gradually I somehow picked up readers, and eventually, with *Self-Portrait in a Convex Mirror*, I won the three main poetry prizes and was suddenly certified as a poet after not counting as one for so long.

Several of your books, including my favorites, have the dedication "For David," who I imagine is David Kermani. You two have been together a very long time, and I'm interested in what you've learned from that long relationship. For some context of where I'm coming from, you've been together longer than I've been alive—I'm really single and really like it—so I'm curious what kind of knowledge a deep partnership brings.

We complement each other. As you may have noticed, David is all about business and getting things done and details. I'm the other way— I'm sort of lazy and get around to doing what I'm supposed to be doing. So I need somebody to push me into shape. I think I'd known David for about three months before I noticed he'd been balancing my checkbook for me, which I never asked him to do. He just naturally gravitates to this kind of activity. He is a typical Capricorn.

And what sign are you?

Leo.

Me too! How did your relationship with David change your life and work?

I guess it changed my life by making me try to be less distracted and lazy and helping me to do the work that I wanted to do. And also making it easier for me to do it, because he's handled so many practical

36

aspects of my life. We're sort of complete opposites, and are attracted by the oppositeness of the other.

I really love the Charles Eliot Norton lectures you gave at Harvard, which are collected in *Other Traditions*. In the one on Laura Riding, you talk about the necessity of misreading her poems, or at least of reading them against how she might tell you to read them: "This is what happens to poetry: no poem can ever hope to produce the exact sensation in even one reader that the poet intended; all poetry is written with this understanding on the part of the poet and the reader." What kinds of understandings are possible through miscommunication?

That's a pretty big question. Certainly the possibility of miscommunication has to be taken into account, both in writing and in communicating verbally. One has to admit that it is there while trying to get beyond it.

The poets in *Other Traditions*, such as John Clare, Thomas Lowell Beddoes, Riding, are all classed as "minor poets," in that they all require a special handling to appreciate. They also all had rather dramatic, tormented lives. That kind of careful attentiveness, or special handling, seems like part of all you do.

I suppose in those essays I wanted to try and make amends for the misunderstandings they endured, having experienced some of them myself. Also, it makes a good story.

Art is not just a social proposition,
but an ethical proposition that
involves ethical choices; therefore,
the proper response to the work of
art—whether it's any good or not, or
whether you like it—has to do with
whether you think it is right or not.

Bill Berkson (b. 1939; d. 2016) was a poet and art critic who provided a vital, intergenerational link between artists and writers in New York and California. Throughout the sixties, he wrote for *ARTnews* and *Arts*, and later frequently contributed to *Art in America*, *Artforum*, and *Modern Painters*. His books of criticism and lectures on art include *The Sweet Singer of Modernism & Other Art Writings 1985–2003* (2003); *Sudden Address: Selected Lectures 1981–2006* (2007); and *For the Ordinary Artist: Short Reviews, Occasional Pieces & More* (2010). Among his numerous volumes of poetry are *Portrait and Dream: New and Selected Poems* (2009) and *Expect Delays* (2014). He was professor emeritus at the San Francisco Art Institute, where he taught from 1984 to 2008.

Bill Berkson

When we were in touch at the end of last year, you were thinking about humanity and writing about the artist Robert Arneson—

Well, I can't think about humanity as in "what would be good for humanity," or whether humanity, as in the Anthropocene, has caused all this trouble for the world—for flora, fauna, land, and water alike. What I have thought about is that particular people have humanity in their work, or exhibit humanity, which might be called humaneness. I guess that is a vague enough term, but it seems to hit home. When you say it to other people, they seem to know what you mean. It is of course in the neighborhood of love, good will, and care, or even something like having a good heart, but also assumes rage, lust, and the beastliness of survival. I've been playing with it; I'm not sure if in Arneson's case it's his humanity or his humanities, because he is so multiplicitous. I don't think it's inextricably linked to what is called humanism with a capital *H*, which seems to be a can-of-worms term, because if you're a humanist in the late twentieth century, early twenty-first century—at least in the academic cloister—you are, like lyric poetry, out to lunch.

We did an interview a few years ago. I was twenty-one or twenty-two. The distance from then to now feels like multiple incarnations of myself—that five years for me was an immense amount of time. When you think back to yourself in the interval between twenty-one and twenty-seven, what does that period of your life seem like?

I was talking to Larry Fagin the other day, and he brought up his time—I think it was between 1962 and '65—of being in San Francisco as part of the Jack Spicer circle. He talked about how in his sense of who he was then and who he is now, it is disproportionate to the actual time span. I said, *Yes, that is very much like between 1960 and '66 for me.* Your early twenties are really a continuation of the prolonged adolescence that American boys have. It's an extension of your teen self, or anyway it was for me. I hadn't learned any better by the time I was twenty than when I was sixteen. The assumption, or even the presumption, was that later I learned better. There are certain things that I did then, and I can't say I regret doing anything, because then I wouldn't be here with you now, enjoying my life in the way that I am.

I was apparently some sort of beast as a really young boy and as a preteen. I was horrid. My favorite cousin died at ninety-six a few weeks ago. I was reviewing our e-mail exchanges over the past ten years or so, and there was one place where she said, *Everyone thought that the proper place for you was Alcatraz. You were a spoiled brat.* So when, if ever, did that change? I think I was displaced in some way for a while, I didn't know what my place in the world was or who to look to. Anyway, in my twenties I was still teen-like, and there was a mass of conflicting directions to go in—identity confusion and all that. And I was acting way ahead of myself and my actual capabilities, ahead of what I actually knew. But I always had, as I've come to realize, some sort of stabilizer. Under the rubric of humanism, there's a term you don't hear very much, which is common sense. I never really went crazy. I never really self-destructed, or was other-destructive either. The stabilizer that accompanies common sense I liken to those moments when driving and I might be on the verge of making a mistake, or somebody else is in the wrong lane, and my wrist just flicks; I've swerved into the appropriate place to avoid disaster. So it's like a little compass within me that may be my guardian angel, because I didn't cultivate it. I think biographically what happened in my later twenties is that I shifted from being the protégé, or the plucky new kid on the block indulged by older artists, to being among my peers—people my own age, of a contemporary culture. It was there, in some ways, that I was socialized. I wasn't so much a beast.

How old were you when you started hanging out with the older poets?

40

Nineteen or twenty—I would have been nineteen in the spring of
'59 when I came back to New York and took Kenneth Koch's workshop,
and that was pretty much it. Then I met the New York School, so to
speak, in the persons of Frank O' Hara, Jimmy Schuyler, and artists like
Larry Rivers, de Kooning, Johns, Rauschenberg, and so on. Then in 1960
I was working for *ARTnews*.

Why do you think those older artists took you up?

For one thing, I had committed myself to poetry, much under Kenneth
Koch's encouragement, because he made it seem like a perfectly normal
thing to do, not something glamorous and not something that you had
to dress up or dress down for. He was really quite reasonable about it.
Plus, he seemed to think I was good at it, or that I could be. Then I met
Frank O'Hara and became friends with him, and Frank O'Hara thought
that if you were his friend then you must be a great artist of one kind
or another—either a poet or painter or dancer or what have you. It had
to do with his will to be present and accounted for; as Morton Feldman
said, *One remarkable thing about Frank O'Hara is that he really wanted you to
be great.* I think he had a sense of his own glory, and he wanted, further,
to bask in *your* glory. It was exciting and a pleasure for him to declare
how marvelous somebody was, so he could just about convince you that
you were. But there were a lot of people whom Frank wanted to believe
were glorious who just weren't, even though he liked the idea that they
were. I don't know that I was all that marvelous then; I mean, I had had
two or three years of writing poems that were striking in some way,
the poems that went into my first book. Then I got mixed up trying to
be everything at once in my midtwenties and I didn't really write that
much poetry, and what I did write is interesting in its way—there are
one or two things I really like—but I think that there was a three- or
four-year period where I was involved more with a fancy social life,
and kind of a wild sex life, than with writing poems. At a certain point
my flick-of-the-wrist trick worked; I had been in a quasi nosedive but
snapped out of it. In the meantime, I got to know a lot of the artists—
I got to know Alex Katz and Edwin Denby, and Frank very well, but
then he died—and for a year or two I knew the artists better than

the poets. I was writing a lot of art criticism then, and when I started
teaching at The New School, increasingly poets my own age were
coming to those classes, and that is how I met Anne Waldman and
various other people. That was terrific, because I was supposed to be
teaching these people, my exact contemporaries, who
at the same time were teaching me.

How old were you when you started teaching that class?
Twenty-four.

**So many of the artists who I think of in that scene—and who I'm
very interested in—are these big, overwhelmingly gay personalities.
I wonder what that was like for you?**

I liken it, and I think appropriately, to my and other people's experience of black music: you encounter it and say, *Gee, this has fantastic energy.*
So there was this great expansive camp sensibility, and also with it was
that kind of expansive sex—sex was right out front. The reason it was
so attractive to me is I was coming from a rather repressed environment.
It wasn't like where you came from, a Southern churchgoing repressed
environment; it was tidy, urban, upper-middle class, a somewhat com-
placent, if stylish, culture, full of advantage, as I was. Except that certain
things nagged at me, like *What is going on here?* and *What do I do here?* and
realizing that I had all this energy in me and didn't know what to do
with it.

I wasn't money hungry—I knew very early on I was not going into
business. So, encountering people who were just interested in literature
and writing poetry and going to concerts, jazz clubs, the ballet, and
watching all sorts of sublime old movies was exciting. You didn't think
of it as the gay community—probably, if everybody was going to
John Button's house to watch a Busby Berkeley movie on late-night TV,
I might have been the only so-called straight guy there. There might
have been one or two women. I'm there because Frank had said, *Let's go
to John's and watch this movie,* and I'm already into those movies, which
were then beginning to be released at the New Yorker, Bleecker Street
Cinema, and other places. 1930s movies carried this fantastic energy,
and a lot of that energy was the energy of talk—those are pictures that

really talk and talk fast; they have great lines. I was as responsive to that as anybody. And there is this whole business of song and dance, which really led straight to what Andy Warhol did in the Factory, where you have these people who are not really all that good—Ruby Keeler as a dancer or Dick Powell as a singer—but they've got this idea of, *Let's put on a show! I'm going to get out here and dance!* It was so charming, but also encouraging to people like Jackie Curtis, who must have thought, *Oh, I can be a star too!* That was terrific.

I couldn't have defined black music or camp behavior—in the way that Frank or John Bernard Myers behaved, or John Ashbery when he permits himself—as exercising what really, at least in some respect, is compensatory culture. In other words, these are people who are, as they would say now, *oppressed,* who are pushed aside, punished, or otherwise brutalized and dehumanized—and in order to assert their humanity they act out, or they develop these routines, one of which is jazz, to express their pain, although there is also the joy of doing it, in itself. In my earliest experiences of both black music and gay culture, I knew nothing about their pain. I was innocent of their pain, so I just enjoyed it, and that gave me a lot of leeway in my behavior, as I adopted a lot of those mannerisms. I delighted in shocking people with how outrageous and how unpredictable my behavior could be.

Like what?

Suddenly doing "Frank"—his voice or a flip gesture. When I first met John Ashbery in Paris, we were sitting at a table, maybe Café de Flore, just Frank, John, and me, and John sort of leaned in and said, *What really is going on with you two?* And in my best Greta Garbo imitation, I said, *I am a woman in love!* That is something I could do. Actually, I can still do it, because I still think, *Why not!* I like to put all those divisions into question, because most of them are stupid divisions. But back then it was more for the shock of it. I think that John Ashbery, for instance, thought, unlike Frank or Ginsberg even, that the lines of identity should be clearly defined. But somehow or other, early on, whether it was aimlessness or just a multitude of possible selves, something in me knew that I could play among the selves. That was also probably where I misled myself in my early twenties, because I was trying to live this downtown life as a serious poet, writing about art and working for *ARTnews*, knowing the artists and seeing the shows. The typical thing was to go to a painter's show and then the New York City Ballet, and the next night a Cage or Morton Feldman concert, or the Five Spot to hear Ornette Coleman—this could all happen in a day. I have appointment calendars from that time, and it's amazing to look at them. Still, my sexuality stayed uptown. I didn't like downtown girls, I didn't like sullen girls in leotards and berets, and I wasn't gay, so at a certain point in the night I left downtown, hopped in a cab, and went to some bar or club uptown, where the girls were. That was a lot of fun, but it was also sort of dissolute. And sometimes the two would get mixed up, but life was compartmentalized, largely.

When did the compartments get deconstructed or merged?

I thought I was building something like a straight version of Cocteau, I was taking on a role, something of a dandy. I had great suits. There was no merger, but at a certain point I was spending more and more time with the poets who mostly lived on the Lower East Side— this was '66 or '67—and finding that we had a lot of shared culture. See, the older New York poets were into classical music. Frank wasn't really interested in jazz. He would go along because his friends were going to the Five Spot. I remember when Bob Dylan hit, and Frank wasn't interested in that at all, not the way that Allen Ginsberg was. I was really seeing more and more of Ron Padgett, Ted Berrigan, Anne Waldman, Lewis Warsh. It was more a rock-and-roll culture, pot and psychedelics instead of alcohol. That was a big change—so at that point, in '67 or so, this uptown life was no more. It didn't go with poetry, not one bit.

It's interesting to think of you as a young terror, because when I read you, I think of you as very graceful. I've always been much more volatile. I have these big feelings, and I like art that has them too—

You haven't stopped really, but when you first appeared in my class, the first thing that struck me was, *Gee, he behaves like the gay guys I knew at the end of the fifties and early sixties, and nobody behaves like that anymore— how terrific!* The other thing, and probably why I reacted to you, was your arrogance. Because somebody should have taken me aside, Frank or somebody should have said to me, *Come off it*, when I was acting excessively intolerant, rude, or somehow above or below my station. So I recognized that in you, and if I was hard on you, it was because I thought, *Better to nip that right now*, so that you have the chance to let it go. It might save some time. The thing is, you behave as though it *matters*, if something is either good or occupies or doesn't occupy what you see as a good social space. If you look at those Richters we looked at once and say, as you did, *This is just meant for corporate lobbies*, I know what you mean. There is something deep in me that responds the same way, but at the same time, at the San Francisco Art Institute I was likely to say, *Well, okay, but painting, in particular, has to be somewhere, and the place where it will be traditionally is in some locus of power, which usually means where the money is.* The thing is, all those things that we talked about are tantamount to saying that art is not just a social proposition, but an ethical proposition that involves ethical choices; therefore, the proper response to the work of art—whether it's any good or not, or whether you like it—has to do with whether you think it is right or not. It's really weird to me that my saying so gets blank stares, or rings up censorial to some people, as though you were going to put the art in jail—no, nor do I put someone in jail because they behaved badly at a party. You just say, *Fuck that, I think I'll go talk to somebody else.* The upside is: *Great, tell me more! That's marvelous!* Or, *Nobody ever said that before, in that way!* People like Tom Hess or Harold Rosenberg or Frank O'Hara understood art as a kind of behavior, that art was some sort of social gesture. But boy, there are rooms full of people who don't get it, won't get it, and think art is about something they learned in school.

In one of the early lectures in *Sudden Address*, you talk about how when you were a young writer, Guston's process related to your way of writing—as opposed to de Kooning's—and I wonder how has that changed over time. Do you still write that way?

In a way, yes. I met Claudia La Rocco at the Edwin Denby evening she organized, and she told me she began as a journalist working for the Associated Press and was called into the editor's office and told offhandedly, *You're the dance critic now*. I always think that's a great way for any critic to begin—on assignment, as it were. At the Associated Press, she exercised her skills as a fast writer. The reason that I didn't become a journalist like my father, after four summers working at International News Service and then at *Newsweek*, was that I realized that I would never be really fast at writing a story. I just had to work it out; still do. With poetry, if I have a story to tell, if I have a narrative, I can get right on it and pretty much get at least a fair first draft. If it's one of these more or less abstract poems, it doesn't get any easier. Art writing never got any easier, really—

I'm glad to hear that! [Laughter.]

So that business of being an inchworm, and recognizing a fellow inchworm in Guston, was true for a long time. I finally got to some degree of fluency. I was just talking about this with Musa Mayer, looking at the Gustons in her apartment, and talking about how for Guston in the 1950s there are very few paintings. It is probable that he did ten or twenty times as many paintings in his last decade as he did in all the previous decades. I guess it was you who asked me, *How many books have you done since 2000?* Meaning, mainly in the years since I had a lung transplant. It wasn't as if I made some sort of resolution to be productive, but I've had fourteen books come out since then, including some little chapbooks, and I'll bet that I've written lots more poetry than in all of the sixties and seventies. I really started to roll in the eighties—more confidence, more commitment, more clear-sighted. Then there was a moment when I had been doing so much art writing and so little poetry that I put the question to myself: *Am I even interested in writing poetry?* It wasn't any sort of test, but I had that spring semester off, and then the whole summer, and I just started writing poems. In the midst of that I thought, *Oh, this is the most interesting thing to do, and there is tremendous pleasure in it*. I had that revelation and just didn't look back.

How did your relation to language change when there was more of a sense of physical urgency?

I don't think it was a matter of urgency, not in the sense of facing mortality and needing to achieve something before I die. If there's any urgency, it's just that the vistas have opened up so widely. There's so much to do.

Was your first awareness of language as something to be aware of from talking and from the radio?

Yes. It's interesting; there certainly was a lot of talk around the house, and we listened to the radio and went to the movies, my parents and I. I remember I had these moments—I think they were, collectively, my Saint Augustine moment, because somewhere in Saint Augustine is a passage where he says, *I heard the language of men.* He was just a boy, and it was as if the speech around him was a foreign language. And I remember that feeling, whether it was my parents talking or older people talking; sometimes I would feel like, *Why are they talking like that?* Or, *How can you say those things?* I had a kid's cynicism about my elders and their talk. At the same time, I was capable of talking grown-up talk—discussing politics and such—at quite an early age. Still, I was in another space, observing and hearing human talk as if I wasn't really connected to it, almost as if it were something for me to listen in on. I think that my poetry has to do with that to a certain extent. John Ashbery's does too—that is where I feel a kinship with him, that early on, at one time or another, each of us felt a distance from ordinary communication, or even from the sense that anything really was being communicated. But there were all these words and all these phrases. In a certain way, that foreignness, the alien quality, became beautiful and elicited, elicits still, a kind of sympathy. At first, the strangeness was framed as a language—spoken or written—that is beautiful, even though I don't really know what it's about; I don't know what it means, or what it's for. Then it became an attractive proposition, that it is not for anything: it's just there to be assembled and reassembled, and out of that assembling you feel a connection with the words, for the way they are put together, that seems to ring bells, and that one can give back out as something everyone knows as both strange and real. I guess that is the humanity of the situation. And that is the real stuff in poetry, to me. When I get a sense of that in a poem, whether it's one of my own or someone else's, that is poetry.

It's every time the same problem right from the start, because the artwork is different and you have to negotiate it, once again, in front of the blank page. Each time you have to find what's an important aspect and what's not. Each time you have to decide what to ignore.

Yve-Alain Bois (b. 1952) is a critic, curator, and historian whose writing marries close attention to form with rigorous theoretical analysis. He's curated the exhibitions *L'informe, mode d'emploi* (1996), at the Centre Georges Pompidou, and *Matisse and Picasso: A Gentle Rivalry* (1999), at the Kimbell Art Museum, among others. His books include *Painting as Model* (1990); *Formless: A User's Guide* (with Rosalind Krauss, 1997); *Matisse and Picasso* (1998); *Art Since 1900* (with Benjamin Buchloh, Hal Foster, and Rosalind Krauss, 2004); *Ellsworth Kelly: Catalogue Raisonné of Paintings, Reliefs, and Sculpture: Vol. 1, 1940–1953* (2015); and *Matisse in the Barnes Foundation* (2015). He is currently an editor of the journal *October* and professor of art history at the Institute for Advanced Study at Princeton University.

Yve-Alain Bois

What would you say was an important early aesthetic experience?

Well, I don't know if it's true, but my mother dates from when I was
five one particular thing that I still remember: a totally serendipitous
visit to the Musée National d'Art Moderne. We were living in the South
of France and visited my grandparents in the suburbs of Paris every
summer. My parents were poor, and that was the time for sales, and we
would do the tedious thing of clothes shopping. In order to make us
accept it, my mother would also take my brother to museums—but not
art museums; it would be a science museum or the planetarium or the
aquarium. Art was not in the picture.

One day we were going to the Musée National de la Marine, at
the Palais de Chaillot, and it was closed, and the next museum down
the street was the Musée National d'Art Moderne. I remember still
today things that I saw then. I think I was at least seven or eight, in
fact, as we were certainly living in France by then—my early childhood
was spent in Algeria. There is a work of art by Gustave Singier—it
wasn't even a good work of art—that struck me to the point that I still
remember everything about it. I've not seen it since that time, yet I
still remember it perfectly—only recently, thanks to the museum's
collection going online, did I see a reproduction of it: it perfectly
matched my recollection. When I was working on the exhibition
Rendezvous [2003] at the Guggenheim, I sent a fax to a colleague at the
Pompidou describing my memory of it, and right away she sent me
the name of the work, just from my description. I also remember a

gigantic allover work by Jean-Paul Riopelle—the French were very proud of this French Canadian artist, who they thought was the equivalent of Pollock. When I saw a Riopelle exhibition at the Pompidou many years later, I recognized instantly which painting it was, one of his best. There was also Brancusi's studio in the basement of the Musée National d'Art Moderne at the time, which I went to see again every time I went to the museum—before it moved to the Pompidou—as a kind of pilgrimage. Those were all shocks that had a very long-term effect on me.

I got interested in art that way. I always liked to draw. When I was a teenager—around fourteen—I had a total fascination with Mondrian. There was an expensive book on Mondrian that I pestered my grandfather to give to me for my confirmation; I still have it. It's a terrible biography by Michel Seuphor. But, you know, I'd not seen any Mondrian paintings in person yet. Two years later, in 1968, I saw the retrospective in Paris. It was supposed to be in the spring, but it was postponed to the fall because of the events of May '68. I think my first piece of art criticism dates from then: a letter to the editor of the Huguenot journal *Réforme*, protesting against a review. By that time I was already an abstract artist.

So you were painting?

Yeah, I was a painter.

What were your paintings like?

They were grids. They were a bit op. They were just terrible. I stopped for a couple reasons. One of them was that I was offered a show in a gallery in Paris when I was sixteen. I knew what I was doing was completely derivative. I had seen a film when I was much younger, *Prélude à la gloire* [1950], about the rise and fall of this child prodigy musician called Roberto Benzi. I've never seen the film again, but Roberto was presented as a genius who was conducting La Scala when he was like ten years old and of course ended up badly—I don't remember the details, it's been more than fifty years since I saw that movie. When I was offered this show I thought, *I'm not going to be the Roberto Benzi of abstract art—I don't want to be a circus animal!*

50

Another thing that happened was that every single time that I'd
done something I thought was mine, I would find out a month, six
months, or a year later that the same thing had been done by someone
else ten, twenty, fifty years before. I wanted to know who did everything
first. I thought, *You can't be an artist if you have this question, this is a question
for historians, not for artists—I'm not ever going to be a good artist.* So I stopped.
Even though I had been encouraged by many artists to continue.
I became very shy later, but in those years I was fearless. I would write
to artists, *I like your work, can I come and see you.* I visited many artists that
way. And usually they remembered me later because I was so young.
For example, thirty years later François Morellet recognized me as the
inquisitive teenager.

I was living in the South of France then, but every time I'd be on
vacation I'd go to Paris to see art, starting at fourteen. Once I brought
my portfolio to the Galerie Denise René—that was the main gallery
for geometric abstraction and op art and kinetic sculpture. Denise
René herself wasn't there, but her sister was and said, *We are opening
our Galerie Rive Gauche on the Left Bank tonight, why don't you come?* I was
staying with my aunt and uncle, and the rule was I could do whatever
I wanted during the day but I had to be back for dinner. So I went
home for dinner all excited about the invitation to go to this opening
later, and my uncle said, *Absolutely not!* My aunt interceded in my favor
and said, *Well, I know that my friend and colleague Jean Clay will probably be
there, because he knows a lot of these artists; why don't you take Yve-Alain, and if
Jean is there you leave him, and Jean will bring him back home.* I was praying
in the car that this guy "Jean" was there—and he was! That night he
introduced me to a lot of artists, including Morellet.

So Jean Clay was a colleague of your aunt?

Yes. They were both working at *Réalités*, a journal like you'd have
in a doctor's office. Jean did a lot of very interesting reporting. In fact,
he wrote the first article ever to appear in France on minimalism.
He was also doing a journal on the side of *Réalités* called *Robho*—very
interesting. He was preparing a special issue on Lygia Clark, and he gave
me translations of her texts, and I got fascinated. When Lygia came to

Paris, I met her, and she became one of the most important people in my life, a kind of surrogate mother. I met her in the summer of '68 when she was coming back from the Venice Biennale, very depressed by that but also because her ex-husband was dying.

Then I came to America for a year after my graduation from high school, from 1969 to 1970. When I came back to France, my parents had unfortunately moved from Toulouse, a wonderful city where I spent my adolescence, to a town called Pau, which I completely detested. At that time, if you went to university, you were required to stay in the same place as your parents. I was miserable there. I found a way to come to Paris—you had to either study something that was only taught in Paris, or you had to go to what they called the grandes écoles—ten or so different grad schools independent of the French university. One of them is called the École Pratique des Hautes Études, which was where Roland Barthes was teaching. I went to study with him.

What did you propose to work on with Roland Barthes?

You're right to ask that. You could be a student there without even having the *baccalauréat*, meaning you could arrive as a five-year-old genius mathematician and be admitted if they found you interesting. The professors didn't need a special degree either—Barthes did not have a doctorate when he started teaching there. It was quite a remarkable institution, a safety valve for people who couldn't quite fit into the system. In order to go there you had to come with a project, which you presented to the professor with whom you wanted to work. Your proposed advisor interviewed you and told you one of three possible things: *I like you, you're project is good, I'll take you*; *I like you, your project is interesting, but it's not for me, go see my neighbor*; or, *I don't like you, your project stinks, fuck off*. I know I had several projects, but the one Barthes took was on the typography of El Lissitzky, the Russian constructivist. I didn't know Russian whatsoever, and not much of anything else either. I was nineteen.

What had you read of Barthes at that time?

All the semiological and presemiological work—the early Barthes. I was also very impressed by Umberto Eco at that time. *The Open Work* was published in 1965 in France, and I was bowled over by that book. It taught me a lot, actually—how to figure out things I wanted to do. I was also interested in modern music, about the role of chance in music and so on.

What was your experience of studying with Roland Barthes?

That was really quite extraordinary. The thing about the École Pratique des Hautes Études is that there was no "coursework." That didn't exist. The only obligations you had were to go to your seminar, one seminar, once a week—you could attend others as an auditor— and have a project you were working on. You never even had to do a presentation—in fact, I never did any, because I was too shy. After being absolutely *not shy* about going to see artists of all kinds—recently the Reina Sofía published my correspondence with Franz Erhard Walter from when I was eighteen. *Unbelievable*. I must have been an impossible kid. That was very different than when I was with Barthes. I was very quiet. I also had a kind of psychological breakdown at the time. He was very generous, an extraordinary professor. His idea was that he was not there to transmit knowledge to us—you could go to the library for that. His job was to show you how one wrote, not in terms of style—he wasn't going to tell you how or where to put a comma—but what it entailed to actually write a book or an essay. Every year he would arrive himself with a project. So he'd say, *This year I'm going to write a book on myself. I don't want to do it as an autobiography, I want to do it as a set of index cards about my work. For next week, I want you to find words that begin with A that you think go through my work*. We'd bring in our *A* words and talk about them together. That's an example—this is the way he started working on the wonderful *Roland Barthes par Roland Barthes* [1975].

When he was working on *Fragments d'un discours amoureux* [1977], we looked at two texts by Freud, "A Child Is Being Beaten" [1919] and "Psycho-Analytic Notes on an Autobiographical Case of Paranoia" [1911]. We discussed those Freud texts a long time—four or five weeks. After that Barthes said, *This leads to nowhere, I'm not going to use it*. I remember one of my classmates saying, *Oh, Roland, you can't do that to us! We worked so hard on these texts—we looked at every sentence, every word*. And Barthes said, *Yeah, but it's not working for me—it doesn't fit into the architecture I'm beginning to see. It's not lost time, though, we enjoyed doing it, we all learned from this, it just doesn't work for this particular project.* That was a lesson. I wish a lot of graduate students had that kind of experience instead of writing dissertations with thirty pages of footnotes because they just want their advisor to know that they've done their homework.

One of the things that is very interesting, and I only thought about it recently, is that among the fifteen or so students who were in my group that studied with Roland, about half ended up creating and editing journals.

Maybe because it was so collaborative?

He wanted the seminar to have the atmosphere of something like a Fourierist community, which it wasn't, but this was a part of his dream. Many people speak about his *voice*—he had a very beautiful, welcoming, warm voice. The seminar would always start the same way: he would arrive with a half-smoked cigar that he'd light and then start talking, inventing new concepts all the time, but never in a dogmatic way, always with a lot of self-doubt—it's hard to describe. Then he went to the Collège de France, which he really hated—it was a big circus, he hated the atmosphere. Lectures, not seminars. People would wait an hour outside to make sure they'd have a spot. It was like he was on display. We come from the same background, Huguenot, so I knew *exactly* how he felt. And he was miserable.

How did you start working with Hubert Damisch?

It was Barthes who suggested I go to Damisch's seminar. I had never heard of him at the time—he had not published a single book then, and only a few articles. Barthes said, *You should go check out the seminar of Damisch. He's a little too talkative, but it might interest you.* And I did go, and I was completely blown away. It was really exciting. Damisch became my second advisor, because what I did with Barthes, the typography thing, was what was called a *diplôme de l'école*, the equivalent of an MA. After you had the *diplôme* you could start a PhD, which I also did on El Lissitzky and Malevich. Barthes and Damisch were coadvisors of my dissertation.

How did you decide to start the journal *Macula* [1976–1979]? What kinds of positions were you trying to stake out with it?

There were several things: at the level of artistic practice, we felt that everything was stale, because it was dominated by Supports/Surfaces artists—they had become Maoist, which was ridiculous. Their descriptions of Bob Ryman in Maoist terms was too much for me. Supports/Surfaces was supported by the *Tel Quel* group, which was very dominant intellectually, so you didn't see much outside that in hip galleries. We felt most of the Supports/Surfaces were not very talented and some of them rather stupid—the Maoism was just the tip. Then there was the dreadful art history situation: it was dead, and unbelievably nationalistic. Art history was about French art and French art historians, so nothing was translated from Panofsky, Schapiro, Riegl, et cetera— nothing that was not French. Also, the academic structure was completely pyramidal. André Chastel was in charge, a very interesting scholar to be sure, very learned, but totally against Panofsky. He was reading everything and at the same time preventing everything from being translated. French scholars then, for the most part, were simply not reading things that were not published in French.

What was it that was so threatening about that way of approaching art history?

Anything that wasn't French was felt as unworthy. Or maybe threatening because it had some ideas. Chastel was at the Collège de France, and he managed to appoint his friend Jacques Thuillier, who once started his keynote address to students with the advice, *Beware of ideas*. I remember that! That's the way it was. Art history was completely dead.

Art history was dead, art practice was blocked by a group occupying the entire field, and art criticism was idiotic. It was totally impressionistic—nice talk about what a writer had had for breakfast and how it influenced how he or she looked at a painting that day. *Journalistic*, no *rigor*, no *accountability*. You can say whatever you want and that's it. Art criticism in France is still pretty bad. There was also another tradition that irritated us—I don't think it exists anymore, because the notion of the public intellectual has disappeared—but it used to be that French novelists and philosophers would write prefaces for artists' catalogues. Derrida was someone who was very important for me personally, and he helped me a lot, but I'd say, *When you write an essay on Freud, you do your homework, and when you write an essay on art, you don't—why!* At the end of his life I must say he did, but it took a while.

How did you and Jean Clay start *Macula*?

Damisch's seminar was key. As was normal at the École, its topic changed every year. First year I attended it was the Bauhaus. Second year, it was the semiology of art, which was very interesting. Another year was looking again at perspective, which led to his book *L'origine de la perspective* [1987]. He was very energized, lot of new stuff all the time. There were a couple of artists in there too, including Christian Bonnefoi, who was an important member of the group. Also, something I forgot to mention about the atmosphere then, and which explains in part the historical role of Damisch's seminar: the lack of information about modern art as a whole. It was extraordinary, because there was nothing to be seen. It's hard to describe. Before the Pompidou there was basically no American artist in a French public collection. There was one cubist Duchamp, and after that, nothing. No Mondrian. There was only one pre-1910 Matisse, and not one that I particularly like, *Le Luxe I* [1907]. The lack of information was spectacular—and Damisch, with his formidable knowledge of twentieth-century art and also of American criticism, gave us much to munch on. For *Macula* we felt that we could translate art criticism from America and elsewhere, and have theoreticians speak about art, to address all these things. We borrowed some money for the first issue, and the sales of that issue paid for the second, and the second paid for the third. We stopped not because we didn't have any money, but because we were tired of having to retranslate everything; we couldn't get good translators, and it was just too tiring.

There were four issues of *Macula*, but how many copies were there of each? I have no sense of its scale.

I think it was about four thousand.

I love the anecdote in the introduction to *Painting as Model* in which you talk about translating a portfolio of Clement Greenberg's criticism on Jackson Pollock and then getting into an argument about it with Hans Haacke. At that moment, what was it that was appealing to you about those Greenberg texts?

There were two things: by comparison to the complete impressionism of French art criticism, there was some rigor, some attempt to seriously describe what was there. *Description* was not the forte of French art criticism after, say, Félix Fénéon. It was just, *I like it!* Without the slightest attempt to explain why this was so. Well, what do I care about your response if you give no reason for it? So in Greenberg there was rigor, although, contrary to what many people think, he was not very good about the materiality of the work. He'd often say things that were completely wrong, which led him to be criticized by artists, for instance Barnett Newman: *You said my paintings are "dyed," that's not true! Rothko's are, not mine!* But it was an attempt to put some order to the mess, even if you don't agree with his genealogies. What attracted me particularly about the idea of publishing all of his texts on Pollock was that you could see him grappling with something that he did not completely understand at first. He didn't like the "allover" in the beginning. At first he was quite critical of it, actually. So that was fascinating to see— someone coping with something that is completely new and requires a change of mind. Also what was impressive to me is the degree to which even though Pollock was his friend, he could say, *I don't like that*, and still they could remain friends. That would have been completely impossible in France at the time—the idea that you could disagree and remain friends. The French world today is still extremely clannish: *If you're not with me, you're against me.* This kind of openness, which is typical of American intelligentsia, is actually one of the main reasons I stayed in America.

How did you meet Rosalind Krauss?

I met her in 1978, and we published a translation of her essay "Notes on the Index" [1977] in *Macula* in 1979. She was in Paris for the summer to take this famous class at the Sorbonne on French language and civilization. I met her at Jean-Claude Lebensztejn's place.

When you met her and were exposed to her thought, what struck you about it?

It was just so *intelligent*. And she was a Francophile, reading what I was reading—Roland Barthes and Derrida and Foucault—it was amazing to see someone from America interested in all these things. Of course, I was interested in American art criticism. I still have the *Artforum*s from when I came to America for the first time in 1969, 1970. Those were the years of minimalism, postminimalism, all those things, which was also the moment when Rosalind became an important critic, so it was fascinating to discuss all that with her.

So, art history in France was a moribund discipline, but French philosophy at the time, variously referred to here as critical theory or poststructuralism, was coming to the fore. I'm interested in your experience of the work being done by Derrida and Foucault at that time and how you became engaged with it.

I suppose that for a student of Barthes and Damisch, that was immediately part of the landscape. Reading Foucault, you were stunned by the intelligence of what you're reading, without the distance to know that sometimes he could be wrong. Later you would find out that sometimes he would cherry-pick historical facts; there are some moments in *The Order of Things* [1966] where you can now see that he'd twist something to fit the structure he wanted to emphasize or underline. But then, you would just read it. That was the only obligation you had as a student, to read this stuff. And it was not even an obligation in the sense that you were asked—it was an obligation that you felt, in order to be part of the conversation. I was mortified when I came to America to find students asked to read these complicated essays at top speed. It had taken me three months to digest *De la grammatologie* [1967], and they were asked to read it in one week. *Impossible!* Of course they could not understand it, and the result was garbage—a theoretical bouillabaisse that came out for years afterward.

So when you came to the States, it was to take a teaching job at Johns Hopkins?

I came for one year. Nancy Troy was an old friend, and she was moving rather unexpectedly to Chicago. Michael Fried called me and asked me if I'd like to come for one year.

How did you know Michael Fried?

Nancy had introduced us a few years before at a dinner at her place. The first thing Michael asked me was, *Who are the artists that you like that you think I don't like?* I said, *Maybe Richard Serra and Robert Ryman*, and he said, *You're right!* It was really strange. He also asked me, *Who are your friends?* And of course I named Rosalind, though I knew he had a big conflict with her. But he had read some of my stuff, and, nevertheless, he asked me to come for a year and then asked me to stay. I said yes.

In the introduction to *Painting as Model*, you especially acknowledge your dialogue with Fried, and I'd like to know more about that.

We disagreed on many things, but he actually enjoyed that I was not a clone. We taught together and the students didn't know what to do. I was a young guy and he was the big professor. I remember one day he said, *We'll read the most important essay in American art criticism, Greenberg's "Collage,"* and I would say, *It might be the most important, but it's also completely wrong!* Once I assigned Fredric Jameson's first long essay on "postmodernism," and there was a student who wanted to look good for Michael and was endlessly trashing the text. Michael got irritated and said, *Listen, young man, if and when you manage to write something as brilliant as Jameson's text, then you can talk like that; I don't agree with him, but that's not the way to criticize an essay!* He was very passionate, but also very funny—people don't always know that about him.

A lot of your early essays were translated into English by Craig Owens and published in *Art in America* in the 1980s. How did that come about?

I met Craig Owens and Douglas Crimp at the same time actually, through Rosalind. I met them in the late seventies. They were both brilliant. Craig then started working at *Art in America* and was my translator. At that time, to tell you the truth, he was a bit arrogant. There was something overly ambitious—like a social climber within the intelligentsia. I remember him saying, *I'll show them!* But that completely disappeared when he got sick. I didn't like his essay "The Allegorical Impulse" [1980] when it was first published; I thought it was superficial, like he wanted to cram too many things into the mold, though now I understand better what he was trying to do and can appreciate the heuristic value it had. But I did not at the time.

When you arrived in the US, what did the intellectual landscape of art discourse look like to you?

When I arrived, I was very surprised. I had fantasized about America as a place where, because of museums and all that, there would be a lot of knowledge of twentieth-century art. But I found there was no one teaching twentieth-century art. Except Rosalind, at CUNY, and Leo Steinberg was giving undergraduate lectures at Hunter. There was no one teaching twentieth-century art at Harvard or UCLA. At Yale there was Bob Herbert, who was really a nineteenth-century person, even though he offered a seminar on twentieth-century art from time to time. I was completely baffled.

Also, orthodox reactionary art history was very strong—I had not expected that. I knew Meyer Schapiro, Leo Steinberg, and Michael Fried, and I thought that was normal art history in the United States. What I found was almost everywhere as dull as in France. But there was a big difference: in France everything was completely pyramidal, so a single man and his lieutenants were governing all positions at all universities and museums all around the country. To be a curator of eighteenth-century French porcelain designs at a museum in Sèvres, you were appointed by the same group as someone who wanted to do modern art history in Paris. Damisch and his group were the only people outside of that. Lebensztejn was inside, which means he had to do a lot of things he probably would not have done otherwise, but even so he was marginalized, and it took him a while to become a full professor. It was really a bad situation. By contrast, in the United States, there were lots of little pyramids. *And* there were a lot more people, so if I could speak to five people in France, there were fifty here.

You sketch out three intellectual trends in the early 1990s in *Painting as Model*: "anti-theoretical," "theoretical," and "a-theoretical." You

60

witnessed the rising waters of "theory" and its backlash in American art history and criticism. What was that like?

I was horrified. Students were reading two hundred pages of Derrida one week and two hundred pages of Foucault the next. Also the translations were terrible. Spivak's translations of *De la grammatologie* was so ridiculous that students would quote something to me from it and it would be precisely the opposite of what Derrida was saying. Richard Howard's translations of Barthes are just *monstrous.* He is so famous as a translator and I have no idea why. My attitude to teaching was, *Not many essays, let's just get one right—I'd rather you get one essay right than get one hundred wrong. Let's take this essay by Foucault, or Barthes, or whatever you want, but not a salad!* Because all these people were not the same—they disagreed! "French theory" doesn't exist! This is a wrong concept. It's an umbrella that covers different things. There is more disagreement between Barthes and Lyotard than between Camus and Sartre or whatever.

Of course, because of this fetishization of theory, there was a lot of *decoration*—people felt obliged to endlessly quote the same stuff: a little Lacan here, and a bit of Deleuze or Althusser there. That was really against my education, because the way Barthes taught us to write was that you don't just bring theory; you had to have a reason for it, and the reason changes with every object—there is not a single recipe you can apply to everything. For that he was often criticized as "eclectic," but for his students that was one of the great values of his teaching. Of course I was very sympathetic to the interest in these things; I was not going to say, *Don't read Barthes or don't read Derrida,* but rather, *You have to do it with the amount of energy and time it requires to do it, rather than having a whiff of theory.* When I'd say this, American friends would tell me, *Oh, you've become a reactionary art historian.* Quite to the contrary, I'm just wanting these things to be used in the best way.

How do you think the discourse has changed over the last few decades?

Obviously, identity politics has changed the whole discourse. I don't have any fundamental criticisms of identity politics, but it's not something that I feel easily drawn to. I guess it's my *French universalism*. [Laughter.] That has changed the way things are discussed. Obviously also the "global turn"—which I'm interested in, but it's not going to change my way of thinking about Mondrian. I'm glad these new avenues are open, but it doesn't need to affect me fundamentally. A lot of things have changed for everyone on the left after the fall of the Berlin Wall, which is bizarre, because it's not like Russia was thought of as an economic paradise by anyone. Nevertheless, this was a kind of public ending of a utopia—*Socialism will not exist, capitalism has won*. That is something that I think has affected everyone. I speak about this with Benjamin Buchloh, who describes the falling of the Berlin Wall as a big trauma or historical marker. I think it's true, but I don't quite know why. What is certainly true is that the utopian fantasy of the left, which I had like anyone else, especially as a kid who threw stones in '68, is gone. So is the idea that whatever you can write might have any kind of effect … it's not *despair*, it's just far less confidence in the power of words.

I also think that art history is ten times smarter now than it was twenty years ago. So, not everything is *gone*. There are a lot more people interested in many things, many mixings of fields, which has been really helpful. I'm always very glad by the fact that art historians now pay attention to what conservators say, and vice versa. Conservators now consider the historical context when making repairs so they don't stupidly make mistakes. Thirty years ago I'm pretty sure that Bill Rubin didn't even know where the conservation department was located in MoMA—and that he'd never gone there. And the conservators would never have dared to ask him anything like, *Should we varnish this Braque?* Now there is a dialogue. The interest in the materiality of art is something you can see in a lot of new art history.

That has been a recurring component of your writing: attending as closely as possible to the material specificity of an object.

That comes from Barthes, frankly.

Where does Roland Barthes discuss the material specificity of an artwork?

Not of visual artworks, about which he did not write much anyway.

But he talks about the material specificity of a sentence—he speaks about the *word*. He wrote to me once: "*Je crois qu'on censure le plaisir quasi-nutritif du mot*"—I believe we repress the quasi-nutritional pleasure of the word—underlining "*nutritif*," and you can sense this "food" part of the word in the way he writes. This attention to the specificity of the text at a micro level—that's Barthes. Images—no. But he did say that the reason he himself started to paint is to have some appreciation of the materiality of painting. And I don't think he did it for a long time.

How have you found different ways to apprehend that materiality through language?

There is no solution. It's always very difficult. *Language is always a failure.* [Laughter.] There is no progress. It's every time the same problem right from the start, because the artwork is different and you have to negotiate it, once again, in front of the blank page. Each time you have to find what's an important aspect and what's not. Each time you have to decide what to ignore. What to emphasize. Where you should split hairs and where, on the contrary, you can gloss over. Every time it's completely new. My conviction that this is very important has not changed—and it never will. When did I start really to take that into consideration? I think it probably comes from my early fascination with Mondrian. My approach to Mondrian at fourteen was following the clichés of the time, seeing Mondrian as a kind of saint who was making very "pure" work that was completely immaterial. Then, looking at the works, you realize that they're painted and the texture is important. Unfortunately, very many of his paintings were badly restored in the fifties and almost killed. That's because of the prevalent interpretation then that Mondrian was about "design": if you scratch your brand new Porsche, you have it repaired; if you had cracks in your Mondrian, they were repaired, often in terrible ways. You can see that Mondrian painted his white planes with different textures; sometimes the brush-strokes would go in opposite directions—in one rectangle they would be vertical and in the neighboring one horizontal. That was to avoid having the white become neutral or the same all over, and to make sure the light would hit each white plane differently. In short, there is a reason he did that. I think that becoming aware of this, as a kind of rebellion against the completely nonmaterial vision of Mondrian, is when it started for me. Also, discovering the work of Robert Ryman, at the time of *Macula*, in '76 or '77—his work really taught me to be attentive to texture and all that.

It does seem like the commitments and sensitivities to aesthetic experience you gained from art of the sixties was used to see historical paintings differently.

It's completely true. A great fascination with these aspects of painting lead to this desire for myopia—like looking at a lot of Cézanne with the help of people like Lawrence Gowing. It pays off to look at things in detail, rather than having a distant view, because you understand the way things are articulated, the way the artist tries to build this signification into the nitty-gritty aspects of the thing.

I'm thinking about the book and exhibition you did with Rosalind Krauss, *Formless: A User's Guide*, and also *Art Since 1900*—do these alternative narratives of modernism or postmodernism need a mainstream foil to remain operational?

The thing with "postmodernism"—I never felt it was an accurate concept. I always felt that everything that was called "postmodern" was just modern. In Jameson's definitions of "postmodernism," he uses James Joyce as an example—so if Joyce is "postmodern," what's modern? According to his definition, Piranesi is "postmodern," Manet is "postmodern"—quotation, distance, historical short-circuits—all these things are modernism itself. In the US the definition of modernism was so narrow that it ended up meaning only "approved by Greenberg"—a tiny river ignoring millions of things around. It's only if you totally followed Greenberg that you could decide that Duchamp is not a modernist. I was pissed years later to discover that the editor at MIT Press had taken out the quotation marks around my use of the word "postmodern" in *Painting as Model*—because I *always* use it with quotation marks. Basically, the concept was built against the straw man of a modernism so narrowly defined that it became useless. If you take Dada out of modernism, what kind of modernism is it?

64

With regard to *Formless*: it's not that everything was going to be pulverized by simply looking at Bataille's concept of *l'informe*. We thought it was not a matter of destroying the house, but just reshuffling the cards. What happens if you put one of Warhol's *Dance Diagrams* [1962] next to Pollock and Smithson and Kazuo Shiraga? Or a Fautrier next to a Fontana? Let's make bizarre connections that would not be morphological but would be structural. That was the idea. Because both Rosalind and I have never been interested in morphological resemblance—which is why we fought with Georges Didi-Huberman in the book/catalogue—but rather with structural relationships. That is what we wanted to see: *Is it possible to make an exhibition that emphasizes structural relationships rather than morphological ones?* That's always been my understanding of what formalism should be.

Forgetting the historical baggage of the term for a moment, if we were to start a renewed engagement with "formalism," where should we begin?

I would immediately ask people to read Russian formalism. In America it's disgusting how little of it was published. There has been no good book on it since Victor Erlich's *Russian Formalism* in 1955—*nothing*. There is this wrong perception that they were antihistoric, anti-Marxist—not at all. They were very concerned with social issues, and it's not at all exclusive. Read the fantastic text of Jakobson and Tynianov about literary evolution, for example. As a matter of fact, read whatever translations you can find of Tynianov: what he has to say of parody or of anachronism will blow your mind. Then I'd go from there to French structuralism.

At this point, how do you regard or define what constitutes a work of art?

[Laughter.] You want a definition of art?

Yes.

I don't know if I have one, actually. In that sense, I think every work creates the condition of discourse that should respond to it, so I don't think it's possible for me to give a definition.

So how do you distinguish between the qualities of works, like,

This painting is better than that painting?

Well, that's a different question. That is a question that is probably being asked right now by everyone who makes quality judgments, and there is no real answer to that either, except for the Kantian one. It's only because of seriality that something can be said to be a better representative of something than something else. Let's say I'm in front of ten Pollocks, and I can say that this one has more openings in itself, is open to more questionings, or more directions, than that one. And as a result *this* one is better than *that* one.

So it's from within its "type"?

Well, that is the way every judgment is made. That is why connoisseurs become better: because they have seen more. They can see better what makes a great Matisse than someone who has seen less Matisses can. The food metaphor is perfectly apt, it seems—Barthes again!

We're in this room, and there are a lot of different kinds of objects in this room. Some of them are rectangles hanging on the wall and they are called "paintings," and some of them are rectangles on the floor and they're called "rugs"—what is the distinction between those things, in your understanding or experience of them? Which is another way of asking, *What is art?*

On that level I'm very traditional. The painting is on the wall.

So for you, art is an a priori category within which you can make distinctions?

Yes. It has a function. It's a priori because it has a function.

What is that function?

Ah. To make us live a better life. [Laughter.]

Really? It's humanism?

I'm an inveterate humanist. You know, for a very long time, being a formalist was being a reactionary guy who just likes "forms" and is a disgusting hedonist—*Yes!* A life without the pleasures of appreciating art is really sad, but it doesn't mean that you disassociate from the rest of the world either. I don't think it's necessary to throw into the trash the traditional definition of art—it's necessary for it to be challenged constantly.

But doesn't Bataille's concept of the formless throw the traditional definition of art into the trash?

Sure! Bataille does. And he had terrible taste! Really bad. Did you ever see his book *Les larmes d'Éros* [1961]? Terrible. There is the anthropological definition, *Art is what is designated as such by a group*—that was Marcel Mauss's definition, and that suits me fine. My group being art historians, art critics, intelligentsia, whatever.

Do you identify more as a critic or historian, or do you not think that is a useful distinction?

It depends on the context. Damisch actually said the same thing: *Sometimes I prefer to be an art historian because art critics are so ignorant, and sometimes I prefer to be an art critic because art historians are so stale!* [Laughter.]

One of the things that really annoys me, when I go to see exhibitions today: there is a degree of complete déjà vu. You go to see shows and say, *This has been done before!* And there is no knowledge on the part of the new generation. Big stars doing something that was done *exactly* the same, twenty-five or forty years ago. Maybe that goes back to my complaint as a failed artist.

Art history offers vivid descriptive strategies for thinking about black cultural production by getting at its specific materiality, and I think that these means are sorely needed in a society in which blackness is always already spectacularized and too often denuded of particularity.

Huey Copeland (b. 1976) is a critic and art historian whose work focuses on modern and contemporary art, particularly its imbrication with constructions of blackness in the visual field. A contributing editor of *Artforum*, he has also published in *American Art, Art Journal, Callaloo, Camera Obscura, Nka, October, Parkett, Qui Parle, Small Axe*, and *Representations*, as well as in many exhibition catalogues and essay collections, such as *Modern Women: Women Artists at The Museum of Modern Art* (2010). His book projects include *Bound to Appear: Art, Slavery, and the Site of Blackness in Multicultural America* (2013) and a pair of volumes in progress on the intersection of race, gender, and the aesthetic: *In the Shadow of the Negress: Modern Artistic Practice in the Transatlantic World* and *Touched by the Mother: On Black Men and Artistic Practice, 1966–2016*. Based in Chicago, Copeland is an associate professor of art history at Northwestern University.

Huey Copeland

When you approach writing about a work of art, what's your process?

As a critic, my first step is trying to engage the artwork as much as
possible in person, and to record my reactions, thoughts, and questions
over time in a running tally, almost like a journal. After several engagements with the work, when I think I know what I'm seeing, *then* I start
to read everything that's been written about it, both in order to understand what central facts or features of the work have gone unremarked
and to see what things I've noticed that other people have noticed
too—*Have they dealt with them in ways that I would want to or not?* In other
words, I have to understand the discourse around the work and then,
once I've absorbed that, I can get a grip on what my observations add up
to and how they might constitute an intervention into the literature.
That usually leads to questions that take me to archives, histories, and
theories that help further contextualize the work, though, of course,
I always end up turning back to the piece to test the rightness of my
interpretations, to make sure that they hold in front of the art.

As for the process of writing itself, I often find myself initially
moving between two sets of notes: one set engages with the work itself,
while the other examines its historiography. When I begin putting
them together I think, *In what order should these ideas be presented?* That
tells me something about what my argument is and the narrative
strategy I need to pursue in composing an account. My investment in
the *texture* of writing—its moods, rhetorics, and style—owes much,
I think, to my love of literature, particular the language of Toni

Morrison and J. M. Coetzee, and to my graduate training. I was lucky to work with T. J. Clark, Darcy Grimaldo Grigsby, and Anne M. Wagner, my primary advisor, at the University of California, Berkeley. I was drawn to their modes of art historical inquiry because I am interested in the social history of art and in compelling prose, which they all pull off brilliantly.

Through their examples and their mentorship, those of us studying modern and contemporary art were not only pushed to think about what our discursive interventions were, but we were also implicitly expected, I think, to develop our own writerly voices. If you read Anne's work, it's very *voicey*, for lack of a better word—she has an inimitable writerly persona, and you can really hear her coming off the page. In a way, I think graduate training for many of us there at that time—folks like Elise Archias, Matthew Jesse Jackson, Eve Meltzer, and Bibiana Obler—was, in part, about *voice lessons*. We were thinking about how we could develop overall narrative structures, argumentative structures, and even sentence structures that could not only speak to the complexity of the work we were describing, but also engage the reader.

For me, the aim of art historical writing—as Anne put it to me more than once—is *to argue and explain*; although hardly unique to us, my friends and I half-jokingly referred to it as "the Berkeley Way." So, the imperative to speak persuasively and clearly to a wide variety of audiences is something that's part and parcel of my training and is an extension of my ethical commitment to the recasting of the field from a black queer feminist perspective. One of the most rewarding engagements with my work came from my own father, an erstwhile statistician by trade: he read *Bound to Appear* and sent me all these Post-it Note commentaries that were just wonderfully incisive. He deeply grasped the argument that I was making and its importance, even though he did complain a little about having to use the dictionary more often then he would have liked!

What was an early important aesthetic experience that made you recognize that there was something special about looking?

[Laughter.] Ah yes, the true story of the magical moment when a

70

young boy discovered the *wonder of art and felt moved beside himself*—

It doesn't have to be "art"—it can just be something you *looked* at.

Well, I'm joking with you, of course, but it's funny that in responding to your question, I started to slip into the kind of language Glenn Ligon deploys in his *Narratives* [1993], frontispieces to autobiographical texts that were never written. Glenn's work, in fact, has been and continues to be an important touchstone for me in lots of ways. When I was an undergraduate at the University of Michigan, the museum on campus acquired a wonderful set of four prints by him, all using lines from the 1928 Zora Neale Hurston essay "How It Feels to Be Colored Me." I knew a little bit about African American art history at the time, but I was just bowled over by seeing this work in person: the sumptuousness of the way those pieces were printed; how they used language to produce an image; and the fact that they were so clearly engaging, twisting, and *détourning* previous aesthetic antecedents, especially Jasper Johns's alphabets—Ligon was taking that system and using it to produce lyric from a black positionality that effectively turned lyric inside out. In looking closely at and writing about those works, all of these concerns came to the fore and made me incredibly excited: they opened up a world of like-minded interlocutors working through questions of race, language, history, identification, and the aesthetic in ways that had not seemed possible to me before. It was engaging with those works—picking them up and holding them time and again in the print study gallery—that made the space of art and art writing seem incredibly necessary, urgent, and freshly accessible to me as a gay black man.

Your book *Bound to Appear* examines four installations in-depth: Fred Wilson's *Mining the Museum* [1992]; Lorna Simpson's *Five Rooms* [1991]; Glenn Ligon's *To Disembark* [1993]; and Renée Green's *Mise-en-Scène* [1991]. Your analysis specifically emphasizes the spatial dynamics of them—presenting them almost as live theatrical experiences—rather than dealing with the documentary ephemera or the individual objects. How did you decide on that?

I wanted to reconstruct a bodily, phenomenological, and relational experience for the reader, one that assumes a spectator who is both informed about and activated by the installations. To put it another way, I wanted to engage the works from the perspective of an idealized yet specific viewing subject, who then narrates an experience of what it could be or was like to engage the work. Of course, I say "could be like" because these are works that I did not see in their original instantiations. Which means I'm working with subsequent reinstallations in some cases, or with the remains, those objects and ephemera, as you put it, which are compelling in their own right, but must be considered as parts of an unfolding ensemble. For me, trying to think through the spatial and affective experiences held out by these ensembles was really important. Thanks to a bit of archival digging, I was able to access floor plans for the works, and in certain instances I would roll out brown kraft paper on the floor and map out the relationships between objects—*Okay, four steps over here, or a foot over there*—to really think about how all of that would have informed viewers' experiences.

What I am getting at, I suppose, is the amount of imaginative projection, or "critical fabulation," to use Saidiya Hartman's apt phrase, that is involved in making works of art that can no longer be directly experienced come alive for the viewer. I was aiming to position the reader so that she's led through the work in my writing. At the same time, because it is *writing*, there's always the opportunity to step back from and redirect the work's narrative unfolding. Even with those qualifications, there are risks to such a writerly tack, particularly that of overdetermining the experience of the work, but I think those risks are worth taking, because otherwise you don't get a sense of the affective atmospheres engendered by the installations, an issue that has hampered previous interpretations of these works. In writing about *Mining the Museum*, for instance, I spent a considerable part of that chapter just trying to give an account of what it might have been to move through the spaces, something *hardly anyone else had ever really tried to do* aside from the authors of the original catalogue documenting the show. Most other writers just zoomed in on the installation's individual tableaux—say, Wilson's famous juxtaposition of slave shackles and a silver tea service—which then stood in for the installation as a whole. By doing that, *Mining the Museum* gets reduced to a few images and robbed of its materiality—which is of course exactly what the installation was about—so instead, I tried to emplot the viewer right in the thick of the work.

How do you regard the role of description in that project?

Description is central to the work that art historians do, and not only in the senses of ekphrasis or formal analysis. The challenge in *Bound to Appear* was to produce a kind of description that both offered an accounting of the look of the works and the logic of their opening onto the world without being prescriptive, instead creating opportunities, I hope, for further dialogue and dissent based on the visual evidence. So, the descriptions are meant to be polemical—even if provisional— and in their very texture, they begin to model the arguments that the book articulates formally and structurally. That's carried through in the way that each chapter is put together; the one on *Mining the Museum* has about as many sections as the installation itself. I don't announce that parallelism in the text, but it allowed me to organize my narrative in a way that was responsive to the very object that my work was engaging and becoming an extension of.

There's an aside in the introduction where you say: "To my mind, the modes and methods of art history matter to the project of African diaspora studies because they emphasize the merits of looking with sustained attention to objects in all of their multiplicity." I want to talk more about that, because I don't see very many people making interesting claims for why art history as a methodology or a field of inquiry is urgent today.

Well, I think that in this ostensibly post-everything moment, it's important to remember that there are still important skills— ways of thinking and looking and engaging with the material—that come out of disciplinary traditions, no matter how biased or myopic those traditions might otherwise seem to be from a black critical perspective. Art history is, in a sense, a deeply colonial project, but its means and modes can be taken up and repurposed for a variety of ends. I don't think they're *neutral* by any means, but I don't think they are inherently despotic in and of themselves. Those tools can help us rigorously engage the work of black artists, which often suffers from a dearth of critical analysis that, to paraphrase Rosalind Krauss, honors their work on the signifier—*What is this painting by this artist, or this particular sculpture and not that other one, doing, precisely, that's compelling?* That matters for understanding the particularity of black folks' achievements, the moods and tones and shifting emphases of their practices across a *longue durée*. Art history offers vivid descriptive strategies for thinking about black cultural production by getting at its specific materiality, and I think that these means are sorely needed in a society in which blackness is always already spectacularized and too often denuded of particularity. There's a way in which the topically focused "'issues-of' discourse" that characterizes far too much of the literature on black culture actually reduces unique aesthetic acts to a set of generalities that reflect neither the multiplicity of the work nor of black being.

Early in *Bound to Appear* you discuss Michele Wallace's characterization of the "visual" as a "negative scene of instruction" for African Americans. Do you think that's why the lineage of black art criticism is so much harder to locate than important work on music and literature?

Wallace's notion of the "visual" as a "negative scene of instruction" is quite useful insofar as it lays out a framework for theorizing the complications black artists have confronted and that any artist, for that matter, has to negotiate if they want to work with or on or through conceptions of blackness. But I don't think that means that we should underestimate the incredible richness and multiplicity of black visual cultures, discourses, and traditions that have, of course, often been ignored by the powers that be. Such elisions mean that we have to work harder to construct histories, to be creative in the face of willed amnesia, and to think seriously about the historical conditions of visualization in which artists are working. Literary scholars like Phillip Brian Harper and Hortense Spillers, who have echoed or anticipated Wallace's critique, understand a certain resistance to the visual within African American critical culture as a response to the kinds of murderous scopic regimes directed at black bodies. Taking these accounts seriously means thinking differently about what the visual in fact is as it's actively practiced within black cultures, and, to my mind, doing so requires an interdisciplinary approach to African and diasporic art. If you're considering Ligon's work, for instance, you have to know something about literature, music, and performance as they intersect with and inflect the visual. In his practice—as in so many other modern and contemporary practices formed and deformed by blackness—there's a constant shuttling between aesthetic modes while acknowledging that all of them are liable to constrain black being. This is where my work intersects with Fred Moten's indispensable writing, in its attention to those fugitive spaces for autonomy, for resistive articulation, that are always already present within and through the visual when heard, felt, and thought otherwise.

How do you see the place of your self in the writing, or rather, how do you understand the role of scholarly "objectivity" in your writing?

That's an interesting question. In the last few years, I've been really compelled by the way that Karen Barad thinks about objectivity in her book *Meeting the Universe Halfway: Quantum Physics and the Entanglement of Matter and Meaning* [2007]. She's a queer theoretical particle physicist trying to create an encounter between postcolonial and feminist theories, performance studies, discourse analysis, and Neils Bohr's philosophy-physics. She quickly dispenses with an ideal of objectivity in a Newtonian sense, the idea that you can be truly distanced from anything you're observing. Instead, she says, we have to embrace theories of relativity and quantum mechanics that underline the contingencies built into our perception and understanding of a thing. Barad teaches us that even saying *what an object is* is completely dependent upon your relationship to it and the apparatus you are using to measure it. *But,* if you can take all that into account, you can actually say something that is objective from within that very qualified perspective. That's actually been really helpful and freeing for me:

while *Bound to Appear* tries to perform objectivity in the classical sense—you know, distanced authorial "I"—there are other ways to bring myself into the writing that make it more rather than less objective in Barad's sense—if I understand her!—because I'm disclosing the conditions of the apparatus.

This is an issue I've continued to think about as I work on *Touched by the Mother*, a book of new and previously published essays in which I occasionally appear as a character, raising the question: *When does the acknowledgment of my own position within the writing become a distraction from an actual engagement with the work?* "Outtakes" [2008], the essay I wrote about posing for Lorna Simpson, was trying to balance that. It's not about gossip or name dropping or *Oh my goodness, I know Lorna, isn't that fabulous!* Of course, it *is* fabulous, but that piece was trying to grapple with what it means to be the subject of "your" artist's work and trying to figure out how you can narrate that experience critically so that the reader has a sense of your implication in the argument and thus the attendant strengths and liabilities of your reading of the work. Someone else could have made a similar argument about how masculinity matters to Lorna's practice, but *I* only came to that interpretation because of the experience I had of posing for her. So, these days, I'm interested in asking, *What are the conditions of social encounter or engagement that make certain kinds of writing and thinking possible, and how do we responsibly bring them into view?*

This question was at the back of my mind as I read *Bound to Appear*, because the kind of information that you are relaying evidences close consultation with the artists themselves, especially because you yourself didn't see those installations. It felt almost like you were writing out of a relationship with the artist as much as out of a relationship with the art.

When it comes to factual information about the works and the experience of them, I want to hear what the artist has to say, of course, but I'm always going to check it against published and unpublished records to get a more complete picture. So, sure, Glenn has an account of how the boxes in *To Disembark* were made, but let me talk to Jim

Donahue, the guy who actually built them, just to get his take, and let me go look at curator Phyllis Rosenzweig's files at the Hirschhorn Museum and Sculpture Garden, where the work was first shown.
I think in many ways the thing that I'm after when I talk to artists about their work is a sense of tone—the tack that they take toward their work, how they think about it, how they inhabit it, and how they see themselves moving through the world. That's what I think is really useful about those conversations, because they give you insight into how a work came into being. But I'm always taking the things artists say as performative utterances intended to do a certain work for them at a certain moment in their trajectories.

The dynamic between you and the artist is not a "historical" relationship. Everyone's alive together, and, to me, that means you're in a relationship that's different than traditional art history. "Contemporary art history" seems like an oxymoron.

In the case of *Bound to Appear,* even though I now know the artists, we're still talking about stuff that happened more than twenty years ago. It's contemporary in the sense that we're all, yes, *alive and here in this moment,* but when they were making those works I was in high school, and I was not aware of them, and Lord knows I wasn't thinking about slavery! So there is a distance you're working with that necessitates a turn to secondary literatures, archives, and records, because even the recent past is not static and shifts over time. If you look at an artist's CVs from 1991, 2001, and 2011, it's likely three very different lists—the early accomplishments start to fall out if they've been successful, because they want to reframe their career to emphasize the developments in their work that are most important to them now. To me, this underlines how even after twenty-something years the very nature of what a history is and how it's presented or understood is not fixed and can't be presumed. That fact does, I think, require the skills of a certain kind of historical tracking. I think with the artists in *Bound to Appear* it was, in part, about working with them to get access to both memories and records in order to construct that history and to produce a frame for that moment. So there are all these kinds of distance—and one could

debate whether they're properly historical or not—but they require
the same tools as history does to transverse, to understand, and to
reconstruct the context that mattered to the work. With contemporary
art, I still try to ask, *What is it that this work is doing in response to or despite
of its particular conditions of possibility?* I think that's a question that I'd
ask of something made yesterday, and of something made a thousand
years ago. It can become a little more difficult to say, *What* really *were the
key conditions of possibility?* given all the possible blinders thrown up by
our sense of the exigencies of the immediate present. But, I think it's
still important to try to articulate an understanding of what you take
those conditions to be, because they inform why you're writing about
the work and why you think it matters in the first place. Does that make
sense?

**It does. I don't have any skin in the game in distinguishing between
"history" or "criticism," but it's interesting to see how you conceive of
it for yourself.**

You know, some people are really hung up on this art history/
criticism distinction, and I just am not. I think my process, whether in
a critical response or a historical engagement, is the same, though there
are of course differences in the kinds of sources to which I turn and the
kinds of research I feel compelled to undertake in any given instance.

**Maybe the distinction is what a writer feels accountable to? When
you're writing about an artist who you know, who is alive, aren't you
writing for their approval to some degree? Doesn't that change what or
how you would write, compared to if they were long out of the picture?
I'm not saying this is better or worse, just that it has an effect—**

For sure, but I think, in the end, you want to get something right
about the unfolding of the work and what it's doing out in the world.
If you've done your work to develop a relationship with the artist,
they'll trust you to do that and to be responsible to it, but they won't
impose their own sense of things—*I want it to be narrated like this.* That's
rarely happened to me, even when what I'm saying is critical, or doesn't
show the work in the best light for promotional purposes. I want to be
accountable to the artist in not getting the facts about the work wrong,

or misrepresenting their own thinking about their practice, even if I don't agree with them. I think ultimately, though, I want to get the work right for the reader, for the viewer, who in this day and age is bombarded with information and text. Why should they be reading what you have to say? Well, because you've done the work and are trying to translate your experience of it, to, again, argue and explain in prose as clear and as vivid as possible. To my mind, that's part of your responsibility to the reader and part of your craft as a writer. It's not to say that I think of my own writing as something that is supposed to be as aesthetically compelling as the thing I'm on about, but I want my writing to have some excitement on its own terms, even as it's speaking to the interests of the work.

I think it's unbelievably clarifying to use the legacies of slavery, and contemporary artists' engagement with it, as a lens for writing art history. How did you start incorporating that legacy in your art writing? It's not something I've ever seen done before.

When I started graduate school, I knew that I wanted to work on the generation of black artists featured in *Bound to Appear*, but I hadn't found a structural framework to think about their practices, other than something vague like "identity." It all came together in the context of a seminar I took with Saidiya on histories of slavery. I ended up writing about Frederick Douglass for that class, but by the end I realized, *Hey, many of the artists I'm interested in all did installations about slavery in the nineties—what's up with that? Okay, that's actually a topic!* Nowadays, there's lots more exciting work being done around questions of art and slavery in the nineteenth century, but at the time there wasn't much recent scholarship beyond the *Image of the Black in Western Art* series [1976–2014], especially with a contemporary US focus. Because of that I had an intense disidentification with "Americanist" art history, which, to me, often seemed to proceed as if slavery never happened. At the same time, I was being trained as a modernist, and I was like, *Hey, you modernists, what allows for the making of the modern world? Slavery!* But not many folks in art history were contending with that fact either.

In many ways, I think what you see in my work or, say, Richard

Meyer's or Julia Bryan-Wilson's—all of us kind of doing our own version of the Berkeley Way—is an attempt to ask, *What are those forces that are constitutive of modernity, such as slavery, homosexuality, or labor, that have not been sufficiently countenanced by the discipline, even though they are central to both art and politics?* In my work, I wanted to underline that contending with slavery not only allows us to understand what these particular artists are doing and what they're preoccupied with, but also enables us to reckon with the *actual history of this country* as opposed to some myopic art historical construction of the cultural field that has no relationship to political economy or overarching social structures.

Of course, there are plenty of artists who engaged the history of slavery prior to the artists I write about, but it was Green, Ligon, Simpson, and Wilson's particular way of engaging that history that I was interested in: making the past highly discursive and taking up these strategies associated with minimalism, conceptualism, and institutional critique. These artists were engaging with the difficulty of representing slavery through means that emphasized the difficulties of representation itself, an ideal conjunction of thematic, formal, and conceptual problems that allowed me to think in ways that art history had not tended to before. *What if we took seriously histories of slavery and colonialism and the ways in which they inform and deform not only contemporary but contemporaneous aesthetic practices?*

In other words, we have to think differently about art given its relationship to the history of trans-Atlantic slavery. Fred Moten has brilliantly explored these questions in his book *In the Break: The Aesthetics of the Black Radical Tradition* [2003], which mattered deeply to my work in *Bound to Appear*. As Sampada Aranke nicely put it in her review of my book, taking slavery seriously means wrestling with the fact that the entire object world is black, has been constitutively *blackened* in some way. What do you do with that astonishing proposition, and what are its implications for art historical practice? *Bound to Appear* moves in one direction in search of answers, but it's a question that continues to drive my work. My other current book project, *In the Shadow of the Negress*, asks, *What happens to the Paris–to–New York narrative of modernism if we say it's not*

80

possible without slavery and the exploitation of black female bodies? That's the motor of it.

Bound to Appear is perhaps the first instantiation of an attempt to fumble toward something like a black radical art history, one that understands slavery as the beginning of the end of the world. This is an important, ongoing, cataclysmic moment that we really haven't dealt with culturally, socially, or politically, for the most part, but the art historical record actually shows us all kinds of evidence of engagement, traffic, and transfer. So, for me, it's about trying to bring the right kind of optics to bear to be able to see all of that. To be able to see the things that are right in front of you.

When enslaved people count as "objects," it really changes the way we discuss what constitutes an object. One distinction you use is that between the "object" and the "thing," though it seems to change slightly throughout the book.

Yes, exactly. I think the difference is a little bit shifty, as it should be. Certain people want to draw very hard and fast distinctions between "thing" and "object." I guess I'm not a nominalist in that way. Moten, in "The Case of Blackness" [2008], is really illuminating on this score when he draws on Heidegger to think about the "object" as something that's calculable, and the "thing" as somehow exceeding such economies. I was interested in how artists mobilized and *thingified* objects in order to create links between personhood and property. The installations I wrote about in *Bound to Appear* create the possibility for seemingly implausible exchanges or relationships between the viewer and the object world that pose all kinds of questions about naturalized modes of identification. When you're looking at, say, *Five Rooms*, which features large glass jars of local rice varieties perched on stools as if they were bodies, surrogates for captive subjects, the question becomes, *What would it mean for a spectator to "identify" with this jar of rice?* It's an absurd question, but that's precisely the point. What does it take to think about and craft some sense of one's entanglement and relationship with this world of things and with humans that have been excluded from the embrace of personhood?

I think everyone carries around a working definition of "what art is," but they never say it out loud, because it's really embarrassing and kind of stupid to be like, *This I believe*, but nevertheless, I want to know— how do you understand what art is?

I don't want to get into any kind of metaphysical thing, so if pressed, I guess I'd say that art is a mode of sensuous human expression that means.

"A mode of sensuous human expression"—sounds good. What does that "means" mean?

That it "means" for the person who made it, or that the work imagines an audience to receive its message. The "work" could, then, be anything from a designed object to a spontaneous gesture. Of course, "art" as a category is so overdetermined and culturally specific that to talk about it in general terms can be like going down a rabbit hole. I will say, however, that it's a particularly exciting time in my corner of the discipline because there is lots of really interesting writing being done on artists of African descent by people like Moten who are not trained as art historians. I think that can be fantastic, because we need to disrupt those disciplinary protocols that, historically, have not served black people particularly well anyway. I'm excited to see folks in performance studies, African American studies, and literature engaging with and posing questions of black art. At the same time, there is now a critical mass of black critics and curators and art historians of my generation— like my Chicago sister-girls Naomi Beckwith, Romi Crawford, Janet Dees, Erin Gilbert, Lee Ann Norman, Krista Thompson, and Yesomi Umolu—so we can begin to have those expansive multisensual conversations about aesthetic phenomena that carry the discipline forward and, hopefully, beyond itself.

I do think that art is, fundamentally,
about ethics. We keep getting told
it represents humanity at its best.
But it also represents us at our worst.
Many works of great beauty were
designed as ideological assault weapons.
Many are the equivalent of empty-
calorie junk food, meant to neutralize
us with pleasure.

Holland Cotter (b. 1947) is one of the most sensitive and insightful chroniclers of contemporary art, paying special attention to art by racial and sexual minorities, as well as from other cultures. Throughout the eighties and nineties he contributed to *New York Arts Journal*, *Arts*, and *Art in America*. He started freelancing for *The New York Times* in 1992, became a staff writer in 1998, and is currently the paper's cochief art critic. He received the Pulitzer Prize for Criticism in 2009.

Holland Cotter

I want to start by talking about your early life and your relationship with poetry. How did that connection with language begin?

It started at home. I grew up near Concord, Massachusetts, outside of Boston. My parents were a very young postwar couple. My dad had just started medical school when I was born, so there was no money to speak of, but they were resourceful. They were book readers, museum goers, and they loved music, especially jazz. While my dad was in school at night, my mother would read my younger sister and me poetry at the dinner table—just a routine thing that she did. Her taste in poetry included Emily Dickinson, which she thought would appeal to us because her poems were short and had references to nature, but also the language is so startling—it wakes you up and makes you listen. I got a lot of Dickinson early on.

My dad had worked as a lifeguard at Walden when he was in high school, and I biked over there all the time, so Transcendentalist figures were in the air. Thoreau the abolitionist, Bronson Alcott the utopian— all those people were neighbors in my mind. Also my aunt Helen was in her eighties when I was about eight, so she was alive at the same time as Emily Dickinson. Because she was a Victorian she had memorized vast amounts of poetry, Longfellow being a favorite. She knew *Evangeline* [1847] and *Hiawatha* [1855], which has all these wonderful special effects in it—that semi-invented Ojibwa that Longfellow got out of lexicons and incorporated into the poem. The birds and animals *talk,* and Aunt Helen had mastered the art of impersonating them.

It's so strange—about three days ago I was talking about that poem, and how incredible the sounds in it are.

Yes, they are! So I was getting that, what language can be and do. I became an early reader from all of those things.

At what point did you decide that you would be a writer or a poet?

It just followed. Dickinson was my model, because her hymn rhythms are easy to imitate. My grandfather, bless his heart, would take my poems and have them typed up at his office, and then put them into little folders, and my parents kept them for a lot of years.

When you started moving into high school and then college, were you already involved with art, or were you mostly focused on poetry?

I was also into art at that point because my parents regularly took me to the Museum of Fine Arts and the Isabella Stewart Gardner Museum, in Boston. Their routine was to drive into the city on a Saturday morning and leave me at the MFA. They'd just plunk me there and go on their way to do their city thing. In those days, in the 1950s, museums were empty and silent. I knew the guards because they saw me so often, and they let me just wander where I wanted to go. I went everywhere, on self-curated tours. My tastes changed over time, and my interests. But I always loved the Netherlandish altarpieces that were like windows with shutters, and the big wood Buddhas sitting in a circle in the walk-in Japanese temple hall, which is still there. But it all started with mummies—

It always starts with mummies!

I was there for the mummies. And because this was Boston, with its possessive sense of local history, I would go to look at *Paul Revere* [1768], the John Singleton Copley portrait. I loved history—the idea of history—and the idea of art being historical matter, that objects were containers of information, lost but discoverable stories. I don't think I reacted to art objects primarily in terms of beauty and form—I probably did unconsciously—but my interest was, *What is this about? What is going on here?* You go to see Copley's *Watson and the Shark* [1778] and there's this astonishing life-and-death narrative happening in front of you: *Why is this guy in the water? Who put him there? Why don't they pull him out?* It just fascinated me.

So you were doing this around the age of fifteen?

Oh, younger—ten or eleven.

And did you ever write poems in relation to the artworks you were looking at?

I don't remember doing that.

Once you went to college, what was your intent?

I went to Harvard with the goal of studying poetry with Robert Lowell. I had written a review of his book *Life Studies* [1959] for the high school newspaper, many years after the book had come out. My grandfather had a Robert Lowell connection of some kind and sent him the review, and I remember getting a note of thanks—as you can imagine, I couldn't believe it. So that's where I went to college and that was my only goal.

And what was it like working with Lowell there?

It was good. He only taught a graduate writing seminar, and I was a sophomore, so I was this little kid in a room with these older students. I was completely tongue-tied. He was in good shape that year. He had some psychological disabilities that meant he sometimes left halfway through a semester. But this year, 1967, he seemed okay. He spent much of the class time talking about poems by other, older writers—and he was a wonderful out-loud reader. He critiqued our work in class. But I was too shy to give him much. I waited till the end of the semester, and then I mailed him a batch of things.

Were you also studying art history?

No, although the first course I took in college, sort of by accident, was an art course. As freshmen we had a science requirement. I didn't know what to do about that. I'd flunked high school chemistry twice. So I combed through the catalogue and came up with an anthropology course, which qualified as a social science or something. It was called "Primitive Art," and was cross-listed with the art department. And that's what I took. It met in the campus ethnology museum, which has great collections of West African and Central African masks. As part of the class our instructor would show us films of masquerades and then send us out into the museum to track down the masks we'd seen danced. That was my first formal education in art. I loved it. It was also my first exposure to African art—the "encyclopedic" MFA didn't have any—and to art as an interactive phenomenon. It doesn't just stand there; it *does* something. It doesn't just exist in space; it happens in time. I eventually began to understand that all those altarpieces and Buddhist sculptures I'd been looking at for years were interactive too.

You have written continuously on African art over the years, so it's interesting to realize this was your first introduction to art history. How did you start becoming engaged with contemporary art?

Well, then there was a gap. I graduated from college in 1970—by that point my college roommate and I had become lovers and we lived together as lovers for a year and a half at school. He was a preacher's son and a history major. He'd spent time in Africa before we met, and was studying modern African politics. So along with my seeing older objects at the Peabody, he was telling me about what was going on in Africa right then, in the present. And this was the sixties, the postcolonial liberation moment, a very exciting, volatile time. He was on top of all that.

Were you always interested in politics?

I had a cushioned upbringing, for sure, but I was a fairly observant kid, and a few realities made their way in. Like everyone else in 1963, I saw the news: African Americans being fire-hosed by police in Birmingham. A year later, when I was in high school, I took a bus through the South with a friend, and that was a serious eye-opener. Also, thanks to older friends, I was reading James Baldwin in my teens. And being gay made me aware, very early, that the larger world I lived in was unfriendly to difference of any kind, period. That sensitized me to a lot of things. It scared me, and pissed me off.

Did any of your political interests specifically relate to gay rights?

Not specifically, no. Politically, Harvard was way behind the times about many things. News of Stonewall just didn't get there, or didn't get broadcast until long after the fact. There was probably a gay community on campus, but I didn't know about it. Anyway, I've never really felt part of any community, including an art community. I'm not at all unsociable, just not much of a joiner.

What did you do after you graduated?

My partner declared himself a conscientious objector to the Vietnam War and was required to do alternative service. My father, who was a doctor, got him a job in a hospital near Boston, in a factory town on the Charles River. During high school summers I'd worked in hospitals as an emergency room orderly, so I took a job there too. We rented a small apartment nearby and lived there for three years.

That sounds very romantic.

In retrospect, it was. We listened to lots of music—we were both into opera—and read. And every day we were involved in these care-taking situations. Hospital work was paycheck work, yeah, but it was much more than that—it was human contact work. *Hands-on, you-me, we'll do this together. When I tell you to lift, lift, and we'll get you into bed.* That kind of thing. I still think of it as the most satisfying job I've ever had, the one that felt the most worth doing, every day. And in a way that school wasn't, it was a moral education, a lesson in first and last things. Basically, it was the same education that Walt Whitman writes about in "Specimen Days" [1882], where he records the experiences he had as the equivalent of a volunteer psychiatric nurse in army hospitals during the Civil War. His job had a lasting effect on him; mine did on me. I think art schools should require all students to do a semester of similar work as part of the curriculum. If they did, new art would look very different from what it does today.

After the job was over, we went to Europe. We just had to get out of this country. We traveled around for a year or so and, among other things, went to tons of museums.

So this puts us at 1974?

Right. While we were in Europe, my partner decided to do graduate work and got into in a program in North Carolina. I wasn't ready to move there, so we went separate ways geographically. I didn't want to go back to Boston either, so I flew to New York. I stayed first with my sister, to whom I'm very close, then crashed with friends, and I've been here ever since. I did odd jobs—temp work, stuff like that. I was a bank messenger for a while down on Wall Street. I worked in a daycare center. I taught English as a second language at City University of New York at Borough of Manhattan Community College. That was a night job, and a great experience.

Why?

The students were older adults who worked days and came to this two-year school in the evening to get college degrees, then went home to take care of their families. They were smart, dedicated, and, by the time they got to me, *tired* people. I was helping them with written class assignments. The teaching felt completely collaborative, the way hospital work had. I'd never really examined the mechanics of language before: how you can organize it efficiently, make it persuasive, communicative. Working with them taught me that. I hope some of my teaching helped them.

So, how did you start writing about art from there?

In, I think, 1975, on the subway, I bumped into an old friend who had just moved to New York to go to graduate school at Columbia. Back in Boston he had started a tabloid-format arts magazine and was trying to get a version of it off the ground here. He asked if I wanted to help edit it, and I said, *Sure.* It was a multi-arts publication, so it included poetry, interviews, fiction, book reviews, music, and art reviews. We needed an art writer, so that's how I started. And this was my introduction to the New York art world.

And how did New York and the New York art world look to you?

The city was a wreck. A class war, directed at the black and immigrant Latino population, was underway. Really, it's still underway. By that point, I was living with someone new, an artist, down near Wall Street, in an old tenement a couple blocks below the World Trade Center. Many of our neighbors were artists of one kind or another. Some of them worked with Robert Wilson. And people were constantly coming through. My upstairs neighbor periodically had Bread and Puppet people down from Vermont camping in his living room. Through him I met Ray Johnson. My next-door neighbor brought

Harmony Hammond and Paul Thek around. Creative Time was doing installations and performances on World Trade Center landfill. Technically, SoHo was the contemporary art world, but there was this whole other world further downtown. And history was rich there. Great ghosts. We lived near where Herman Melville was born; Edgar Allen Poe and his teenage bride had stayed in a rooming house a couple doors down; Coenties Slip, where Ellsworth Kelly and Agnes Martin lived in the 1950s, was a short walk away. Anyway, I started to write about art while working on the magazine, which was called *New York Arts Journal.*

It was like learning on the job.

Totally.

How long did you do that?

The magazine lasted just a few years. There was very little money. We initially distributed it ourselves, lugging it around to bookstores. My friend and I were the staff, along with a few Columbia students getting course credit as volunteers. When you called our "office" you were calling a dorm.

As you were teaching yourself to write art criticism, who were your models for how to do it?

The critic I was reading the most was Edwin Denby, even though he was mostly writing about dance. I liked Jill Johnston a lot too. So in general my model was dance criticism. To some extent, it still is.

Of course, Denby was also a poet. Did looking at Denby hip you to the entire tradition of New York School poets writing art criticism?

Yes. I didn't know about it until I started to read him. Somehow through him I got turned on to John Ashbery's criticism in *New York* magazine.

That period of Ashbery's poetry is among the most dazzling in the English language, but it took me a long time to see the virtues of his art criticism, which just seemed so much more grown-up or something, in a way I didn't connect with.

Because the critical language was more functional, expository?

It was just so *clear*, and it took me awhile to understand how hard that is to pull off.

I've always thought that his criticism was absolutely crucial adjunct material to the poetry, if in no other way than in the sheer variety of subjects that he covered as a critic. He'd write about standard modernist shows, the stuff any critic in a mainstream publication has to write about because it's what readers presumably want to read about. But he'd also focus on off-the-radar figures like Jean Fautrier, and Anne Ryan, and Jess—and on unusual subjects like Japanese folk art, and Émile Gallé vases, and the Prinzhorn Collection. And he wrote about it all the same way, with the same enthusiasm, as if it all mattered equally to him.

That could equally describe your own criticism. Going through the archive of your writing, it's like, *Oh! Korean ceramics and Bauhaus weavings and historical African carvings and gay performance art*—and they are all done with the same level of care.

I learned from his example. As time went on I started to ask for something more and different from criticism, but it was certainly encouraging to read him in the early 1970s. Your other weekly mainstream choices then were Harold Rosenberg in *The New Yorker* or various disciples of Donald Judd. And that was all, essentially, formalism: you know, *This a good painting; that's a bad one.* This kind of writing could be made to sound tough and sexy, but if you gave any thought to what actually was being said, it was bogus. It was mostly about, *Look at me.* Young critics often start out from this place; I did. It can make you feel powerful. Later, you figure out that wanting power is a problem; *the* problem. Generosity is the answer.

Anyway, apart from very early, essentially self-published reviews, I got my start as an art writer with *Arts Magazine* in the early 1980s. By this point my then partner and I had broken up and I'd moved to the East Village—we'd been together for seven years.

That's a twenty-five-year marriage in the gay world.

Breaking up was devastating. It always is.

Did it affect the way that you wrote, either poetry or criticism?

It made me write more, because I needed now to make a life for myself, which partly meant keeping busy. By this point I'd published

a couple of things in *Arts Magazine*, so I asked the editor, Richard
Martin, if I could do a monthly reviews column, with the East Village,
which was then having its moment, as my beat. He said, *Do it.* The *Arts*
experience was eccentric and interesting. They had a minute office on
Madison Square Park, and, as far as I knew, almost no one was ever in
it. And it was hard to get anyone on the phone. So you either mailed in
your copy or slid it under the door. The next thing you knew, it was in
print—

Unedited!

Yeah, pretty much—misspellings, everything. Here's how I'd
communicate with Richard: I'd write him a note saying, *I'd like to review
the following shows.* By return mail, I'd get the same note back with a
handwritten annotation: *Great!* That was it.

That sounds so sketchy!

It was good, easy—I liked that mode of communication, the
way I like e-mail today. *Arts* paid next to nothing, but always paid
immediately, first of the month, before an issue was even out. This was
important, not just financially—though, believe me, we needed every
cent we could get—but psychologically. It meant that in some small
way you were being treated like a professional, not jerked around, and
made to wait and beg as happens too often to critics now.

Then after awhile I started writing for *Art in America.* The painter
Stephen Westfall, who lived in the East Village and wrote for the maga-
zine himself, advised me to wait until I'd assembled a year's worth of
Arts clips, then send them to Betsy Baker, *Art in America*'s editor in chief.
I did exactly what he told me, and Betsy invited me to write, gallery
reviews initially. The first time she asked for a feature-length article,
I said no. I felt I wasn't up to it. I knew how much I didn't know.

**Is this around the time you decided to go back to school for art
history?**

Right. But first some other thing happened. I found a full-time,
sort of secretarial day job at an academic computer center. I always
liked having a nonart day job. And at this one I loved the people I was
working with. I mean, some tech nerds were on their own very remote

planet. But it was also a racially mixed group of gay/straight/trans ex-hippie, pro-union social worker types. I've stayed close to them, which is one reason I've never felt the need of an art-world social life.

And there was a lot of time free for traveling. I went back to Europe, and then to Japan, where I stayed mostly out in the countryside, visiting small-town temples and shrines, with Tanizaki and Simone Weil in my backpack. I was learning where all those Buddhas I'd hung out with at the MFA came from and seeing equivalent images in their temple-homes, where people left fruit and water for them, bathed and dressed them.

How old were you then?

Thirty-something. I was getting restless writing only about contemporary art and felt I needed to expand my reach if I was going to continue with art writing at all. So I dropped by Hunter College and talked with the head of the graduate program in art history. She said, *Why don't you take one course and see how you like it.* I did. Ancient Greek art. I *loved* it. I nose-dived in; total immersion. In, like, two months, I reread Herodotus, Hesiod, Homer. I spent my weekends taking notes on pots at the Met. Then I signed on with the master's program. And, being the committed generalist that I am, I took courses in everything.

One course was in Islamic art, taught by a professor named Ulku Bates, who is Turkish. By that time I'd been to Turkey and North Africa, so I'd seen Islamic art in situ. Now I was learning about its content: what it means to people; how and why they connect to it. After the course was over I said, *I know this is the only Islamic course you teach, how can I study more?* She said we could do an independent study. When I asked her to suggest a subject, she said, *One thing that really fascinates me is Mughal pavilion architecture in Kashmir, up in the mountains—the topic is wide open, almost nobody has been doing work on it.* So I went to Kashmir and it was glorious. This was '84, just before it became impossible to go there—during the trip Indira Gandhi was assassinated and a lot of trouble started. From Kashmir I went to Nepal and India, where I visited some very early Buddhist sites, which intensified my interest in that area. I wrapped up the CUNY degree and went into the doctoral program at Columbia to concentrate on South Asian art.

And did you become involved with Buddhism philosophically or spiritually, or was it just an aesthetic interest?

No, I'm not a Buddhist. Louise Bourgeois once said something like, *I don't believe in God, but I have a religious temperament.* And that sounds right to me, going back to when I was ten, sitting with those Buddhas and feeling they weren't just objects. They were animated with the energy of the people who made them, and worshipped them, or just plain loved them, like me.

Also, I've got to say, the more I studied non-Western art in school, the more I became aware of how utterly unchill the idea of "spiritual" was within Western academic precincts. It wasn't just ignored. It was disdained. Ad Reinhardt a "spiritual" artist? *Don't even think that thought.* Which automatically, for me, made the thought absolutely worth thinking hard about.

So in the eighties and early nineties you're writing articles for *Art in America,* and you're starting the PhD on Buddhist art at Columbia, but it's also the time of the AIDS crisis. How did that impact your thinking and life and work?

It's still hard to talk about this. AIDS pervaded everything, daily. Friends got sick. People went through cycles of despair and denial. My old college lover tested HIV positive and died. Although we had long been with different partners, we had stayed close. The day he got his test results he called. This is before there were life-extending medications.

With your history of working in hospitals, what kind of activism were you engaged with?

I wasn't attached to GMHC or any organized program. I just did what everyone did, one on one: visited apartments, brought food, took people to clinics, spent time with them, fed pets, wrote checks. The loss is still incomprehensible. The East Village today is a ghost town for me. My faith in the American government, what little I ever, ever had, was shot to hell and never recovered. Thanks to ACT UP, some faith in activism, and art as activism, survives.

You often write about marginalized communities and art of other

cultures. I wonder if during both the AIDS crisis and the culture wars that focus was intensified or clarified?

Again, being homosexual, and knowing it practically from infancy, shaped my view of the world. I have had all the benefits of white male privilege, but I stand outside the range of heterosexual privilege, which is so taken for granted in American culture as to be all but unspoken of, yet is at the same time aggressively protected and promoted. For this reason, for as long as I can remember, I've identified with outsiderness. This goes way beyond the intellectual. It's temperamental. I don't *think* it. It's ingrained. And I identify with outsiderness wherever I find it, not just when it's related to sexual preference, but also to class, race, gender, disability, belief, and place of origin.

And I know this is a factor in determining my interests in art. My interests are very broad, as is my definition of what is art. But I think that what attracts me, in a general way, is art that's made under pressure, emotional, or social, or political. And often—though by no means always—this art emerges from "marginalized communities," including marginalized communities of one. Within a Western secular context, such communities would include religious cultures, present and past, across the globe.

So I'd say it's personal experience, more than a sense of deliberated ethical responsibility, that makes me choose what I write about. My frequent starting point is: *Wow, this is stuff is fabulous; I should tell people about it.* And writing gives you a chance to dive *into* fabulousness, take a crash course in it—every week! I always say that my job at *The New York Times* is a salaried form of continuing adult education, and I mean it.

Did you stop writing poetry?

Pretty much. No time. Maybe later.

You were writing these long articles for *Art in America*, and then you start writing reviews for *The New York Times* in the 1990s. The forms of those publications—not only the length, but the context as well—are very different. What was that transition was like?

It was hell. Betsy was always very generous with word lengths. I remember working on something and calling her in a panic and saying, *I've got six thousand words and I'm not near the end, what should I do?* She said, *Keep going till you feel you're done.* And she ran it. I'm so grateful, for many, many reasons, that I got to write for her—it was a high point.

How did she help you learn to write?

Mostly through encouragement. I don't remember her doing much line editing. She would make occasional comments—*You might want to expand this*—then leave it to me to self-edit. But having her read it, and approve, was huge, in terms of giving me confidence. In a way, she's still the audience I write for. She knew what kind of writer I am—I'm not going to hand in a rough draft, because I'm too insecure, or controlling, to let anyone see something unfinished. I have to hold on until I've polished this thing as much as I can, and that means it's going to be late. It just *is.* I can't do it any other way.

So I get my first assignment at the *Times*—this was in 1991; I was a freelancer—and it was to write about a show of South Asian art at the Met. The show had maybe fifty objects. I was told I could have six hundred words and needed to file it in three days. I thought: *Six hundred words—that's the size of, like, an extended photo caption—and I won't be able to even get started on what there is to say!* It took me seventy-two almost sleepless hours to write, rethink, rewrite, recount, reduce. It was very tough, and it kept being tough for a while.

If we were to diagram one of those reviews, would we find a set of strategies that you use to tackle them?

Fortunately, but also unfortunately, you do develop strategies, which can easily harden into formulas. There are certain conventions in newspaper writing that you pretty much have to stick with, like coming up with an establishing statement that lets readers know what you're writing about and makes them care enough to keep reading. There's more pressure on the top than ever now, with people on cell phones reading fast and itching to click on the next item.

What is the role of description in your criticism?

Important, because basically that's the "language" part, but I wouldn't say it's my main interest.

What would you say is your main interest?

Ideas, content, including history. More and more my interest is in how the past relates to the present—how old art is pertinent to what is happening in the world, and in my life, now. Whatever the date, there are the same basic human stories. It's built into the art phenomenon: *Somebody made this. Someone was here.* Our big museums, the ones that have the resources for broad-spectrum views, should use their permanent collections to tell difficult, comparative, and inclusive stories. Instead, they lean on the "beauty" button and keep you moving. Art doesn't speak for itself. If it did, the Met's African and South Asian galleries would be packed every day. They aren't.

It's hard to explain, but it seems like there is a strong ethical sense in your criticism.

I do think that art is, fundamentally, about ethics. We keep getting told it represents humanity at its best. But it also represents us at our worst. Many works of great beauty were designed as ideological assault weapons. Many are the equivalent of empty-calorie junk food, meant to neutralize us with pleasure. This is as true in the past as in the present.

And of course, who gets represented and who doesn't in museums is an ethical matter. The "encyclopedic" Met has no African Americans in senior curatorial positions. The Whitney Museum of *American Art* is only now acknowledging the existence of South America. MoMA, after a certain amount of critical shaming, has taken to cosmetically plugging in a few non-Western items here and there to keep us squawkers quiet.

How do you feel the climate of the art world, and of art criticism, has shifted over your writing life?

As for the mainstream art world, the changes I can think of offhand are the same ones everybody's aware of. In the forty or so years I've been around, it's grown unimaginably huge, rich, and professionalized. It's a giant product generator. One result, people say, is that criticism has been drastically smallized, made irrelevant. I do think this is to some degree true of the old thumbs-up-thumbs-down model as applied to individual artists or formal categories—painting, say. For me, the most interesting writing now tends to be aimed at larger targets: institutions, political developments, modes of thought. Conversely, though, I find there's more room now for the personal voice. This shift may have roots in the AIDS years, when any divide between personal and political became impossible to sustain.

How did you bring your personal voice into criticism?

Maybe after I came out in print. In 1994, for *Art in America*, I did a bunch of interviews with gay artists and I identified myself as gay, not because I thought I "should," but because emotionally I couldn't *not*. I needed to. That's all. This was a time when theory-driven writing had gained traction. In general, I find theory hugely interesting, a real vista opener. But as an off-the-shelf literary style it's restrictive, like legalese. And it's addictive. I've mentored some young critics and encouraged them to wean themselves from it, to try to find a voice of their own, a personal vocabulary, plain or not. I say: *Don't be afraid of "I," which doesn't*—does not—*mean indulging your ego, because who cares about anybody's stand-up ego? Just own the art you're writing about. Make it yours, and ours.* Figuring out how to do that can be your ticket out of the art factory.

For me, an art experience is defined by the consciousness of the person who made it disclosing itself to you through the decisions involved in making it. That is kinda spooky. And that entails a level of belief, and if that's not there, I'm not interested in it as an art experience.

I agree. And I feel that way about art writing. I think it can channel some sense of the consciousness that goes into the making of art. And it can convey a writer's "level of belief." There's nothing hifalutin, or mystical, about this. It's basic. An art writer can translate an art experience into words, into a reading experience, the way Denby and Johnston did with dance. Yeah, the translation is a different experience, a lesser one maybe, but it's the experience of people who were *right there* for the original, nose to the glass, the way I was as a kid looking at Van der Weyden's *Saint Luke Drawing the Virgin* [ca. 1435–1440] at the MFA. I was thinking, *Okay, I know this scene is made up, but it's also real. The curve of the baby's fingers—Van der Weyden must have seen that. Saint Luke must be someone he really knew. Mary's house, with the rug and pillows, must have been his house.*

In a painting, everything in it is there because somebody wanted

it to be there, and furthermore, they wanted it to be *precisely* like it is. There is a class of artists I think of as "gateway drugs" to art, where the artist's mind and heart are so foregrounded that you can look at their work, even as a child, and get some sense of what art is—for me it was being seven years old looking at reproductions of Van Gogh and thinking, *It's like a sunflower but it's also someone's feelings, and I can tell that by how it looks.*

My version of your gateway Van Gogh was Matisse's *Blue Window* [1913]. When I was in grade school, we were given boxes with postcard-size reproductions of lots of paintings. The one that stopped me was this Matisse—the most abstract picture of all. I got that it was an image of the real, everyday world, but filtered through very strange eyes. The sense of depth was off. The shapes were weird. I could name some of them—table, window, trees—but some I had to guess at, invent—play with, in other words, the way I was already learning language could be played with in poetry. And this was at a time in my life when play was realer than reality and helped me deal with reality. It gave me a place to retreat to, and to look out from, free from fear. When you don't feel fear, you see everything more clearly.

Art opens us to otherness, and not just the
simple sense of otherness of the different
subjectivity of the artist that produces
the art object, because the artist, too, is a
divided subject. The artist's unconscious,
as much as his or her conscious mind,
determines the work.

Douglas Crimp (b. 1944) is a critic, curator, activist, and
historian whose work helped define postmodernism
and institutional critique, having named the Pictures
Generation with his exhibition *Pictures* at Artists Space
in 1977. His books include *AIDS: Cultural Analysis/
Cultural Activism* (1988); *AIDS Demo Graphics* (1990);
On the Museum's Ruins (1993); *Melancholia and
Moralism: Essays on AIDS and Queer Politics* (2002);
"Our Kind of Movie": The Films of Andy Warhol (2012);
and the memoir *Before Pictures* (2016). He was editor of
the journal *October* from 1977 to 1990 and is a professor
of art history at the University of Rochester.

Douglas Crimp

When in your childhood did you have your first interactions with art?

There was no art in Coeur d'Alene, a small town in the panhandle of Idaho. I grew up in the fifties, in an educated, middle-class family, but they knew little about art—my mother hung a large "brushstroke" reproduction of a Bronzino portrait of a young man in our dining room because she thought the sitter looked like my grandfather. The nearest city to Coeur d'Alene is Spokane, Washington, which, as far as I know, still doesn't have an art scene. Seattle is the nearest city where I could have seen art, but I didn't go there until the 1962 Seattle World's Fair in the summer before I went to college. The World's Fair included art exhibitions; that was my first exposure to "real art."

Where, then, would you locate early important aesthetic experiences?

When it came time to go to college, I applied to universities that had undergraduate architecture schools. I got a scholarship to Tulane, and that's where I went. In my first year I took a required course in the history of architecture, in which I first saw lantern slides of architecture, and I loved it. I transferred the next year to art history. The art department at Tulane included both art history and studio, and it had an MFA program. I fairly quickly fell in with a crowd of studio art graduate students and began going to galleries in the French Quarter. There is an art museum in New Orleans, but I have no memories of it—it was then an extremely provincial museum, as I recall—so my first important encounters with art in museums were in New York.

And it wasn't until I came to New York that I saw dance or heard classical music.

I did see some theater in New Orleans, because Tulane had a very fine theater department at that time; most of the faculty left and came to NYU around the same time I moved here in 1967. *TDR/The Drama Review* was originally the *Tulane Drama Review*. *TDR* did special issues on figures like Genet and Ionesco; Michael Kirby edited a Happenings issue—this was very advanced for the midsixties. Richard Schechner, who is still teaching performance studies at NYU, was a young professor of theater at Tulane when I was a student, and a very radical one. I vividly remember that he brought Ellen Stewart to New Orleans, and I met her at a party. Because of that, when I came to New York, I went often to La MaMa.

There are many things intertwined in a life; I'd like to focus on just three: art, writing, and sexuality. How did each of those emerge and interact for you?

My education in Idaho was rather primitive; Idaho is a rather primitive state. It is one of the most right-wing states in the country. My high school girlfriend was Marilynne Robinson—

Wow!

We were best friends, were in classes together, went to the junior prom together. She wrote an essay that's in her recent collection *When I Was a Child I Read Books* [2012]; she recalls her education very fondly. She was from a somewhat more sophisticated family than mine. It's because of Marilynne that I went away to college. Her older brother, the art historian David Summers, went to Brown, and she went to Pembroke, and I thought, *Well, if Marilynne is going away to college, then I'll go away to college too*. People didn't normally do that in our town. I couldn't even get any guidance on how or where to apply. I had to figure it out on my own. Frankly, when I got to college, I was a fish out of water. People were so far ahead of me in terms of the kind of education they arrived with. I think I got a scholarship because there was a sort of affirmative action for people from states that were underrepresented—that was their notion of diversity at the time.

Were you reading literature in Idaho?

No. Marilynne was. We didn't *have* to read much in high school.
I wasn't like most people that I know now, who were "bookish" children.
I didn't read a lot, and I'm still a very slow reader. When I got to college
I really struggled to keep up. But I do remember that, although it was
not easy for me, I was considered a good writer from the beginning.
My professors praised my writing. That gave me a degree of confidence.

As to my sexuality, I made a very good choice when I decided to go
to college in New Orleans, which had highly developed bohemian and
gay cultures. I didn't go to gay bars initially. I went to sailors' bars with
the art school crowd, some of whom were openly gay. Even in the early
sixties, New Orleans was an easy place to come out, if you could say *any*
place was an easy place to come out for a kid from Idaho. I managed to
have something of a gay identity and a gay life. I would go on my own
to the French Quarter and hang out with drag queens in bars, and I
became comfortable with the scene. I enjoyed myself. I didn't struggle
as many men of my generation did with wanting not to be gay, because
from the beginning I got a lot of pleasure out of being gay, and I decided,
I'm not giving this up.

Was there a moment when you first felt or thought, *I'm gay*?

I knew I liked boys when I was very little. But "gay" was not a word
I heard, of course. I don't think I encountered the word "homosexual"
until I was in high school. I remember that in my high school there was
a very effeminate guy that was picked on—and I knew it was about his
sexuality and that that was *my* sexuality too, but there was no way to
understand it. There were no representations of it available to me. It
was something that I had to deal with entirely on my own. I had very
strong attractions to guys, but I didn't act on them. It turned out that
my best friend in high school was gay, too, but I didn't know it. I found
out much later.

Before Pictures seems to have both an emotional and an intellectual
motivation; at the same time, might those two impulses be in tension, or
have different functions?**

I see the polarity in this book not as "emotional" and "intellectual," but something more like "autobiographical" and "critical." The components are, on the one hand, autobiographical anecdotes, and, on the other, an actual enactment of criticism. In returning to things that I did in my first decade in New York, I regard them from my present perspective, and often tackle issues that arise for me only now. For example: in the Agnes Martin chapter, which springs from the fact that I did a small exhibition of her work in 1971 and visited her in New Mexico, I analyze her film *Gabriel,* which I didn't encounter in 1976 when she made it, but only when I set about writing that chapter.

I was interested in putting together two aspects of my life that were fairly difficult to negotiate in my first decade in New York—my art-world self and my gay-world self, at a time when both those worlds were highly experimental. I experienced innovation, experimentation, and transformation in the queer world and the art world simultaneously but mostly separately. I had to figure out how to make my two worlds, if not *cohere*, at least not be absolutely in conflict. My hope for *Before Pictures* is that it will provide a "queer history" of both these worlds by putting them in conversation. I expect it might change how we think of seventies gay culture, which we know mostly from the work of historians who write about the flourishing of gay politics. It might also change how we think about the art world of the seventies.

I had several different motivations for writing the book. One is that, in my ACT UP days, I made a whole bunch of younger friends, people mostly twenty years younger than me. I experienced the extraordinary explosion of gay culture during the seventies, but they didn't. I talked about it, they asked me about it, and on a couple occasions people said, *You should really write about the gay seventies in New York.* That is not only because of their interest in what I was saying but because we were all horrified by the new narrative that was being put in place by gay conservatives. This narrative held that the seventies represented our immaturity, an immaturity that led inevitably to AIDS, which in turn made us grow up and mature, become good citizens who wanted to get married and settle down and behave ourselves. I opposed that narrative in all of my AIDS writing.

This was happening around the time that queer theory was invented. I began teaching gay studies at Sarah Lawrence College in 1990 and then taught queer theory at the University of Rochester, and I was very much aware of all the conservative gay journalism, which was also antitheory, anti–queer theory.

It was for popular readership, for magazines.

Books, too. In writing a book about gay culture in the seventies as I experienced it, I had a goal entirely beyond telling my own story. I want to reclaim that era of gay life in the positive light in which I experienced it for its present radical potential. It is a political goal. So that is one origin of the book. Another is that, like anyone, I have my amusing stories, stories I've told over time. In 2004 my friend Yvonne Rainer, about whom I was preparing to teach a course, gave me the manuscript of her memoir, *Feelings Are Facts* [2006], which is very moving. Someone I was close to publishing an autobiographical work made me realize that such a thing was not out of the question for me. But I try not to call *Before Pictures* a memoir. The book is a hybrid of memoir, history, and criticism—and, importantly, pictures. There are over one hundred and fifty illustrations: reproductions of artworks, fashion photographs, film stills, pictures of architecture and dance, snapshots of me—and wonderful photographs that Zoe Leonard took for section dividers, of the five buildings I've lived in in New York and the nearby subway stops.

I'm interested in how *Before Pictures* relates to the larger presence of memoir as a mode of critical writing and increased interest within the larger culture at the moment. Look at the popularity of critics like Hilton Als, Wayne Koestenbaum, or Chris Kraus—there is a huge interest in memoir. Or would you characterize the current direction of art criticism differently?

I'm not sure I could characterize a "current direction of art criticism" at all, at this point. Apart from writing this book, which I've done over the past ten years, I've been writing about dance. So I probably don't pay as much attention as you do to recent art criticism. To the extent that I do, it's pretty much limited to an academic sphere. I teach in a PhD program; although it is interdisciplinary, the primary interest of many students is contemporary art. Many of the books my colleagues and I teach from are by academically trained art historians—by the scholar-critics who write the *October* books, such as Branden Joseph on Robert Rauschenberg, Carrie Lambert-Beatty on Yvonne Rainer, or Devin Fore's *Realism after Modernism* [2012]. My close colleague Rachel Haidu wrote an *October* book on Marcel Broodthaers. And then there are the books by my own former graduate students, like Darby English. I tend to think of recent art criticism as following this academic model. Probably what you're talking about is a reaction to that, which I perfectly understand.

Another aspect of contemporary culture that *Before Pictures* relates to is the mythology of New York in the seventies. There is an obsession with the work that was made in New York in the seventies—*when lofts in SoHo were cheap, and so much art had a specific spare aesthetic—*that I find exhausting. To have lived through the seventies in New York and then experience this reification of it must be rather complicated.

For a period I, too, thought there was something of an obsession with the 1970s, but I've recently felt that we've moved beyond it. Of course, there are certain artists working in the seventies that graduate students who are your age are particularly drawn to, and some of those artists are still making great work—Joan Jonas, for example. When I began writing this book in 2005 and for the following five years or so I felt that it was dovetailing with a more general interest in the seventies, but I'm not sure we're still there.

Certainly, though, it was possible to live in New York in that period as an artist or a critic or a choreographer and have a lot of free time and a good-sized living and studio space—it *was* cheap—in stark contrast to what it's like now. I actually thought for a while that I would be able to support myself by writing art criticism. I don't know how anybody does it now. I don't know how young dancers, especially, can manage to live and work in this city. Another reason the seventies might seem like a golden era is that it was before AIDS. And because it was so affordable to live here then, lots of gay people got by on part-time jobs and were able to stay out until five in the morning cruising and having sex at the trucks or the piers. That's what I did then. So questions like *What's become of New York?* or *What's become of gay life?* retroactively cast that particular decade in a particular light.

How did you see that manifest in relation to the recent *Greater New York* show at MoMA PS1 [2015–2016], of which you were a cocurator, which seemed to incorporate that seventies nostalgia as part of its premise?

Long before they invited me to become part of the team, the three other curators decided they didn't want this iteration of *Greater New York* to be one more "emerging artists" show; they chose to disrupt that expectation by adding a historical dimension. PS1 was approaching its fortieth anniversary; returning to its founding moment in 1976 prompted the very questions that we're talking about—New York City, then versus now. *How do young artists manage to work New York today? To what extent does their work engage with the issues that the city today confronts us with—extreme income inequality, lack of affordable housing, racism?* That is what Peter Eleey presented me with when he approached me for the project. One reason he thought of me was that he came to PS1 in 2010, just at the time that Lynne Cooke and I did the exhibition *Mixed Use, Manhattan* [2010] at the Reina Sofía in Madrid, and he really wanted to bring it to New York, but it wasn't possible. It was a major disappointment to Lynne and me that we couldn't find a venue in New York for the show, which was, after all, *about* New York. So when Peter invited me I thought, *This is an opportunity to bring some of that material back to New York. Mixed Use, Manhattan* was not a seventies show; like *Greater New York*, it began in the seventies and came up to the present, but there were works like James Nares's *Pendulum* [1976] that I had discovered while working on *Mixed Use, Manhattan* and was very happy to be able to bring to New York. It became a kind of keynote for *Greater New York* because it was the work you encountered in the double-height space just off the lobby.

How do you see the relationship between criticism and art history?

During the period covered in *Before Pictures*, I was struggling against a Greenbergian model, a model that posited a historical necessity in the progress of art, which in turn determined which art "passed" and which art "failed." That teleological view was something that I didn't give up, even if I gave up the kind of art that Greenberg and his followers were interested in. I discuss this in the book's final chapter, explaining that when I was writing the essay "Pictures" [1977] I still wanted to make a case for the historical logic of the work. This is something I no longer want to do, because it is simply not why I write about art today. In my AIDS writing I gradually adopted a more personal voice, and that continues not only in *Before Pictures*, but in my previous book, *"Our Kind of Movie": The Films of Andy Warhol*, and in my current writing on dance. Much of the writing is almost minutely descriptive, and out of that description grows my analysis. I attend to my subjective experience of the work and also to the question of the subject in the work—what the work does *for* the subject or *to* the subject. The turn toward the subject that emerged with poststructuralism absolutely continues to inform what I do, but it informs it differently than it did when I was first reading poststructuralist theory in the seventies.

I think of myself as both a critic and an art historian, probably more a critic than a historian. I'm trained as an art historian and I train art historians, but my work since I finished college has always been on contemporary art. The people who wrote about contemporary art when I began writing art criticism weren't art historians for the most part. I studied very briefly at the Institute of Fine Arts at NYU around 1970, and at that time you were not allowed to work on a living artist. Art history basically stopped when the last generation died. Now, more than fifty percent of people who study in art history graduate programs in the United States declare their field as "contemporary"; all other periods of art history are sadly dwindling. So when I said that my take on contemporary criticism has very much to do with academic art historians writing about contemporary art, that is because we've now produced a couple of generations of critics who are academically trained in contemporary art, who've written dissertations about contemporary art, and tend to use the prose style that is often disparaged as "academic." I think you agree that I don't write that kind of prose.

You're a very clear writer.

Of course, so-called academic writing can be perfectly clear too, and it must be said that not all of us academics write the same way. Rosalind Krauss is an academic art historian—trained at Harvard, teaching at Columbia—and she is a wonderful writer. I enjoy writing and I work hard at the craft of it. I wasn't reading literature in Idaho but I did learn my grammar, and that has served me well. I hope some of my pleasure in writing comes through for the reader. I try to get my students to become cognizant of style when they write, because so much of what they are reading has a dissertation-like style, the style of a first book that has been slightly adapted from a dissertation. I want my students to find their own voices. I don't want their writing to be that kind of predictable, impersonal, nonidentifiable voice that is fairly standard in academia. There also are, of course, people who write "academic" prose very beautifully—there is great precision combined with serious scholarship clearly readable in the writing, and that can be a joy to read.

As you were learning to write about art, especially at the very beginning, when you were an editorial associate at *ARTnews*, who were you reading as models?

I began reading art magazines in college because of my friendship with studio art students. I'm a complete autodidact as an art writer. I read *ARTnews* and *Art in America*. *ARTnews* did not, of course, cover only contemporary art—it included a wide historical range, including things like Leo Steinberg's 1972 "The Philosophical Brothel" on Picasso's *Les demoiselles d'Avignon* [1907], and Linda Nochlin's 1971 "Why Have There Been No Great Women Artists?" When I came to New York I had the extraordinary luck of almost immediately getting a job at the Guggenheim. I wasn't initially a curatorial assistant. I was more lowly than that. When Diane Waldman was working on a Roy Lichtenstein exhibition, she came to me to help edit the catalogue and was impressed by my work on it and hired me to be her curatorial assistant. Diane was very good friends with Betsy Baker, who was the managing editor at *ARTnews* and commissioned me to write an article on a Georgia O'Keeffe exhibition at the Whitney, which was the first thing I ever published.

Betsy was a terrific editor, and she took a chance and gave me the assignment—I was extremely lucky. A few years later I became a regular reviewer. *ARTnews* had a policy of reviewing every exhibition in town every month—*imagine*! The reviews were extremely short, just five or six lines. It's really tough to say anything at all in that amount of space. You'd be given a list of exhibitions to review and you had little choice in the matter. Shortly after starting at *ARTnews* I became one of the writers of the "New York Letter" for *Art International*. There I was actually able to choose artists I had an interest in and write a longer form of journalism, in which a thematic thread might run through the monthly column.

I didn't know much about the differences between the various magazines. Even an opposition between *ARTnews* and *Artforum* was not something that I fully understood, though I think I looked up to *Artforum* because it seemed to be the more truly intellectual journal. I was reading Rosalind Krauss and Annette Michelson in *Artforum* before I met them, and I knew I wanted to study with Rosalind because of her writing for *Artforum* in the period after she broke ranks with Greenberg and Fried. By the time I went back to graduate school to work with her in 1976, I was part of an art-world milieu that was very different from hers. I was part of the downtown art world, the world around Helene Winer and Artists Space; *Pictures* comes out of that. Rosalind knew nothing of those artists until I wrote about them—she learned about them from me.

What's interesting about *Before Pictures* is that its perspective is qualified in all kinds of interesting ways. By contrast, when I went back to reread *On the Museum's Ruins*, I was surprised at how invested it is in its own authority and the authoritativeness of its readings.

I was part of a very specific world, the world of *October*, when I wrote those essays. I was influenced by my colleagues and very much in sync with them. Also, the eighties were a time of important political stakes, so my writing was very polemical. Essays like "The Art of Exhibition" [1984] and "The End of Painting" [1981]—really all of the essays in *On the Museum's Ruins*—are polemical; I am definitely arguing a position. My leaving *October* was such a traumatic experience that I had to reinvent myself, or refind myself, become a different person and a different writer afterward.

How would you describe the nature of that trauma?

I was pushed out of *October*. I edited the AIDS issue in 1987 single-handedly. It became far and away the most successful issue that *October* had ever done—it sold the most copies, got the most attention, and immediately became an *October* book. My fellow editors came, I think, to resent that success, and particularly the fact that for a new group of readers, *October* was "Douglas Crimp's magazine," not "Rosalind Krauss and Annette Michelson's magazine."

Becoming an AIDS activist transformed me intellectually. It transformed what I wanted to work on, and it brought me, methodologically, closer to cultural studies. I was bringing that perspective to bear at a time when Rosalind and Annette had more or less withdrawn from the day-to-day work of the magazine—they had grown tired of it. The pace of putting out a quarterly magazine is relentless. After they pushed me out by refusing two of the papers from the conference "How Do I Look? Queer Film and Video" [1989], they brought in five new editors to replace me. That took much of the burden off of them, and eventually that group of editors brought in their former students—a whole new generation of people to bring material to the magazine. *October* never published much unsolicited material; it doesn't operate the way most academic journals do. It was never a peer-reviewed journal. It's a big job to find things you want to publish, especially if your notion of what is right for your journal is as narrow as it always has been for *October*. It became narrower still after I left. The interdisciplinary aspect that characterized the first ten years largely disappeared. Annette is an intellectual with very broad interests—in music, film, literature, politics, and art—and she gave the magazine a breadth that I feel it doesn't have anymore, even though she is still there. It's now much more a visual art publication—and a high-modernist one, at that. At the time they forced me out, *October* was my job, so I suddenly found myself jobless, without an income.

Presumably it was also a huge part of your social life, at least in

the art world.

It was my art-world identity. But by then of course I had begun to move into a different world, the world of AIDS activism, the queer world. I left *October* in 1990, and *AIDS Demo Graphics* was published that same year, so you can see where I was at that time. Luckily, I got the Sarah Lawrence gay studies position just at the moment I needed a new job. I wasn't paid very well at *October*, so it wasn't like I suffered financially by moving into the academy. But I hadn't finished my dissertation, because I had put it on hold when I got drawn into the AIDS activist movement. Once I began teaching at the University of Rochester, I really needed a PhD. All of this happened so quickly, and for a few years I really struggled. And I should also say: I loved editing a magazine. I had no desire to become a professor.

One of the pieces I appreciated the most in *Melancholia and Moralism* was the essay on the AIDS quilt, and your ambivalence about it. At the end you wrote: "I have to ask of this representation what I ask of all representations: to whom is it addressed?" How do you think of that in relation to your writing: To whom is your criticism addressed, and *Before Pictures* in particular?

Nearly everything I write is written initially as a talk, even the chapters of this book. For example, the *ARTnews* chapter was written as a keynote address for a conference in honor of my friend Henry Abelove's teaching career. Henry taught for years at Wesleyan and was a very beloved and influential teacher. He was one of the editors of *The Lesbian and Gay Studies Reader* [1993]. His fields were history and English, but he was a major instigator of queer studies in the academy. One of Henry's greatest loves is poetry, especially Frank O'Hara and James Schuyler. I'm not a poetry reader. And while I'm a cinephile, Henry doesn't go to the movies. He reacts badly to images that move. So I wrote a chapter about my cinephilia—in the company of my first boyfriend—and my simultaneous sense of alienation from the *ARTnews* poet-critics, thus about my love of movies and Henry's love of poetry, my inability to read poetry and Henry's inability to see movies. I wrote the talk thinking about Henry and imagining an audience of his former students who would be giving papers at the conference. So there are often very concrete "listeners" in my head when I'm writing. I think my prose style comes partly from my sense of how it will sound when spoken and thus its "sound" as you're reading.

To shift for a moment: to write autobiographically is not to write about one's self necessarily, but to write about one's self in relation to other people. That opens a can of worms, ethically, regarding how to represent others. I'm interested in how you thought about this in writing *Before Pictures*? I'm thinking particularly of the scene from the *ARTnews* section where you describe having sex with David Kermani, who was John Ashbery's boyfriend, and then having an unpleasant encounter with Ashbery afterward. It wasn't a particularly sweet story, nor sweetly told; does that matter to you?

Sure, it matters. I hope I don't seem mean-spirited toward anyone. There are stories that people will undoubtedly not like to read about themselves. I no longer have any connection to Ashbery and Kermani—they are historical personages to me now. It's a very long time ago that I knew them, and in any case, I never knew them well. Some of my resentment toward Ashbery likely comes from the way he titled my first essays in *ARTnews*—I should be over it by now, of course. I think he was just fooling around, not caring at all about what the authors had written, and he titled my piece on Georgia O'Keeffe "Georgia Is a State of Mind" [1970]. Really bad punning: Georgia is a state, and "Georgia on My Mind" [1930]—*awful*. If that's surrealist poetry, then you can have it! The story I tell is true, but I suppose it could seem overly gossipy— although lots of memoirs are full of far more vicious gossip.

Of course gossip has been theorized and reclaimed within queer theory too. And I guess Ellsworth Kelly, on whom you wrote a chapter, is now dead—

But he wasn't when I wrote the chapter about my brief fling with him; even up until the time I was seeking image rights he was alive.

Can I clarify: You said Kelly was mainly into "shrimping" sexually with you—that's sucking toes, right?

Yes.

Well, that sounds silly and sweet.

I didn't know Ellsworth after that brief period in 1973. He was shy about his sexuality then—I don't mean shrimping, I mean being gay. I have no idea whether or how much he might have overcome that shyness as years went by. I don't know, would something like that embarrass you?

No, but clearly I don't embarrass easily.

I admire Ellsworth Kelly enormously, and I assume that comes through in the chapter.

To go back to reconciling art and activism, how did you return to writing about visual art?

At a certain point I couldn't work on AIDS anymore. I think that happened to a lot of AIDS activists. We burned out. And I no longer felt qualified to teach about AIDS; you couldn't responsibly deal with AIDS from the perspective of white gay men in New York City, which was the perspective of my AIDS writings. In 1996, after I had been teaching in the Visual and Cultural Studies Program at Rochester for several years, *October* did a special issue on visual studies. It infuriated me because it was so nakedly *anti*–visual studies—claiming that visual studies constitutes a deskilling of art history, that it is just vulgar identity politics, and so forth. It was one of their questionnaire-format issues, but they didn't invite anybody from Rochester to participate, even though ours was the founding program of the field.

Partly in response, I wrote a piece called "Getting the Warhol We Deserve" [1999], which also responded to Hal Foster's *The Return of the Real* [1996]. It was my first reengagement with *October*. My essay was about the stakes of criticism, about making it clear *why* you want to make the argument you're making. I asked, in effect, what Foster's stakes were in making the argument he made about Warhol in *The Return of the Real*. I proposed a cultural-studies approach to Warhol that would locate him in pre-Stonewall queer culture in New York, a culture that included Jack Smith, Ronald Tavel, the Theater of the Ridiculous, and so forth. Starting with that proposal, I began studying Warhol's films, and by the time I published "Getting the Warhol We Deserve,"

I had also published an essay on *Blow Job* [1964]. Warhol is, of course, a thoroughly canonical figure, but I wrote about a noncanonical aspect of his work. My reengagement with art was through cultural studies and queer theory, and my Warhol book is really a queer-theory book.

Something I thought a lot about while reading *Before Pictures* was the role of the interpersonal in what then becomes registered as clean, official art history, or culture in general. How do you see that relationship between the personal and critical?

Networks of personal relationships influence what one writes. Maybe it's a little different if you're writing about the Renaissance, but even then it will depend on who you studied with, what sort of program you teach in—your take on how history should be written is inevitably determined by your subjectivity, and subjectivity is relational. With contemporary art, we all live in this world, or these many overlapping worlds. What gets revealed in memoirs or autobiographies—or by scholars going back to a particular moment and researching in the archives, looking at letters and other documents—might well change our understanding of what has been the accepted narrative up to that point. This process is always happening, and the notion of "objectivity" is consequently overthrown. The fact is that your view can only ever be partial, in both senses of the word.

In the last essay of *Melancholia and Moralism,* you talk about seroconverting in the late nineties after years of AIDS activism and incredibly intimate knowledge about risks and safe sex. Your explanation for *how* that could happen was "because I am human." It made me wonder: *Where does art connect to that place of humanity? How do you understand art's human function?*

As I said, the poststructuralist—or call it postmodernist—turn toward the subject has been increasingly important to my work. Art opens us to otherness, and not just the simple sense of otherness of the different subjectivity of the artist that produces the art object, because the artist, too, is a divided subject. The artist's unconscious, as much as his or her conscious mind, determines the work. Art challenges not only our sense of the world but of who we are in relation to the world and to otherness in the world, and of who we are in relation to ourselves. But how you analyze that is a new question each time you are confronted with a work of art, because every work of art opens us to otherness differently. Maybe some very bad works of art don't do it at all. Their muteness or unanalyzability stems from the fact that they mean nothing to you—Jeff Koons's *Balloon Dog* [1994–2000] doesn't open me to anything. It tends, on the contrary, to close me off, to push me away, to say, *Get me out of here.*

I can't imagine doing a kind of social history that doesn't involve periodic moments of very intense looking—describing everything that can be seen, and leaving nothing out, as far as your vision can tell. Otherwise, you haven't dealt with the thing, you've only dealt with the parts that accord with the history you've come to affirm.

Darby English (b. 1974) is an art historian whose work unlocks new dimensions of American art through a rigorous attention to form. His books include *How to See a Work of Art in Total Darkness* (2007); *1971: A Year in the Life of Color* (2016); and *To Describe a Life: Notes from the Intersection of Art and Race Terror* (2018). He also coedited the volumes *Kara Walker: Narratives of a Negress* (2002) and *Art History and Emergency* (2016). He is the Carl Darling Buck Professor in the Department of Art History at the University of Chicago. English also serves as adjunct curator in the Department of Painting and Sculpture at The Museum of Modern Art, New York.

Darby English

What would you point to as an early important aesthetic experience?

When I was a child, we went to The Cleveland Museum of Art. My favorite experiences were of strolling through those galleries with parents who enjoyed this very much. They weren't necessarily always equipped to provide detailed information about the art we were looking at, but they were only too happy to indulge their only child in this way. At a certain point, it must have been clear that I was the person who needed this experience the most, but I was never made to feel as though my interest was a burden to them. I don't recall having a lot to say about it—ever since I could talk I have had speech impediments, and this predisposed me to keep words to myself—but I loved looking, in a deep and abiding way. I guess I looked really hard; I certainly wanted to look often. My first real loves were Dutch landscape paintings by Ruisdael and Van Goyen, which I revisited almost on a pilgrimage basis. I was mainly looking at paintings; it took me the longest time to learn how to see sculpture of any kind. The *Portrait of Tieleman Roosterman* [1634], by Frans Hals—I saw it again recently, and it's still to me as completely fixating as ever. Looking back, I feel that a painting like that appeared to me as something like *mitigated truth*.

What do you mean by that?

The works that first taught me that art is a special and crucial part of the real world were realistic paintings—they promoted the realness of depicted figures and spaces while giving, and maybe even flaunting, evidence of an artist's intervention, evidence of an individual personality's interpretation of . . . *whatever*. That truth could be sensed and not merely stated or displayed was already a considerable development upon everyday understandings of truth, in my world. Now I could think about truth reconciled with felicity; reconciled with opinion; reconciled with differentness. That frees you up in your relationship to truth in the unreflective, common sense. That's important when you're different, when all the evidence you have suggests that one's sense of things isn't so common.

Looking back, I think that whatever that sense was—a confirmation of sensibility or something—it's one of the most crucial insights I've ever received. That truth wasn't one thing, there wasn't a one truth, even about the way the land and the sky outside look, or the way that guy sitting over there looks. There's something absolutely discrete about him, but you and I will find different things to be interested in when looking at him, when treating him as though he were merely a view. Something about the proliferation of mitigated truths in a museum, for me, confirms one's right to take a different kind of interest in the things and beings of the world, as long as one sees what, in them, is singular and discrete and not subject to alteration under the pressure of a view. This is a right that needs to be protected fiercely. Art may protect that right more fiercely than any other institution in the culture. Anyway, for me, art has something to do with the individual's right to *differ*. I feel very lucky to have lived a life that affirmed this early on.

It wasn't just painting specific. Teachers affirmed this. At some point in high school, I turned in a paper on Joseph Conrad in which I described a scene that seemed to me green by calling it "verdant." No big deal, just a word somewhere in something that I'd written. But the teacher called me aside to thank me for using such a beautiful word; probably part of the thanks related to the correctness of the usage, too. I didn't then and don't now know what to make of this. It wasn't the "day I became a writer"—actually, it increased my anxiety about writing, because I then wanted to always produce papers that moved her in that way. But something happened.

Were you writing outside of assignments—poems or stories?

Yes. There was a literary magazine at my school. I contributed poems, which were terrible. I think I even knew then that they were terrible. I got one or two published. The faculty advisor took me to be responsible enough to be an editor. My best friend and I ended up coediting the literary magazine for a year or two. So now we were arbiters of literary taste in our little microculture. We'd have meetings to review submissions, and we took this very seriously. There was also a little popularity nonsense going on, like, *There's no way we're going to print anything by that asshole*. We were cultivating a sense—our own respective senses—of what "good taste" meant in English-langauge writing. But we were also perpetrating our taste. That became uncomfortable after a period of time, and I resigned before my senior year. I didn't want to be outside other people's use of language, judging it up or down. At that point, I started listening to a lot of music, mainly for lyrics at the time, because I had quit all my instruments except for one. And I read a lot of "real" writing, mostly nonfiction. From my time at the literary magazine, I learned something about myself that has remained true: I dislike deciding things for other people. On the one hand, to me that's a scary kind of power, rarely used for good; on the other, it's so completely enchanting to me to watch how people who are not me make choices in navigating the landscapes we share—landscapes such as a language, or a neighborhood, or a work of art. I love a minor difference.

What was particularly important to you at that time?

At that point, I was reading a lot of art criticism.

In high school?

Yes. I got a copy of Peter Schjeldahl's *The Hydrogen Jukebox* [1991]— amazing to me because it was this sparsely illustrated thing full of freely felt, deliberate, and forcefully put words about art. It took me forever to reconcile the essays' claims with the art they're ostensibly about, because this writing was so autonomous. A very interesting encounter for a child to have with subject-driven language; something for me to think about, maybe, in relation to my present-day fear of autonomous art writing. I also read George Kubler's translation of Henri Focillon's *The Life of Forms in Art* [1942] at that time. I was totally mystified and in love, but probably had no idea what I was reading. I did understand the attempt, however, to describe the problem of verbalizing the ineffable in concrete things. It's a perennial problem, too. Didn't know that then, either.

The thing about *Hydrogen Jukebox* is that Peter is one of our greatest writers on painting. His Manet essay is a way of narrating the experience of painting as an intersubjective experience, through close attention to form—that seems close to what you're doing in your newest book, *To Describe a Life*.

That essay was very important to me, along his essays on Chardin and Morandi, which do the same thing. Looking back—*What was I getting from Peter Schjeldahl's essays?* The same thing I was getting from James Merrill and James Baldwin and Ellison's nonfiction at the same time—the sense that *it's not about you*. Some art is doing things—things unrelated to its depiction or the criticality of its sheer positioning vis-à-vis a charged site—things that it wants people to know about in detail. In trying to tell them, because the art can't tell them itself, one cannot, I feel, limit the account to descriptions of the art's own means, whatever the fuck those would be. Art exists for the people who will come along and try to come to terms with it, to describe its attempt, and to find a context for this attempt as part of an effort to ascertain its impact on something beyond itself, beyond art. That context in turn belongs to history, which is a complex of contexts, but in the end history is only a perspective. One person's view of what it took to bring now about. I feel like Peter's respect for the art's core modesty about its situation amid all this, about its dependency on attempts made or not made, is exemplary. He's going to tell you what he thinks, but he doesn't start out with that. And he has no time for pathetic, academic hang-ups.

It's never prescriptive.

At its best, it's a deeply empathetic project, which has to do with producing a legible and durable record of something that's been fully considered. *I'm not going anywhere until I've seen everything that this thing has to show me.* It's most often a *thing* with Schjeldahl, but of course sometimes one needs to make the same commitment to describe a situation adequately.

In a book like *1971*, when I'm talking about color painting and color sculpture and trying to think about the historiography of color, a similar kind of commitment was required. The book looks closely at writing about color; of course; all that writing is happening in a social context that's structured by "color" in a strong racial sense. I can't imagine doing a kind of social history that doesn't involve periodic moments of very intense looking—describing everything that can be seen and leaving nothing out, as far as your vision can tell. Otherwise, you haven't dealt with the thing, you've only dealt with the parts that accord with the history you've come to affirm—you've come to the object for something, taken only what you needed, and left a great lot behind. My project forbids that kind of selectivity, at least up front. Obviously at other, early stages of research, one must make decisions, and that means making choices from among what's available—not only to see and describe, but also to feel and think. If the work is any good, if it exists for some reason that makes a claim on history, then there'll be a lot. When someone is faced with a lot of something, she has to make choices.

When you went to college, did you intend to study art history?

I was surer about studying English and philosophy. I ended up with two majors, trading English for art history. I went to Williams College, which is known for a rigorous and rigorously traditional kind of art history that was cultivated by academic men and museum men. Are you noting the emphasis on *men*? White ones. But I got the solidest of foundations there. I took the survey in the first two semesters of my freshman year—if we ended in the twentieth century, it was probably with the late work of a nineteenth-century painter. There was no modernism, really—at least not available to the undergraduates. I was required to buy a copy of Steinberg's *Other Criteria* [1972], *thank God*, but I can't recall reading it in a classroom setting, the sensibility of which almost every page of those essays would gravely offend. And there was utterly no thought of contemporary art in the official art historical narrative. No courses on contemporary art until the fall of my last year: one was taught by a brilliant painter, Mike Glier, who was himself in the throes of postmodernist art theory at the time; the other was for graduate students and cotaught by Linda and Hartley Shearer. So it was late in school, during that first term of the last year, that I caught a glimpse of an art history that occupied a full-bodied and relatively unanxious relationship to the present. Following the surveys, I took memorable courses in the art of the Dutch Golden Age, history of architecture, all the French painting from Robert to David and his followers—which is so little art, when you think of it—and other European painting. Again, a solid training not much modified from the canon of objects and writings established during the century of the founding of the discipline. Things were similarly conservative methodologically, with the exemption of some discourse theory, some film theory, and the core works of English-language feminist art history. Linda Nochlin was an early hero. I needed reading and courses well beyond art history in order to learn how to think about language, race, class, and sexuality. The difference between art criticism, which I do not do or even value particularly highly, and art history, which I regard as a staple of cultural history and try assiduously to practice well—this difference was not taught. Looking back, that strikes me as odd.

Two big interventions or so occurred in my sophomore and junior year. The first one was Abigail Solomon-Godeau coming from Santa Barbara to teach a course in the graduate program that some undergrads such as myself were permitted to take. She put art history in a historical perspective, not only alongside other moments in its own disciplinary life, but alongside other social practices. And she was just fucking brilliant. I learned modernism from someone who was hard at work dimensionalizing it. Hers was a pretty vigorously anti-institutional modernism, and there was this awareness that art history was an institution, one defined and refined and promulgated through procedures like majoring in it, and assimilating masters and master narratives—continually reinstituting instituted knowledge.

And there was a concomitant awareness that there had to be other ways of caring deeply how art has been made, presented, and understood through time. Abigail never attacked our curriculum outright, but from the reading and the learning she directed, it was clear that that curriculum was an institution inviting critique. Another kind of white cube, if you want. That was massively helpful, because I hadn't until then the language to narrate my complaint about the curriculum. By "complaint," I probably mean all the standard young skeptic questions, like, *What about me? What about now? What about all the ways of power? What about the stuff that so much of this writing elides or mitigates in advance?* And I was both nervous about and discouraged from bringing in language from philosophy and political theory, where I was spending all my spare time.

This was the mid-1990s. Disciplines were splitting and recombining. A good number were being straight-up invented. Until this two-part moment, I knew this, but couldn't reconcile it with my greatest academic love, and let me tell you—that was hard. So, the second big thing was Debra Bricker Balken, an independent scholar based in Cambridge, coming to teach a course on museology during Winter Study of my junior year. In that class I read Douglas Crimp's *On the Museum's Ruins* [1993], which was more or less hot off the presses. I read it really fast and it blew my brain apart, and I turned to Douglas's *AIDS Demo Graphics* [1990] next. These books look differently at institutionalized art politics and political practices involving art; they develop a language of critique for the forms that constitute art as well as those that constrain it. The museum book was assigned very early in the course, but I stayed with it, as it stayed with me. The feeling was somehow, *This is what I've needed all this time.* Queer life on that campus was *very* good in those years—*God, was it good*—and I was reading queer theory in political theory courses, but didn't know how to adapt it to anything. Douglas's work showed me how. Douglas's AIDS work is largely anticipated in the museum book, but that book hit me at the same time that the difference between being gay and being queer snapped into view. Anyway, it made it possible for me at last to imagine

an art-oriented intellectual practice that was fully open to what I
needed from political theory, and that militated against the closures
I experienced in art history. That was when I decided to apply to the
University of Rochester to work with Douglas. It's the only thing that
I *knew* I wanted to try next. Of the postcollege options I was qualified
to pursue, only that one felt urgent. I had something to figure out. I'm
still figuring it out, and it's every bit as thrilling now as it was then.

A funny thing happened when I first got to Rochester, cat and all. In
my first academic meeting with Douglas, naturally he wanted to know
what I was thinking about working on. I'm like, *Museums, duh! That's
our thing, right?* And the first words out of his mouth, which he said with
a kind of confused sweetness, were, *Darby, you know, I don't think about
museums anymore.* Flat out. If he said a thing about what he *did* think
about, I don't remember it. All I knew was that my Ruby and I lived
in Rochester now, so that I could think about museums with Douglas
Crimp, who himself doesn't think about museums anymore. Somehow
I was able not to worry too much about that. I mean, there we were.

Not long after that, I needed a subject for a paper I had to write
in one of the two classes I was taking with Douglas that semester.
I realized I was still thinking about a Glenn Ligon installation I'd
seen at the Williams College Museum of Art as a college kid. The total
exhibition was titled *Glenn Ligon: To Disembark* [1993]—it comprised the
wanted ads from Glenn's *Runaways* [1993] series, for which his friends
provided him with descriptions of Glenn, the sort of thing they'd say
in a "missing person" report; it had the music-box shipping crates,
which reminded you first of Judd and then of Henry "Box" Brown, a
slave who was shipped to freedom in crates of similar proportion and
construction. If you didn't already know about Brown, which I did not,
a label nearby schooled you. Ligon's first text paintings made directly
on the wall were also in that show. I think it was one with a Zora Neale
Hurston text, either *Untitled (I Remember the Very Day That I Became Colored)*
[1990] or *Untitled (I Feel Most Colored When I Am Thrown Against a Sharp
White Background)* [1990]—one of those two. Oilstick applied directly to
plain white gallery walls, Glenn's selection and Glenn's hand revivifying

Hurston as a kind of elevated graffiti. And the whole complex of art objects was a whole. I was like, *What the fuck?* This show had haunted me in the quietest way. Looking back, I think it was the vividness of the intersections in the work—past with present, minimal art with lumber, freedom with unfreedom, literary aesthetics with visual aesthetics of low and high kinds … And it was extra great in a way because I had no discourse explaining it to me. It just happened—again and again, because I returned a lot—and then sank in. Three whole years passed before I tried formulating a single sentence about it. Maybe we should all have to wait that long between having an experience and tap-tap-typing out random junk about it. Not because what I eventually wrote was so great, but because during this gestation or whatever, the work and the experience had grown into this incredibly thick, rich, personal and intellectual resource that was my own.

Anyway, this exhibition had really nailed me at Williams, but I never had any place to think about it, since the curriculum allocated such a tiny space for contemporary art. So I decided to write my first seminar paper on Ligon's work. Douglas said, *That's good. I know Glenn*—who kindly got his gallery to send me all of the slides, all of the press, and not only the citations for the entire bibliography, but the texts and books, as well. There weren't tons then, so in a box I could carry home I got the whole extant Glenn Ligon research archive. Then I read what passed for a literature about Ligon's practice, and I was flabbergasted by the lack of attention to form in virtually all of it. *Flabbergasted.*

My primary experience with this work had been totally form based—a phenomenally rich, extended intensity. None of what I myself felt the work to be, or do, or mean was reflected in any of the writing. Every critic or writer who encountered it seemed to take it as an opportunity to reflect on the demographics of the art world, or spout random givens about blackness, maleness, gayness, or whatever. Generalizations about abstractions—*Great.* Seriously: generalization after generalization, barely one of them inflected by the texture or character of the various works under discussion. In a way, dealing with this has been my problem ever since—pointing it out, correcting

129

for it, theorizing preventative measures we might take, as best as one writing person can do. At this point, I should probably confess that it's a revisionist project—revising racist arts-and-culture writing by black people as much as revising racist arts-and-culture writing by nonblack people. And, to be clear, what's racist about it is its perpetuation of the racist norms that condone generalization and dismissal through disattention to specificity, alterity, variance, and just plain change.

Your book *1971: A Year in the Life of Color* is a revisionist reengagement with late modernist color painting and sculpture, which was off-limits in art history for a long time because of its associations with Clement Greenberg and Michael Fried. But a critique of the Black Arts Movement also drives the book. I would love to open that up a little bit. How did you first encounter the rhetoric of the Black Arts Movement that you felt the need to react to it so strongly?

The first encounter? I was an upper-middle-class black kid in rural suburban Cleveland—which was *not really a thing* when I was a kid in the late seventies and eighties. I was just going along and doing my music lessons, doing school, hanging out with friends—all of whom are white. There's music everywhere in your life—in the car, in the bathroom, in the living room, even in the garage—some of it's black and some of it's not. You just like it or you don't. The people who help your family to constitute a neighborhood are all white people; you see nothing of conflict between your parents and these people. You have your crushes and your nemeses, all of whom are white. Then there's some party, staged by someone's parents right around the time everyone is getting hormonal. I'm at this party, and at some point I'm in a gaggle of boys, and this kid Brian and I realize that we want to touch the body of the same girl, who is white. And it turns out that Brian has a certain right-of-way in that situation. I didn't know this until I acted, or spoke as though I were about to act, on my own interest in the girl in question. That's when Brian let me know he had right-of-way. I responded by pushing him down a short flight of stairs and running away from the fight that surely would have ensued if I hadn't run. So, like Hurston in that line that Ligon appropriated for a painting, I remember the very

130

day that I became colored. The day I was made to realize that there was something about the apparently minor differences between him and her and me that wasn't minor at all. At least not on that occasion.

Well, that's all very abstract. I came to the language of black essentialism around the same time, through some school exercises. It either was clear or was made clear that it was inviting me to join it, to enter into its fold. By then I was committed to the fantasy that I don't color my tastes, because good and bad things weren't colored accordingly in the world where I formed. Things are *mixed* there. I was formed in a mixed and overwhelmingly peaceful place. We did everything that interested us until our interest changed direction, and then we did something else. For that reason mainly, I like that which keeps *open* the question of cultural location.

The first time I encountered strong black cultural formation—as a thing that I was expected to want to be a part of, to feel at home in—was high school. There was a Black Student Union. Later, my college would have its own version. My relation to both was fraught. Already the "union" tells you a little about the historical pedigree—this is a vestige of the systematic collectivization of black students in a situation where each person would otherwise be left to her own devices, which was a very dangerous situation in the sixties and seventies. You had to have your *people*.

Everybody with a difference from the norm, wherever they happen to be, deals with this. Like, *Are you a joiner or not? What are going to be the terms for joining or choosing to remain perpetually in a negotiated liminality between yourself and the various groups you might join?* Frankly, it's much harder to go on one's own and stay one's own course. But that was my choice, and for that choice I was made to feel uncomfortable by a majority of the other black students at my school.

Then at Williams, the resident advisors in my dormitory, from the very beginning, were both like, *Darby, are you going to go to the BSU orientation for new students?* Not particularly flatly, I said no, but I didn't give a reason. I didn't even go to see. I think because I didn't want to be in a formation. My luck so far in life had been such that, socially speaking, I could go where I wanted to go and work my way into whatever scene. The way my parents would say it, when I walked into a room, I saw everyone as a potential friend. Not that I'm super extroverted or outgoing; I just am comfortable with people as they are in the world as it is. Doubtless this bears some ultimate relation to the way I myself want to be treated. I've been lucky to experience less targeted racial violence than a lot of people in my social category.

So my first encounters weren't with black power ideas of an original vintage, but they were with the contemporary vestiges of that. The first time I studied it was when I was at Williams taking a comparative religion course with a lesbian theologian, Reverend Dr. Thandeka, who taught Eve and the Snake—a famously important and very difficult course. We read feminist comparative religious theory, like Gerda Lerner. We read Audre Lorde—I read "Uses of the Erotic" [1978] for the first of what must now be a couple hundred times. That class changed me as a person in the same way that *On the Museum's Ruins* had changed me as a baby art historian. I realized that black feminism, and a queer black feminism especially, was closer to my heart and experience than anything else I'd ever read about identity of any kind. I would need a lot of time to figure out what was going on in that connection. I think now that it may have had to do with the distance I felt, both historically and experientially, from black American male certainties about the world into which we're born, certainties about how the world feels about us, certainties about how we ought to orient ourselves in response to it. I just don't know all that stuff; or, rather, what I do know doesn't yield certainties of that kind. It recently became possible for me to say this about a revered colleague and friend, Fred Moten: Fred *knows things* about blackness that I just don't know. And I can't write as though I do. And if you're going to try to make me feel bad about that, then that's on you, but know this: it isn't going to work.

It is fascinating to contrast your work and early formation with Fred Moten's deep connection with the Black Arts Movement through the work of Amiri Baraka.

I want to broaden it beyond Fred. He's by no means the only

practitioner who can be associated with such a starting point. He's the most nuanced and rigorous of those thinkers, in my opinion, but he's not alone. I'm so grateful to be in dialogue with him, strained and minimal as it is. I can't imagine better luck as a scholar than to be in dialogue with one of the smartest people in the world about the stuff you, too, are trying to think about as hard as you can. He's willing to disagree. He's willing to tell me, word for word, what he doesn't buy about my arguments. He can't get on board with a lot of things that I think and do and try, but he's respectful in a way that stands out. That's Fred's humanism and *his humanity*. They combine into something fierce, and fiercely necessary. Wheras I'm not convinced that Baraka can be described the same way.

I love hearing that, because I feel like people won't disagree like that about art right now. If there are fights, it's not about art—it's about a kind of righteous indignation around political issues in proximity to art, but it's not about the art itself.

I have a similarly strong response to what feels like an absence of spirited debate about art, which produces that nauseating ease with which folks will shame you for disliking something that's on trend in whatever way. I had a moment of release from this just yesterday, but it was quickly followed by another very "now" frustration, which is born of people denying that something is interesting because they don't want to look at it—or, better, be seen by it. I'd been to Gladstone Gallery to see a Thomas Hirschhorn show, *De-Pixelation* [2017–2018]. Just as I started looking at the things right in front of me, my "more-of-the-same" eyes flashed clear. Then it was different, a different Hirschhorn. He's thinking of something else, in a new mode, on a different scale, with a different language. It wasn't an environment of any kind. There's something gravely serious about the approach that he's taken, both to making the things that are on view and making them available to viewers. And there's a very simple concept at the heart of it, which is de-pixelation—which takes the stuff that's pixelated in our news images, like the horrors of war, and de-pixelates it so that we can deal precisely with what is horrible about the horrors ostensibly "depicted" in what actually are redacted photographs and video feeds. He's pointing to a core conflict in our relation to the image culture we inhabit: we condone its mitigation of the very truths we use it to document.

After Hirschhorn and a good deal else, I was having drinks with friends, all of whom had seen the Gladstone show, hated it, decided it had no complexity. Turns out no one had looked at anything. They just didn't look at it. Technically, we were talking about the art in the show, only all of it was being seen through a scrim comprising everything they already knew about Thomas Hirschhorn before arriving. Somehow, all of it was clear even to shut eyes: what he was up to, what he had to tell us, how the telling went, how to assimilate it post-encounter. On one level, I *get* it: there's too much art that's telling us things about ourselves. I have my own problem with that disposition toward the viewer. But I like art more than I like avoiding conflicts as expertly as possible—and I *really* like avoiding conflict! Anyway, it was a disappointing conversation, but the company was unbeatable. What are you gonna do?

The way that I engage with a lot of art writing is as the embodiment of a worldview, almost as a form of fiction—the world the writer would like to inhabit. From that perspective, thinking about *1971*, I see that as showing the kind of attention and consideration I would like to exist in the world. The reason you can write that way in *1971* is that a color-oriented art asserts an overwhelmingly formal experience, which has to be attended to in a particularly intense way. That is not the way that art is written about now, or, in many cases, asks to be looked at.

I don't think art has to—wow, this is a much larger claim than I expected to hear myself making—but, I don't think art has to make the plea for attention on its own. That color-driven art *seized* attention. Those works entail a quantum of concentration and demand a quantum of concentrated focus. One had to accept the terms of an immersive proposal—*This work proposes an immersion, are you up to it?* One had a choice to make, and it was hoped that one would choose immersion. But I also feel that there's an obligation to attend even where attention

134

isn't being seized, even in the absence of that proposal. I think it's what we're supposed to do anyway. Art wants attention, and I want to provide it with a supportive environment.

Well, that is borne out most beautifully in *To Describe a Life*, which I think is a really stunning work of art writing. Part of what's so brilliant is that you're lavishing a kind of close formal reading on objects that don't even seem to ask for it.

Or *warrant* it?

Or seem to warrant it. There are moments when you're gearing up to doing a close formal reading of Pope.L's *Skin Set Drawings* [1997– ongoing], where I was like, *Really? This is what we're doing?* But I went with it, and suddenly you get to the point where—*It's paying off!* It seemed like that was your intention: *I'm going to bring to bear a level of attention on these things that don't even seem like they deserve it.* That somehow seems like an ethical or political move.

It is. They're not arbitrarily chosen. They're chosen because I do think that, despite perhaps *seeming* unlikely to withstand that kind of long and lavish attention, each work under consideration has worthwhile things to say to us about being in this world, right now.

They have things to say to *you*.

That's a very helpful corrective. They have things to say to *me* about how I ought to think—not *what*, but about *how* I ought to try and think, about what is happening in the world right now, which is an epidemic of disregard for specific human vitalities. I don't think the art has to formulate a specific demand for us to behave as though there is one to respond to, or honor. I don't think one needs to be doing journalistic biography of dead people to talk about mass execution, to talk about what's at stake in the visualization of real lives that matter, that can continue to matter even after they're ended. The visuality itself of abruptly ended life is also extremely complex, important to be able to think about now, and in this I am recalled to Hirschhorn, and specifically to the import, for his latest project, of recentness. Fresh death. Though it's terribly hard to remember, the individual people that we lose are never fully gone. Memory work bears them passage into what is a future for them and a perpetual present for us. Maybe in *To Describe a Life* I am trying to think about how to suggest that the relative endurance of works of art are powered by a similar sort of *durability*—they're not monumental, they're not made of permanent materials, they're not strident in their disposition, but they have, or want, *staying power*. Art power evolves with culture change. So maybe what has staying power are these objects' implications. I think their invitations—the kind of looking and thinking that they invite us to do—are important factors to attend to right now.

The introduction includes an explication of *Tipping Point* [2016], Zoe Leonard's sculpture made of a stack of fifty-three copies of James Baldwin's *The Fire Next Time* [1963]; it's one of the finest pieces of art writing of this century. Just *so fine.* Partly I think that because I hated those book stacks.

A lot of people do.

What it made me realize was not only that I had not really looked at them or thought about them, but even if I had, I don't think I would have come up with the same reading that you did, which was so *deeply felt*. It was an affirmation of what writing about art can do, which is model the experience of one consciousness engaging with an object as an embodiment of multiple other consciousnesses—sorting that through. You bring into that not only Zoe Leonard and James Baldwin, but all fifty-three people who owned those books before Leonard acquired them. It really captured something profound about art. I'm not even sure if the context exists in the present art world to receive what you're doing in *To Describe a Life*.

This is the most amazing thing I can hear, that somewhere on the page was evidenced the work I attempted to do as a conscious, reflective, curious looker, to figure something out about this sculpture, about how it came to have huge significance for me. I decided a long time ago that I write for the future. All I want is for people down the line to know that someone took this very seriously.

For instance, I want for people to know that someone was looking at Glenn Ligon's first text paintings and *not* deciding that, say, the affinity with Jasper Johns was perfunctory. When I was reading all the writing on Ligon up to December 1996, most of it was capsule reviews. Richard Meyer's catalogue essay for the show at the ICA Philadelphia was the only scholarly text. And it was serious: Richard did his homework, he looked long and hard. But his essay strung all the work together in a way that gave rise to some suspicion on my part. I wondered, *Is it really so much of a thing, all these* different *things Ligon has done? What about the mechanics of the appropriations all over the practice?* Richard's and my difference on this score came down to method. In figuring out precisely how Richard's piece frustrated me, I learned what I now know about the lack of integrity in what we sometimes call an oeuvre. Farewell to the oeuvre! But like I said, that was method.

Elsewhere in the first wave of Ligon literature, what made the most indelible impression was the sheer racism of a review by Michael Kimmelman of a show including some of Ligon's early text paintings. Kimmelman writes something like, *There was this and this and a text painting by a young black artist called Glenn Ligon that suggests the unlikely source of Jasper Johns.* Of course, there's nothing "unlikely" about Jasper Johns having been a source for Ligon. On a really real level, all I'm trying to do in what I've done on Glenn's work is to say to some student in the future, *Okay, you've seen one version of this art's genealogy, wherein black artists don't warrant comparison to white artists, because how could a black one even know about a white one? Here's an alternative.*

I mean, to be responding to what you were saying when you said, *I don't think there's a reader in the art culture of now for this*—that's fine. I wish there were. It would be nice to encounter kindred spirits more often. I've found that that's not reasonable to expect from art readers right now. They're after something else, something that's not what I do.

I would love to know more about what brought you to use Simone Weil's *The* Iliad, *or, The Poem of Force* [1939] in your essay on Kerry James Marshall's painting *Untitled (Policeman)* [2015].

Weil was introduced to me in a seminar on French critical theory that I took in graduate school with the critical theorist Tom DiPiero. I peeked at the essay on the *Iliad* then and maybe didn't really find what

I was looking for, whatever that was. But I kept it close, all of the Weil, because it's at once very weird and powerfully true. For the longest time, whenever there was a new pile, I would pull it out and stick it on top. For years and years, I was *about* to read all of the Weil. Jacqueline Rose's collection *The Last Resistance* [2007] has an essay on Simone Weil written just as a sort of a tribute. I'm greatly indebted to Rose's thought and writing—her commitments to thinking about the creative enterprise that sets itself up *in between* conflicting entities, and her commitment to advocating for artists—mainly writers—who create in impossible situations. And she understands that, underneath it all, Freud was one of the finest prose stylists of the last century. Jackie's whole project is a model for me. I try to think of my commitments as being to people with a similar positionality, like being black in the wrong way, or being black at the wrong time, or being black at the wrong place. Often these become impossible situations, if they don't start out that way. Not as much gunfire as in the places that hold Rose's gaze in those essays, but other violent deployments of force are very much the norm.

Anyway, I saw Kerry's painting unfinished, and I left the studio thinking he was making a takedown of the police. All I really knew was that he was making a painting of a cop and that I still despise the cops. For what it's worth, the cops have given me a lot of good reasons to despise them. I was like, *Can I come back when it's finished?* He called me to come see it the morning it was shipping out to Miami for an art fair. I walked into the studio and saw immediately that he hadn't been doing what I wanted him to be doing. I felt some resentment. I felt the force of my own need for this painting to have been some kind of equal but opposite strike against the police. It's utterly ambivalent—*utterly ambivalent*. Really unshakably so. At some nearby moment, I recalled Weil's words about the figure she describes as the man of force and the recipient of his force. On her account, force turns both into stone; there's no breaking down the recalcitrance they achieve in the face of one another. It must be that I felt the force in me was equivalent to the one that I projectively attributed to the police, and I *felt* it in a way that I had never felt it before—walking into Kerry's studio and encountering an ambivalent image of the police. I felt myself standing squarely in front of the painting, trying to change it around into what I needed. And it wasn't complying. I don't even know how to express how grateful I am for that, now that I've taken a period of time to look at it and learn from it. I live for that.

I tend to be wrong about a great deal of what I think I know. Kerry's painting doesn't *know* things about blackness and policing. It doesn't *know* things about race and policing that everyone in the culture knows to a certain degree. I'm glad there's finally a monument to not knowing some of that stuff—a nonmonumental monument for not knowing. The approach that the painting takes to our knowingness and us is oblique: we're witnesses to this clenched scene, we're not the addressee. And I just love Weil's words, and found them adequate to this conflict, her conviction that, when force is on the move, master and slave both turn to stone. The violence and the mentality that that arrangement adopts, it's all-pervading—but at a certain level of ontological inter-relation, there is no power difference. That's more than a little bit fucked up, but it's also powerfully true.

And like many things in Weil, it's figured as strangely impersonal. She's someone I've been reading over and over since I was, like, nineteen years old, but lately she's felt like oxygen. There's a line in *Gravity and Grace* [1947] where she says, "Every being cries out silently to be read differently." I really felt that was the core of your project.

Differently every time? Differently from—

Differently from however it's being read.

Yes, exactly. In other words, every reading produces the fantasy of an alternative reading that competes—for what thing, we cannot say—with the reading one has just performed, with another's reading or one's own reading on a different occasion. In any case, there is the always present conception of the same text perceived from a different point of view. For Weil, and I think for all serious readers, this truth about reading, an inescapable fantasy, serves both as a menace and as a thrill. In this very limited way, works of art differ very little in their effects from texts.

In *To Describe a Life*, you draw an equivalence between the individuality of a subject and the individuality of the work of art.

I suggest one. And it's by that suggestion that the "life" in the title may seem a double entendre. I'm fine with that as a provisional suggestion. The only way it works as a title is by way of the double interpretation—life as we know it and the discrete existences of specific artworks. I guess it shows through that I'm always still puzzling through *The Life of Forms*. Focillon's project in that book has aged extremely well. It may even be more completely of our time than it is of its own, because we have survived the reigns of countless narrow formalisms. The art that no formalism can contain enjoys a greater freedom in the aesthetic and interpretive schemes of the present. There *is* a life in forms. That's just axiomatic for us today.

You *feel* it.

What I have come to love about that book is the number of ways Focillon has to formulate the vitality that he sees and feels in a really astonishing range of objects—spaces, shallow relief, painting qua painting. There's something ecstatic about the methodology. It's deeply queer, his refusal of any available formal disciplinarity.

There is a footnote in *To Describe a Life* that includes a beautiful little snippet of a Kay Ryan poem. I was interested in your relationship to poetry, and how it figures in your thinking about writing.

It's simple: I go to poetry in search of an economy that I find it hard to generate on my own. My friend Hamza Walker, who graciously reads a lot of my drafts, says he's always adding water, to dilute them, thin them out, clarify them. I've also recently begun to purge my dependency on adverbial modifiers; they just don't need to be there. I favor short-line poetry, a poetry whose saying achieves palpable substance with as few words as possible. I'm not interested in poetry's metaphors so much, in part because I'm very bad at metaphor—bad at tracking it and bad at doing it. Relatedly, I dislike the distraction of metaphor in writing whose primary aims are description, analysis, and interpretation. I just think it's diversionary. There's no time for that. The poets whose work I need nearby when I am writing, these poets tend to be practical realists who approach their subjects directly. Books by Ryan and Louise Glück are literally always within a few steps' reach. They think about thinking and look at looking; what keeps them on the move is the dimensionality of the things and beings of the world, which makes a peculiar kind of comfort out of the fact that there is *always* more to think about and to look at. Other constants include Harmony Holiday, Frank O'Hara, Mona Van Duyn, Alice Notley, and Tony Hoagland.

For me, great poetry takes you out of syntax as you know it, shows you what else language can do, takes very seriously what it cannot do. It can be a great help to narrate frustration, so that it's not just debilitating noise. Words can do so much more than we let them do—single words, even. And autonomous images made from words, not to metaphorize, just to describe differently. I have learned *so much* about what I do and how I do it, as someone living an art life, from Kay Ryan. There's a poem called "Least Action" [2003]. It's equally about vision itself, this huge and hugely pertinent subject, and about the nature of any attempt to effect something, which is so micro. It goes:

> It is vision
> or the lack
> that brings me
> back to the principle
> of least action,
> by which in one
> branch of rabbinical
> thought the world
> might become the
> Kingdom of Peace not
> through the tumult
> and destruction necessary
> for a New Start, but
> by adjusting little parts
> a little bit—maybe turn

that cup a quarter inch
or scoot up that bench.
It imagines an
incremental resurrection,
a radiant body
puzzled out through
tinkering with the fit
of what's available.
As though what is is
right already but
askew. It is tempting
for any person who would
like to love what she
can do.

Just that phrase "tinkering with the fit / of what's available"—rather than needing always to revolutionize everything at once. Not just least action "versus" maximal action. The poem is pointing to the sometimes shocking effectiveness of the smallest adjustment makeable. I think I come back to that poem when I need to be reminded about what kind of change art can actually make. I do believe in art's effectiveness. I do believe that it can be actually politically efficacious. But it doesn't achieve effectiveness or efficaciousness through a cause-and-effect kind of directness. It does not, nor has it ever. Where it concerns things that need changing, art is but a means among other means. Art sends word: *We have a situation*. Word has to reach someone. It must be received and translated up, or over, or out—transformed somehow. Some amount of telephone gaming will be necessary between the creation of a change-oriented work and some change. How much can I really do with this writing? I will do everything that I can do, but that will never be equal to what is needed.

Ryan's poetry, in particular, is adapted to the conflict between the appetite for change and the world's recalcitrance. In a poem called "New Rooms" [2012], Ryan talks about how nice it would be if everywhere we go we could just tack up the rooms we know. Thing is, the windows and doors in the rooms we know won't sync with the windows and doors in the new rooms where we find ourselves. What do we do? We have again and again to learn new rooms, to leave the old rooms behind. We have to let go. Maybe this pertains to an experiment in the writing I am doing now: giving poetry a place instead of shunting it off-camera. I don't have a message about the role poetry's playing, except to say that I am thinking with poems all the time. It's surprising that I don't have a poetry book in my pocket this morning, because usually I do. It's become very crucial, because I have a hard time with "feeling" words.

What do you mean?

Words for feelings, like names for my feelings. My therapist observed a long time ago that when I talk about pleasure or frustration or excitement or anxiety, my discourse is conspicuously devoid of feeling words. I leap to an intellectual level as quickly as possible. Poetry has been a help in that department. Probably I choose the poetry I choose because much of it proceeds from a patient narration of response, in the real, to stuff that occurs immediately. Occurrences that leave no time for abstracting everything into a nice parcel of intellectualization. I think that what we've been talking about, and I think sharing between us, is a conviction that without access to one's feeling words, very little can be done in art writing that's actually faithful to what we need to relate.

To be a good critic, you have to have
a touch of ressentiment, as Nietzsche
would say. Not personal envy, but
social antagonism.

Hal Foster (b. 1955) has been a force in American
art criticism since the late seventies, bringing
psychoanalytic and poststructural theory to bear
on contemporary art and its historical precedents.
In 1983 he edited the anthology *The Anti-Aesthetic:
Essays on Postmodern Culture*, which helped frame
postmodernism within the arts. Foster wrote for
Artforum (1978–1981) and was a senior editor at
Art in America (1981–1987) before becoming a
coeditor of the journal *October* in 1991, and contributes
frequently to *Artforum*, *October*, and the *London
Review of Books*. His books include *Recodings* (1985);
Compulsive Beauty (1993); *The Return of the Real*
(1996); *Design and Crime* (2002); *The Art-Architecture
Complex* (2011); *The First Pop Age* (2012); and
Bad New Days (2015). He is the Townsend Martin,
Class of 1917, Professor of Art and Archaeology at
Princeton University.

Hal Foster

What was an early important aesthetic experience for you?

I grew up in the middle class in Seattle in the 1960s. My best friend, Charles Wright, came from a family that owned art; his parents were the primary collectors of postwar work in Seattle—Bagley and Virginia Wright. They had extraordinary pieces, like Robert Morris's *Box with the sound of its own making* [1961] and James Rosenquist's sculpture *Tumbleweed* [1963–1966], which was made of barbed wire and neon light. I barely knew what art was; certainly we didn't have such things in our house. One day—I was twelve or so—I wandered into their living room, and there was a painting on the wall that knocked me out. I didn't know what it was, really, but I did know it was gorgeous. It had blocks of color—oranges and yellows, whites and blues—like fire and ice forced together quietly but explosively. And I had these two thoughts back to back: *This is the most beautiful thing I've ever seen*, and *Why do they have it and we don't?*

Oh my God!

The moral of the story—and, like all primal scenes, it is partly real and partly fictive—is that I became a critic at that moment. To be a good critic, you have to have a touch of ressentiment, as Nietzsche would say. Not personal envy, but social antagonism. I had the sense that this thing of beauty was not for everyone—that it could not be possessed by everyone—and that angered me. I should add that, to their great credit, the Wrights gave the painting, a Rothko, and much else besides, to the Seattle Art Museum; I visit it every time I'm in town. In any case, my experience of aesthetic wonder was cut with a feeling of social discontent, and I think that made me a critic.

That's astonishing.

Isn't that true for many critics?

I've never heard anyone say it out loud!

Well, the origin stories I've heard from other critics and historians usually involve some collision between the aesthetic and the social, even or especially when they attempt to deny it. It's pretentious to say, but this is where I feel an affinity with critics like Baudelaire and Benjamin: they were bourgeois men who fell out of sympathy with their own class. They looked back at bourgeois culture with a mixture of longing and disgust that gave their writing a critical charge it wouldn't otherwise have had.

What did you do with that experience at that point? Did you then start studying art? Did you start trying to make art?

No. My first love was writing, but I was also interested in art. I became an art critic because it was a way for me to do the first through the second. Culturally the middle-class suburbs were a desert, but somehow middlebrow magazines like *The New Yorker* and *The New York Review of Books* made it into homes like mine, and I was captivated by a critical voice that sometimes appeared there—a voice like Susan Sontag's or Joan Didion's. These voices tended to be women's; they had an edge; it was critique, not high culture, that I heard. I wanted to be part of that conversation; I wanted to *sound* like that.

One aspect of Susan Sontag as a stylist is that she makes being really smart seem sexy.

Yes, she made critique sound cool, but then so did others, like Rosalind Krauss. I was an undergraduate at Princeton, and Rosalind was there as a visiting critic. This was the mid-1970s, and back then art history departments didn't know what to do with contemporary art. Princeton brought Rosalind in to tell us a little bit about it. I first saw her in 1975, and I thought, *That's what a New York intellectual looks like, sounds like, acts like. That's for me.* It was that critical voice again—sharp, conceptual, present, lucid—that got me. It seemed to speak the truth about the new, to cut it clear from the given.

A crucial thing to understand about my generation of critics is that for us critical theory *was* the avant-garde. It was the most advanced front of the culture, more intense than anything in the arts. We consumed Barthes and Benjamin and pored over Derrida and Foucault, to the point where most of us spent time in Paris. We learned French. We went all in. Critical theory also seemed to continue the revolts of the 1960s by other means. If they were beaten back politically, they could at least be developed theoretically. Critical theory kept that hope alive for us. That's why we were so invested in it.

What was the intellectual terrain of the discipline of art history as you experienced it at Princeton in the seventies?

There was very little relation between art history and contemporary practice, and almost none at all between art history and critical theory. Theory had only arrived at the university, and when it did come it was mostly repelled, certainly at places like Princeton. But there were whispers of theory even there. My favorite professors were on to it, mostly in French, English, and comp lit, but it was haphazard, and it all came at once: Benjamin with Derrida, say, or Lévi-Strauss with Foucault, and at first all as a way to read literature. This was a time of translating and sorting, which meant it was also a time of new journals, like *October, Critical Inquiry, Representations* . . . It was very exciting.

Harold Bloom spent a term at Princeton when I was a junior. This was soon after he had published *The Anxiety of Influence* [1973], and just when I had begun to glimpse a similar Oedipal dynamic, a related historical agon, in art history. Bloom made it come alive in relation to poetry, and under his influence I wrote my senior thesis on the influence of Yeats on poets like Ted Hughes. After I graduated I attempted to map his model onto art, but it didn't work: his idea of the relationship between present and past poetry was rhetorical in a way that didn't translate to the visual. And, of course, it's a "boy" model—it's all about the struggle between fathers and sons. I discarded it as soon as I came to New York, in large part because I plunged into a scene led by feminist artists. Nevertheless, I remained very interested in how artists find an entrance into art history.

It makes sense you were attracted to it, though, because he employed a psychoanalytic framework, which becomes a major component of your later work. Were you involved with psychoanalysis by that time?

No, not yet. I came to New York in fall 1977, which was a moment of extraordinary rereadings not only of Marx and Nietzsche but also of Freud. That rereading came through Lacan, but then Lacan was also a subject of critique in French feminist theory—e.g., Luce Irigaray and Michèle Montrelay—and in English feminist art and cinema—e.g., Mary Kelly and Laura Mulvey.

I gravitated downtown and came into contact with the Pictures artists—Barbara Kruger, Sherrie Levine, Cindy Sherman, and others. This scene was driven by mixed feelings of suspicion and fascination— with art, film, mass culture, everything. Feminist film criticism led the way, and *Screen* magazine was important to some of us. It was clear that we needed a theory of subjectivity if we wanted to reflect on the different movements that had emerged since the sixties—civil rights, the women's movement, anticolonial struggles. We needed an account of how subjectivities were produced. Hence the turn to psychoanalysis for me and for others.

This scene was led by women. Not all of the artists were theoretical by any means. Cindy Sherman is not theoretical, but her work is. It is obviously concerned with questions of sexuality, identity, and representation; it always was. I was close to Barbara Kruger and Craig Owens, and soon we were in touch with artists in London like Mary Kelly and Victor Burgin. There was a whole group of us, and in order to come to terms with the new feminist art all around us, we began to work both with psychoanalysis and against it.

You came from Princeton to New York and started writing criticism, but you also got an MA in English from Columbia.

I began to write criticism immediately because I was arrogant enough to believe that I could. People thought I was older than I was because I *sounded* older. It was a relatively inauspicious time for *Artforum.*

148

Phil Leider and Michael Fried were long gone, and Rosalind Krauss and Annette Michelson had departed. *Artforum* was in flux.

The academy was also in flux, in distress, really, as there were no jobs. I went to Columbia because I wanted to learn more about critical theory. Edward Said was known to teach the Frankfurt School and the French theorists, so I was drawn to him. I was in the small seminar in which he first presented *Orientalism* [1978], and it was extraordinary to experience this invention of a whole new discourse. That's when I thought again, *This is what I want to do*. Said represented for us what a real intellectual—a political public intellectual—could be.

In 1981 you became an editor at *Art in America*. Was that through Craig Owens, who was also an editor there at the time?

No. Craig became an editor only several months before I did. We met at the Institute for Architecture and Urban Studies in the late 1970s. I credit Betsy Baker here, the longtime editor of *Art in America*: she saw that there was a new interest in critical theory in the art world, and that the art magazines had to respond somehow. Betsy wasn't inclined to it temperamentally, but she understood that it had to be given space— hence the hiring of Craig and me. We were kids; he was thirty and I was twenty-five. Even so, for the six years or so that we worked together at *Art in America*, it was the center of critical thinking in the New York art world—apart from *October*, that is, which we were involved with as well.

It doesn't get talked about in the way *Artforum* does, but *Art in America* in the eighties seemed like a fascinating place where very different kinds of writing were going on at the same time.

Yes, but it was a struggle. Other writers were hostile to us. And then soon enough we were all overwhelmed by the market. Once Wall Street was deregulated under Reagan, there was a lot of money in the art world—throughout the 1970s the art market was as depressed as the rest of the economy. The idea that art could be an investment, part of a portfolio, became widespread. There were collisions between critical claims and financial forces, and to mediate it all at an art magazine reliant on gallery ads was difficult. Some of our artist friends were taken up by the new market, and we had to think hard about the relationship

149

between critical advocacy and market value. Craig and I eventually left the magazine for the academy in order to be free of such pressures. Little did we know that we would be a commodity there too.

By that time—this is now the mid to late 1980s—the academy had become interested in critical theory. It went from hostile to intrigued, and that's when many of us—Douglas Crimp and Benjamin Buchloh, among others—returned to graduate school. Of course we also wanted to pursue historical projects that our exposure to critical theory and contemporary art had opened up. Some of us studied at the Graduate Center at CUNY. It was in the city, it was cheap, Rosalind was there, and so was Linda Nochlin, but the real draw was the cohort of students. It was a site where contemporary practice, critical theory, and art history could be put in dynamic interrelation. Essentially, we taught each other.

The Graduate Center at that moment is almost mythical in art history—a combustible mix of interesting people in a place that gave them a lot of latitude. What was the process of deciding to pursue a PhD with Rosalind Krauss?

The Graduate Center still had the feeling of the old CUNY, where people from different backgrounds could become activist intellectuals. It was free of the taint of elitism associated with the Ivy League, which was very attractive. And though it was contentious, the Graduate Center was not antagonistic. We were interested in different artists, different movements, to be sure, but we came together for discussion, and we took each other very seriously. Even though Rosalind was sometimes seen as a difficult mentor, she wasn't for me. For the most part she treated us as peers in these debates, and she learned from us too. Since then I have believed in the seminar almost as a micro-utopia; if people treat one another with respect, it is a great medium where collective thought can be created.

There were so many different propositions in play at the time. And sometimes the situation became sectarian: you were either a Debordian or an Althusserian, either a Lacanian or a Foucaultian, and so on. The tribalism could be fierce, but we also understood that the arguments made all the discourses stronger. That, too, has remained an important point of reference for me: that we needed each other, needed different models of theory and practice, needed to sort them out, to see how they matched up, to see what we could do with them.

What each of us did, in our various ways, was to let our contemporary commitments guide our historical research. Certainly Rosalind was one model—the way her investment in minimalism allowed her to construct a new history of modernist sculpture. But there were others too—for example, the way T. J. Clark used his Situationist involvements to rethink French painting of the mid to late nineteenth century. Or even Michael Fried—the way his insistence on late modernist painting opened up an account of "absorption and theatricality," as he terms it, since Diderot. I didn't agree with him, but I admired him for his project nonetheless.

The kind of art history you were developing in those seminar rooms, which became associated with *October*—that was not a foregone conclusion for how to write art history at the time. There were many other scholars who were antagonistic to this theoretical approach you were taking to the discipline, and some of them were also teaching at the Graduate Center. So I have a hard time believing it was all so "Kumbaya."

Sure, there were tensions, and we were aware of them, but they incited us more than inhibited us. We were also confident that we were on the side not of the *good*, exactly, but certainly of the *smart*.

This goes back to our feeling that critical theory was the avant-garde and that art history was literally old school. That's how the old guard in the academy and the art world saw us, too—they were threatened. Sometimes I wish I could redo some of my more polemical statements, but I also appreciate the way that we were almost compelled to take strong positions. The academy seemed inert to us; we thought it needed to go through the same kind of institutional critique that art had gone through. And we took very seriously the notion of a politics of theory— how discourses can actually change institutions. Many now say that *we* are the academy—*we* are the canon, *we* are the problem. Maybe. But we wanted to open up art history to what it had suppressed—radical ideas, often to do with questions of class, sexuality, and race—and that work is never done.

I think that's very interesting, because one thing that runs through your criticism—from the earliest stuff in *Art in America* to your most recent book, *Bad New Days*—is a focus on questions of authority, in the sense that *you want it*. As though you believe that art or culture is built of antagonisms, but that you also want to be the one who comes out on top.

When I look back I sometimes see an ultraleftism of theory in our early work—whereby the right theory alone somehow counted as the right politics, and the right politics was authoritative. I succumbed to that tendency at times. But the question of authority is a tricky one for my generation. Of course we questioned it—the death of the author and the critique of originality were our cardinal beliefs—but, as you suggest, we also wanted authority, the authority of critique. By the way, we critics drank that Barthes-Benjamin Kool-Aid to the dregs; most of our artist friends only pretended to drink it. We thought, *They use photography. Photographs are multiples without an original. We've solved the problem of "value" in art.* Meanwhile, Richard Prince numbered every series in a limited edition. We sang the anthems of the death of the author and the critique of originality, while artists like Richard hummed along.

Sometimes in the 1980s, with feminist criticism, postcolonial discourse, and queer theory, a voice that sounded authoritative was deemed to be authoritarian, and I think that slippage was unfortunate. Of course I want to question authority when it is simply presumed, but I also want to support it when it is earned. I believe in expertise, and today many kinds of knowledge—cultural as well as political—are too quickly attacked as elitist. Of course, in this moment it is also crucially important to ask who gets to speak—indeed, to ask who is present to speak at all—and people like me should shut up more and listen more.

One of the things that I appreciated in *Design and Crime* is when you articulate the "schizophrenic" thread running through art history as a discipline: you have parallel arguments for art's formal autonomy on the one hand, and the foregrounding of social-historical context on the other. You conclude by arguing for a "strategic autonomy," which I interpret as saying simply that you believe that art needs to be seen as a special, specific thing—that art is not *everything else.*

I wrote that text about the antinomies of art history at a time—this was the mid to late 1990s—when we were involved in the debate about visual culture versus art history. Here my *October* colleagues and I were seen to be rearguard, because now, two decades on, we appeared to defend art history, not to attack it—to defend it against a collapse into visual studies, against a relativizing of art by media images. The point of my essay was that this tension between art and culture was in fact structural to the discipline, that visual studies was on the inside, not the outside, of art history at its best—think of Aby Warburg, Michael Baxandall, many others. "Strategic autonomy" was a play on Gayatri Spivak, on her notion of "strategic essentialism"—that at times, for political reasons, one has to claim aspects of an essentialist identity. So, too, I thought, at times, for cultural reasons, one has to claim aspects of an aesthetic autonomy. I think most artists would agree, even ones who are most committed to politics or most involved in mass culture, that the work that they do as artists is semi-autonomous, that every artist must develop his or her own language. I think most critics believe the same thing about criticism.

If we take "strategic autonomy," wherein the boundaries of a work of art are figured like a permeable membrane with the social-historical conditions on the outside, what still lies inside that makes art its own special thing?

Its own histories, for one thing, its own reservoirs of forms. Most of the artists I take seriously look backward as well as forward; in fact, sometimes they go back in order to move ahead. This is a very old dynamic in art history, and it is where the conservative and the radical are no longer in contradiction. One makes a break in an art form, but in that very break a new connection to the past is forged.

I just completed a book of conversations with Richard Serra, an artist who has transformed sculpture beyond recognition. But unlike his peers, such as Robert Smithson and Robert Morris, and his predecessors, such as Donald Judd and Dan Flavin, Serra held on to the term "sculpture": he sees his practice in relation to the history of the medium, and he finds connections there not only to moderns like Brancusi but also to ancients like Myron. His is not a "postmedium condition." Serra wants us to experience his sculpture *right here, right now*—what does "site-specificity" mean otherwise?—but he also wants that experience to reawaken key moments in past art, to bring that reserve of thoughts and feelings into the present. Maybe that's what I sensed when I looked at that Rothko—not just a beautiful painting, but somehow, within one painting, *all of painting*.

How has your writing evolved? It seems like the more you've written, the more attention has been paid to the writing itself.

I've always cared about the writing. I'm a writer first, a critic-historian-theorist second. That said, I've never wanted the writing to be self-involved or involuted; I've always wanted it to be as lucid as possible—difficult but lucid. That's what I heard in the critical voices that so impressed me as a young person—I found this conceptual clarity in Sontag, Krauss, Annette Michelson, a few others. Also, for my generation, theorists like Barthes, Derrida, and Foucault were the great *writers* of the time. Certainly there are moments of subjectivity in such work—Barthes played his subjectivity immaculately, like an instrument. But I don't like it when criticism becomes subjectivist; that's not much more than sensibility criticism come again.

Many people think we are in a "postcritical age"; they even hope we are. I understand the fatigue with the negativity of criticism, but mostly that fatigue is laziness—and an anti-intellectualism that is far more American than apple pie ever was. It's obvious that we need criticism now more than ever. When I was young you could pick up *The New Yorker* and read Sontag, or pick up *The New York Review of Books* and read Didion. Now you pick up such magazines and you get . . . Peter Schjeldahl? Jed Perl? David Salle? I admire Peter and David as writers, but they aren't critics. I blame the editors: they've given up on the critical part of the old public sphere; they've given up on criticism.

How do you distinguish between those two things—a writer and a critic?

The best critics—Baudelaire, Benjamin, Barthes—are great writers, so I don't distinguish there. I do distinguish, as Benjamin did, between commentators and critics. Most critics are in fact commentators; they might be beautiful writers, like Schjeldahl, but that's *it*: they tend to be belletristic, concerned with sensibility, suspicious of political positions and allergic to theoretical ones. Forty years ago spaces opened up for critical writing, even at big publications. Now that space has shrunk. Of course there are all kinds of online reviews, but in many ways that pluralism has watered criticism down. I'm fine with *Hyperallergic*, say, or *The Brooklyn Rail*; they have a service to render. I just don't see them as critical projects.

As someone who teaches art historians now, how do you see the relationship between those as roles or mentalities—the critic and historian?

For my cohort the roles were not opposed. One was a critic of contemporary art *and* a historian of modernist art; the contemporary and the modernist still spoke to each other. That gave the criticism footing in the past, and the history relevance in the present. That connection is stretched thin now: in the academy the modernist and the contemporary are distinct fields. People like me were raised halfway in the art world and halfway in the academy; now many people interested in contemporary practice and critical theory are formed in the academy alone.

You've said that this extended eighties period is not a "historical object" for you—which makes total sense to me, because it's your life and you're embedded in it.

I understand that for younger people it is a historical object. It's not for me, and not only because I lived it in part. It's not for me because I think it's a mistake to historicize prematurely—we don't know yet where that work will stand in the long run. Remember the famous line in Hegel: *Art for us is a thing of the past.* Every generation has to ask that question: *When does work qualify as art? When does work settle down in its historical place? When are we distant enough to know?* Part of me hopes that it never is—that that place can always be questioned. But then most of us agree on the absolute greatness of Manet, Cézanne, Matisse, Mondrian, Pollock, and so on. When does that happen, and how? At one point in our conversations Richard Serra says, *You never know how long you get. Duchamp said thirty years, Warhol said fifteen minutes. You don't know.*

You were one of the founding editors of Zone Books. How did Zone originate, and what were your intentions with it?

I was formed not only as a critic but also as an editor. In some ways my so-called career was launched by an editorial project, *The Anti-Aesthetic,* in 1983, and, again, I worked at *Art in America* for several years in the eighties. Zone, which began in 1985 as a magazine and soon developed into a line of books, was an intellectual initiative. In part it was articulated against *October,* which was largely influenced by Derrida and Barthes. Zone was developed under the aegis of Foucault and Deleuze instead; it was both more historicist and more philosophical in its orientation than *October.* We also translated key French texts important to the poststructuralists that were not known to Anglophone readers: Bergson, Bataille, Canguilhem . . .

In many ways Zone issued from the intellectual comraderie of four guys—Michel Feher, Jonathan Crary, Sanford Kwinter, and me. At that time New York allowed for that kind of intimacy. After several years we diverged a bit, and I came to see *October* as the setting for my own work, so I jumped over as an editor in 1991.

I was looking at the books on my shelf published by Zone in the eighties, when you were involved. They include: Gilles Deleuze's *Masochism: Coldness and Cruelty* [1967]; Henri Bergson's *Matter and Memory* [1896]; Henri Focillon's *Life of Forms in Art* [1942]; Erwin Panofsky's *Perspective as Symbolic Form* [1927]; and of course the books by Georges Bataille.

Bataille was one figure shared by Zone and *October.*

Except they engage very different versions of Bataille—for instance, *October* never touches all the weird stuff on magic and religion.

October was interested in Bataille the dissident surrealist, the Bataille of *Documents* [1929–1930]. Zone was involved with the postwar Bataille of *The Accursed Share* [1949], *Theory of Religion* [1973], and other books.

When you moved to *October* in 1991, Crimp had left as the editor. What in your mind were the parameters of that project, and where were you interested in steering it? It takes on a different identity at that point.

Douglas departing was a real blow to the magazine. Certainly it revealed some limitations of the editors, but at least they saw they had to change. I was invited in with Benjamin Buchloh and Yve-Alain Bois. Rosalind had old commitments to minimalists and postminimalists, but for the most part she had fallen out of contact with contemporary artists. Benjamin was bound up with conceptual and institutional-critical artists like Dan Graham and Michael Asher, so he brought in that dimension of the neo-avant-garde. Yve-Alain had personal connections to neoconcrete artists like Lygia Clark and Hélio Oiticica, so he expanded the international frame of modernist practice. They also had particular European commitments—Benjamin to German art from Dada to Richter and Polke, Yve-Alain from Russian constructivism to contemporary French practice. Maybe as an American I was less hostile to questions of mass culture; certainly I was a Pictures Generation person. The early nineties was the moment of "abject art," and I was alert to that work in a way the others were not. In that moment the body came into play in a new way: with the attacks on the welfare state, the indifference to the AIDS epidemic, and the unraveling of society under neoliberalism, the damaged body became a cipher for a damaged body politic. In this light—or darkness—I wrote about Robert Gober, Mike Kelley, and others in ways that I think somewhat mystified my colleagues. Also, I was more interested than they were in the culture wars—and in its ramifications for us. What do we do when "identity"— the very thing we had so often critiqued—becomes central politically and artistically? In part I helped the journal stay relevant.

The aims of *October* and the stakes of those intellectual battles weren't consistent over the last forty years—what's that trajectory, and how do you see it functioning now?

Generally speaking, for its first ten years or so *October* was the key site where contemporary art and critical theory were brought together: to parse the relationship between postmodernist art and poststructural criticism was the *October* project then. The second decade expanded the practice-theory nexus—for example, to feminism and psychoanalysis. During that time we also opened up the modernist field to movements that were somewhat occluded, like Dada and constructivism. We also performed new readings of movements that were well known— rethinking surrealism through Bataille, for instance. This historical dimension of *October*, at once documentary and revisionist, has always been important, and continues to be so, I think. The next period was inflected by culture wars—which were also canon wars—and we had to find our footing in relation to these shifts. It was during this time that we took up institutional questions such as art history versus visual culture. We also reanimated old formats like the roundtable and the questionnaire to make the journal more open to other points of view. We have always prized critical rigor, but it was important to include other voices too.

The last thing that I want to ask you about is *Art Since 1900*. There are a number of things one could do to consolidate power around intellectual positions, and writing a textbook is probably the most straightforward one. There you're essentially laying it out: *This is our canon, and this is how we talk about it*. I'm interested in the process of that and how you approached it.

I get the Foucaultian point that power is bound up with knowledge, but why leap over the knowledge part so directly to the power part? *Art Since 1900* is a digest of the life work of four—and now, with David Joselit, five—important modernists. Is that simply a power play on our part? Give me—give us—a break! Also, can you construct a canon out of the scores of entries that make up the two volumes? I bet not. Certainly I couldn't.

The textbook is often critiqued, rotely, because it is not comprehensive. But how could it be? I grant that the title—*Art Since 1900*—sounds very inclusive, but that was an imposition of the publisher. Our title was much more focused—"Modernism and Its

Discontents." It is our take on things, of course, but it is set up as a puzzle of pieces that can be put together in many different ways. There's no teleological trajectory, no correct grouping. Sure, there are blind spots, but we're upfront about our own limitations. I think it's taken up as a canonical statement because some people need the *October* editors as a foil. Which is to say that a good part of the criticism is projection—but, then, it often is. Unfortunately, I'm as Oedipal as the next guy; I grew up as an antagonist of Greenberg, William Rubin, Fried, and others. I know what it's like to need a bad object. But it's hard to group the *October* editors all together. We're all so different. "Octoberite"—what does that even mean?

I'm very interested in what new formations of practice, criticism, and history will emerge out of this period of reaction and insurgency. I can't articulate them; it's not for me to articulate them, but I see them out there. It has to do with different people who come with different topics, sometimes with languages that others share, sometimes not. Welcome to the new barbarians!

There's no seam between what
is called "description" and what
is called "interpretation." You
start saying what this thing looks
like, and before you know it
there's significance leaking out of
every sentence, and you're going
somewhere.

Michael Fried (b. 1939) is a critic, art historian, and poet whose work helped define the discourse on modernism. In dialogue with Clement Greenberg in the 1960s, he wrote art criticism for *Arts Magazine*, *Art International*, and *Artforum*, famously attacking nascent minimalism in "Art and Objecthood" (1967), which remains a foundational text of twentieth-century art history. His books include *Absorption and Theatricality: Painting and Beholder in the Age of Diderot* (1980); *Courbet's Realism* (1990); *Manet's Modernism: or, The Face of Painting in the 1860s* (1996); *Art and Objecthood: Essays and Reviews* (1998); *Why Photography Matters as Art as Never Before* (2008); *The Moment of Caravaggio* (2010); *Four Honest Outlaws: Sala, Ray, Marioni, Gordon* (2011); and *What Was Literary Impressionism?* (2018). He is also the author of four books of poems, most recently *Promesse du Bonheur*, with photographs by James Welling (2016). He is the J. R. Herbert Boone Professor Emeritus of Humanities and the History of Art at Johns Hopkins University.

Michael Fried

I'd like to know about your childhood—what did your parents do?

I grew up in the Bronx. My father was a lawyer. My mother became a junior high school teacher. My father was actually born in a shtetl, came over to America at seven. He went to law school—very intelligent man. They were a representative sort of middle-class, professional-class, New York Jewish family. I have a younger sister who became an outstanding high school science teacher—we would have had to be idiots to not go to college; the values at home were of a completely serious intellectual kind.

Was your experience of being Jewish mostly cultural, or were you involved with it spiritually?

I would say it was merely cultural. My dad's parents lived two houses away. I was very close to them. They had the two sets of silverware—one for meat, one for dairy—and we went to temple on the High Holy Days and had Shabbas dinners because of my grandmother. None of that ever took with me. The simplest way I can put it is, it would make me unbelievably happy to learn tomorrow that Manet was Jewish. [Laughter.] In other words, a strong sense of Jewish identity, but also one that is unbelievably shallow—that captures it perfectly. From a very early age there would be the big bar mitzvahs and the family weddings, and I always felt that this extended Jewish world had nothing to do with me. I knew instinctively there was some other world for me— which I eventually learned was called Paris.

They made me go to Hebrew school three afternoons a week, which

I completely hated. In regular school, though, I was a totally good boy. I was the kind of kid who if the teacher said, *I'll leave the room for five minutes, I don't want any of you to talk*—I'd *never* talk. But Hebrew school was another story. I was very close with my parents. They were wonderful to me, and they would take me to Manhattan on the weekends. We went to two places: the American Museum of Natural History and the Met. As a kid I drew better than anyone else in class. When I was eleven or twelve I painted in oils every Saturday with a painter named Jan de Ruth, and a few years after that I went to the Art Students League and did watercolors. I'd go to the Met with a pad and I'd copy pictures. It was clear early on that I *loved* art.

Later, at moments when I came closest to thinking about being an artist, what came between me and it was the whole physical side of art making. For example, I found completely daunting the idea of stretching canvases. Look at early Darby Bannards—he made all his supports. Frank Stella made all his own supports, then stretched the canvases. Even today, as I say it to you now, I feel anxiety.

Here is something else: think about Morris Louis. Living in a house in suburban Maryland near Washington. He taught painting but the family was also partly supported by his wife, who was the principal of a Hebrew school. He's come to the end of the *Veils* [1954–1959]. He's trying to move toward what will eventually become the *Unfurleds* [1960–1961]. Then he goes on to the *Stripes* [1961–1962]. Then in September '62 he dies so suddenly of cancer that he never gets to prune his work—he never gets to throw out the unsuccessful stuff—so every piece of canvas that he ever painted on during those years exists. What you see are scores of enormous canvases on which he's tried *this*, it didn't work, so he tried *that*, it didn't work. One thing that no one thinks about is how much money it costs to do that. You have to believe in yourself to the extent that you're prepared to throw away a lot of money on all that canvas and paint that didn't work out. I realized very early on that I didn't have that mentality. I'd be thinking, *Oh, shit. I better not ruin this! This is a piece of really good watercolor paper that costs three bucks*—at a time when three bucks meant something—*so I'd better not mess it up*. If you think that way, you're dead. To be an artist you have to have a different mindset. From the start you have to think, *I'm worth any fucking amount of three-dollar paper!* Things like that just knocked me out of being an artist.

When you were going to museums as a child, what paintings first made you understand something about what paintings are? Or what art is?

My favorite painting at the Met, which was just complete magic—I can recapture the feeling even now—was El Greco's *View of Toledo* [ca. 1599–1600]. I couldn't believe that a painting could do this—it was like a whole universe. When I was copying pictures, I would very often choose a picture, such as an Ingres, because it looked copyable—strong profiles. I just loved the whole physical existence of the pictures—that they were not reproductions.

What about your early relationship with language? When did you realize that you wanted to be a writer?

My father wanted to be a writer, so writing was a value in my family. Even in public school I was always trying to *write*—I would write something that had alliterations or internal rhymes or whatever. Writing always mattered to me. I belonged to a generation that was tremendously science oriented; in high schools in the fifties, bright kids were channeled toward the sciences. At a certain point my father was worried I was too into science. In 1954, the year I turned fifteen, he read about Louise Bogan bringing out her *Collected Poems*, so he bought a copy and left it around the house. I found it and started reading Bogan's poems—I didn't know that's why he'd done that, he only told me much later. I completely *loved* them—I have them in my head to this day.

Could you describe what struck you about them?

Yes, they completely encapsulate what I would today call my poetics: they were short, intense lyrics—not discursive, *lyrical*. This is what, in a certain sense, painting and poetry have in common; as Hazlitt says in an essay called "On the Pleasure of Painting" [1821], "One part of a picture shames another." What he means is, *It has to be fucking perfect.*

[Laughter.]

It can't be, *This is a wonderful painting, but the left eye is slightly wrong.*

Well, every now and then you see a painting where you'll say something like that, but the pressure is always on to get everything *right*. That's what a lyric poem is like; you can't have a great lyric poem where line twelve sucks. It can happen, it's bound to happen, that some lines may be stronger than others—even in Mallarmé—but the ideal, the drive, is to make something that has no weak spot. Then, too, for both painting and poetry, if a work is *merely* perfect it will probably be academic. So on top of that it has to be *intense*. If you can make poems or paintings that are intense *and* perfect, you've done something. In a way, it's a very simple aesthetic that I've always operated with. That's what Anthony Caro's sculptures are about—all the trial and error is to get it just right.

That is a beautiful way of explicating what you call "syntax" in Caro's sculptures, which is largely that every part is meaningful in relation to every other part.

That's absolutely right, and that's exactly how he thought about it. Caro was not verbally articulate—we were very close from the early days because he saw that I completely got his work, but he also appreciated talking with me because I could find words for what he was doing. He would literally write them down. It was a wonderful relationship for both of us.

Were you going to study poetry when you went to Princeton?

I went to Princeton thinking I'd be a scientist. I discovered very, very quickly that out of the eight hundred kids in the freshman class, there were like four hundred who could do physics better than me, so that was not an attractive career path. But I took the introductory Shakespeare course, and I got an A plus—that's when I realized I was good at this. I started to write poems just out of the blue. The second year I took creative writing. Leslie Fiedler was there, and he was wonderfully supportive. He delivered me by hand to R. P. Blackmur, and I became a Blackmur student, and I wrote poems for him. I won the poetry prizes at Princeton. By the time I left I knew that I wanted to amount to something as a poet.

But did you consider yourself a poet?

A great question. Yes and no. I can now say, *I'm a poet,* but there were whole decades where I couldn't quite. I thought, *How can anyone ever say, "I am a poet"?* It seemed to me to be the greatest, most desirable distinction in the universe. Seeing a shrink in my midforties helped me get past a dysfunctional overvaluation of the idea of poetry. So did my close friendship with a remarkable poet and poetic intelligence at Johns Hopkins, the great Allen Grossman. Grossman had no sympathy at all for my writing poems and putting them in a drawer. It just seemed stupid to him. That was a big help in coming out. Of course, I still think what I just said about being a poet is true, but living by it was not useful in any way.

One thing about being my mother's son—the Depression hit the moment my parents graduated from college, so they belonged to a generation for whom the deepest truth of life was the Depression. What my mother took away from that was, *If you want something, you better go for it. No one is going to hand it to you.* There was actually a wonderful moment after my sister had had a daughter; we were visiting her in Boston along with my mother and father. Several of us were sitting on the bed in a motel room, and the baby started to reach for a doll, so Ruth, my wife, handed it to her, and my mother said, *Don't do that—if she wants the doll let her go get the doll.* That was my mother. [Laughter.] Once she did say to me explicitly, *Michael, within five miles of where we are sitting, here in the Bronx, there are a thousand little Jewish boys your age who are just as smart as you, and only a very few are going to end up doing anything that counts.* If there's anything I deeply believe, it's *that*—it's not about being gifted, it's about what you do with your gift. If you have some particular endowment, lucky you, but there are like a million people with an endowment for painting who don't become Frank Stella.

How did you meet Frank Stella at Princeton?

I submitted a few poems to the college literary magazine, and I got a message back saying they were publishing them and that there would be a meeting for anyone involved in the magazine in two weeks. I walked into this small room and there was a group of intensely interesting people—the cream of Princeton, really. Sitting on the couch was this tough-looking guy who said nothing, in fact barely looked up, making abstract drawings with a magic marker on a big pad. I had gone to the Art Students League, but I'd never seen someone make abstractions before. That was Frank. Afterward I asked one of the other students who knew him, *Does he want to be a painter?* The guy looked at me and said, *He doesn't "want" to be a painter—he* is *a painter—that's who he is.* Very quickly Frank and I became close, and through Frank I met Darby Bannard.

Were you reading art criticism?

We were reading Clement Greenberg. Remember, *Art and Culture* [1961] hadn't been published yet—we're talking '56, '57, '58. The alternative was *ARTnews* and horrible Harold Rosenberg's warmed-over existentialist rhetoric—and we hated that! The greatest luck of my life, in terms of a single encounter, was meeting Frank, because it was a kind of instant initiation into modernist abstract art. I discovered very quickly that in fact my default setting was for abstraction—I've never had to think about abstraction. From the first moment I encountered it, I *got* it.

So when you meet Frank Stella you're writing poetry, and are you also painting?

I wasn't painting, but through Frank I met Stephen Greene, who was teaching painting at Princeton, and he was terrific. I took one studio course with him, but my paintings were nothing special. New York was only an hour away, and we all went and looked at art there. I began taking art history courses, which I loved. At some point in 1957, '58—I was eighteen going on nineteen, it was my junior year— I decided to write to Clement Greenberg. It was sort of like my mother again: I could imagine her saying, *So you'd like to meet Clement Greenberg. Figure out how to get in touch with him. Just do it.* I probably got his address from Stephen Greene, and I wrote saying, *I'm a junior at Princeton and I'd like to come and meet you.* A week or so later, a postcard—his favorite medium—arrived saying, *Here's my number, call me, arrange to come.* But I got cold feet and did nothing about it. Then about two weeks later I got a follow-up card saying, *Some of my cards seem to have gone astray* …So I went and visited him. He was living at 90 Bank Street in the

Village and was revising the essays that became *Art and Culture*. There were paintings and sculptures in the apartment, including a smallish sculpture by Theodore Roszak, and he asked me what I thought of it. And I said, *Actually, I don't like much like Roszak—I don't think it's very good.* And he called to his wife, *Jenny, Jenny, this guy can see through Ted Roszak!*

[Laughter.]

I didn't realize that that was how you won your spurs with Clem. Greenberg was a shit and a bully and all those things that people say, but he could be wonderful to you at the beginning. It was only when you became someone in your own right that he would turn against you. My senior year he was invited to give the Gauss Seminars in Criticism at Princeton, which undergraduates don't normally go to, but he put me on the list, and I went. And I got Frank and Darby invited. Frank was in New York—that's the year leading to the stripes—but he came down for most of the lectures, and that's how Greenberg met them both. And then, through an error of judgment by the board of selection, I was awarded a Rhodes Scholarship, so I went off to Oxford, which I hated. There was Frank making stripes, there was Darby making his early pictures, there was New York exploding artistically, and I was eating sausages in the Middle Ages, where it felt as if nobody had ever heard of Manet, much less Pollock.

It must have been Greenberg who gave me a letter of introduction to Hilton Kramer back when I was at Princeton, when Hilton was editing *Arts Magazine*. Hilton had me write some trial reviews, which must have been okay. During my two years at Oxford, where I didn't read for a degree but played a lot of tennis on grass and also met the woman, Ruth Leys, I would soon marry, Kramer had me write two short book reviews, I realize now not to lose touch with me completely. Then I moved to London for a year, and for maybe thirty bucks became a special student at UCL, studying basic philosophy with Richard Wollheim, who became a friend—that was a great year for me, 1961 to 1962. That was when I realized that I wanted to get a PhD in art history, but I wasn't ready to return to America yet. Then, just as I moved to London, the position of London correspondent for *Arts Magazine* came open, because Alan Bowness didn't want the job anymore. Out of the blue I got a short telegram from Kramer offering me the position, and suddenly at twenty-two I was writing a monthly "London Letter" for *Arts*—unbelievable. It paid seventy-five dollars, which covered my share of the rent for an apartment I shared with a British friend. It's hard to imagine how cheap big cities were during those years.

You're right, I can't imagine.

Frank could support himself on some house painting, rent a small studio in the Lower East Side, and still have enough money to make paintings. I probably lived that whole year in London for about three thousand bucks—for everything, apartment, food, movies, even some traveling. And I'm the London critic for *Arts*! So the very first show I go to cover, the dealer says, *Come join us for dinner afterward.* And I'm stunned—*I get dinner too!* We go to an Italian restaurant, and I'm seated opposite a surly looking guy in his midthirties who says, *When are you coming to see my work?* And I think to myself, *This may not be as great a deal as it seemed.* But the next weekend I go by underground to the guy's house in Hampstead, and of course it's Anthony Caro. There are two early abstract pieces in his courtyard, *Midday* [1960] and *Sculpture Seven* [1961], and I'm completely blown away. He comes out of the house and I say, *You're a great sculptor, and the yellow one's a masterpiece.* After that I saw Caro regularly and developed a deep passion for his work. At the end of the summer of 1962 I returned to America, started graduate school in art history at Harvard, and also began writing a monthly "New York Letter" for James Fitzsimmons's *Art International*. I also got back in touch with Greenberg, who said he liked the "London Letters"; met Ken Noland and other artists; became seriously interested in the work of Morris Louis, who had just died; and everything just fell into place. I would fly down to New York once a month, stay with Frank and Barbara Rose, who were then married, and Frank and I would spend two days going around galleries. If all I had wanted to do was write up what Frank was saying, I would have had a different career, but it would have been a distinguished one. He was so smart. He *is* so smart. Then I would fly back to Boston, spend two days writing up my "Letter," and return to coursework at Harvard. It was a marvelous routine.

It seems like *Art and Culture* flattens, in every sense of the word, not only Greenberg's previous criticism but our whole understanding of midcentury American painting up to that point. When you were first writing criticism in the late fifties, early sixties, what did the landscape look like, in terms of the possibilities and models?

The truth is, I didn't know a hell of a lot. Really, what Frank, Darby, and I knew was *ARTnews*, whose dominance was tremendous—Harold Rosenberg and "X Paints a Picture," the rhetoric of which was completely useless. I cannot express how distasteful I found Rosenberg.

What was important to me, in addition to Greenberg's writing, was what it turns out had been important to Greenberg, and that was T. S. Eliot. Eliot's critical essays are relatively short, with a handful of brilliantly chosen quotations, and a fantastic ability to sum up and condense. Quite apart from his analytical intelligence, there were two skills Greenberg had to a superlative degree. First was the ability to characterize the work of a painter or movement without detailed descriptions of individual works, but in a way that made it clear that a tremendous amount of close looking and hard thinking supported every statement. The second skill, part of his journalistic gift—I'm using "journalistic" now not at all as a pejorative—is that he was brilliant at finding thrilling ways of starting an essay. The essays begin and just like that—you're in the middle of an argument by the time you're halfway through the first paragraph. It's an incredible ability—very, very rare.

If we take the whole of Greenberg's work and ask, *All right, let's see, what did he say about Pollock? What did he say about Newman? What did he say about Rothko? What did he say about de Kooning? What did he say about Gorky?*—it's sometimes surprisingly little. His great distinction is that he saw how important their art was, and of course he more than anyone understood how tremendous Pollock was, and so on. But if you had to make the case for Greenberg as a major writer even about Pollock, what he had to say comes down to relatively few paragraphs. What are the great essays? "Cézanne and the Unity of Modern Art" [1959], "The Later

Monet" [1956], and above all "Collage" [1959]—he was *prescient* about contemporary abstraction and wrote powerfully about it, but he was *brilliant* about that earlier moment, the passage from impressionism to the emergence of cubism. Right from the start, I felt that the greatest critical essay on art I would ever read was "Collage." And of course Greenberg was a force in the studio, as lots of artists have testified.

In 1965 I organized a show of paintings at the Fogg Museum of Art at Harvard by Noland, Olitski, and Stella with a long catalogue text, and then two years later—1966 to '67—I got truly inspired and wrote in quick succession essays on Morris Louis and Caro; "Shape as Form" [1966], on Stella's *Irregular Polygons* [1965–66]; an essay on Olitski; and finally "Art and Objecthood." That's quite an outpouring, but for years I had mixed feelings about them, probably because they operate in a completely un-Greenbergian way. *I'm about to write an essay about Frank Stella's new eccentric shape paintings. How they have come about is in every way dialectical. In order to understand this, we have to go back to the cave paintings—* not really, but almost. I mean, most of the essays begin by wheeling huge pieces of artillery into place—like World War I. They have none of the zippiness of Greenberg, none of his flair for vivid opening paragraphs. They're much more like, *If you're serious, you're going to hang in there with me while I work on the problematic of shape. And if you're not up to this, then fuck you, because this is going to take some doing.* Now, of course, I see that heavy-duty quality as a particular strength of those essays. But it took me a long time to go back to them.

I would love to talk more about the role of description in writing criticism and how it's evolved in your work.

When I started writing criticism, I realized fairly quickly that I loved generating an argument by describing. I loved the *project* of writing description—I still do. I don't think it's that common a gift, but if you can do it, then there's no seam between what is called "description" and what is called "interpretation."

Exactly!

You start saying what this thing looks like, and before you know it there's significance leaking out of every sentence, and you're going somewhere. I loved that, almost technically. And I also realized, of course, that that was not what Clem did, so it was just a beautiful stretch of uninhabited country.

Take my essay on Stella's *Irregular Polygons*: in order to get what I think they're doing, I have to describe them, and in the course of doing that, or in order to do that, I have to develop a certain armory of concepts. The other rule that I have—in the fall of 1966, Ruth and I went with Frank to his studio, and the *Irregular Polygons* were there. Ruth asked, *So, Frank, why did you go from the stripes to this?* And I had to practically shout, *No! If he's going to answer your question, I have to leave. Otherwise, you have to withdraw the question.* I'm the critic—it's for *me* to figure out what the paintings are up to and why Frank made them the way he did, what his intentions were in doing so. I might be right and I might be wrong, but it's my job to try to work it out. It's hard to keep that attitude completely intact when you are friends with artists. But for me, that's always been very important. I want to be the one figuring out what's going on, and one major vehicle for accomplishing that is a certain sort of "motivated description," to use a phrase of Svetlana Alpers's.

It becomes a way of modeling the activity of looking as cognitive experience—

Yes.

—which then opens up the dynamic of beholding as a psychologically charged one.

That's completely right. And that touches on something that's very, very important. If someone said to me, in the most general terms, *What do you think is new about your writing about art?* I would say that more than anyone I'm aware of—with the exception of Gombrich, who operates completely differently and whose writings I don't especially like—I've opened up the topic of the relationship between the work and the beholder, which is to say the topic of what happens *this* side of the painting. No one before me seems to have found this discussable in a rigorous way. It's very tricky to get that right, because what you're having to do is analyze structures that are built into the picture, structures that elicit something from you, that have the beholder in view, but are nevertheless not simply a function of the beholder's experience.

I'm writing an essay on Georges de La Tour's *Penitent Magdalen* [ca. 1640], which is at the Met. In your book *The Moment of Caravaggio*, there is an analysis of Caravaggio's *Penitent Magdalen* [1596–1597], which I also love, and which is so closely related to what I am writing— it made me realize that these structures actually live *inside* the paint- ings. It was a confirmation of my own experience and showed me that you're not making this up.

Completely—I would like to feel that anybody reading the art history I've done would come to feel that. In other words, I'm drawing this *out of* the pictures. At the same time, doing this requires a particular stance toward the work of art, a certain sort of frame of mind. Let's say we're talking about a picture. Well, the crucial thing is to find a way to open yourself to what it is doing—*Open yourself to the picture, don't be afraid.* The whole of art history as a field discourages that approach—*That's too subjective, that's just you.* Art history considers itself a discipline—whatever that means; its entire rationale is to rule out that sort of approach. German art historians especially are often very uncomfortable when they hear me speak. For most of them, it feels like what I do isn't objective—it's not *Wissenschaft,* it's not science. *There's no method,* they complain, *you're just saying what you see.* I say, *That's exactly right!* Except, let's just add to that, *I'm trying to describe and account for what's actually there.* There isn't a "method" other than trying to open yourself to the picture and draw forth from what's there to be seen. It's pretty basic, but the field doesn't much like it.

The other thing that's impressive about "Art and Objecthood"— which ranks with Greenberg's "Collage" as one of the great American essays—is that your argument is so sensitized to the fact that bodily, visual, and cognitive experience are profoundly intertwined.

During my time at Oxford, when I first became interested in philo- sophy, some of the interesting younger people there were reading Merleau-Ponty. So I started reading him too—he wasn't translated yet, but fortunately my French was just about adequate to the task. I read the three key Merleau-Ponty essays for painting: "Cézanne's Doubt" [1945], "Indirect Language and the Voices of Silence" [1952], and "Eye and Mind" [1961]. This was extremely fortunate; I could not have read anything more useful, because my own basic response to art was, from the first, *bodily*. And what Merleau-Ponty was saying was, *Don't forget for a moment that you are an embodied being, and seeing and perceiving are bodily activities.* It was so emboldening to absorb that theoretical justification at that early stage. My early Caro essay for his show at the Whitechapel Gallery in 1963, for all its crudeness, is all about the sculptures in relation to the body.

In all my seminars at Johns Hopkins, I'd always start by saying, *The most important thing I'm going to teach in this class is that you have a body. And I'm going to teach you how your body works. For example, I want you to shut your eyes and feel where your behind stops. Now, I want you to feel where the chair begins. It's the same, right?* There's absolutely no way you can make that distinction. You see what that means right away—*The body and the world are intertwined, so don't fall into the trap of thinking there's just a subject and an object.* That's why it makes me so happy to hear you say that. *Yes, I feel that way.* That's also why I regarded Rosalind Krauss's charge of "pure visuality" in my work as being complete horseshit—the writing refutes it at every point. I never bought into this idea of "disembodied visuality"—what could be stupider?

The strange irony is that the arguments for minimalism depend on that same phenomenology, coming out of Merleau-Ponty.

That's right. That's where aesthetic judgment comes in. You can say, *Wow, this stuff is intensely bodily in its appeal or address to the viewer,* but that is neither here nor there with respect to the issue of artistic quality, of the work's success as art.

I don't know if you experience this with any irony, but "Art and Objecthood" *got* **minimalism in such a deep way. You understood exactly what it was doing, and no one really refutes that. What everyone disagrees with is your evaluation—that you disapproved of it.**

I think that's completely right. The valuation could be wrong—

173

that's up for grabs—but I still stand by it.

To go from "Art and Objecthood" to _Absorption and Theatricality_— part of its sophistication is that it figures paintings in an intertextual web of contemporaneous criticism. In fact, running through your work there is an extensive use of contemporaneous criticism and artist's writings. While you have this extreme sensitivity to physical and visual experiences, you are also bringing in an awareness of language as it bears on the "artwork."

When I wrote "Art and Objecthood" and first formulated my attack on theatricality, I had read some Diderot but hadn't yet realized that he and I were on the same page, so to speak! Nevertheless, from early on I understood that the relation of the work to the beholder was going to be an important concern for me. This first became clear when I was very young—still an undergraduate—thinking about the artist who's always meant the most to me, Manet. What I couldn't stop thinking about before I had anything really to think with was that in painting after painting, there was a figure looking at the viewer in a certain way—it happens again and again. If I had said that to anybody in the world of art history, they would reply, _Yes, of course—we all know that—the figures look at us. Big deal. Are we supposed to give you credit for noticing that?_ What I would want to say back is, _You know it and you don't know it. You do, in the sense that, yeah, you're aware that they're looking at you, but you don't find that to be anything worth thinking about._ It has the structure of _We all know that._ Which brings us to an iron law of intellectual life: whenever something has the structure of _We all know that_, it also has the structure of being completely un–thought through.

So I knew from the beginning that whatever I would eventually write about Manet had somehow to take that seriously—because something out of the ordinary was happening there. _Why would these figures be looking at us in that way?_ I didn't know how to describe that yet, but I wanted to know why at a certain moment—1860—in a certain place— Paris—ambitious painting should have taken this particular turn. This also meant that Greenberg's notion that modernist painting began with Manet because of his pursuit of flatness—a very influential claim even among art historians who liked to think they disagreed with Greenberg—couldn't be exactly right. Eventually I developed the notion of *facingness* as crucial for Manet. And it also meant that in order to understand why this should have happened around 1860—why the presence of the beholder before the painting became a certain sort of issue precisely then—I had to begin earlier. I had to go back in time, to track the developments that led up to this. Dialectically, as I like to say.

First, though, I wrote a PhD dissertation on Manet's use of sources in earlier painting, another widely unacknowledged but utterly unexamined aspect of his art, and by way of committing art historical suicide published it in a single issue of *Artforum*—Phil Leider's idea, for which I will always be grateful. Then I thought I would move a generation back in time and write about Courbet, but after a few painful months I realized I couldn't carry that through, because I was constantly writing paragraphs that said things like, *In order to understand this we have to go back to the eighteenth century*. Finally I realized that something fundamentally important first took shape around the middle of the eighteenth century, with what was called the reaction against the rococo, and it seemed to me that if I moved back there and then inched forward dialectically I would finally get to understand why Manet's figures look at the beholder the way they do. So I made the leap and immersed myself in the eighteenth century. And, in a great stroke of luck, I found waiting for me there the wonderful Diderot— the first great art critic, and, beyond that, maybe the most attractive genius in the history of thought. So *appealing*, so *smart*, such a great writer—thrilling to read. It quickly emerged that for him the crucial issue was precisely something that I had already raised in "Art and Objecthood," namely the relation of the work of art to the viewer. This was a breakthrough moment for me.

Of course, all of this had to be thought through historically, which in the first place led to *Absorption and Theatricality*. Here's a simple example that I used with my students: take David's *The Oath of the Horatii*, 1784. My claim is that it's his decisive attempt to make a Diderotian picture—dramatic but not theatrical. But by the mid-1790s, ten years later, his former student Delécluze, who became an art critic and who wrote an important book about David, tells us that David thought the composition of the *Oath* was *un peu théâtral*—a little theatrical. So, was David right in 1785, or was he right in 1796? Is *The Oath of the Horatii* dramatic, or is it theatrical? It's a trick question: the right answer is to refuse the question.

Because to answer the question is in effect to become a contemporary critic of the picture. But you're not a critic in the 1780s or 1790s—you're a historian trying to understand something two hundred plus years later. What's important is to figure out how the *Oath* or any other picture was viewed and understood in its own time or at some later moment. And you can't do this by taking sides. Half the art critics who wrote about Millet in the 1860s said, *These are amazing pictures of real peasants absorbed in shoveling shit*. And the other half, including Gautier and Baudelaire, said, *These are phony, theatrical little figures pretending to be peasants, pretending to be absorbed in shoveling shit*. So who is right? Again, it's a trap. It makes no sense to think that it's up to us to decide if they're really shoveling shit—we're dealing with pictures, nobody's shoveling anything.

The important point to understand is that around 1860 the sophisticated art world in Paris was *divided* about this. And that meant that Millet-intensity absorption no longer worked for everyone with a stake in painting. Through reading the criticism you're getting privileged insight into the structures of perception about and responses to art at that time. In other words, the whole trick of *Absorption and Theatricality*, and lots of the art history I've written since, is that I'm trying to understand contemporary arguments without buying into them one way or the other. Diderot disliked Watteau because Watteau seemed to him a ne plus ultra of theatricality. But of course Watteau is *wonderful*. For the historian, the crucial point to grasp is that this was how Diderot felt about Watteau. That's the sense in which when I'm about writing art historically, *I am an art historian*. I'm doing my best to keep a certain historical distance from everything. On the one hand, I'm opening myself experientially to the maximum degree to the pictures so as to become attuned to what the paintings have to tell me, and on the other I'm committed intellectually to a strategy of historical distance so that I can finally claim, *This is what was going on then*.

Your early criticism highly privileges color—for instance, in "Shape as Form" you say, "It cannot be emphasized too strongly, however, that Noland's chief concern throughout his career has been with color— rather, with feeling *through* color—and not with structure," but there's never any pressure placed on what color actually is.

That's really interesting—and it's perfectly true. The moment I entered art criticism was a moment of stunning coloristic achievement—Louis, Noland, Olitski, Poons, for a start. Not to mention Rothko, Still, Newman, Hofmann. When minimalism hit it was as if its secret mission was to expunge color from art. *We're now going to operate with a range between white and pewter with various nuances of beige thrown in*—and people loved that! In fact they still do! Look at the rage for Agnes Martin. If someone said to me, *Would you write an essay about color per se? Laying out your thinking about color*—I'd have to say, *I don't really have any coherent thinking about color.*

That's incredible.

But I recognize it when I see it! [Laughter.] There is an art workshop called Triangle Artists' Workshop, founded by Caro back around 1980. It was held for a time in Pine Plains, New York—a group of painters and sculptors would go there for two weeks in the summer and make art. Caro wanted me to come as a visiting critic, and I didn't really want to do that—I don't like doing crits, because a lot of times I just find so little to say. I love being in the studio with artists I'm close to and admire, but I find it very hard to deal with work that leaves me cold. But I told him that I would go if I could also have a place to paint, because there were certain materials I wanted to try out. For example, I'd never used acrylic gel. I'm very glad I did that, because gel is a weird substance—take a lot of gel and you put a tiny bit of dark blue in it and suddenly the whole thing is dark blue. It's completely counter to anything you think you know about paint before you've encountered gel. While I was there, I discovered something I already suspected:

I don't have valuable color intuitions. On just some very primitive level, if you told Ken Noland, *Don't even think about making a painting, but here are some paints and a piece of paper and just put some dabs of paint wherever you like—just put some touches of color wherever you like,* the result would be beautiful. It might not be a painting, but it would beautiful, and you'd want to take it home and frame it and look at it every day of your life. His feeling for color was so deep, so true. I didn't have that instinct, which was another reason not to venture into painting.

Color is almost *unfair* in that sense, because people have a strong color sensibility or they don't, and there's no way around that. You can't teach it.

In my case I can recognize it and admire it unstintingly but I couldn't do it myself. My two weeks at Triangle were more than worth it, to discover that simple truth in such a strong way. But color per se is just not something I've ever thought about in the sense that you raised, and as far as I'm aware there isn't a lot of interesting thinking about it.

The discourse on color remains strangely primitive. Of course Wittgenstein's late essay is very interesting, but you don't get much farther than that philosophically. That's actually why I love color—it's so *resistant,* to language, theorization, stability.

I think that's deeply right. Simply describing the colors in those early Bannards is so difficult. Here's something I don't believe: I completely don't believe that painting is a visual art and therefore any attempt to capture it in language is doomed—that there's always going to be this fundamental mismatch between images and words. I think that's complete horseshit. But if we take just color, then, maybe, yes. Because it is virtually impossible to describe color. How many reds are there? Is raspberry red the same as cherry red, the same as strawberry red—crimson, scarlet, carmine, whatever. Invariably you're finessing the issue. You might say "reddish."

Color's relationship to language is extravagantly arbitrary and relational.

Absolutely.

I've been reading Wallace Stevens carefully because he uses color

178

words all the time—color is the *hinge* in so many of his poems.

Stevens is a terrific example. If you take one of the greatest of all the color poems, "Sea Surface Full of Clouds" [1924], you realize that what's doing the discrimination at every point are epithets that have nothing to do with color—"chop-house chocolate," "jelly yellow," "too-fluent green." It's a miracle poem, because he's generating the sense of a world of nuanced color without actually shifting the color words themselves, he's just shifting the qualifiers. It's the damnedest thing, and I think that's what you're talking about.

There's a moment in your Caravaggio book where you say, "The exemplary figure of Christ . . . functions in his art as an internal guarantee of fine-grained meaningfulness." Discussing Caravaggio's *Penitent Magdalen*, **you make the point that our knowledge that this represents "Mary Magdalen" infinitely expands the psychological and spiritual dimensions of contemplating it. That made me wonder how these external narratives function within our closely observed experiences of artworks.**

That's completely true across the board. In the first place, you find yourself wanting to say, *What matters in a work of art is only what's in the work of art.* But then you realize that what is "in" a work of art is much more than you could ever hope to inventory, much less give an exhaustive account of. Because, let's take the *Oath of the Horatii*—what can I possibly make of it if I don't know the ancient Roman narrative behind it? Or, for that matter, Corneille's tragedy *Horace* [1640]? Or if this seems too learned, I at least have to know why these characters are dressed the way they are. Or what it means to swear an oath. Or what an elementary family structure is like. It would help if I understood that they are human beings. Are all these things "in" the painting or not?

[Laughter.]

So the whole idea of limiting one's account to what's within the frame cannot be sustained in a rigorous or, say, "hermetic" way. That's exactly the equivalent to the *Magdalen*: the meaning of this picture is inseparable from late sixteenth-century Catholicism, from the story of Christ, from who the Magdalen is. And all of that can be activated by the painting, appealed to by the painting, and exploited by the painting—even if it's not strictly *in* the picture. That's another limitation of Greenberg's thought, because for him everything I'm talking about here is just a matter of *illustration,* which for him means it's artistically irrelevant. It's just illustration that the woman is the Magdalen—but then what *isn't* illustration? What if we saw her as a woman who seems to be a little bit unhappy—that would be illustration too, no? At what point do you reach some bedrock that's *only* within the picture? Greenberg might say, when you reach paints, colors, canvas. But the answer is, *Nowhere!*

It's "turtles all the way down."

A work of art is *permeable* to the world. Let's go further, it's *saturated* by the world, by history, by modes of meaningfulness—that's a much more productive way of thinking about it—so that what you've got is this heuristic, framed structure that can mobilize some portion of that saturation in a significant way. And that's what we are trying to understand and respond to when we look at a painting.

There are also places where you go into paintings soliciting a viewer's "empathic projection," and I'm very interested in that.

It arose this way, thinking about works like Caravaggio's *Magdalen.* The whole rhetoric around Caravaggio's paintings, and I quote my former teacher Sydney Freedberg, whom I greatly admire, is one of "psychological depths"—*No painter ever reached such psychological depths before.*

You want to say, *What are you talking about?* We're looking at a woman sitting on a low stool with her head down. Or an older bald guy with a lot of light on the top of his head—you don't even see his features because they're in shadow. But in both cases we're made to feel that there's something extremely profound and moving going on. But remember, going back to Millet's peasants, no one is actually there— it ain't the Magdalen herself. It's not like you walk into a room and there she is. It's just this picture of a person doing—*what exactly?* But nevertheless there is so much feeling. My question is, *Where is all that feeling coming from?*

180

You.

There isn't anybody else there. What you've got is a development in painting where something's being done within the picture that mobilizes and motivates some extraordinary projection of feeling, of such a sort you feel you're discovering the feeling over there, that it's not in *you*, it's in her and at the same time in the painting. I want to make the claim that this was a profound development—perhaps not absolutely new, maybe that's what it always was to look at a certain kind of Buddhist sculpture, I don't know—but that Caravaggio found himself mobilizing something fundamental in a new way, at least within Western art.

It goes with a point that I've written about in relation to photography and video. What we've seen within the last twenty years or so is what I'm calling the laying bare of empathic projection, in works by artists like Jeff Wall and Anri Sala, where the whole point is to make us aware of what we are doing. In other words, to the extent that for centuries absorption was a basic resource for painting, what I've also called the magic of absorption seems to have definitively given out under the pressures of a kind of "to be seen-ness." If you think of Wall's famous photograph of a draftsman in a comparative anatomy lab, we're meant to see it as having been posed, and, at the same time, as nevertheless mobilizing certain effects of absorption. At a remove, so to speak. In Caravaggio we're not meant to understand what in effect we are doing, we're just meant to project empathically, as we do. With the new art, we are meant to be aware of that projective impulse—I find that extremely interesting.

After your major art historical work, you returned to writing on contemporary art in *Why Photography Matters as Art as Never Before* and *Four Honest Outlaws*. How did you start reengaging with contemporary art?

It's a long story, but here is a characteristic incident. About fifteen years ago I went to the Marian Goodman Gallery with my friend the painter Joseph Marioni to see a Wall show, and on the way out there was a little room with a video playing. I looked in and saw a close-up view of a guy improvising on a saxophone. Even in that first split second, there was *something*. So I walked into the room with Joseph and was like, *Let's look at this for about a minute.* After a minute I thought, *Let's watch it through to the end.* We watched it to the end, and then we watched it again from start to finish—this took thirteen minutes. The piece was by Anri Sala and is called *Long Sorrow* [2005]. Basically Sala suspended the American saxophonist Jemeel Moondoc out on the seventeenth floor of an apartment building in Berlin and had him improvise on the saxophone as if to keep himself sane. I watched this thing about five or six times; then we had to leave. But I couldn't get it out of my head—*What the fuck was going on?* When I came back to Baltimore, I tried to find out who Anri Sala was. My wife, Ruth, was going up to New York the next day; I said, *Do me a favor, go by the Marian Goodman Gallery, introduce yourself, and ask if they have a DVD of* Long Sorrow *that they would be willing to lend me.* Ruth came back with the DVD. Over the next couple of weeks I watched it about five hundred times and became completely convinced that it's a masterpiece. I wrote about it in *Four Honest Outlaws*, which included a DVD of *Long Sorrow*. Eventually I spent the year 2007 to 2008 in Berlin and got to know Sala personally. I think he's a terrific artist, arguably the most brilliant of his generation. There we are. In other words, it was largely a matter of chance that I saw it, though of course Sala had already made his way into the Marian Goodman Gallery. I had never cared about any piece of video before—not at all—but I was blown away by what Sala had done. These are the experiences that, as a critic, you cherish. This is the dream. Nothing specifically led me to video—of course, everything prior in my experience and thinking led me there, but I didn't know that—and then I had to find a way to write about it. Needless to say, this involved detailed description, over the course of probably fifteen or twenty pages. Not using any technical knowledge, just doing my best to make sense of what I was seeing. Not surprisingly, in the end I found myself invoking issues of what I call "presentness," a term that goes back to "Art and Objecthood." But the basic experience was that of a discovery.

I'd like to talk about your poetry, especially the recent collection

***Promesse du Bonheur.* The poems are basically brief gemlike fragments of experience—**

Moments. They tend to be moments.

You've said you see the poems, criticism, and art history as all constituting a single vision. I would love to know more about how you see that.

The vision has everything to do with presentness. This is clearest in the lyrics, I think, which invariably aim to convey a maximum sense of something like reality—I want the sense of a world, my world, to make itself felt in every line—in an imaginative form that the reader can, in effect, take away and live with once the act of reading is done. From early on, brevity seemed crucial to this. And of course I was encouraged in my passion for brevity by the experience of Caro's sculptures, in which just a few elements come together to tremendous effects, as well as by Noland's paintings of circles, chevrons, and the like. Sixties abstraction was a certain sort of model, in other words.

The most surprising thing that happened to me in the course of all my involvement with writing poetry is that at a certain moment, starting in the mid-1990s, the prose poem opened up and presented itself as a medium. Suddenly I found myself thinking about the unit of the sentence and about what you can do putting sentences one after another to make a certain sort of whole. In some cases, it's just a single sentence, as in my poem "The Prince of Homburg" [2014]:

Bugles blare, torches are lit, cavalrymen in above-the-knee boots hasten to their mounts, on all sides lethal violence strains to be unloosed, this happens not just once but many, many times, and no one, not even his most ardent admirers, knows for certain whether or not it will prove possible to awaken the Prince of Homburg from his dream of fame and love without destroying him.

The reference, of course, is to Kleist's stupendous play. What the lyric poems are all about is trying to deliver a moment of experience in the fullest possible way. Whereas in the prose poems, the project is to express a certain kind of thought—you can track the thought as it works itself out, sensuously, as it were. For me, the core value of both is a certain intensity. It's similar to abstract paintings trying to deliver this perfect intense artifact where everything down to the smallest touch or nuance is meaningful. That's a big dream. I wanted to somehow get the idea across that my poetry, criticism, and history are not on completely different tracks.

In most of the poems there is vivid, unpretentious, present-tense description that ends with a reflective or retrospective thought or phrase—"and I was appalled," "But I never did," et cetera—that gives a shape to the poem.

The other structure that relates to that is the inserted parenthetical phrase that also builds in a second temporality.

Is that about creating a distance in the poem?

Yes. Take these sentences from the prose poem "From Michael Schmidt's *Frauen*" [2014]: "On a clear night, needless to say, somewhere in the countryside, far from the illumination of cities. (Michael Schmidt lives in such a place.)" You get this little momentary *jolt* out of the texture of the poem, and it's something that instantly casts the whole poem in a certain light—in this case we glimpse a relation between the poet and Schmidt, if you see what I mean.

I think what I'm trying to ask you about is about the temporalities within the poems, which are ultimately cut between experience and reflection. Suddenly, the thing that was present has been framed by memory and positioned in the past.

I think that's right. If not the distant past, then at least something temporally distinct, framing the poem from within and somehow shifting the poem into the context of the world. It's as if that little parenthesis were actually a frame around the poem, because it's building in a certain kind of momentary epistemological distance.

Take the poem "When Kit Left Darby" [2008]:

After weeks of saying nothing Darby painted a ravishing picture he
    called "Carol's Absence"—a large black
square (with rounded corners) on a pale blue one. I found it
    heartbreaking. But it couldn't bring Kit back.

The second, short, final sentence, "But it couldn't bring Kit back,"
extends so far outside of that original moment and event. That seems
like the persistent logic of the poems—a temporal curve.

I was interested in this moment of reflection very early on. For me
the parentheses play this role. Here's an extreme version, "A Tailor"
[2016]:

At seventy (older then than now), he could still thread a needle
in one pass, holding his arms out straight before him.

The parenthetical "(older then than now)" glosses "seventy," which
was a lot older when I was a kid than it is now—I'm seventy-eight, but
I could go out this afternoon and hit a tennis ball. In any case, those
few words position the poet in relation to the experience, and the
reader in relation to the poem. It's not something I've thought through
analytically, it just keeps happening in the poems.

The process of writing about art
is closest to the process of writing
fiction, because it's about discovery,
not knowing, trying to build a
coherent world from the unfamiliar,
from the edges of what one barely
understands or knows.

Thyrza Nichols Goodeve (b. 1957) is a writer and critic whose creative nonfiction blends feminism, science fiction, and contemporary art. She has also made in-depth interviews with artists a major part of her work, publishing what she calls collaborative conversations with Yvonne Rainer, Carolee Schneemann, Matthew Barney, the Brothers Quay, and Andrea Fraser. Her book-length interview with theorist Donna Haraway, *How Like a Leaf*, was published in 1999. Goodeve has written for *Artforum* (1989–1999), *Parkett* (1996–2001), and *Art Agenda* (2012–2016), and is currently the senior arts editor for *The Brooklyn Rail*. She teaches in the low-residency MFA Art Practice program at the School of Visual Arts, New York.

Thyrza Nichols Goodeve

**What was your first conscious awareness that you wanted to be
a writer?**

"Conscious" is the operative word. It took me a long time to own
being a writer, although I was always writing, from an early age. But
declaring and taking it on as an identity is a whole other thing. I'm
always fascinated when people say, *When I was five, I knew I wanted
to do this.* Because of the nature of my family—I was the only girl
and the third child—what I would do or become was never really a
consideration the way it was for my brothers, who were super bright,
talented, and charismatic. I was kind of invisible and never thought
about becoming something. It was just never a question, until I went
on a term abroad to Morocco in high school and met writers, especially
one guy who kept asking me, *Where do you want to go to school? What do you
want to be? What do you want to do?* Nobody had ever asked me that before.

Certainly, the idea that one made one's life, or lived it, by and
through writing started then. I kept a journal for the first time. My project was on Moroccan literature, so the headmaster, Joseph McPhillips,
said, *You have to go speak to Paul Bowles, because he's the authority on that.*
I did not know who Paul Bowles was. So I went over and met his lover
Mohammed Mrabet, whose books Paul had been translating, and
Mrabet "fell in love" with me. I say "fell in love" advisedly since he
was lovers with Bowles and married with his own family, and I was
just a seventeen-year-old blonde virgin. But I spent all my time going
over and hanging out with Bowles and Mrabet, and then, after I left,

Mrabet wrote me, through Paul, for years, and Paul would translate and transcribe Mrabet's letters, because Mrabet was illiterate. And then Paul and I corresponded. Those letters, writing back and forth, were how I located myself during those years—going from Vermont to NYU to Sarah Lawrence. I started reading then in a way I never had—my brain had literally changed. I shifted from being a preppy jock to someone driven by reading, writing, and seeking.

I went to Sarah Lawrence for creative writing, but the more I became identified as a "writer," the more uncomfortable I felt. For instance, I brought the beginning of a novel to my fiction teacher, and he *loved* it. I was really swept up in Paris and Gertrude Stein and Hemingway, so I was writing something about a writer who was in Morocco who was going through some kind of identity crisis similar to what Hemingway and his generation went through in the 1920s. My teacher identified with it, and he said, *Okay, you work on this, we'll finish it by the spring, and we'll have it published next year.* I stopped writing.

Why?

I don't know why. I became paralyzed. It was like the more the idea of being a writer started to be in my face, the less I was able to be a writer—I started writing short, weird, experimental fiction and eventually just gave up and went the graduate school route—cinema studies at NYU and then the History of Consciousness program at UC Santa Cruz.

How did you find your way to the Whitney ISP?

I got to New York in 1978 as a sophomore at NYU, but then I transferred to Sarah Lawrence and was living up near Columbia. I literally stumbled into the Whitney program because a friend of mine from Sarah Lawrence, Jean Rasenberger, was there. I was studying for a master's in cinema studies at NYU and working as an intern at The Collective for Living Cinema, and one day I went to visit her in the old location on lower Broadway. I remember we were just standing in her studio talking to Ron Clark and David Diao about Lacan, because psychoanalysis and Lacan were the rage, so I was mouthing off in some embarrassing way, and Ron handed me an application and said, *We want you.* I had a studio, but I never really used it. I even stayed an extra semester because Ron and I had gotten so close. At that point I was involved in experimental film and film theory—which came out of my interest in narrative and experimental writing. My understanding of art was formed from those years at the ISP: art was *critical*. My influences were the people who taught there—Vito Acconci, Hans Haacke, Barbara Kruger, Yvonne Rainer, Martha Rosler, and Hal Foster, who was putting together his book on postmodernism, *The Anti-Aesthetic* [1983].

So that's where you met Yvonne Rainer and started working with her?

"Working with her" would be pushing it—hanging out with her, being friends would be closer to the truth. I was so shy and so neurotic. We were all supposed to make an appointment to meet with her, and I kept putting it off. She's an intimidating person. She doesn't mean to be—she's actually very, very funny and goofy as a person—but if you don't know her she's very intimidating. Finally she came up to me and said, *When are we going to talk?*

I was TA-ing at NYU, and I was teaching Hitchcock's *Marnie* [1964] for the first time. It hit a nerve in me because I used to steal as a child, and Marnie, as you know, is a kleptomaniac in the film, so when I showed up to talk to Yvonne I was in tears. And we just went straight to the most personal stuff, which is what Yvonne responds to—which is why I think she and I became so close; immediately we were talking about emotions.

Did you know her work before that?

Yes, because she had come out to speak at Sarah Lawrence and shown *Journeys from Berlin/1971* [1980]. I remember it as one of those weird fisheye-lens moments, because I was sitting way in the back, looking down, and she looked so intense and severe and had such gravitas—I mean, she was this *New York filmmaker*—you know that feeling you have at that age. I watched the film and I liked it with the kind of reverence I had at that point for difficult films, but, of course, it took me many times of seeing it to understand, and now I'd say it certainly is one of the most important films for me. I don't know when

189

her works started to really make sense, but her films and writing were the models of my thinking and being for many years. I see my life as a series of profound encounters—Paul Bowles, the filmmaker Peter Watkins, then Yvonne, Matthew Barney, and Avital Ronell.

You were studying with Annette Michelson at NYU?

Yes. It was hardly a *supportive* experience. I was twenty-three. Her assistant at the time was Allen Weiss, who had a PhD in philosophy, and he used to say he liked sitting next to me in class because it was like sitting next to a lightning rod—in other words, he would never get hit. Annette was infamous for her cruelty, and I was a perfect target. Though her classes were *essential* to me, to my interest in the avant-garde and theory, she thrived on poking at a person's vulnerability. Her methodology was a kind of pedagogical terrorism. The stories are funny now, but at the time it was hideous. When she used to slam her books around on her desk, telling me I was incapable of doing theory, I finally had the temerity to ask, *But Annette, why does it matter to you? So what if I fail?* Later, I realized she most likely had had a crush on me, which explained the combination of brutality and obsessive attention. She in fact lost a seminar paper of mine and voted against my entering the PhD in cinema studies, which was the best thing, because that's when I applied to the History of Consciousness program to study narratology with Hayden White.

What were you planning on writing about?

I was clueless and just lucky I got in—my application was something about "feminist readings of modernist texts." *Snore away*. I really went there because I didn't know what to do—I wish now I had had the confidence to *be a writer*, i.e., write for publications, pursue fiction and nonfiction outside of academia, but that's twenty-twenty hindsight. Emotionally and temperamentally I was totally incapable of doing that, and, no matter how ambivalent and allergic I am to academia, clearly graduate school is how I gained the confidence to put my voice out there. But the truth is, I was incredibly fortunate to land in one of the only PhD programs at the time where someone of my sensibility could be embraced. James Clifford was absolutely instrumental; he identified me immediately as a writer and worked with me that way, so I built up the confidence and began to discover the writerly voice that had been battered out of me by Michelson. Hist Con at that time was incredibly open, nonhierarchical, and responsive to experiment—mostly because of Hayden, and then certainly because of Donna Haraway and Jim. Those two single-handedly made Hist Con a rare, singularly inventive, and rigorous place to read theory, history, science, feminism, antiracism, queer theory, and anthropology and approach these fields in remarkably creative ways.

Could you describe how you started studying with Haraway and what that experience was like?

Again, it came about in a roundabout way. I did not go there to study with her—all these stories make me feel like my life has been one long process of backing my way into these incredible people. Anyway, she is a very beloved person for people who studied with her, because she's so incredibly generous and ethical and takes everybody so seriously. I got there in 1984, when she was on sabbatical writing "A Cyborg Manifesto" [1984]. All we heard about was *how great Donna is*—to the point I was prepared to stay away from her. It was too culty.

The class that I came in with, we were known as the "representation" people. The people before us in Hist Con were all much more political theory people. I felt they were the serious ones, and we were seen as the flaky arty ones. Hayden White used to joke and call me Miss Postmodernism because I was in Yvonne's film *The Man Who Envied Women* [1985]. Then Teresa de Lauretis arrived, who does film theory and feminism, particularly narrative theory, which was what I was interested in, and so people thought that I would be studying with her. Something in me knew that she wouldn't be good—I actually voted against choosing her as the new faculty hire. My experience with Annette gave me a sixth sense; Teresa is just a terribly limited person—selfish, lacking in moral courage, the complete opposite of someone like Donna Haraway. At the time, I was part of the lesbian community—it was my moment of thinking I had found the answers to my troubles with relationships in the fact that I must be a lesbian, which was silly, because after Santa

Cruz I've only been involved with men, and anyway, the same dynamics come up whether one is hetero or queer, so my naiveté was typical of a moment when I could romanticize being a lesbian. Anyway, this does lead to Donna, because my girlfriend at that time got involved with Teresa de Lauretis, who was also involved with another student, who was one of my best friends. We all ended up in a small seminar of eight people on feminism and film theory with Teresa. She put a picture of me from *The Man Who Envied Women* on the cover of her course reader, because Yvonne's work was so important to her. During this seminar she was sleeping with my girlfriend and my friend who was also in the seminar, but Teresa and my girlfriend were lying to me about their relationship, and everyone in the program seemed to know but me. In hindsight, it's simple—they fell in love and all that, and that was their business and that was fine—but she handled it about as poorly as one could. She pulled me into her office and literally said, *Thyrza, you know what you need to do? You have to change your object of desire*. This was my professor! It was like we were all acting out an Yvonne Rainer movie. It was just crazy.

Anyway, I ended up very depressed, very sick, and I was going to leave the program. Academia never really worked for me, and so I was getting ready to leave, and Donna Haraway shows up. She was the chair of the department at that point. She comes up to me—and I always cry when I tell this story—and she says, *Thyrza, I haven't been there for you. I haven't known how to handle the situation. So here's what we are going to do. You are going to come and meet with me in my office every two weeks and talk about your work*. That's what we did. I became Donna's student at that point. I had been doing work on science fiction, hysteria, lobotomy, and multiple personality disorder. *Artforum* called her up in 1989 and said, *We are doing a special summer issue on wonder*—Ida Panicelli was doing it—and they wanted something from Donna Haraway. She said, *Well, I don't really have anything, but I have this student*, and she recommended me. I sent them this crazy seminar paper on lobotomy, multiple personality disorder, and postmodernism. It was a moment when *Artforum* was very interested in theory in a kind of wild way. The issue is something else—

Vilém Flusser and Paul Virilio are also in it. So that's the summer of 1989, when I published my first article in an art magazine, even though it had nothing to do with art. Ida was incredibly supportive and said, *You can write anything you want.* Again, it's like what happened with my fiction teacher—such overwhelming possibility froze me. I felt like I didn't know enough about art, which I didn't. But I did write some stuff—on Rosemarie Trockel's animal videos, wounds, and things like that. Then other people started to ask me to write about art, even though I wasn't trained in it. Somewhere along the line, I moved back to New York, and Jack Bankowsky at *Artforum* asked me to interview Matthew Barney.

I know Matthew Barney has been a major focus of your writing life; what was it like first seeing his work?

Indeed, the interview with him changed my life, like my time in Tangier. It was when I realized I really liked art and liked writing about it, when I realized it was a perfect vocation for me, because I'm such an omnivorous horizontal thinker, undisciplined but interdisciplinary. To write about contemporary art means you potentially can write about anything and everything—science, aesthetics, dirt, pearls, animals, you name it—and do it however you want. This is the period in which I began to position myself as a writer, not an academic; the minute I finished my PhD, I left academia. Matthew's work was a total breakthrough for me. You have to imagine: this was 1994, 1995. This was *Cremaster 4* [1995]—the one with the satyr in it. I'd been breastfed that mythological work is bad, aesthetics is bad, pleasure in consuming or appreciating art is bad, and I knew nothing about Matthew Barney. I was working at the Whitney as a researcher on the exhibition *The American Century* [1999–2000]. Beautiful Mark Fletcher, who was working as an assistant at Barbara Gladstone Gallery, which at that point was in SoHo, brought me down into the gallery's basement, where I watched *Cremaster 4* on a tiny monitor. I just sat there going, *What the fuck am I looking at!* I had absolutely no idea what it was, but I knew there was something profound in it. I still feel that way this many years later. It was astonishing.

This is when I started to separate from the academic and ideological critique platform I had been brought up on at the Whitney program. Because up until that point, my interest in art had always been about "politics"—critical art was the only art. Andrea Fraser, Mark Dion, Felix Gonzalez-Torres, and Gregg Bordowitz were all people who I'd been in the program with in the early eighties.

With Barney, I learned art is about opening up your head and having it explode. The conversation between us just *worked*. I don't know how or why. I'd done all this research and so I had questions, and I was able to pull him out. And at that point he was just learning how to talk about his work, so he had this odd combination of being matter of fact yet saying the oddest things. We'd be talking and all of a sudden he'd go, *Yes, that's the moment the pound cake comes in*, and I'm just sitting there going, *This is fantastic and insane*. And he's the perfect artist for someone like myself—each *Cremaster* was different; research took me from Houdini to biology to Gary Gilmore to the many properties of the hexagon to petroleum jelly, et cetera. It was interesting that his work wasn't about "understanding," but it was about knowing that there were all sorts of formal and mythic systems behind it, and that it was coherent even though it is wildly eclectic. And just the humor of it. Because of that I got very involved in his work.

When you started realizing you didn't want to deal with art on the level of ideology critique that you had experienced at the ISP, what were the models or examples of writing about art that helped you figure out what you were doing?

What a great question. Certainly, again, nothing conscious. I was drawn to writing that was poetic and theoretical—Derrida had been a big influence, but I read him as a poet, not a philosopher. I loved Molly Nesbit's book *Their Common Sense* [2000]; she's still an art historian who I'm interested in for how she structures her work, not just what she writes. Later I discovered through Matthew this incredible writer named Angus Cook, but I haven't followed him or art writing that much. Recently I finally read Diderot and was blown away by how hilarious and odd he is. All art writing, like theory, has always been about the writing for me—the language, what Bill Berkson would call "the word"—being attached to the word. One writer who was super important in the beginning was Neville Wakefield, who was a friend of Matthew's—what a writer! And Louise Neri asked me to write for *Parkett* at that point, which, again, was a place I could just write without being a critic or an art historian. My first piece on Matthew's work, "Matthew Barney 95: Suspension [Cremaster], Secretion [pearl], Secret [biology]" [1995], was me kind of blindly feeling my way along. I started to develop or return to a mode of writing I have done from time to time—layering voices. As far back as when I wrote my paper on Mohammed Mrabet at the age of seventeen, I created different voices and I wrote part-fiction, part-expository essays. Of course, I had no idea this would become a genre of writing. In the late nineties, I wrote an essay on the Internet and vaudeville where I used the voices of vaudeville characters. In order to talk about Matthew's work, I felt I needed to take on different voices as well and started something called "The Cremaster Dialogues," which never turned into anything, but it was what I was trying to do for the Guggenheim catalogue. Nancy Spector, who I went to Sarah Lawrence with, had approached me in the late nineties and said, *We're going to be doing a big show in five years on Matthew Barney's* Cremaster. *I want you to write the catalogue essay.* So then I had an excuse, and basically was invited to the set of each of the *Cremasters* as they were filmed and talked to Matthew throughout it, from 1996 to 2001. I thought I would be able to come up with an interview that would be about the process of his making the whole *Cremaster* cycle [1994–2002], but I ended up getting to know Matthew too well, and I couldn't ask questions anymore. I became bad at it. It was like it just didn't work anymore. And I was bumped from the Guggenheim catalogue. There were many reasons why, but probably the biggest was that I couldn't figure out how to write "an" essay on the *Cremaster* cycle. There was no way I felt I could write, or *wanted* to write, an essay that tied up all the ends, because the whole point of his work—what drew me to it—was that it was like a molecule constantly moving, changing, morphing, layering, connected yet discrete, with everything in *relation*.

195

I still feel there's something I hope to write about it someday.

I was also teaching at the Whitney program during this period—'97, '98—and my interest in Matthew's work was a big problem. You can imagine. Being the juvenile I am, I remember taking a taxi with Benjamin Buchloh and going on about my love of Barney's work knowing full well it would drive him crazy. In hindsight, a pretty dumb thing to do. I had Matthew come and speak to the ISP. It was awkward as hell—he showed up with Marti Domination, the star of *Cremaster 1* [1996], who Ron Clark recognized as a dancer he'd seen at the Baby Doll Lounge down the street. Hilarious. I also asked Ann Hamilton. Later they were taken off the roster of artists who had spoken at the ISP. I owe so much to the ISP, and to Ron Clark, but there's a side of it that's so attitudinal, if there is such a word; it took on the worst part of an academic paradigm where power and arrogance were rewarded. I invited Avital Ronell to come and speak too, and the students were idiotic and rude to her, and hadn't even read her work! It was agonizingly embarrassing. At one point, Ron even got down on Haraway and started describing her work in seminars as relativist. Clearly, I was moving away from the family that had nurtured me, although I was still close with people like Yvonne and Andrea Fraser. In hindsight, I see I was starting to grow out of a one-dimensional view of art. In fact, I was going backward as far as the ISP narrative is concerned, because I realized I was and am a romantic when it comes to art, and that's okay. I had to teach myself how to see and love and look at painting—I've even taken a painting class. Now I adore painting.

This is also when you were working on *How Like a Leaf*?

Yes, exactly. This is when interviewing became my mode. I was writing for *Parkett* a lot. Looking back on those pieces on Cady Noland, Raymond Pettibon, even Sarah Morris, they're not intellectual essays so much as feeling my way through an artwork or a person or something. I started to do interviews for *Artforum*, and I did one with the Brothers Quay, which was great. Donna started to be asked to do things in the art world, and Ars Electronica wanted her to do an essay for one of their catalogues. She said, *Why don't you interview me?* We did, and as we were putting it together, her editor at Routledge said, *Let's make this into a book*, so then that's how *How Like a Leaf* came about.

Could we analyze *How Like a Leaf* as an example of your interview process? I know that you have complex thoughts about the interview as a form. I've read some reviews of it, and I think academics were jarred by how *personal* it is, not only about Donna but also about your relationship. Of course, that is connected to the intellectual and political aspects of both of your work.

I wanted to make a portrait of Donna Haraway where people could understand that her work is about everyday life. It's about how we live. I was frustrated by the experience of teaching "A Cyborg Manifesto" in the eighties, because everybody reacted negatively—*It's so academic, this is so ivory tower*—but all of her work for me was so much about her life, my life, everybody's life. For example, I was very taken and moved by her whole relationship with her first husband, Jay, who she met when she was at Yale; he ended up coming out as gay, but they stayed together. Later he and his lover and she and her long-term companion, Rusten, all shared a house together in Northern California, and I just thought that was so beautiful and so emblematic of Donna Haraway. She and Rusten went through a terrible period of living with and nursing both Jay and his lover as they died of AIDS. Shattering stuff. Haraway lives her work.

How have your ideas on interviewing as a writing practice evolved?

I am pretty maniacal about it. They are really essays—an essay built from the dialogue between me and the other person. I've come to call them collaborative conversations, because they are really built in writing after the initial moment when I sit down to record a conversation with someone. I see the moment when you sit down as just one occasion, just the start, where you lay out material and follow paths and discover new connections. I am like you, I try to read everything, to see what's been said, and I have a notebook in front of me with notes, but once I'm with the person it's, *Okay, now we're here, what's going to happen?* It's similar to teaching in that way. The Brothers Quay said I interviewed out of my back pocket. Digression is essential. That's the magic. Like the title *How Like a Leaf*—how did that title show up? Because I decided to ask Donna Haraway, *When was the first moment that you encountered the idea of the cyborg, experientially?* And she pauses, starts looking around, and says, *It's the moment I realized how like a leaf I am.* Then she starts talking about the veins in her hand and the veins in a leaf, and my jaw is dropping and I'm just sitting there—*This is amazing.* That's what I like. Peter Halley once said to me, *It's like you're a medium, you start channeling the other person.*

One of the stories that you tell about yourself is that you're shy, not confident, but having an exchange with that kind of openness takes a lot of trust in yourself.

I'll never forget when Mathew Barney first met me—he had read the *Artforum* article on lobotomy, postmodernism, and multiple personality disorder—and he said, *You are so different than your writing. I expected you to be this hard-ass.* It was a telling moment, and since, I've been really struck by how confident my voice is in my writing and how confused people are by my childlike, flighty personality, because they expect something I'm not. I learned from Lacan that being *sujet supposé savoir,* "the subject who's supposed to know," is exactly what I have a hard time with, except when I write. But interviewing is also different— it's about *intimacy,* about listening and being with the person, really becoming the person. I may be insecure in certain ways, but I'm very good one-on-one. I'm fascinated with what somebody says and how they say it—that is *essential*—rather than imposing my own idea. But as I said, my conversations are all edited, never straight transcriptions. Journalists are horrified by what I do, because I have no interest in some notion of the "gotcha," where something is published and the person feels violated because of the way the interviewer contextualizes it, or transcribes it poorly, or even because one might not always say what one means. I want the person to have the opportunity to go in and clarify, rewrite, et cetera—because that's where the magic moments can be emphasized and enlarged. With *How Like a Leaf,* I chopped that whole transcript up and just literally created it—it's completely constructed. Donna went over it, but I finalized it. She and I just finished a series of conversations that took me six months to complete. This is so unlike journalism, where it's a rule not to show it to your subject before it's published. I try to help that person articulate what they want to say about their work, which maybe they don't even know they know yet.

Your writing is really grounded in a "personal" voice—how have you approached that in your work?

One doesn't *try* to do this. One just does what one does. It makes me uncomfortable sometimes that the "I" is there, because ideally what I am interested in is foregrounding the subjectivity of my experience, I guess, rather than foregrounding myself. It's idiosyncratic, and I do find that the way art, theory, whatever, intersects with life is the point. Like the essay I wrote so long ago called "You Sober People," published in a book called *When Pain Strikes* [1999], which used my experience as a methadone counselor to explore connections between Donna Haraway's work and Avital Ronell's.

That piece is so intense. Wait, you were actually working as a methadone counselor? I imagined that was a conceit.

I needed money. A friend of mine was working as an administrator in a big methadone company in San Francisco and she said, *Why not try to be a counselor?* In the essay, I tell the story of one client I bonded with; he became addicted to heroin because he had been in a flash flood in LA, and he scraped his back and the pebbles were still stuck in it. They gave him morphine to heal him and he said, hauntingly, *And from that point on, I kept trying to get back to that feeling.* He was a very sweet soul. Anyway, I was doing that while I was teaching and reading Avital's work—in particular, *Crack Wars: Literature, Addiction, Mania* [1992], which is probably my favorite book of all time next to *Charlotte's Web* [1952], and so I put it all together. One needs to make a living somehow.

But then it takes the form of this essay. What were you trying to work out in it, at the level of form but also in the confluence of ideas?

Certainly, Avital Ronell was *the* influence. *The Telephone Book: Technology, Schizophrenia, Electric Speech* [1989]—I mean, is there a more brilliant piece of thinking and writing and making out there? You know it can't be republished because it would be too expensive to

print, because every page is designed differently. *Every page.* I had a
very hard time with the Heidegger part of her work at that point, but
through osmosis it started to sink in. Then I read *Crack Wars*, and it
was the time of early Prozac—Peter Kramer's book *Listening to Prozac*
[1993] was important to me. It's still a fascinating take on Prozac. I was
interested in the way some people refuse to take medication because
they feel like, *It's not pure, it's not me,* so they stay depressed—it sounds
really crazy to those for whom this stuff works, being on drugs and
functional. This is very similar to Donna Haraway's idea of feminism
in "A Cyborg Manifesto"—getting away from the idea of nature as a
separate, pure, authentic space rather than the actuality that we are
fused and merged with technology, and that is neither good or bad
but *is*. So, "You Sober People" was a combination of Donna's cyborg
idea and Avital's discussion of drugs and technology, what she calls
narcoanalysis—putting those two women's work together, but doing it
through the story that I tell. Thinking back now, I think I would never
have written such a thing if I didn't know both people. I met Avital in
the early nineties in California—we were both on a panel put together
by John Muse on Desert Storm. I've sat in on Avital's classes at NYU
for several years now. She is of the most supreme importance to me as
a writer and thinker. And counterintuitively, her work too is all about
everyday experience. Of course, it is the gold standard of literary theory
and philosophy, and yet, her early work on Rodney King and TV; her
seminars on addiction or the "debilitated subject"; her book *Stupidity*
[2002], which she was writing on the eve of Bush's election, or *Loser Sons*
[2012], on the eve of Trump's—she always has her intensely fine-tuned
rabbit ears set telephathically to what is going on. But it's all about
language, close reading. She always says, *If we had six months to read this
sentence together . . .*

    **Bill Berkson is someone important to both of us. I would just love
to know—how did you meet him?**

    I was teaching at the San Francisco Art Institute when he was
there. I had published in *Artforum*. I arrived in Santa Cruz in '84, left
in '88. Lived in San Francisco till '93. This was my period of deep, deep

200

depression. I didn't even try to write a dissertation. I was teaching film at San Francisco State University and coteaching an insane course at the San Francisco Art Institute—a three-way core course with this guy named Ray Mondini and this other woman who was a poet. In a way, it was the worst of the early part of "interdisciplinary" art teaching. Anyway, Bill came up to me one day; he was teaching a course on art writing and poetics, and he asked me to come speak about what I do. I've never been more flattered in my life. I'd read his books and I was so blown away by his writing. Then, when I was teaching at SVA in the MFA in Art Writing program, I invited him to speak to my class, and I realized he was my mentor as an art writer. Especially when he writes about abstraction—his ability to get into little bits of paint and describe it and play with it. His essay "De Kooning, with Attitude" [2000] and his writing on Franz Kline—amazing.

What are different strategies that run through your writing, in terms of how to approach writing about art?

I'm the kind of person who needs something to work off. So often my essays have a quote at the beginning because it's the way I start up. I realized that's why I like writing about art, too: it gives me something to go in and work with, against, and from. Being given a blank slate feels almost too easy, because you can just make anything up. But again, I think it is a confidence thing—I need something to say, *It's okay to start from here.*

The big breakthrough came when I realized one day that I write *with* art rather than *on* art. Like Ellen Gallagher's work, when I was writing about her—her gorgeous early work before *DeLuxe* [2004–2005], the paintings. It's like I kind of go inside of the work and write. But the artist is very important to me too. I realized that I'm really interested in what the artist has to say. I'm not Jerry Saltz and Roberta Smith— they're great at what they do. And that's a confidence thing too— having the confidence to just say, *What I feel and think is all that matters.* That's amazing to me. I don't know how they do it. In that sense, I am the complete opposite of them.

But if there is a strategy, it is called *reading*, because anytime I write,

it is what I read that's worked into the writing. It could be fiction—
I read *The Hunchback of Notre-Dame* [1831] to write that little preface for
the *Cremaster 5* book [1997], for example. But it's also the nerd stuff—
I just love to learn, and every writing assignment is an opportunity
to learn, which is why I prefer to write on things I don't know
anything about.

**You've written so much about works that have a fractured relation-
ship to narrative, both in film and installation. How do you structure the
narrative of telling the story about an artwork?**

That's where it's almost like a fiction writer, where you have no idea
what you're doing, but you let it act on you, you let it go, and from it
structure evolves. You see where it's going, where it wants to go. People
like me use fractured narrative because we write associatively and can't
always make a logical, smooth transition discursively. Arguments are
less what I do then accretions. It comes from my fondness for early
surrealist writing—juxtaposition, tension, not narrative flow. I'm a
pretty bad storyteller. An interesting example is something I wrote
about Matthew Barney's work called "Philosophize with a Crowbar/
Bleed Like a Blade of Grass" [2013], which was a dialogue with characters like the Testicular Hysteric—it's never been published and I don't
think is really successful, because it's not worked through, and in fact
I was asked to rewrite it discursively for Suzanne Anker and Sabine
Flach's book *Embodied Fantasies: From Awe to Artifice* [2013], which I did,
under the very unambiguous title "Twilight of the Art World: From
Representation to Ontology."

**You've done several interviews with Yvonne Rainer, and in one of
them you set up a dialogue between Yvonne Rainer's present self and
her past self. How would you describe the difference between Thyrza
writing about now and Thyrza from the 1990s?**

Yeesh. The irony: as I learned more and more about art and became
a better and better writer, the less access I had to publishing in places
like *Artforum*, which had at one point felt like a home. It's so different.
Basically, it's just age and practice. I'm just a much better writer.
I understand the difficulty and the wonder of language, the humility

it takes to write. I was lucky as a younger person that I had an innate ability to write, but I never used to rewrite, which embarrasses the hell out of me. Avital and I were sitting in a café in Berkeley once and she was working on revision after revision, and I was like, *Really?* What an idiot—writing is only about revision. It is very strange but very exciting to be an editor now and just be immersed in the *work* of what writing is.

But to get back to your question—one thing I think about is how lucky I am to have fallen into writing about art. Daily I think, *What a pleasure and what a gift to engage in dialogues about the questions that upset us in the world through art.* It's just such a privilege to live in a world where people are trying to *make.* That goes back to why the Morocco story was important to me, because before I went to Morocco I just was *being* in my life. After Morocco, it was like, *Oh, you make from your life. Life is about making.*

You call yourself an "art writer" and not an "art critic"—what is that distinction for you?

In some ways it's just a peevish thing, a discomfort with being called a "critic," because I don't think that's what I do—establishing tastes, opinions, judgments. I learned early on that if I write about something I don't like, I'm a *terrible* writer. I sound like a little sophomore brat— I get sarcastic. Robert Hughes is the best at writing about what he hates. I love reading him. But I learned early, writing book reviews for *Bookforum,* that I was bad at it. So, I only write about things that *compel* me. Again, that makes me a lousy art critic, so why call myself that? And I'm not trained in art history. Like Bill Berkson, I write from the place of the passionate amateur—I always feel and want to feel like an outsider, a newbie to the art world, even though I've been writing for twenty-five years, and even now with this position as a senior art editor. But I guess that's the paradox: I am at once always outside the discourse of art—visiting it, never landing as a native—yet when it comes to the artwork I think what I do is write from inside it, through and with its voice, at least when it works. But ultimately I'd go back to what I've said earlier: the process of writing about art is closest to the process of writing fiction, because it's about discovery, not knowing, trying to build a coherent world from the unfamiliar, from the edges of what one barely understands or knows. I adore being given assignments—writing on things I don't know. In fact, I am better, or the writing is more interesting, when I'm in the process of discovery. Laying down a sentence and going: *Where did that come from? Okay, let's see where it goes.* It's all about letting the art lead, that's for sure, and taking you God knows where.

I've always known that nobody is going
to read this because it's about art. They
are going to read it because it's *good*. That
puts me and the genre at cross-purposes.
I know most of the art criticism out
there, and I have no idea why anybody
would read that shit.

Few figures in art criticism are as inexplicably polarizing
or technically dazzling as Dave Hickey (b. 1940). In the
1960s he ran his own gallery in Austin, Texas, called
A Clean, Well-Lighted Place, and was the director
of Reese Palley in New York. He left the art world for
Nashville in the 1970s to be a songwriter and frequent
contributor to *Country Music* magazine, reemerging as
a firebrand during the culture wars with *The Invisible
Dragon: Four Essays on Beauty* (1993). His writing
on art has been collected in the volumes *Air Guitar:
Essays on Art & Democracy* (1997); *Pirates and Farmers*
(2013); *25 Women: Essays on their Art* (2016); and
Perfect Wave (2017). His collected short fiction was
published in 1989 as *Prior Convictions*. He was formerly
a professor of English at the University of Nevada,
Las Vegas, and Distinguished Professor of Criticism
in the MFA program at the University of New Mexico.
He received a MacArthur Fellowship in 2001.

Dave Hickey

You've alluded to the work you were doing as a PhD student in literature at the University of Texas in the 1960s; I want to know a little more about what you were working on.

I was figuring out what I would call a grammatical calculus for describing language in a musical sense, incorporating elements of speed and frequency, so that you're not just counting the repetitions of the word but also how often and how fast words repeat so you can get a much clearer sense of the prose you're describing. It's more like musical notation software. I had passages from Hemingway, D. H. Lawrence, and Gertrude Stein, each in three states of revision. They had all the manuscripts at UT. I thought I could encode all these and, since revisions are presumed to be intentional, make empirical statements about intention by encoding the changes from version to version. *Nobody* makes empirical statements about intention, but I thought that it could be done, and I think I pretty much did it, although I ran up against a lot of problems with my committee. Most offensively, I took exception to a part of Chomsky that he couldn't live without, but I could—I'll give you an example: "I" and "you"—personal pronouns? They're not "pronouns." They don't stand for nouns; they stand for gestures, they stand at the portal between the palpable world and the world of language, and that changes the way sentences are generated. It also creates a kind of tiered system so that sentences that use "I" are first-level sentences; "you" or "it" are in different categories altogether. Shifting into and out of these modes, especially with D. H. Lawrence, seemed to be a good way of demonstrating that, but I couldn't do it without dissing Chomsky—and I did severely want to diss Chomsky. They never let me defend my dissertation, but I wrote it. I learned a whole lot, and I was right.

In several essays, you've referenced J. L. Austin. Is that where your thinking about language then goes? Toward his performative speech acts?

I treat literary prose as performative speech, and I'm interested in what they call the phonotext—*you hear it as you read it.* If you can't hear the phonotext, you don't know what prose is. Many academics don't deal with the phonotext at all, they just read the words. I'm doing a talk at the College Art Association in February [2015] called "Theory and Critique: The Raw and the Cooked," and I come out in favor of the raw theory—no footnotes, so it's lodged into the world, not lodged into other texts through footnotes.

Your analysis of the phonotext comes out of a lifelong love of music.

Yes, and I listen well.

What was the music you listened to as a child?

My dad was a bebop musician, and I was a rock-and-roll person; I could read music, although I can't write it out very well. I just tend to think of things in musical terms. This puts me in a tradition with Monet, Miro, and Braque—people who were basically musical painters. Duchamp was the alternative, and nobody got further on a one-trick pony than he did—a phonotext critique leads you into the tangible world, and for some reason Duchampian critique leads you back into theory. Also, I always thought it was my job to make up jargon and not to use it. I was a serious structuralist in graduate school in the 1960s; I wrote art criticism for nearly twenty years without using "desire," "deconstruction," or any of those words. Finally I was forced into using them because people presumed that you had to use those words or you weren't "serious." I remember the first thing I did that used those words was a piece on Jim Shaw. It talked about representation and jouissance, which are fairly shoddy concepts.

After the work you did on literature in Texas, you went to New York

to work at Reese Palley gallery, and you started writing about art. How did you approach writing then? Is there a connection between the kind of scholarly analysis you were doing on literature and the process of looking at art and writing about looking?

I was learning how to write by studying linguistics, like a painter learning her palette. There may be a connection, since my mother was a painter, but the sequence was interesting. I was doing literature and then I discovered that Ruscha, Rauschenberg, and Johns loved language the way I loved it. I was beguiled by the idea of Ruscha using the *incarnate word*—which is not the referential word but the word as flesh. That seemed to define a particular point of view, which Mapplethorpe and a lot of canonical Catholic artists used.

After you worked in the New York art world for a period, you left in the seventies to be part of the country music scene. What precipitated that?

Boredom. I got tired of invitations I couldn't refuse. I got fired from my gallery job. I got fired from *Art in America*. I started freelancing about music. I describe the moment like this—it was '72 or '73—I'm walking out of a Richard Tuttle show where he has glued weird white pieces of paper to the wall. I'm thinking, *Richard Tuttle or Keith Richards? Richard Tuttle or Keith Richards?* It was as simple as that: it was more fun to write about Keith Richards. The drugs were better for sure. Also, I was really interested in that kind of fame—not in the sense of wanting it, but just in knowing what the mechanics of fame might be.

Doesn't this relate to what was going on with Warhol in New York— this very question of celebrity?

I thought about that a lot with Andy, because he was *the fame guy*. Finally, I think Andy really believed that there was true fame, or true charisma, and that Marilyn or a number of people had this true charisma. Otherwise Andy was an ad guy. He knew you could make people think anything. So the star-making process of the Factory was this enormous bullshit mind-fuck of, *I can make you do that*. Warhol was a control freak. He went off the rails in the midsixties when he discovered that he could make people do things. He could say, *Could you take off your pants, fella?* and the fella would take off his pants and show Andy his dick. For Warhol, who wouldn't do *anything* you told him, this must have been a traumatic disappointment. I think he was angry that all he had built was a bunch of people who would do whatever he told them to.

I've always regarded fame the way Andy did; I know people who have authentic charisma—Rod Stewart has authentic charisma. If you're in the room with him, he's in Technicolor and you're in black and white. I've known a few people like that, but fame is mostly copy and coverage. A lot of the people I know who are famous are like Emmylou Harris, who is an old friend of mine. Emmylou is comfortable one place: on the stage with a guitar behind the microphone. If she's not there, she's not comfortable. I'm sure there is some psychological name for that.

When you started to become involved with people who were "real" celebrities in the music world, what did it show you about art?

The first thing I learned is that there is no qualitative difference between great pop and great art—*good is good.* Second thing I learned was that if you're going to be in rock and roll, bring a friend, because it can all turn to shit fast. I've known the guys from the Eagles over the years just in passing, and they were really good buddies, and that blew up so hysterically. I never would think of writing about an artist the way I wrote about Keith Richards, because the art object is there today, and there will be another day, every day—there will be a new day when the artist dead—so that is a liberation.

Do you listen to music when you write?

No. I used to, but I don't anymore. I hear the words too much.

There's an interesting connection between you as a songwriter, traveling with country music people, and the way that you dealt with the more recent phase of your life as a critic, with the persona of an "outlaw" or an "oppositional" voice.

Well, I named those Nashville guys—Willie Nelson, Merle Haggard, Waylon Jennings—the "Outlaws" in a magazine article. As for me, I'm a hardcore alienated person, although a sweetie pie. I went to grammar school for four years at thirteen different grammar schools, and if you do this, you get good at goodbye. I'm happy to see people who I haven't seen in fifteen years—that's okay. We don't exchange Christmas cards—that's okay. I'm always sad when they die—that is one good thing about digital: the hardest thing to do is to take dead people out of your Rolodex. I remember taking Scott Burton out of my Rolodex and thinking, *Aw, boo-hoo, Scott!* At the same time, this ties in with my feelings about fame: if you would tell me who I'm supposed to be famous *to* or *for*, I could address myself to it, but I'm not really close enough to anybody or any institution to know. Art critics are not supposed to be famous. I have had periods of forty-watt celebrity and they weren't any better than any other time. If you're in a band, you've still got to get up and play. If you're a writer, you have to get up and write, win or lose. If you win, you're in vogue. I know what works: word of mouth, and that is all it is—there isn't anything anybody at Columbia might write that is going to make them famous.

I'm interested in the way "Jeff Koons" is functioning now in criticism, which feels like a funless and a critically unassailable form of hysteria.

I just finished rereading a book I really like called *The Eloquence of Color* [1993] by Jacqueline Lichtenstein, about the seventeenth-century French academy, which was divided between those who believed in line and those who believed in color. The linear people were pedants, and I think Jeff is a pedant. As they would say in the seventeenth century, *He stinks of the inkpot.* He has a terrible penchant for these retro, *Fitzcarraldo*-esque [1982] technological projects that don't *do* anything. How could Jeff Koons and Robert Gober do the same thing—which is manufacture found objects—Jeff to no end and Robert to what seems like profound ends? I don't understand. I used to work at Reese Palley right across the street from Fanelli's, which is where Jeff always was. From the first, I was amazed by the thud of his wit—it was *not there*. People say, *Jeff is so childlike*, and I think he is really like a child, and I don't attach any joke or flattery to that remark. You're always asked by people who collect, *What am I paying for? Am I paying for Rauschenberg's élan?* With Jeff it's clear you're paying for a whole lot of Detroit technology, and that *is* an investment. And Damien Hirst is the same. They both make work that looks like *work*.

I have a hard time with the fluffy art world. A lot of my opinions have changed over the years, and a lot of my contemporaries are not making as good art as they used to. They still do good art, but—

Is that because of the climate in which they are making art, or what?

A lot of it is the production demand. To cite a really good Ruscha drawing: *She Sure Knew Her Devotionals* [1976]. What is that about? It's three graphic locutions of the "shush" phoneme: *sh / su / tion*. That is all it is. It's cool, but not a lot of people know that or care. Is Ed going to go back and do that for two million dollars? Or *Guacamole Airlines* [1976], which comes out as "wacky Molière lines," acknowledging Ed's French descendance. But no longer. Ed is pretty interesting as an artist— serious in his own way, cagey beyond imagining.

You're working on an autobiographical book called *Obit: The Musical*. In *Pirates and Farmers* you said, "My life has no narrative, but it has had some nice vignettes." What is the importance in that distinction?

I've always used autobiographical stuff as a pendant in criticism— I dangle it out there. Using criticism as a pendant to personal narrative is going to be a little harder. I have fallen upon *Tristram Shandy* [1759– 1767], in the sense that my book will begin something like: *I knew I was coming out wrong. I was going to fall out of my mother's pussy onto my ass with a cord around my neck. My mom was going to be rushed off to the ICU, and I knew she would hate me forever*—you know, something *intimate* like that. I'll follow the general tonality of *Tristram Shandy*, of letting it change with my whims.

You put an epigraph from *Tristram Shandy* at the front of *The Invisible Dragon: Four Essays on Beauty*. That book seems emblematic.

It is, and would that I could write that well. This is one of the reasons my work doesn't have much footing in the art world. Who's read *Tristram Shandy*? My writing comes out of Victorian journalism— Ruskin and Carlyle, Charles Lamb and De Quincey. I was so glad when I found them. I picked up De Quincey's *Confessions of an English Opium- Eater* [1821] for reasons other than prose. I was a fan of opium, but reading it I thought, *I can do this! I can write this kind of sentence that goes on for three pages and ends with one word, just like, bam! I can do that!* Then I knew what to do, but it's not a very *fashionable* way to write.

Given that so much of your own writing is grounded in "Dave Hickey" as a character—your anecdotes and personal experiences— do you think it's useful to talk about an artist's life or what they have to say in relation to the art object? Or about yourself as the writer?

I've never regarded myself as much beyond an example of something, and I've always known that nobody is going to read this because it's about art. They are going to read it because it's *good*. That puts me and the genre at cross-purposes. I know most of the art criticism out there, and I have no idea why anybody would read that shit.

I think what has happened is that critique won over theory. Theory died in 1978 or something like that. The whole *kill them all and stand on their tummies* attitude that Deleuze brought to the discourse is what I like about theory. The big problem was that Deleuze and Foucault in particular were translated by Americans who were liberals, and I don't think that either one of them was. They are really too coldhearted to be liberals. I still like *The Order of Things* [1966], where Foucault dismantles sociology as a historical solipsism, but that was a war that Foucault *lost*. Look at *The Logic of Sense* [1969]. It is about the phonotext, and Deleuze lost that one too.

You cultivate this brash cowboy persona, but you're actually a sweetheart, and you really *care*. Why not just be a little sweeter publicly?

Oh, *I'm a sensitive plant*. The world is ablaze to me, and people are kaleidoscopes. I get my feelings hurt, so whatever brashness manifests itself in my manner is to cover that up. I wrote an essay in *Air Guitar* about going to a jam session with my dad—we went to play jazz. The essay made people cry. I wasn't trying to do that, but maybe I'm such a swoony sop I can't help it.

As I reread *Invisible Dragon*, I thought it made total sense as a culture-wars text.

It was intended to be. It was basically the same argument that

Jacqueline Lichtenstein makes in *The Eloquence of Color*: there is a point in rhetoric where language stops and art goes on. Cicero said that his ideal orator need not say a word but simply stand before the crowd to manifest the justice of his case. Out of this premise comes the elegant pantomime of Renaissance painting. That was my argument for beauty. With beauty you're free. You don't have to ask anybody. Why would you have to ask somebody?

The rhetorical move you made in writing about Mapplethorpe during the culture wars was to say, essentially, that the right-wingers looked at this stuff and knew exactly what it was; Jesse Helms was not misunderstanding it.

The essay was heartfelt. If artists can't do dangerous, why bother? As Robert said, *It's pornography*. Patti Smith says something to that effect in her little book *Just Kids* [2010]. I liked Robert Mapplethorpe. He took me to the Spike one night to watch fist fucking. He thought he was going to shock me, but I wasn't shockable. I was terrified, but not shocked. Robert liked to maneuver straight people into very uncomfortable gay situations, and I just figured it was my night in the barrel, and it was so cool to have these bikers think that I was "with" Robert. Those are the people you don't want to lose. Those were important people, as people. When I came into the dealer side of the art world, I was in a tiny minority as a straight guy. I was really there at the tolerance of Johnny Myers, Henry Geldzahler, Klaus Kertess, Andy, and all those gay guys. And where was all the homophobia? In the university. That is why all these gay people were in the commercial art world. I was talking to someone the other night about the catastrophe of AIDS, and what I remember was the battlefield aspect: the gauze and blood, the lesions, bandages, and drip tubes. Those sunken eyes. I had a friend named Steve Reichard who spent five years trying to come out. First time he goes to bed with a man, he gets AIDS and dies in six months. And Steve was a good guy. I literally couldn't believe it. I think the imperial coda of minimalism and the death of all those people changed everything profoundly.

In that context, how did you see the significance of Mapplethorpe's

moving toward "beauty" in that moment?

When I first saw the *X* photographs [1978], I probably hadn't seen more than three thousand pictures of people fist fucking, you know. I wasn't shocked, but Robert was better at it. Pretty obviously beauty set him free—it wasn't just something out of *Screw* magazine. Robert just made 'em eat it.

My ever ready plan B is to move to the beach with some hot guy—it's always on the table so that I never feel trapped into playing this art-world game I don't want to play. We'll see how long that lasts.

That is what I did when I left New York the first time: I went to Nashville. I wrote songs, played in bands, and it wasn't bad. People today are defining the role of the artist as anyone who wants to be an artist—and that won't cut it. The idea that even a thousandth of MFAs are artists is laughable, and that makes it impossible for the people who are regular artists. If you're just a regular artist, whose work doesn't come with a social excuse, or a letter from a doctor, you're kinda fucked.

For me, being banished to Nashville was kind of special, because Waylon Jennings, Billy Joe Shaver, Roger Miller, and Kinky Friedman were my contemporaries. I felt perfectly at home with them. It wasn't like, *Oh, you can't sit here.* Or, *Did I knock the Wedgwood dish off the table?* Or, *Did I puke in your hat?* I was comfortable there, and I had a wonderful woman named Marshall Chapman, who would get me in fights but then she'd fight too. So we cut a swath. Marshall and I were the only two people of our kind in Nashville, except for Waylon, and he was much sweeter than we were.

It feels like there are very few major critical voices guiding the conversation now, which is—as I understand it—different than the art discourse in the "golden days" of the sixties and seventies.

Take a critic like Michael Fried. He is an observant man, with whom I disagree 180 degrees, but *Absorption and Theatricality* [1976] is brilliantly observed—*He saw that?!* He's wrong, but he saw it. The critics that are out there now? Roberta is very observant, but I never get a sense of a metacritical stance from her, and Jerry is a good-hearted village explainer. I probably like Richard Shiff the best for being steady and clear. Christopher Knight is good because he is not afraid—he nearly took the Getty down with facts and figures and e-mails. Peter Schjeldahl is a good critic as a poet, but when he took the *New Yorker* job I told him, The New Yorker *is a narrative magazine. Your first line should be something like: The woman standing next to me looking at the Anselm Kiefer blew her nose.* Peter has never gotten a hook like that past his better self. I do think there are generations that come up feeling entitled. I certainly did—Plagens did and Schjeldahl did, so there are people who never think about compromising. I used to work at a newspaper. They would tell me, *You don't have to work this hard. We can do second best in a daily newspaper.* I'd say, *I can't do second best until I figure out first best.*

Could we talk a bit more about the complexity of pronouns?

I've never fully resolved this with myself, but there needs to be some kind of resolution of demonstratives, with "this," "then," "there," "I," "you," and "one," indicating the level of abstraction. I must have worked for six months trying to determine a level of abstraction of "of," so you could go from the "king *of* England" to the "heart *of* heart"—that is a little easier in French because they use those *faire* forms. It began to seem to me that if there is an ur-form of expression, it is, *I say (this) to you,* so all the sentence goes in the parentheses at the "this"—somehow the depth of that structure matters. The further removed you get from the *I say (this) to you*—from the palpable world—the weirder it gets to read. It's like scholars who say, *One would imagine*—what the fuck does that mean! Or, *One might imagine,* or, *Tomorrow one might have been imagining.* I think I would go with Derrida and say that the text comes first insofar as the way the language is put together, but in an everyday way speech has come to overwhelm the text. I think the weird thing about writing is that unless you are writing second-source scholarly prose, there is no way to do without "me" and "I"—I have never figured out how to do without them. People have accused me of using "I" and "me" as exercises of narcissism. I regard it as an exercise in modesty, saying, *Hey, it's just me—don't associate this with the Pew Research Center—it's just Dave out here in the desert.* If you treat "I" and "you" as demonstrative gestures, then that makes "I/you" sentences basically performative. I think

216

there is a performative cloak around most written prose. I've always really loved Foucault's thing in which he says that before you can start talking about difference, you must start talking about similitude—that the discourse of differences is based on similitudes that are harder to express since we gave away rhyme. Foucault draws that line in the early seventeenth century, where the discourse rises beyond what's like what.

When did you decide to stop writing fiction?

Pretty early on. I had been educated by very good people. I had wonderful professors. I had Jorge Luis Borges, Tom Wolfe, Nathalie Sarraute, and John Graves, who was a great nature writer—these people were beacons of insight. I had a classicist named Bill Arrowsmith, who was a bit of a showoff, and John Silber, who was an erudite monster. I think that the problem of fiction is that you don't know the "I." You spend a lot of time defining the "I"—the speaking voice or the writing voice, or, as in Henry James, when he does "indirect discourse," where he is writing in the third person as if it were the first person, which I also like to do. So you add to fiction the necessity of establishing the "I." There's one thing that Hemingway always did that I respect a lot: he misuses "which" so as not to use "that," flattening the subordination— all the "that"s subordinate, while the "which"s just set aside. There is a great section where he does that in *Death in the Afternoon* [1932].

Is that about creating speed?

It creates speed, but I think it's about keeping everything at the same level of topographical generalization. I'll give you a simple example: I have the newspaper report that he wrote during the war, and it says, *There are cows and calves gathered in the canyon.* The next draft says, *There are cows gathered in the canyon*—the calves are gone because they are self-evident. Next change: *There are cattle in the canyon*—getting everything up to this one level of generalization. Then you apply random specificity to nail it in the world, in the same sense that a vogue sweater has a dropped stitch—almost exactly that way. You might say: *The beach was long and white, and beyond the beach were the breakers frosted blue, and beyond the breakers there were elephant clouds, and there is this little Prince Albert tobacco tin laying in the sand.* The tin of tobacco organizes all this vast, vague generalization. This is an awfully good technique, but it's incredibly artificial. Basically Hemingway paints cubism: this to this to this to this to this—it's all prepositional. However, I always wanted to write like a writer I've never figured out, E. M. Forster. I think *Aspects of the Novel* [1927] is about the cleanest fucking prose I've ever read.

I read it recently! Funny enough, I read it because a painter friend of mine was saying it related to her ideas about painting.

I think he got right down to it. One of the reasons I stopped writing fiction was that book, because the nineteenth-century novel as Forster describes it is a kind of social pornography—you know what is in everybody's heads. You know Elizabeth Bennett's sisters better than you know your own sisters.

One of the things that Forster does at the beginning of *Aspects of the Novel*—he says he's supposed to give lectures on English literature since Chaucer, and he takes that as meaning everything written in English or translated into English: Dostoyevsky, Melville, Proust, et cetera. Everything gets put on this single horizon. I'm interested in moves like that, like the opening of Kubler's *The Shape of Time* [1962].

What *Aspects of the Novel* does best for artists is make clear it's not "you." Painting is not *you*. The novel is not *you*. I had these assignments I gave to my first-year graduate students—first I gave them an assignment to paint a painting in a completely different gender identity than they had. Everyone fucked this up. For the other one, I said, *Graduate students have one problem: you know what you hate, but you don't know what you like. Paint me a painting of what you hate.* And what they painted was always good! They were good because their pissy little personalities were not engaged—they all came out great, and I could never get them to go back to the good stuff that they hated. I think a lot of artists, like Artschwager, really address the issue of not doing what they like.

I still want to understand your transition from fiction—

I found that the longer I wrote fiction the more insistent and flashy my voice became, and I couldn't just turn it down. That makes fiction really hard—you know what I mean. My friend Larry McMurtry says I'm afraid to be boring, and he's right. I can do fairy tales and cowboy

218

songs, rondeaux redoublés and villanelles. What plagues me is exactly the point of ordinary language, which is that the ordinary language just gives you everything, and I want it. I want "percolate," "pissy," and "prestidigitation." I am one with David Foster Wallace in this.

How do you think of the structure of writing art reviews? Is it narrative?

I write reviews like a Wildean dream: *Were we ever to dream of a world in which David Salle was a major artist, it would perhaps look like this.* What I mean is, just the fact that I choose to write it means that I like it somehow. The construction of the essay is then all theory: *What is the theoretical constitution of a world in which these are good paintings?* This always kept a lot of German painting out of my writing—I just don't have the temperament for it.

While I'm reading your essays, I can't see the structure, but I feel it—I know I'm being taken somewhere. How did you get to that?

The structure is in the phonotext. My rules: think of the last line first, hook the first, and keep your promises. That is a lot of my rewriting. If it sounds just pretty good, then I need to go back and play the dominant seventh up top so that the cadence has some sense of fulfillment. You're writing backward, sort of, unless you hit the right word on the first try. Sometimes, though, the easiest things to write about are "difficult art"—conceptual art especially, because conceptual art is *not* intellectual art, and you can just lay it out in words. A lot of Texas writers insist on making their language sound like "literature"— like Cormac McCarthy, where I feel like I'm walking into a stock pond of crème de menthe. I try to avoid that by just resting the prose in the prose. It just has to bubble and flow.

The difference between fine and decorative art is that you can break down decorative art for the parts—you can take off the pearls and diamonds and sell them. When Marxists came to town, all of a sudden "work" became intrinsic value, so to do any labor on your picture became a bad thing, because it was indicative of a bourgeois predilection. That was driven to the bottom of the lake, until Damien Hirst had the sense to do his diamond skull—I don't want to look at it, but it makes a statement. Shameless and articulate. I've known artists that I was so sure were going to do good and they didn't. A lot of that has to do with bad timing. Bad timing, bad decisions, too much heroin, married to a beautician—there are a lot of reasons for a failed art career, and fine materials and handicraft are two of them.

I once wrote something about Ad Reinhardt's interest in *The Shape of Time*; one of the reasons I think artists really like that book is it explains that a lot depends on your entrance into a historical cycle, and takes a lot of pressure off.

Back in California we would say, *You missed the exit*, or, *You dropped into the wrong wave*—you've got to drop into the right wave to become famous. There is an eerie collaboration between you and the wicked sea, and I think that is the same thing you are talking about. What I do not sense in young artists is any group larger than five who feel some affinity with each other. That is how you win: if you have a group of artists with whom you feel an affinity, if one does well, eventually the rest will do well—a rising tide will raise all boats. If you don't, your neighbor can become Julian Schnabel and it won't make any difference to you. From my point of view, New York is not a very nice place to work on art anymore. The thing I like best about Josiah McElheny is that when I met him he wanted to talk about Venetian glass. It was almost as if he could fulfill his desires when looking away from art, and right now I think that's maybe the case.

Can we talk more technically about the process of writing itself?

The biggest problem when I started writing criticism was transitions—*How does it get from here to there?* Gradually I read enough to realize that you don't use them. No transitions. What you do is what I call a jump shift. In an art essay, I will start off with some sort of conversational anecdote, and it will amount to about three hundred words; then you jump shift. An essay I was working on once started off with a little narrative about being in Julian Schnabel's studio while they were tearing out the window to move out a thirty-foot painting. Julian is directing everyone with his hands in the air, and one of the working guys turns and says, *I bet Julian was an asshole in high school*. If you build

220

that up and give it the time to create a little mise-en-scène, then you can just put a dot at the end and start again cold: *Julian Schnabel was born in Brooklyn, New York, in April 1951.* Then you go into that if you have that first hook nailed. My trick is to write paragraphs—don't worry about where they go. After I have paragraphs I put them in order: *Here's the narrative, here's the hook, here's the lede, here's the jump shift*—it's a little train that goes along, and you find the place to hook in another two paragraphs, and then it's the end. That means you are developing these little groups of leitmotifs. If you try to write it rationally, it will sound stupid, because it's *not* rational. It's a set of waves. What I spend a lot of time on is just keeping it close to the ground, so we can go through this, we can go through Julian's background, we can go through the rise of neo-expressionism and get to the place I was ultimately going: Julian's career as a movie director, for which he was rehearsing when he was moving the painting through the window. That was the sort of loose hook that was there—and I'll write it up one of these days, maybe— so I'm sorta going there and I'm sorta starting here. But mostly, if you write good paragraphs, you don't need a transition: you can jump.

You reference John Ruskin a lot, who wrote endless, paragraph-long sentences—what do you see that needs to be in a paragraph to make it a complete unit?

Well, I agree with Henry James, who said the paragraph is the basic unit of writing. James's paragraphs are a bit more portly than mine are, since I believe in the nested theory that eight bars of music is statement, restatement, release, return, and twenty-four bars of music is statement, restatement, release, return. So you're almost trying to write the essay in each paragraph starting from a different point of view. But the thing is to write good paragraphs, and what you want is a good stop at the end of the paragraph, because if it stops well you can go anywhere from there. And you want a good lede, like in any story. The trick in a paragraph, I think, is that they are like sonnets in the sense that they have pivots, or voltas. There is a place in every paragraph where it *turns*. You start out here and you end up there, in a slightly more skewed position. Three-fifths into a paragraph it better start turning—something better start happening. Same thing applies to the essay—three-fifths into the essay, it better start turning. What imposing a rational structure on things does—and Arthur Danto was the main offender in this infelicity—is that the marching prose just soaks into the soil. You have to go back to the visible as much as possible. My preference—which most critics ignore—is to spend a lot of time actually describing the work. If you can describe the work then you have said what you have to say about the painting. You can presume that you are moving right along. So we have the scene in Julian's studio, then you have lots of background—what an asshole Julian was in high school in Houston, where I first met him. I mean, he was not really *mean*; he was just who he is, he has a sense of *drama*—

You met Julian Schnabel when he was in high school?

No, I met him when he was out of high school and hanging around Houston trying to be an artist. Julian was trading his crap to all of his artist friends for their art, and I'm sure they threw it all away—but the ones who held on to it are very happy. So: here is your lede, here is your backstory—such that you need to fill in historical things—here is your description of the work, and if you can't get out from those three points, *you're in trouble!* It sounds a lot more mechanical than it is. A lot of it is prosody and instinct. Sometimes I don't do it at all, but in general I try to start off with that thing I suggested to Peter Schjeldahl—*The lady standing next to me looking at the Kiefer blew her nose.*

When it comes to that setup—the conversational lede, the biographical stuff, and then the description—how do you connect the biographical to the descriptive?

It will connect because you say it does. The narrative pushes it up. You're the boss. That is what you discover, that is why you don't worry about transitions. If it's not there, the words will put it there, and you won't have to do all the shit Arthur Danto does. I think it's fairly important to make your preferences clear; I've written essays where I've essentially said, *In my universe, I don't like this art. But in this universe, I'm going to tell you how it might be good.*

What do you think of the personal essay as a form? Is "art criticism"

something else?

I mostly write personal essays. I find them much more flexible. I really learned how to do it when I was writing slick magazine profiles on celebrities. How do you profile a celebrity? Where do you put in their background? Where do you put in their performance? How do you arrange things like that, without having to say "thus" or "because" too much—*because you shouldn't do that*. Better to describe Roger Miller changing clothes ten times before a show.

The logic of the celebrity profile is "up close and personal"— something more than the public face everyone knows.

Bob Christgau used to say, *You are not the celebrity's friend, you are the reader's guy*. I agree. You are noticing the socks with the holes in them and the bottles of cognac and whatever is around. I think you will find that when you start doing this, it's like dressing a set, that you'll put in the things you want, like how in Julian's apartment there is a lot of North African stuff, but like Jeff Koons, strangely enough, nothing is funny—Julian has *no* sense of humor. There are hijinks, that kind of clunky *I'm going to bump into you in the schoolyard* stuff, but there's not much else there. I actually think that by going into the movies Julian saved himself—his movies are very nice. That is because, I think, Julian's temperament is Diaghilev's—it's the organizer, it's the guy who is casting the parts. He was always trying to make a movie for himself, which purportedly he did in *Basquiat* [1996]. But how and where that connects to the paintings would be the hard part. As I'm writing this essay in my imagination, I'd call the paintings "set dressing."

In what ways is figurative language—metaphor—useful or dangerous in describing art?

Well, I wrote a piece about Lynda Benglis's big poured pieces that come out of the wall, and I ended up having to say the same things about Robert Gober's legs coming out of the wall—they are about a natural world bifurcated by industry. I think that is right in both cases. I'm really an everyday-language person. You don't send out for figurative expression; it arises out of the vocabulary in which you're writing. I think metaphors are forced up out of the prose.

There was something you wrote about the exhibition *Primary Atmospheres* [2010] where you say the object's relationship to its form is that of aspic to its mold, which I thought clicked a lot of evocative stuff together in a very simple way.

That is pretty much the idea, and it's a version of the idea I was talking about with Jasper Johns: *Why does Jasper use letters and numbers and targets?* Well, first, because they are forms that have no originals and I think Jasper liked that, but, most importantly, they are *real stupid*, and stupid nearly always pays off in that sense.

There is something he said to Leo Steinberg about the targets, that he uses them because they are something the mind "already knows," which is the same thing.

Right, and I think that a lot of Jasper's iconography is just an excuse to make sexy surface paintings. I think children will be wondering about whether the target is an asshole for the rest of this century—and in Lari Pittman it occasionally is—but I don't think it is in Jasper's case. I like the logic of the flags: the thing about the flag is not who made it, but who salutes it. The best thing about the target is that you aim at it. You move the whole presence of the object into its extension in space.

To go back to writing: I think you keep your promises. If what you're doing is all out of shape, the reason is probably that there is a promise you made up at the top that you are not keeping at the end. The fat lady in the second sentence must reappear if you're writing literary prose. Everything should be accounted for. But what you do about picking the wrong artists—shit, I don't know. That is why I find negative reviews much more difficult to write than positive reviews. I can figure out the conditions under which something might be good, but I can't explain why anyone would make bad art. I don't have a fucking clue!

When you get into the description part of it, you mainly talk about the physical object itself in a tight frame, as opposed to the exhibition as an entity.

If it is an exhibition, I will usually pick out a typical object in the show. Nuance resides in the single occasion, so I think you're better off just talking about one. This goes back to the advice of Paul Williams, the songwriter: *Never put more than one interesting line in a song*. And there is a tendency to do that—you want to make everything *gorgeous*, but if it's a good hook, just let it *emanate*. If you're being clear and grammatical, don't worry about boring—people can read clear and grammatical very rapidly. If you want to make it hard, make it beautiful and difficult.

You mainly write monographic pieces.

That is what I write lately. I have this very interesting problem now: this story I should have been writing for two weeks, while I've been down here seeing stars and jaguars—which is this story on David Levinthal. It's for the Smithsonian. There is a nice, simple little "Smithsonian essay" to be written. But there is a much more complicated essay to be written about what happens when the stopped time in a toy and the stopped time in a photograph create the illusion of action—it's like a double negative. That is a little more grown-up than the Smithsonian wants, but … There is also the argument to be made that this is Western art because the size of the figure is related to the scale of the ground, so you can use a little-bitty ground to make something look big. That seems simple enough, unless you have been to the Middle East or a Byzantine church—it's hard to describe. Even so, I like to write about things that I like but that I don't understand when I start. When I started writing I did learn some very basic rules, one of which is, *Don't start writing until you are ready to start writing*. The transition from typewriter to computer, which you have never suffered, was that, on a computer, you can just write and erase and write and erase, but it won't get you there because you really need to wait until you have something to say. So—put it off.

Until you *have* to do it?

Yeah. Then you're getting more money per hour and you're not going to be boring. I can't imagine writing boring stuff for a long time. I think the deadline pressure really helps periodical journalism. Were it not for that I would probably still be revising my first little essay.

Before you start writing, do you envision how things go, like how the narrative works?

No, I envision random words—a kind of bouquet of possible meanings. "Turtle," "veranda," "enfilade," or "mountain chickadee"— how they look.

Descriptions?

"Taller than a dog"—just vigorous little shots at observing the art. I remember I wrote a pretty good piece on Mary Heilmann—I've known her for years. I knew her when she lived in El Segundo—all my girlfriends are ranked up and down the beaches of Southern California. I decided that the most persuasive, imaginative image of "Mary Heilmann" would be the Norman Rockwell picture of the little girl sitting out in front of the principal's office with a black eye and a big smile—*that is Mary*. She's such a willful imp that she didn't start painting until she was sure painting was dead. She was going around asking everyone, *Is painting dead?* Then she started making paintings that have no lateral pressure—she was a ceramist—so all her paintings piss off at the edges, which is very effective, of course.

All painters grow up learning discipline: *This is too much, this is too little, this goes in, this goes out, this should go flat*—all of these kinds of decisions. I always thought that Liz Murray had the ability to break every one of those rules. I don't think she ever thought, *This shouldn't stick out three feet*, whereas any normal person would. Liz was perfectly free, and I think that explains her prodigious production. She was really having fun. In a sane world she would be recognized as the greatest art comedian of the twentieth century. The Carol Burnett of art.

How do humor and wit function in both your writing about art and the work of art itself?

I thought early on that John Currin was humorous; now his work just looks frat house. There is art like Ruscha's that is witty, but wit is not going to get you a blow job in New York. Personally, although I traffic in wit, I know that it doesn't really help and that people don't really like it. I come out of Alexander Pope and all of that ongoing ongoingness.

So the idea is just lining all your little cars in the railroad yard and attaching them as they need to be attached. I can't remember the day, but I can remember the feeling, when I got an assignment that I *knew* I could write! When you think, *I don't know if I can write this*, or *What am I going to write about Bachman-Turner Overdrive?*—you're dead. What I did with Bachman-Turner Overdrive was to invent a teenage companion, "Norman," who was much hipper to childlike things, and I would take him—theoretically—on trips with me, and he would keep me from getting too excited about Nils Lofgren or whatever was the latest pop of the day. There are thousands of devices. If the content is too personal, too much grounded in my experience, I'm much more comfortable going into the third person and writing it as "he."

You did that in the introduction to the revised edition of *Invisible Dragon*.

And I did it in the last essay in my short-story book, *Prior Convictions*. The essay was called "Proof through the Night," which I regard as the last great title from "The Star-Spangled Banner"—I was happy about that. *Proof through the night*—don't we all need that! This leads me to something else: one of the ways out of swanning narcissism, if worse comes to worst, is to quote yourself. But you don't say, *I thought . . .* You say, *I have a friend who thinks . . .* Then you have some calm distance— and you never have to say who that person was! You really have a lot of options when you write, but that presumes that you have something in your mouth that you are chewing on, unlike that asshole at Princeton— he's not chewing on anything.

What I'm saying is: a good essay on art is not always a good argu- ment, it is *a good story with implications*—that is what you learn writing celebrity journalism. You are writing a story with available materials, available light.

You just need to understand that as you move on, you are not going to be any smarter than you are today. I'm not any smarter than I was when I was twenty-three, *but* eventually I acquired the confidence that I *was* right. At first you think, *I think this, but everyone is going to hate me.* Then as you grow you think, *But I'm right—fuck you!* That is a good feeling. It gives you more energy if you think you're right about a certain kind of thing.

I don't want to live in a world where everyone agrees.

I don't either! I do *difficulty*. If everyone loves it—*I don't*.

Art is a social form, a thing made by
me that is meant for you. Artists sit
or stand alone in a room for many
hours a day and don't see or talk to
anyone. This is how most of my time
is spent. But there are always others
in the artist's head, worlds of others.
The need to make is not solitary:
*I've made something, and it's for you,
and it's now a part of our world.*

Siri Hustvedt (b. 1955) is a novelist and essayist whose work interleaves reflections on literature with art history, philosophy, and neurobiology. From 1996 to 2004 she wrote art reviews for *Modern Painters*, many of which are collected in the book *Mysteries of the Rectangle* (2005). Her novels include *The Blindfold* (1992); *The Enchantment of Lily Dahl* (1996); *What I Loved* (2003); *The Sorrows of an American* (2008); *The Summer Without Men* (2011); and *The Blazing World* (2014). Among her books of essays and nonfiction are *Yonder* (1998); *A Plea for Eros* (2005); *The Shaking Woman: Or, A History of My Nerves* (2010); *Living, Thinking, Looking* (2012); and *A Woman Looking at Men Looking at Women* (2016).

Siri Hustvedt

There is an essay in *A Woman Looking at Men Looking at Women* where you offhandedly say that your mother used to call you "too sensitive for this world"—I'm wondering about that and how it relates to your early aesthetic experiences.

That particular essay, "Becoming Others," is about my mirror-touch synesthesia, a form of synesthesia that wasn't named until 2005, although obviously people have been walking around with it forever. It's a physiological phenomenon: if I see another person slapped on the cheek, I have a sensation in my own cheek. I also have strong physical responses to colors—once while looking at a shade of turquoise in Iceland, I had a revolting crawling sensation all over my body. Everyone responds to color, but my mirror-touch sensations probably exaggerate the response. At the same time, I can't jump out of myself and check what it is like for you. When I was growing up, it never occurred to me that other people didn't feel what they saw.

So you experience visual things as tactile sensations?

Yes, that is the definition of mirror-touch synesthesia. There are many forms of synesthesia. Some people translate musical sounds into colors. Others see letters and numbers in color—*F is green; L is yellow; 3 is blue; 7 is black.* The colors are subjective. Everyone has her or his own. The great physicist Richard Feynman had that form of synesthesia. He once said he wondered what his students saw when they imagined a formula, because for him it was ablaze with color—lovely, no?

It's possible that this sensitivity increased my interest in looking at paintings. I grew up in a house in Minnesota with a Norwegian mother and a father who was a professor of Scandinavian literature and language. Munch was everywhere—not *real* Munchs, of course, but books and prints. My earliest exposure to a painter was to Munch.

That's a good one.

A very good one. I also drew and painted. When I was maybe fourteen, I made a painting of Jesus on the cross I was particularly proud of. A couple of years later, I saw a Munch painting of the Crucifixion and realized that my painting had been directly stolen from an unconscious memory of it—every figure was in exactly the same place with the same gestures. I understood how unconscious borrowing works; all those Munch images must have settled deep inside me for me to unknowingly make a bad copy.

We had other art books in the house; they were mostly modernist artists—all men, of course. I remember looking closely at a Cézanne book my parents had and loving it—I still love Cézanne. The Minneapolis Institute of Art and the Walker Art Center were nearby, so many of my adolescent art experiences took place in those institutions. Goya's *Self-Portrait with Dr. Arrieta* [1820] at the Institute had a powerful and haunting effect on me. He portrays himself as desperately feeble, almost swooning, seemingly near death, and the physician behind him is so tender—I have lived with that image for many years. When I was perhaps fifteen or sixteen, I saw a Mondrian show at the Walker. The curator had done the viewer the great favor of including early Mondrians, so when I walked through the show I witnessed his development—from trees and horizons to abstraction. It was a profound experience for me; I felt as if I was *seeing* the artist's thoughts.

When I was seventeen, I spent a year in Bergen, Norway, and attended gymnasium there. After Christmas, while I was still on vacation, I used money I had saved to take a ship to Newcastle, and from there I took a train to London. I stayed in a youth hostel and went to museums. It was a great adventure because I knew no one in the city. At the Tate, I saw Turners for the first time in real life. I remember them vividly. Looking at those Turners, I was drowning and on fire

232

and completely alive.

How did your relationship with language relate to these vivid visual experiences?

I decided to become a writer when I was thirteen. I think there was something about the withdrawal and retreat into text I liked. Even now, I notice that although my husband can watch two or three movies in a row if he is engaged in the films, I find it difficult to take in more than one. The experience is *too big*. The abstractness of language and the immediacy of visual images should not be confused. They are different, both in terms of ontogeny and phylogeny. I was deeply irritated by the art-world fashion in the seventies and eighties for looting textual theory, mostly French, to discuss visual art—that was a grave mistake. There may well be a relation between my immersion in written language and my hypersensitivity to images, color, and the real world.

How did you decide to become a writer?

Reading. My reading obsession began early, but around twelve, thirteen, I felt as if a switch had been flipped in my mind. Everything printed was suddenly accessible to me. I remember thinking, *Oh, wow, I can read little print!* For all children, that time of life is a moment of burgeoning brain development and greater emotional and intellectual maturity. I couldn't have read philosophy, of course, but I could read long English novels, which are mostly what I read.

Is that when you first got hooked on Charles Dickens, on whom you wrote your dissertation at Columbia?

Yes, I read *David Copperfield* [1849–1850] the summer after I turned thirteen. My father was studying the Icelandic sagas, and the family spent an entire summer in Reykjavík. The city library had lots of English books. My mother recommended titles, and I read them. I read dozens of novels. I read all the time. I never stopped—in part because I had insomnia; it never got dark, and my diurnal rhythms were screwed up. So I stayed up and read long books in three or four days: Jane Austen, Mark Twain, the Brontës, Dumas, Dickens. That summer I decided to become a writer.

Were you drawing and painting before that?

Before then, when people asked me what I wanted to be when I grew up, I always said, *I want to be an artist.* There are several artists in my novels. I think they reflect my old longing to make visual art.

Your book of essays on painting, *Mysteries of the Rectangle*, is so great. I have relationships with many of the artists and artworks you write about, so I was able to read about your experiences with them and hold them against my own. It made me realize how important it is to me to verify art writing against my own experiences.

When you read a description of an artwork, even a highly detailed one, you invent an image, which is inevitably different from another person's image. This was once vividly illustrated for me when a group of German artists made art based on works by my character Bill Wechsler in *What I Loved.* Their images had nothing to do with what I had imagined while writing the novel. It is important to recognize that in a narrative, artworks are part of the artist's character. They say what the artist cannot say. This is my relationship to a novel while I am writing it—the book knows more than I do. When an artist is working well, the artwork knows more than she or he does. It defies other forms of articulation.

Recently a gallery asked me to write about an artist. I replied, *It's not that I find this work bad—it's good and lively and worthwhile—but it is not mysterious to me.* In other words, I am only interested in writing about art that escapes me, art that I don't fully understand, that keeps me looking. Therefore Goya. He is an artist I can never quite get my hooks into, an artist who continually eludes me. This is true for literature as well— the books I return to are the books I need *again.* When I read them, I don't fully understand what is happening to me or how it's been done.

I think it's very clarifying when you write that "a work of art is always part person"—explaining that our relationship with an artwork is never "I-to-object," but rather an artwork is a "part-object/part-you."

Exactly. It's not a mystical idea. It is simply that an encounter with a work of art is an encounter with the traces of a human consciousness and unconsciousness. I've written several times that we don't treat works of art as we treat chairs, even beautiful chairs. An artwork is there only to be taken in; it is a "part-you." It is the "quasi-you" in a dialogical relation.

When you recognize the "part-you" of an object, you're connecting it with the life of the person who made it. Something I think you do with a lot of nuance is describe that connection in a way that is fleeting and not reductive.

I would like to stress that it's not biographical. It is rather that the relation between a spectator and a work of art has an intersubjective quality. *Intersubjectivity* happens between one subject and another, and it is this in-between, relational quality I want to stress, and that, of course, changes over time. As you were saying, when you know a painting, care about it, and have an established history with it, and then you read what I have to say about it, you remember what you felt and thought in the presence of the painting. It is unlikely that your feelings or thoughts are identical to mine, but they may press you to see what you hadn't seen before. The error is to treat art objects as if there is some higher, objective view of them. Let's face it: even sophisticated art critics often pretend they have an authorial, third-person view, from which they can make objective declarations about what *the thing is*. I adamantly *refuse* to do that. To be clear, I think I have as much authority as many others. I am not devaluing my own thoughts. It is rather that I believe that kind of art writing is founded on a false philosophical premise. That is something quite different.

When did you first begin writing about art?

In 1995. Karen Wright, then editor of *Modern Painters*, had read my first novel, *The Blindfold*, in which my narrator describes her experience with Giorgione's *The Tempest* [ca. 1505]—a painting that has obsessed me since I was nineteen, when I saw a reproduction of it in an art history class. Karen thought to herself, *Here's a novelist who can write about art*. She began to call me with writing suggestions. I was working on a book and put her off. I kept saying I was too busy. Then she called about the big Vermeer show in Washington, DC, and I thought, *Siri, you would be mad not to do it*. It was a great assignment because Karen told me to pick just one picture to write about. I walked into the press showing with my little badge, wandered through the show of twenty-something Vermeers. I was in a state of stupefied wonder, but I finally parked myself in front of *Woman with a Pearl Necklace* [ca. 1662–1665] and remained there for a couple of hours, looking and thinking and dreaming. It's a great painting filled with sacred, quiet, secret joy. Then, I saw an egg shape in the windowsill. None of the other paintings with windows had eggs. I checked. I also recognized the woman's hand gesture. I felt certain I had seen something like it in Siena. And then the word came to me: "Annunciation." Arthur Wheelock, one of the curators, was wandering around, so I asked him, *Has anyone ever thought of this as an Annunciation painting?* I explained my reasoning about the woman's hands. He turned rather white. I think he did see exactly what I meant, but he said, *I have always thought of this as a Eucharistic painting,* and walked off.

I went home, wrote the piece, which is a narrative account of how I came to my thoughts about the painting. Excitedly, I FedExed the essay to Wheelock. He never answered me. But a few weeks later, he did an interview about the show and said, *Someone recently pointed out to me that it's an Annunciation painting.* There are three points to be made here: one, my argument convinced him; two, he should have answered me; three, he knew there was a name attached to that "someone," and he should have mentioned it. Art museums do not like intruders. I discovered a foggy face in the left-hand corner of Goya's *Third of May 1808* [1814] and wrote about it as a hidden self-portrait, sent other people to see it—they saw it—but I was met with striking hostility from some art historians and museum curators. Territorialism exists in many disciplines, but to be honest, I generally find the sciences more welcoming than the arts and humanities. It may be because scientists have become the masters of culture and can be benevolent, while people in the arts and humanities struggle with feelings of inferiority and feel threatened.

So your sense is that you're treated with suspicion or condescension because you are not "properly credentialed" to make certain art historical claims? Like, *Who is this person with their own thoughts on Vermeer?*

236

Wheelock knew I was right, which is why he changed his mind.
I know that essay made the rounds, and I heard through the grapevine
that it changed peoples' thinking about the painting, but I'm not sure
anyone has ever given me credit in print.

**This is going to sound a bit strange, but when I was reading your
essays in *Mysteries of the Rectangle*, I thought, *She is trying to make
an actual contribution to the way we understand paintings*. That's not a
feeling I have when I read most criticism.**

Yes. In my collection *Living, Thinking, Looking*, the essay "Embodied
Visions: What Does It Mean to Look at a Work of Art?" [2010] is a
philosophical statement about what happens between viewer and
artwork. But, in fact, for me, nothing is ever finished. Every essay is on
its way to another. I never want to close off discussion, which is not the
same as saying I have no thoughts or beliefs—I certainly do. What I
mean is that there is always room for change, for another perspective,
a new piece of understanding that will alter what I have said before.
I am convinced I am on the right track, that art experience is an
intersubjective relation between an "I" and a "quasi-you." This is true
for all works of art. There is always an other hiding within it. Therefore,
philosophical reflections, as well as psychological and neuroscientific
research into self-other relations and the nature of human perception
itself, are not extraneous to understanding what it means to look at art
but essential to it.

**One of the reasons I am so attracted to your writing on art is how
attentive you are to its emotional qualities, which, as you note in several
places, have been mostly been denigrated in discourse.**

In art writing, the denigration of emotion is common, and the
denigration of emotion is also denigration of the body. This is certainly
not an original thought—feminist scholars have written at length
about the identification of the body and emotion with women and
the intellect and the spirit with men, and that great divide, the mind/
body problem, has haunted the West since Plato and is still alive and
well in our culture. Art by women has often been dismissed as too
emotional and corporeal. There is a move now in both the sciences and

the humanities to recover the body as crucial to thought. The "mind" is not a neo-Cartesian, ethereal substance hovering over the low, debased, material body but essential to so-called mental experience. A friend of mine, the neuroscientist Antonio Damasio, has researched people with damage to their prefrontal cortices who lost feelings of empathy and guilt. This results in an inability to make sound decisions and plan for the future. Feeling is vital to reasoning and judgment.

Narrative doesn't work in visual art in the same way it does in literature. For instance, take Giorgione's *The Tempest,* which has a famously strange relationship to narrative. How do you understand narrative in painting, especially when it's then translated into writing?

A painting is there all at once, but one's attention cannot be on the entire painting all at once, so looking becomes a sequential act of focusing on various parts of the painting, and there is usually a verbal description that follows the attentive eye. This is different from other arts such as music or the novel that unfold in a sequential, linear way. In a painting, narrative movement is created from the relational elements within that static image. For example, Giorgione's *The Tempest* has a diabolical triangular motion, created by the spectator in relation to the two figures in the canvas: the woman in the painting is looking up and out at the viewer, the man to the far left of the picture is looking at the woman, and the viewer is trapped in a kind of erotic gazing mechanism. The man looking at the woman serves as the spectator's double. Like the viewer outside the painting, he is drawn to the woman on the other side of a river. He's dressed. She is partly naked, nursing a baby—God, that's an amazing painting! It generates a spinning narrative trap that goes nowhere, just round and round. It's a locked image. Some narrative paintings are open—you can leave them. It all has to do with how the narrative field is defined.

I don't know if this is paradoxical or not: when we look at a work of art we are communing with another consciousness—that of the maker, separated by time and space—but I also don't think people make art in the first person as *themselves.* How do we square those two things?

On this question, Kierkegaard is the unparalleled genius. The

238

last essay in my most recent book is on Kierkegaard's pseudonymous writing. I ask: *Who are the pseudonyms?* He speaks of them in various ways, but they are not he. They do not articulate his views. In this way, Kierkegaard is a philosopher-novelist or a novelist-philosopher. When a novelist writes, she becomes another person, and that ability is not limited to artists. I have asked myself an interesting question: *How is the ordinary, imaginative plurality of self related to the pathology of multiple personality disorder?* It is now called dissociative identity disorder, because "multiple personality disorder" was too creepy, was overdiagnosed, and for a time took on epidemic proportions. There is considerable empirical evidence, however, that there are people who harbor several personalities with different physiological attributes— one has asthma, another doesn't, for example. This should challenge our view of human beings as singular. In my essay "The Delusions of Certainty" [2016], I wonder if a novelist who is writing in the voice of a character for several years develops physiological signs related to that character. We have no idea. You have to ask the question before you can research it. No scientist has asked the question. You're right, though. I think plurality is a normal feature of reflective human consciousness.

I don't know if within literary circles this is a really dopey reference, but someone who is a major influence on me is Mikhail Bakhtin, who seems to prefigure a lot of what you're talking about, regarding the dialogic imagination and polyphony in novels.

That's a terrific reference! Bakhtin is a thinker who has had an enormous effect on me. One of my favorite quotes from him is, "The word in language is half someone else's." For Bakhtin, words are alive and charged with the meanings of others. You give a word an idiosyncratic meaning; the other person adopts it and then returns it to you with his own inflection. I believe this is the way to understand language. Bakhtin also had the great intelligence to pay attention to how words are shot through with power relations and how authoritarianism creates the stilted and dead discourses we see all around us— the ossified rhetoric of power.

Your writing crosses several disciplinary boundaries; I imagine

you as an air traffic controller for ideas. How do you see where you sit intellectually within these different discourses?

It's true: I am a fly in the ointment, a constant irritant. We had a scientist friend of mine here for dinner last night. The two of us were arguing about neurobiology, how to frame certain questions. In neuro-science, I went from zero—literally knowing next to nothing—to lecturing on the subject for people in various fields who respect my work. He said to me, *After being your friend for all these years, I've understood that what you do is decide you're going to master something, and you do. Then you become critical. And then you go on to the next question.*

It's vital not to be afraid to ask fundamental questions that may sound stupid. In 2016, a scholarly book on my work by people in various disciplines came out from De Gruyter. One scholar in the collection notes that I am prone to saying the obvious: *What am I looking at? How can paint have this effect on me?* What she fails to understand, I think, is that when I make an obvious statement, such as *A painting doesn't move*, I am insisting on the fundamentals required to build a larger philosophical structure. Let's say there are five hundred questions in a problem. A lot of discourse begins at question two hundred fifty-seven, which means it's sitting on two hundred fifty-six other questions that have supposedly been answered, but if you go down the ladder, you see almost immediately that they haven't been solved. Question two hundred fifty-seven is founded on a rickety piece of equipment.

Recently, I gave a grand rounds lecture in neurology at Mass General in Boston. While I was there, I also visited a group of research scientists doing work on dementia and Alzheimer's—highly specific, significant work. I told them, *The reason it is important for you to read literature and philosophy and psychology even though you spend your days shaving brain tissue or studying shadows on fMRIs is not because I think everyone should become a cultured polymath. It is because I think knowledge from other disciplines will help you solve problems in your own work.* I call this "reading against myself." I have laboriously worked my way through texts I find turgid and unpleasant—symbolic logic and various arguments in Anglo-American analytical philosophy, for example—not because I "like" them or because I agree with them, but because I know that my reading of this material has given me a mental flexibility I would never have had otherwise. So many people are locked into one train of thought; not just in the sciences, in the humanities, too. Inevitably, locked-in people run into a problem that is insoluble from that single point of view, but if they call in a couple of mates from other disciplines, those outside visitors may take a look at the dead end and say, *That's not so hard!*

That is why we need each other.

We need each other, yes, and that's why all artistic and intellectual life is a form of collaboration. Nothing comes from nothing. That is the other thing to hammer home: no one invents him- or herself.

What do you think art is?

Long before there was art as we think of it, people were making things. I gave a series of lectures in November at the University of Tübingen and was taken to a museum with objects that had been found at an anthropological dig near the city. The beautifully illuminated museum cases were filled with tiny carved animals—forty thousand years old. It's hard to explain how moving those little horses and bears and bison were—and a hedgehog, my favorite. The animals were immediately identifiable. Why were these people making those animals forty thousand years ago? Think of it—writing is only about fifty-five hundred years old. We don't know why, but those people represented their world in sculpture. They had music, too; they made flutes.

When we talk about art today, we often think of the art world with fancy people and good wine and elegant clothes and vast sums of money, but the urge to make something is where art begins, and it always takes place among others. Art is a social form, a thing made by me that is meant for you. Artists sit or stand alone in a room for many hours a day and don't see or talk to anyone. This is how most of my time is spent. But there are always others in the artist's head, worlds of others. The need to make is not solitary. *I've made something, and it's for you, and it's now a part of our world.* And the meaning of the thing that has been made is created by our collective social reality.

How do you understand the strangeness of how people end up

doing what they are doing, or being who they are? Like you, a girl from Minnesota, who is living the life you are. Or anyone really. How do you think about the mysteriousness of that?

That is a way of asking, *What is the self?* Although it's inelegant and inadequate, the word to keep in mind is "socio-psycho-biological." Each part of that hyphenated adjective blurs into the next because everything is ultimately physiological.

We are mammals limited by our evolutionary heritage and the organic realities of our species, but we are also dynamic creatures that change in relation to what happens to us. A story is not just a verbal narrative; it is part of the body. Culture becomes you materially, in the way you walk and talk and gesture and inhabit yourself. Much of this is unconscious, but it is inculturated and physical.

"Socio-psycho-biological"—is there space for the spiritual in there?

I'm not only a synesthete. I'm a migraineur. I've had Alice in Wonderland syndrome, visual hallucinations, and euphoria before migraines—none of which I regret, by the way. I regret the pain, but auras have enhanced my life. I think of transcendence as experiences that take me out of myself. I believe there are forms of collective experience, including art, that transcend the loneliness of being, that lift you out of your singular organism. That is the magic of what Kierkegaard calls reflection. Kierkegaard was so reflective it pained him. He wanted more immediacy. He wanted to live more in the moment. What he called "the unhappy consciousness" is the person who is continually running back and forth in time—recollecting the past and anticipating the future—but never living in the now. Kierkegaard wanted to be a Christian, in the deepest, darkest sense, so much so that his ideas don't resemble most other forms of Christianity. But the traveling Kierkegaard worried about—that racing back and forth in time—is what the imagination does. The imagination has tremendous mobility, and for me it is a form of spiritual consciousness.

Were you raised going to church?

Yes, Lutheran. My parents were not pious. In fact, I never really knew what they believed. I agonized as a child over the terrible

242

Abraham/Isaac story. It kept me awake and miserable for weeks. *Why would God ask Abraham to murder his child?* A Sunday school teacher told me that the story meant that we had to love God more than our parents. I knew I didn't. Finally, I told my mother about it. She looked at me and said, *Nonsense.* I was so relieved I skipped down the stairs to my room. Lutheranism has a frightening transparency—there is nowhere to hide. You have a direct, not mediated, relation to God—a heavy burden. I was happy to be rid of it. When I became a graduate student at Columbia, I knew nothing about poststructuralism and felt ignorant in relation to my hipper fellow students, but I had read a lot of philosophy, and I knew my Bible, which is a great help if you are studying literature. By that time, I would have described myself as a secular person, but I had had a religious education. At St. Olaf College, where I was an undergraduate, every student was required to take three religion courses. I read Martin Buber for the first time in one of those classes, who remains one of my great beloveds. So let's just say: it was not a waste of time.

I think the context of black life is different, and I honor that. If we get into politics today, Black Lives Matter and these movements, they are telling us that black people are being killed exponentially. You're going to tell me that doesn't *affect* artists in some kind of way? Or doesn't affect the materiality of art if you're a black person?

Kellie Jones (b. 1959) is a curator, critic, and art historian whose work focuses on reevaluating the contexts and legacies of African American artists. Recently she curated the acclaimed exhibitions *Now Dig This! Art and Black Los Angeles 1960–1980*, which appeared at both the Hammer Museum and PS1 (2011–2013), and *Witness: Art and Civil Rights in the Sixties* (2014), at the Brooklyn Museum. Her books include *EyeMinded: Living and Writing Contemporary Art* (2006) and *South of Pico: African American Artists in Los Angeles in the 1960s and 1970s* (2017). She is an associate professor in the Department of Art History and Archaeology and a fellow with the Institute for Research in African American Studies at Columbia University. Jones received a MacArthur Fellowship in 2016.

Kellie Jones

You organized *EyeMinded* in four sections, each introduced by some-one in your family, followed by a piece of their own writing. I don't know of another critical anthology that's organized around the family unit. It signals a certain emotional, intellectual, and almost mythological framework from which you emerged—*This is my sister, Lisa Jones; my father, Amiri Baraka; my mother, Hettie Jones; and my husband, Guthrie P. Ramsey Jr.* You grew up in this context surrounded by artists; when did you feel like you had an awareness of art or aesthetics as a special thing?

It was always just part of life. There's a picture in *EyeMinded* that I love, with my sister and I just flying into Paula Cooper Gallery as little girls in 1969. To me, that really encapsulates how I felt about it. That art world was a fun place if you were a kid. There are cool adults, they're not really paying attention. They're having fun, and there's always art. There are studios: Al Loving's studio, Norman Lewis's studio, which I remember vividly. These were just fun spaces, because they were about *creativity*. And in a way, nothing was off-limits. Right? That's what creativity is. To be surrounded by that as a kid is *magical*. I think you also know that people *work*—that creativity doesn't just happen. People work *very hard* at it, and they often don't get paid. I grew up on the Lower East Side. A lot of these artists started on the Lower East Side and then moved to SoHo and Tribeca later to get larger spaces. We're running in and out of those places. They're great. They're huge. I just finished an essay on Elizabeth Murray, who was my elementary school art teacher; her first husband, Don Sunseri, was my woodshop teacher. They were our neighbors for a while. Artists were always there. They were always making something. Elizabeth was supportive of me for her entire life. She helped me get my very first show as an independent curator. She wrote about others—one of the first essays that she writes is about another friend, Candida Alvarez. I think about these people as being very supportive of each other. Al Loving had just passed away before a show I curated with his work in it, *Energy/Experimentation: Black Artists and Abstraction 1964–1980* [2006], opened, but when we were talking about it he thanked me for being on this journey with him and the people of his generation—as somebody who grew up in it, who could understand it from the inside.

It took me a while to realize you could be a part of the art world without being an artist, that there were jobs for people like curators and writers. But it was really about forging that path for myself. The only person I knew at that time who was a curator was Lowery Sims. I started working at the Studio Museum in Harlem, and that was a place where you could actually see people of color who were in this field besides artists—because I knew so many of the artists. I went to Amherst College during the early years of coeducation. One of the things about a small liberal arts college is that you can do what you want, and so I made up a degree that was black studies, Spanish, and art history, and that's what I've been doing ever since.

One of the interesting things about the world you describe is that there's not *an* art world: there are a bunch of art worlds that people build for themselves out of their communities. As a child, you split your time between a Lower East Side bohemia with your Jewish mother and a black nationalist context with your father in Newark. How did you experience the relationship between those things?

They were just different worlds. I think kids are always flexible—more flexible than you think. They can really process things quickly, because they're new in the world, right? All the sedimented realities that we know as adults, it doesn't really pertain to them. They're in the world right now, living that world. It's just, *This is what you do.* We were obviously really participating in that world in Newark: being part of the African Free School, marching on African Liberation Day. We were there all the time, being part of that. Also, our grandparents were there. They were also migrants. They grew up in segregation. They were born in the teens, in Alabama and South Carolina. They had seen things that we would only find out about later, reading, not necessarily from them. Their idea was, *You're going to change the world, too.*

What both the people in Newark and the Lower East Side had in common was a belief in art making a difference in the world. We marched in New York for certain things, and we marched in Newark for other things—but it was about art making a difference in the world. That's what joins those worlds for me. They looked different, and they required different things of you in terms of how you participated. Whether you're in the play *Slave Ship* [1967] that my dad did—as children, we added the sound effects. My sister and I always remember that: you go into this dark room and you scream and you're part of the play. [Laughter.] *That's cool.* Then you go to a Baptist church with your grandparents—you dress up and eat candy and are quiet. Then you're back to the Lower East Side, and you do art.

One thing you've written and made exhibitions on is this dynamic between a certain generation of African American abstractionists and the way that relates to other discourses of black identity as it becomes manifest in art, specifically representational imagery that was seen as more politically relevant than abstraction. I'm seeing a connection between those multiple locations of your childhood and your ability to hold those different types of art making in relationship to each other, without making them hierarchical. It's not like, *This is the only politically effective way of doing art.* You write beautifully about those multiple tracks. How did you balance that as a writer?

Probably because I lived it. Maybe that is the childhood part of me that was able to switch and see all these things and say they were all effective in their own ways, and they also had things that didn't work in their own ways. I think it's really interesting, especially since *EyeMinded* came out, that the role of figuration and all kinds of classical agitprop, social realist, or at least figurative types of art are now important again. There's always a role for that. It also doesn't cancel out people from making abstraction at the same time. And it doesn't mean that people aren't always searching for a more just society. Some people don't do it in their work, or abstraction *is* their version of it.

I think I might have learned that from somebody like Norman Lewis. I remember him saying, *You don't have to put your activism in your art*—and he struggled with that for years. His generation was dedicated to making abstract art but could march on a picket line protesting The Metropolitan Museum of Art's show *Harlem on My Mind* [1969]. At a certain point all black artists more or less had to live in Harlem, they weren't living downtown. So to create a show called *Harlem on My Mind* with no African American artists in it, who were actually living in Harlem, was pretty ridiculous. So they're going to protest that, but that doesn't mean they have to make a painting about it. Even though society really wants them to, because that's the kind of art it wants to see from African American artists, right? There's a story about Norman Lewis's abstract expressionist colleagues telling him, *You need to go make a lynching painting, man.* But in fact, if I put on my art history hat, for the most part, that was never African American artists' predominant mode—making art about violence—because they experienced it every day. It was more like art was a sacred, a fun, and a creative spot. *Yes*, you want to be part of a discourse that is antiracist, antiviolent, antihomophobic, whatever it is. But your art can also be about pleasure and love.

I'm interested in your relationship to language. Particularly having two parents who are legendary writers, it seems like it might be complex becoming a writer yourself.

Well, language was always *very* important—that's for sure. I think I actually had it easier going into art history, being an art historian and a curator. My sister, Lisa Jones, is the one for whom things are more complicated, because she is a playwright, a filmmaker, an essayist— she's doing all the things that the parents do. But luckily she's the best writer ever, so it works. I just love her mind and language—she is so inspiring. She also taught me to write. She is the first person who told me, *You just need to dump that mind on the page.* In fact, I now teach that to my students: *Dump your mind down on the page. Don't think about grammar. Don't think about anything. Just think about getting it out of your head onto the page.* They always struggle with that particular part.

It seems like maybe because you weren't writing "creatively," you could develop your voice as a writer without comparing yourself to what your family was doing.

I never set out to be a writer. I thought I was going to be a diplomat. When I became a curator, I wasn't even thinking about writing, but then I wrote a lot. I always thought that was just part of curating, but now I realize, *Not necessarily.* When I made the choice to be in academia instead of being full-time in museums, it was because I realized that I liked writing and I liked ideas and I liked *that* part of the curatorial process. The ideas, the history, the research—finding things out, the detective work.

So, you're in high school, and you're making art and in a milieu of people making art. Then you go to Amherst and find that you have to invent your own discipline. What was that like, and how did you decide to build that path?

Well, even in high school, when you took art history, it was the same: you're reading art history books, probably H. W. Janson, *History of Art,* and there are no people of color in the narrative. Later Janson decides to include William T. Williams—and William T. Williams says, *I will only be in it if you include Henry O. Tanner,* and that's how it starts to change in terms of African American representation in such texts. Other than that, any person of color is very ancient—they're Egyptians, they're Mayans, that's it. So you decide you're going to study art history in college. Is it any different? *No.* What I did was go abroad. In my junior year I went to Latin America, and I studied Latin American art in Bogotá, Colombia. Then I went to California—you could actually study some Latin American art in California at that time. You could study African art, which I did, at Amherst even—John Pemberton was there, a very important Africanist who focused on Nigeria. There were people who were in black studies, teaching about African life or sociology or politics; Asa J. Davis was one. Andrea Benton Rushing, who advised my senior thesis, focused on African American literature. There was also the idea of diaspora, particularly the African influence in Brazil. You could study those things, but you couldn't really study the visual arts. What I did is my own independent studies, and I interviewed artists like Al Loving, Norman Lewis, and Jack Whitten.

What was the purpose of doing those interviews at the time?

To find out what they thought about art. They were right there; I knew they would do it. I could finds ways to get the Latin American piece in school, but the African American piece I think I had to make up by myself. Although there were a few books, including James A. Porter's *Modern Negro Art* [1943] and Samella Lewis's *Art: African American* [1978]. David C. Driskell's *Two Centuries of Black American Art* [1976] was used for many years as a textbook, even though it was an exhibition catalogue.

Does Robert Farris Thompson's *Flash of the Spirit* exist then, or does it come out later?

Flash of the Spirit is published in 1984, so it is later. I still have the first copy that I bought at a bookstore in Harlem, Liberation Bookstore, in the eighties, when I was a curator at Jamaica Arts Center. I did a show called *Deja Vu: Haitian Influence in Contemporary American Art* [1989], and I invited Robert Farris Thompson to be a guest essayist. I had already read the book, and then I ended up studying with him in graduate school.

Right; you go to Yale to work with Robert Farris Thompson. In fact, the wonderful early essay of yours on Basquiat is dedicated, "For RFT," which I imagine is him—

Yes!

I would like to know more about what that experience was like and how influential it was on your approach to writing art history.

Huge! [Laughter.] First of all, he is an amazing writer. He's an amazing researcher also. What I learned from him I think reinforced one of the things that I had learned as a child, which was to always support people. In his class, there was never a "wrong" answer. He

250

may not agree with you—*Well, that's interesting, but what about this?* The classroom was a place to hear all sorts of perspectives on different things, and his classes were always amazingly popular. I was his head teaching assistant for three years, and we had up to a hundred and fifty people in the class. There would be great things going on: you'd have people doing capoeira, you'd have all sorts of people doing guest lectures or concerts in the classroom. He didn't say, *Go see this*, because it was New Haven, not New York. He brought things right into the classroom for you to see. He was one of the first people, along with Arnold Rubin, Doran Ross, and others, who really began to teach African art within art history departments, as opposed to departments of anthropology. Also, he starts really focusing on this idea of masquerade as something that was performative, not just the mask as something that we fetishize. He wrote about differentiating between "masking," which is the dress up, and "masquerade," which is the performance. Those things are related, but they're distinct parts. It's not like you just have this carapace and that's it.

Now, I'm going to tell you his biography: first he goes to law school, then he goes to graduate school for art history. Starting out, he's supposed to be a pre-Columbianist. *Why?* Because you can't study African art in an art history program.

Did he go to Yale to work with George Kubler?

Yes! He goes there to work with Kubler and then decides that he's going to study Africa. Kubler says, *Good luck*, but then he does it. He made himself up, too—it's easy for me to do it, he'd already done it!

Well, the other thing Thompson does is situate these objects and performances as part of a whole metaphysical construct—he doesn't discount their spirituality. I think that that's rare for people writing about art of any sort.

But his project also has a political edge. If you look at some of his early writings from the sixties, he's really mapping African American creativity—which was not generally talked about. He really asks, *How do people make work when they've been enslaved for hundreds of years? Well, this is how we can start to see it* . . . Then he moves away from that discourse about slavery into things that are more affirming. I think he wanted to focus on what was created, not what was unable to be created, because of African American enslavement. He also brings in the rest of the world, because this is a way that you can also narrate what creativity is. I think his whole diasporic push is not denying that slavery exists, but saying, *Let's look beyond that at what creativity is.* Because if you look at some of the discourse around that time or earlier, it was as though black people never made anything. Today, I have a class that goes back to the seventeenth century, but the discourse of the sixties and seventies is that African Americans never made anything of value—they had no history. So what people like Thompson do is intercede in this through research to show us that that's not true. That also allowed all of us who have studied with him a platform to move things further along.

Your dissertation was called "Flying and Touching Down: Abstraction, Metaphor, and Social Concern" [1999]. I would love to know more about all those parts: abstraction, metaphor, and social concern.

The dissertation compared the work of Mexican and African American artists, combining conceptualism and cultural nationalism from the sixties into the eighties. As an undergraduate, I wrote a senior thesis on comparative mural traditions of African American and Mexican artists. I start with the idea that these are already equal things. You have those earlier traditions in the thirties, which are about a cultural nationalist reconceptualization or revalidation of the lives of Latin American and African American people. African Americans are very excited when the Mexican muralists are working in the US, because they recognize, *Here are some people who are looking at their own ancient traditions and then making new art out of them.* In that moment, you can see African Americans looking to Africa as an ancient tradition and making art out of it as part of Harlem Renaissance narratives. They're also "documenting," for want of a better word, the contemporary lives of these people. You see that in the thirties, and it doesn't go away. I revisited it through conceptualism in the sixties through the eighties, thinking about David Hammons and Senga Nengudi in the US and people like Felipe Ehrenberg and also the *grupos* movement on the Mexican side.

Your writing really feels like it has a job to do, which is to create a context and a set up information that didn't exist before. When you take up that task, I think you're assuming a specific responsibility to try and represent where the artists are coming from. And that seems different from what we often call "criticism."

I've never really thought of myself as a critic, actually. I've written maybe one piece for *The Village Voice*—a review of an exhibition at the Studio Museum in Harlem in the 1980s. I don't know if I would call myself a critic because I don't feel that I'm "critical" in that way. I do feel like I'm more of an advocate. Much of the writing I do is in catalogues for artists, which is something celebrating them. That's a different kind of writing than to write a review in a newspaper or a magazine.

When you start working on African diaspora art histories, it's like what Grey Gundaker said in her book *Signs of Diaspora / Diaspora of Signs: Literacies, Creolization, and Vernacular Practice in African America* [1998], and I'm paraphrasing: *When you scratch the surface, it's not that there's so little information. There's so much it's almost overwhelming.* She works in anthropology and was also a student of Thompson. I like that idea. I like that detective work. With *South of Pico*, it took me a while to finish because *Now Dig This!* kind of happened to me in the middle, but I just got so interested in those stories, particularly the stories of black migration. Another one of my heroes is my colleague at Columbia University Farah Jasmine Griffin, who has a book called *"Who Set You Flowin'?": The African-American Migration Narrative* [1995], which discusses how African American literature reflects on black migration. For Griffin, migration is the urtext of African American modernity in the twentieth century. I wanted to understand how that idea was manifest in art, particularly when I realized you just have to go back one or two generations to find that, as Maren Hassinger says in *South of Pico, We all came from the South.* How is this aspect of American life registered in art both as a discursive idea but also in its materiality?

I don't think that makes the writing any more or less insightful than

something with a different purpose; it just acknowledges that it has a different job to do. How do you see what you do as a writer, or the function of being a writer on art?

I write about what I see, what I like, what I think needs to change—there are opportunities to do different kinds of writing in that way. I enjoy writing about people for whom there is very little already said, and so you get to make it up. You think about what the artist is trying to do. How does that relate to what's gone before? Do I think about changing the way art history is narrated? I guess I do.

One thing is that by curating shows, we get to actually see this stuff, which otherwise you might only know from an image or description in a book or archive. One of the great gifts of *Now Dig This!* was just giving people the chance to actually see what this art is, and let the object exceed whatever narratives are attached to it.

That's part of the tradition that I come from. Thinking about these people like James A. Porter—he doesn't start Howard University's art department, but he's one of the important early figures. These people are historians, artists, and curators. They have to do three jobs in order to get all this out there. David Driskell does the same, Samella Lewis does the same. Now, by the time I come along, I can drop one of those—I don't have to be an artist. I was trained as an artist in high school, but I can actually drop it. And the people who are generations after me can actually be only one of those things. It's okay for them. But how can I teach students this history without making the opportunity to show the work? And also, with an exhibition like *Now Dig This!*, it allowed me to go to collections. If you're just writing a book, are you going to have entry to the Whitney Museum of American Art to go into the storage and see their collection? *I don't think so.* But if you're working on a show for the Hammer Museum—*Great, come on in!* And that is the way that students get to see this work. Or even me: with *Now Dig This!*, there was a piece by Noah Purifoy I'd always seen in books as a small, black-and-white reproduction. *Okay, let's go see it.* By the way, it's four feet tall and it's ochre. It's actually not freestanding, it hangs on the wall—you don't know this until you see the object in person. We write about objects sometimes without seeing them because we have no access, but if you see them, like you say, the object always exceeds what's been written about it, particularly in the case of these artists.

When you are working with young historians and writers, are there any tools or recommendations that you have for them about how to write about art or these histories?

There are all sorts of ways you can write about things. There's not *one* way. For me, I think the framing I really value is *context*. I wrote an essay recently about Elizabeth Catlett, who everybody thinks they know. But, for instance, if you look at the context of, in her case, segregation—*How was she making art in the forties and fifties as a woman, and what was that like?* She was also a great writer—in Spanish as well as English, by the way. I think this also goes back to art history's inveighing against biography, but if you're a black person and you're making art in 1942, can you actually go to a museum and see art? If you look at the history of American art and think, *Why does work by Elizabeth Catlett or Norman Lewis look different from some of these other artists? Or, Why are they really still interested in figuration? That's so passé*—there are reasons for that, for what that work was doing for them, what that work was doing for African Americans, and for progressive people in general. To understand that I think you really have to look at biography. Jack Whitten talks about how he never goes to the museum until he comes to New York in the sixties and goes to MoMA. *Why?* Because Birmingham doesn't let black people into its museums, or its general libraries, for that matter. Later, he finds out you can go on certain days, but why doesn't he know that? Because they don't *want* you to know that. Elizabeth Catlett is teaching in New Orleans at Dillard, the historically black university there, and she wants to take her students to go see Picasso's *Guernica* [1937], which was visiting the New Orleans Museum of Art, in a place called City Park. But guess what? City Park is not open to black people. She figures out a way to get a bus to take them right up to the steps of the museum so they don't actually *step* in the park. One of those students is Samella Lewis. What does it mean to be an artist or to study art when you can't have access to the "great" works of art that are supposed to be so canonical and important? Or even just look at something and how it's made? How do you access that?

We are all doing the same thing, we are all writing about art, but there are just different ways in. If you're writing about Mark Bradford or Jennie C. Jones or Hank Willis Thomas, that's different, maybe, because that idea of segregation is no longer such an issue, but what else is happening for African American artists? For instance, Hank Willis Thomas's cousin is killed when Thomas is first starting out as a professional artist. He's like his brother. *Does that not affect you as an artist?* Well, we can talk about it because, *guess what,* the work that he made right after that is all about that. If you don't go back to that fact, then you seem like a really bad researcher. But I don't think it's the only way you have to talk about this art. You can talk about it any way you want, but for me, I think the context of black life is different, and I honor that. If we get into politics today, Black Lives Matter and these movements, they are telling us that black people are being killed exponentially. You're going to tell me that doesn't *affect* artists in some kind of way? Or doesn't affect the materiality of art if you're a black person? In *South of Pico,* I make a comparison between David Hammons and Chris Burden representing the violated body. For the most part, African American artists didn't deal with that violated body in art—because their bodies are getting violated all the time in life.

It's like Judith Wilson writing about black artists depicting the black nude. Do you think your experience growing up with artists predisposed you to see the complexity of the relationship between the art and the life?

Absolutely. Recently I've seen how my mom, Hettie Jones, addresses this in her writing about emerging as a feminist and as a woman artist, in *Love, H: The Letters of Helene Dorn and Hettie Jones* [2016]. What's interesting about it is that us kids really don't figure too much in her narrative. She talks about the difficulties of being a woman artist. I think going forward, those are some of the ideas I'm going to keep writing about. Recently everybody I'm interested in is named Elizabeth—Elizabeth Catlett, Betye Saar, Elizabeth Murray—they all actually have three kids, and all continue to work. They figured out how to continue to make art as mothers. Even if they had a change of medium—Elizabeth Cattlet and Betye Saar both become printmakers until their children are older, and then they both go into sculpture. Interestingly, Elizabeth Murray's work becomes huge; it's kind of the opposite for her. Historically, when we talk about women artists, we really don't want to talk about them as mothers—*We don't talk about it with men, so we better not talk about it with women*. I think actually I'm moving in the opposite direction, because the fact that these women continue to work and be productive with not one, not two, but *three* children—and with Elizabeth Murray, she's making some of her most outlandish and largest work ever—I think we need to really reevaluate this idea of motherhood and art and not be afraid to go there. My thing is to go where people aren't looking. *You're looking at that; I am going to look over here. Why not?*

I was trying to assert a public "I" that
was mostly female. At the time, and even
still, the female "I" is always considered
to be an involuted, self-interrogatory,
memoirist's "I"—rather than an "I"
that's burning through the world.

Chris Kraus (b. 1955) is a writer and filmmaker
particularly known for her first-person fiction in the
novels *I Love Dick* (1997); *Aliens & Anorexia* (2000);
Torpor (2006); and *Summer of Hate* (2012). Her two
books of collected essays are *Video Green* (2004) and
Where Art Belongs (2011). With her collaborator Hedi
El Kholti and her former husband, Sylvère Lotringer,
she is the major engine behind the influential press
Semiotext(e), where she founded the Native Agents
imprint. Her most recent book is the literary biography
After Kathy Acker (2017).

Chris Kraus

In *Video Green*, you have a little essay called "Shit on My Sleepmask" [2001], in which you talk about carrying around three of Kathy Acker's notebooks before they went into her archives at Duke. From that I take it you've been working on *After Kathy Acker* for a long time.

I tend to work on things for a long time, a long gestation period. It's been twenty years with this book—since 1997. *I Love Dick* had just come out, and Kathy died, and the confluence of those two things affected me strongly. I was living in Los Angeles at the time, and Sylvère was coming to visit Kathy as she was dying in a clinic in Tijuana. Even though I didn't personally visit her there, I went down with him a couple times, so I saw the situation. It was devastating to see her life end that way—I don't think there is any possible happy death of cancer at the age of fifty. That kind of radicalized me, and I wanted to write her biography right away. Luckily, I did interviews then, in San Diego, with people she'd known when she lived there in the sixties and early seventies. I talked with Mel Freilicher, and David and Eleanor Antin, Martha Rosler, Len Neufeld in New York—all those early friends, lovers, and associates—twenty years ago, when all the antagonisms, rivalries, and feuds were still fresh in people's minds. I gathered incredible material, but it sat in the closet because I couldn't see a clear path toward writing the book. Did you notice how different the tone of that essay, "Shit on My Sleepmask," is from the biography? Back then I was just wildly empathizing with Kathy, and my first impulse was to write it in a rush of complete identification. That didn't go very far. I hit a wall,

259

and realized that coming so close on the heels of *I Love Dick*, with all of our mutual friendships and associations, there was something a little too incestuous about it, and it would probably be better to just get on with writing another book. So that's what I did.

After *Summer of Hate* came out, I wasn't ready to start another novel. Someone in the UK invited me to write an academic monograph about Kathy. That made the material interesting and available to me in a new way. Suddenly, writing it as a biographically infused critical work, or critical biography, I thought, *Oh, yeah, I can do that! It's not overwhelming*. When I got into it, I realized it was a lot more than a monograph, because I still wanted to go deeper. But the suggestion that I write it from a more distanced vantage of a critical reading changed everything and made it possible: I found working on the book with that distance was, paradoxically, the best way to come closer. You can only identify with another person in the first degree so far until it becomes false. Somehow, reaching back in time through the construction of her work helped me to channel Kathy in a primary and witchy way—to the point where sometimes I'd type "she" but *felt* like I'd typed "I."

Of all your writing, on the surface this book seems to have the least to do with "Chris Kraus" as a character, but I felt your presence while reading it. Actually, some of the descriptions you use for Acker's work seem to mirror your own concerns as a writer, like when you say, "Disinclined toward conventional narrative ... Acker worked and reworked her memories until ... they became conduits to something a-personal, until they became myth." Did writing this book give you a different perspective on your own writing?

Our writing is very different, but of course there are similarities. Like Kathy, I was stumped and repulsed by the idea of writing conventional narratives with made-up plots and invented characters—but then again, so are a lot of people. We each found our own ways. Acker is a much more psychological writer. I've never written about my childhood or family background, and those were the primary building blocks of her work. She goes back to these stories over and over again. My writing draws from real-life events, but it's highly constructed

260

and edited. Unlike Acker, I don't have recurring fugues that migrate between novels. She shares that in common with William S. Burroughs. It could be I'm finished with writing from life, and working on Acker's biography is kind of a bridge to the next thing.

I've wondered about that, because as your books proceed from *Dick* and *Aliens* to *Torpor* and *Summer of Hate*, they become increasingly distanced on the level of form. In the first two, the protagonist is named "Chris," and the narrative is told in first person. In *Torpor* and *Summer of Hate,* what would have been the "Chris" character is now named "Sylvie" and then "Catt," and other characters come into focus.

The real key is that the first books were written in real time, and the later ones weren't. In *I Love Dick* and *Video Green*, everything flows from an account of the real time of writing: *I am sitting here and looking outside my window and the phone rings and it's blah* ... So the writer is the protagonist. In *Torpor*, Sylvie's and Jerome's stories are equally weighted. It's about two people's lives, with their subplots and backstories. I was very conscious of working with tense, and it became a way out of writing in real time. The strange use of tense in *Torpor* was appropriate to the book's subject, historical trauma. I remember discovering the Romanian poet Mihail Sebastian's diary, written during the German occupation, and he writes out this great line by Dante Gabriel Rossetti: "Look in my face; my name is Might-have-been." I remember Sylvère using this strange, "would-have-been" tense, and he mentioned that many of his old friends who'd been hidden as children in France used it also. The *futur antérieur*, a future that's been foreclosed by the past. Tense became the whole structural key for writing that novel.

It's funny, people say my work is *so personal*, but the form is everything. The form is really how I arrive at how I'm going to write and what the book is going to be.

I see your entire body of work as a dissection of our fantasies of "the personal." It makes me think of the early books you edited in the Semiotext(e) Native Agents series, which have been really big influences on me as an artist and a writer—especially Cookie Mueller's

Walking Through Clear Water in a Pool Painted Black [1990], Lynne Tillman's *Madame Realism Complex* [1992], David Rattray's *How I Became One of the Invisible* [1992], and Eileen Myles's *Not Me* [1991]. These are people writing in the first person, but it's not *about* them.

Exactly. The presence of the narrator leads you through other material. The New York School poets did this, and they took it from the French poets of the 1920s, who in turn grabbed it from the ancients. There's a long tradition of first-person narration that has nothing to do with memoir. When I started Native Agents in 1990, I was trying to assert a public "I" that was mostly female. At the time, and even still, the female "I" is always considered to be an involuted, self-interrogatory, memoirist's "I"—rather than an "I" that's burning through the world.

How did that series originate, and how did it evolve?

First, I published my friends! When I got to the end of that list, people arrived through mutual friends and connections. Eileen Myles introduced me to Michelle Tea, and said, *You have to publish this book*, and I did—*The Passionate Mistakes and Intricate Corruption of One Girl in America* [1998]. By 2001, that mission felt finished, at least for me. When Hedi El Kholti joined us at Semiotext(e), things changed. Hedi brought in some classics of gay liberation from France in the seventies, and new international writers like Abdellah Taïa. Since then, we've had a much broader vision of what Native Agents should be. Hedi and I work on that list together, with contributions from Sylvère, who's more focused on theory. What we do now is very particular, although harder to put into words than the initial idea. The books all feel like manifestations of larger issues, as they play out on an individual level. You'll notice we don't publish any domestic dramas about the dilemmas of life on the Upper West Side. [Laughter.]

Early in *Video Green* you say, "Whereas modernism believed the artist's life held all the magic keys to reading works of art, neoconceptualism has cooled this off and corporatized it. The artist's own biography doesn't matter much at all. What life? The blanker the better. The life experience of the artist, if channeled into the artwork, can only impede the artist's neocorporate, neoconceptualist purpose. It is the

biography of the *institution* that we want to read."

I think that's still pretty accurate.

In that sense, writing this biography of Kathy Acker seems almost like an intervention in a certain kind of art discussion.

I don't know. People will always write biographies of writers. My friend Robert Dewhurst is writing an extraordinary biography of the poet John Wieners. Robert mentioned to me, *You can tell on the first page what the focus of the biography is going to be. If it starts with the birth and the lineage of the parents and early childhood, it's probably going to be a psychological biography.* I knew right away I didn't want to do that. Of course Acker's family background and childhood come into play, but the real juice is, *How did she invent herself and create herself as a writer?* So I begin when she's twenty-three, living in New York, keeping her first notebooks and training herself to be a writer.

But you mentioned the role of biography in art criticism. I don't think you need to know an artist's biography in a literal way to consider their work. But you do want to understand their intentions. Looking at an artwork, I'm always trying to penetrate the presence of the artist within it. Behind presence, of course, is intention: *Where are they trying to go? What are they trying to do?* To understand that, you need to situate the artist in place, time, and context. Writing about Paul Thek in *Aliens*, I described his projects and collaborations in a pretty conventional, art critical way, but then came to a point where I began to imagine him in his loft south of Tribeca in the 1970s, looking at his soft, flabby, forty-five-year-old body in the mirror. He wrote about this in his diary, and I leapt into it.

That discussion of Thek was particularly striking. Something I'm always curious about is the persistent problem of what it means to write about other people's lives. What are the limitations, and how do we register them in our writing?

You can speculate. Writing about R. B. Kitaj's paintings in *I Love Dick*, I didn't know anything about him, and we weren't in touch, so I just made up a story, based on what I saw in his work. Now that I'm more of a "professional" art writer, I do things on commission and work in collaboration with the artist. I always try and talk with the person. Sometimes our dialogue comes into the text directly, and sometimes it flows underneath it. I think the artwork itself is always an artifact of a process—and that's why we like it.

I'm always intrigued by the backstory. Writing the essay "You Are Invited to Be the Last Tiny Creature" in *Where Art Belongs,* I set myself up as the group's chronicler—I sort of volunteered for that job. There were dozens of conversations. Eventually, my own point of view enters into it. For example, I was fascinated by the difference between Jason Yates's artworks and most of the others'. Jason had done an MFA at ArtCenter, while the others had come to art in a more naive way. Looking at these works side by side, there's a visceral difference. *What is it?* The difference seemed fascinating to me, and somehow definitive. Even within this level playing field of a collective gallery, the work of someone who declares himself an artist is more powerful than someone who hasn't. A matter of intention, I think. So the chronicle is ultimately pretty subjective.

What is so nice about that as a strategy is that a "chronicle" gives you a structure that allows the story to unfold. Conventional art criticism, like a "review," doesn't often have that kind of narrative pull.

Of course, there's a difference between a long piece like "Tiny Creature" and a catalogue essay. Still, people always make work in a context: not just of their personal, family, and relationship histories, but their choice of peers and their influences. You have to explore that context to really appreciate the work.

That's what I found most impressive about your Acker biography— how sensitively you describe the people around her and the layered dialogue that fed their work.

I definitely wanted to knock out the singular myth of the "great artist" that biography often supports and perpetuates. I was always looking for shared culture, shared influences. Kathy ghosted Catullus in several books—but she wasn't the only one to discover him! He'd been newly translated in the late 1960s, and his explicit, direct, first-person poetry was read pretty widely. Likewise, her use of phenomenology—

she got it from Alan Sondheim, who got it from Keith Sonnier, who got it from Robert Smithson! This doesn't detract from her genius. But it's important to write context into the picture. There's a whole clusterfuck of influence going back decades, generations, and centuries. One of the ways we falsify and mystify the biography of the artist is to believe that their invention is so completely singular. Yes, in some ways it is, and that's what makes it important and interesting, but it doesn't exist in a vacuum. As you say, there was a large group of people talking about ideas then, at a very high level—these ideas were in the air among an extended group of friends in New York and other cities.

"A whole clusterfuck of influence" would be a great subtitle for this book, actually. The other thing that is so brilliant writing a book like this about Kathy Acker is that she herself, through her strategy of incorporating appropriated text into her own writing, already acknowledges and enfolds the complexity you're talking about. This is a detour, but I can't resist: in *Aliens & Anorexia*, the "Chris" character, while making small talk at a party, mentions that she's the great-grandniece of Karl Kraus. Are you really?

I don't know. I'd like to think so. It's possible: my father's side of the family came from the same outside-of-Prague neighborhood that his family came from. Anyway, he's a spiritual great-granduncle.

Like you say, there are very few things about your early life in your books. I'm curious: When did you first started engaging with literature? And what was an important early experience with language?

My father taught me to read when I was three. He didn't go to college, but he would have loved to be an intellectual. He worked for Cambridge University Press and brought books home for us. He subscribed to *The New York Review of Books*. He trained me to be very precocious, so I was always a huge reader. Which is probably why I postponed writing for such a long time—it was so expected. But I couldn't find the right way to do it until *I Love Dick*.

I had very powerful experiences with literature. In New Zealand, I inhaled the writings of New Zealand modernists like John Mulgan, Janet Frame, and James K. Baxter. Reading their books on long bus trips and looking out at the same landscape they were talking about. Reading was always the way I could be most alive. George Eliot's *Middlemarch* [1871–1872] had been a childhood favorite book. One of my first art projects in New York was a performance piece adapted from *Middlemarch*. When Sylvère and I got together, he introduced me to a lot of French literature, theory, and culture.

Can you describe the *Middlemarch* performance?

I was studying with Ruth Maleczech, of Mabou Mines, and this piece was the precursor to my 1980 play *Disparate Actions/Desperate Actions*. Mabou Mines had this brilliant acting idea of "tracking"— using one text as the subtext, completely opposed to the text that you're speaking. The subtext determined your gestures, your moves and demeanor. I used Ulrike Meinhof's famous Stammheim prison letter as the literal text, but was playing Dorothea Brooke under the surface: her walk along Yew Tree Lane when she realizes she's made a mistake by marrying Casaubon. I think I imported that acting idea into writing. The idea of tracking, which probably started with Brecht, seemed incredibly powerful. It made acting seem truer, because in real life it's never *one thing*—it's always this confluence of things at the same time, so to perform that confluence, rather than to pretend to perform a singular thing, seemed genius to me.

How did you explore trying to translate that into writing, the contradictory confluence of a text and subtext?

Maybe not literally, but definitely I feel that each book I've written comes through a "character mask." I guess they'd call it "voice," if we were in an MFA program. But it varies from book to book, and it can take a long time to find it. That's why I don't bang out book after book—so far, every book has come from a different place, and I have to discover who's telling the story, and to whom, and for what purpose.

I reread *Middlemarch* last summer—it's one of my most beloved books. What's so striking is the highly nuanced moral and ethical sense that the characters have, that Dorothea has. There are scenes later in the book where I get an almost an erotic thrill from the *morality* of her actions. I feel like there is similarly an elaborate sense of ethics and

266

morals in your writing, even as the characters are mostly interested in being outsiders. How do you understand the moral universe of your writing?

It's true! My work is so nineteenth century. But the question of ethics has always been important to me. Channeling the Platonists, Simone Weil writes about her search for the Good. I think a lot of the action in my books entails people trying to find their way toward the Good, the right course.

I was fascinated by the point you make about Acker's early books, that they had a secret, vitally important, male interlocutor, and I couldn't help but think of that in relation to *I Love Dick*.

I didn't see Kathy and Alan Sondheim's *Blue Tape* [1974] until years after I'd written *I Love Dick*, but there were strong similarities. Kathy crushed heavily on Alan, and they made a video about it. Definitely writing to "Dick" made it possible for me to become a writer. I'd made half-hearted attempts before that, but it wasn't until I had a real addressee that the gates opened and I felt like I could go on forever. And I've continued writing secretly to a person, or a few people. It's another acting technique—the "silent partner," someone from your own life who you superimpose over your scene partner. And then you use whatever emotion comes up. Acting is super relational, but so is writing. *I Love Dick* is relational in a really direct way, but still keeps that sense of talking to someone.

I asked you about your early reading, but I'm curious about what early important aesthetic experiences you had.

I used to love seeing plays, and would get crushes on certain actors. The empathy loop between actor and audience is incredibly powerful. And then, in New York, I guess it was poetry. Even though I wasn't writing, most of my friends were poets, and I worked for a while at the Poetry Project. I went to the readings, read all the books, and adopted their snobberies.

One of the things that you write about in the Acker biography is the elaboration of her public persona. On the one hand, she probably rightfully believed that fame was necessary for her to make a living, but it also seemed like it took a toll on her reputation.

That was the dilemma. She knew that her work was extremely difficult and noncommercial, but she wanted to be commercially published, she wanted to be famous. So, reinforced by her editors and publishers, she constructed an elaborate, flamboyant persona that she believed would carry her work to a larger audience. And in some ways it did. But it turned out to be a devil's bargain, because an image becomes frozen in time. She was known as the mideighties postpunk princess, and by the nineties it began looking dated. The new Penguin Classics edition of *Blood and Guts in High School* [1984] does not have a glamour photo of Acker on the front cover. It's a more distanced and haunting image of an anonymous figure. Twenty years after her death, people can start separating Acker's image from her work. Even the first round of scholarship was very fixated on her image. Of course, at the same time, Acker loved her own image. She loved dressing up and being photographed. She wasn't exactly a victim.

How have you related to your own increasing notoriety, or the image of "Chris Kraus" in the world?

I'm trying to duck it.

Well, unlike Kathy Acker, you're not taking photographs of your back tattoo while wearing Victorian lingerie. But because your work uses "Chris" as a character, it seems unavoidable.

I've always loathed the idea of art stars and media icons. It mystifies culture, makes it much less accessible. And it's gotten worse, carried over into the literary world. There's a deluge of coverage for a few heavily promoted titles, and then a next round of stories on the phenomenon—coverage of the coverage. I think people should be as transparent as possible about how this happens. And about how artists and writers actually support themselves. The adaption of *I Love Dick* for TV makes the "Chris Kraus" character unavoidable. I'm not going to recant it, or trash people for reading things into the book I'd never intended. But I need to live without being locked into that image. Images are antithetical to the present, and what writing does is give you the present.

Throughout your writing, there are people taking care of other artists' work after they die. That happens very literally in the essay "Posthumous Lives" [1999], on Penny Arcade and Jack Smith, but it recurs in different ways, for instance in your writing about Paul Thek. Writing a literary biography seems like another form of that. I'm wondering what you think we owe our friends' work when they are no longer in the world?

Starting the book, I put the Voltaire quote "To the dead we owe only the truth" on my corkboard. Corny, maybe, but that's what I was going for.

I've spent a lot of time with your film *How to Shoot a Crime* [1987], which includes footage of Sylvère interviewing two dominatrixes, Mademoiselle Victoire and Terence Sellers, because I'm writing about Sellers, who died last year. It's such a terrific little portrait of her.

Yes. There's a great scene toward the end when, after talking for a long time, they get into a spat. Sylvère asks Terence, *Why do you have to be right all the time?* and Terence says, *Don't you? Twenty years from now there's only going to be this videotape of me when I'm thirty years old, talking.* At that moment, you see her taking herself seriously as an artist in a way that escapes him.

Am I right in thinking that your interest in BDSM was artistic and intellectual before it was something you explored sexually for yourself?

It was more of a sexual and social interest.

How did becoming involved in S&M change your relation to the early avant-garde writing and theory that valorized it? Or the transgressive writing you published?

I didn't go there. Maybe someday I will, that kind of delirious and sensuous description—Acker went there, and that's the part of her work that I relate to the least. She became involved in writing about "sacred sexuality" in this the kind of Bataillean way. For me, S&M was more practical. When I moved to LA, Sylvère and I were still involved—we were still legally married and each other's most intimate relationship. I wasn't looking for a husband, and there didn't seem to be a lot of arenas allowing for the kind of sexual friendship in the same way that S&M does. Especially in the LA art world! People were so primitive about relationships—what they meant and *should be*—which was always terminal, leading toward moving in together and getting married. In the straight world, there are not the same nuances that you have in gay male culture of overlapping friendships and sexual relationships. BDSM didn't lead to intimate friendships, but at least within the brackets of "play," the contact was extremely connected— it wasn't like having drunken bar sex and never seeing the person again. There was a real exchange and listening and intimacy that doesn't usually occur with other kinds of casual sex. People who are drawn to it tend to be really smart but crippled in other ways—often being a dom is a brilliant compensation, being extremely present in one arena when you can't be present in others. It also helped me revise my presence and image. I was trying to get out of the "serious young woman" role that I write about in *I Love Dick*, toward a sense of myself that would include sexuality—it's so problematic for someone who grew up as a feminist. Turning sex into a game or character mask was incredibly helpful. The doms I would play with were engaged in this project of making me more conventionally femme—the costumes, the hairstyles, demeanor. It was more palatable to me as a game. Really, it was genuinely helpful, a kind of therapy. Although lately, I've started thinking about the aspect of grief that's involved in S&M. I was already working on *Torpor* when I started having these adventures. I was dealing with grief and historical trauma, and many of the people I played with then had experienced recent grief, recent losses. I'm sure that has something to do with it . . . that S&M is an indirect means of working through grief.

That's fascinating—and makes sense to me emotionally. I really liked the way you describe S&M as "emotionally high-tech" in your essay "Emotional Technologies" [2002]. There is something about playing out those power relations directly, as opposed to masking them behind other social and institutional structures, that can be very liberating.

I agree. Many people are tourists in that country, but some become natives.

270

One of the things that absolutely drove me crazy was the notion of pluralism that dominated art criticism in the 1970s—*anything goes*. I was completely obsessed with torpedoing the idea of pluralism.

Rosalind Krauss (b. 1941) is a critic and historian who reoriented the discipline of art history by incorporating structuralist, poststructuralist, and psychoanalytic theory into an analysis of modern and contemporary art. She began as a critic for *Artforum* in the sixties, in conversation with Clement Greenberg and Michael Fried, before breaking away to cofound the journal *October* with Annette Michelson in 1976. Her books include *Terminal Iron Works: The Sculpture of David Smith* (1971); *Passages in Modern Sculpture* (1977); *The Originality of the Avant-Garde and Other Modernist Myths* (1985); *The Optical Unconscious* (1993); *Formless: A User's Guide* (with Yve-Alain Bois, 1997); *The Picasso Papers* (1999); *Bachelors* (1999); *Perpetual Inventory* (2010); *Under Blue Cup* (2011); and *Willem de Kooning Nonstop: Cherchez la femme* (2015). She is University Professor in the Department of Art History and Archaeology at Columbia University.

Rosalind Krauss

Can you can recall an early important aesthetic experience that made you conscious of visual pleasure?

I think the most important aesthetic experience I had growing up in Washington, DC, was having The Phillips Collection available to me, which is very beautiful. It was in a house, and upstairs they had bedrooms, and one was filled with Paul Klee paintings. I would sit on the rug in the bedroom and look at these Klees—it was just fantastic.

What were you responding to in the Klees?

The way that each one was about something very specific and very different—I just found the range in them so beautiful.

How did you start writing?

I started as a journalist. I was the head of the newspaper in my high school, and then at Wellesley College I was the editor in chief of *The Wellesley News*. That kind of percussive writing was very important to me. Every Wednesday, I would go to the printers and write headlines to fit the columns. I always felt that I was a writer, but I became more of a writer as I wrote art criticism, which I started very early with *Artforum*.

One thing that is interesting to me about coming out of journalism is that precision and concision are vital.

Absolutely.

When you went to Wellesley, did you already know you wanted to study art history?

Actually, I wanted to be an artist. Then, in the course of working in studios there, I realized that I didn't have it, *at all*. At that point I got interested in art history. When I finished at Wellesley, I went to Harvard, and Michael Fried was in my class. We became friends, and he recommended me to Jim Fitzsimmons, who was the editor of *Art International*, and then eventually to Phil Leider, who was editor in chief at *Artforum*.

Writing art criticism then was a really wonderful experience. You'd wander into an exhibition that you had to write about, and it might have been somebody you didn't know a *thing* about, and you'd have to just figure it out. The first example of this was that I was assigned to review a Donald Judd exhibition. I was just stymied by it. How to deal with this obviously incredible work that I didn't have any vocabulary for, and that I didn't have any kind of context in which to put it? I had to invent my own context. I found it really good to go cold into an artist's work and not know anything about it, and have to respond to it in some way that would be relevant.

When you arrived at Harvard, what was it like?

The major professors were Sydney Freedberg, who was Renaissance, and Seymour Slive, who was Dutch baroque. For me, the most important person was John Coolidge, the director of the Fogg Museum of Art, who ran this incredible seminar where we traveled around with him, through Albany, Utica, and Buffalo, visiting collections.

Was it spent looking closely at objects, or at the museum spaces themselves?

Well, we went to see collectors and dealers. In the case of New York, we went to Christie's and things like that. Partly it was sociological, because what we learned was how Coolidge presented himself to all of these people. I mean, it's like he *entertained* them; he showed us that you can't just go into somebody's collection and sit there like a dumbbell. You have to really give them something in return. It was really great.

How did you first encounter Clement Greenberg?

I met him at Harvard; Michael Fried introduced us. He was very friendly and open and receptive, so when I would go to New York to do my critical work, I used to see him every afternoon and we'd have a drink together. I got to know him very well. He said this wonderful

274

thing to me that I recorded in *The Optical Unconscious*—I asked him what he thought of some essay by Barbara Rose, and he said, "Spare me smart Jewish girls with their typewriters," which I felt was *so great*, and I never forgot it.

Did you feel that you were also a smart Jewish girl with a typewriter, and that this was a way of putting you in your place?

Yeah, of course I did.

During the seventies, all the young critics who came up under Greenberg—you, Fried, Rose—were trying to distance themselves from Greenbergian thought in different ways. But aside from Greenberg, what else was going on in criticism that you were reacting against?

One of the things that absolutely drove me crazy was the notion of pluralism that dominated art criticism in the 1970s—*anything goes*. I was completely obsessed with torpedoing the idea of pluralism. It seemed to me, and I think this is something that Wölfflin says too, that not everything can happen at the same time. "Sculpture in the Expanded Field" [1979] was part of this, and "Grids" [1979] was too. I think my need for structuralism had to do with finding a way to demonstrate the inevitability of one, and *only one*, possibility.

How have the pleasures and possibilities of aesthetic experience shifted for you, from the time of you looking at those Klees as a girl to today?

It never did. It was really constant. What it made possible was my very close relationships with certain artists. I had close relationships with Robert Smithson and Richard Serra. They really liked the way I intuited the recursive drives in their work. It was Richard who recommended me to curate his first exhibition for The Museum of Modern Art. I don't remember when exactly—'86? When we talked about it, I said to him, *My nonnegotiable conditions are that you do your lead pieces in lead and not steel and that you display your work in one per room and no more.* Because I experienced a big Richard Serra exhibition at the Centre Pompidou where it looked like an iron shop—you saw one work through another. It was just a mess. His need to reconstruct his lead pieces in steel is absolutely a misunderstanding of the importance of those works.

How did you understand critical work as related to or distinct from the historical work that you had done? Because it seems the reason you would be allowed to write a dissertation on David Smith at that time was that he had died and it was a bounded body of work.

Harvard said the only way I could do a dissertation on Smith was to do a catalogue raisonné, which was a really incredible job. I did a catalogue raisonné, and in 1977 Garland Reference Library just photographed the pages and published it as a book. Some of the pages have these funky photographs that I made myself. Now the estate of David Smith is going to do their own catalogue raisonné, which sort of puts mine in the junk heap of history. I'm glad I did it. It brought me very much closer to the work. Of course, then there was that horrible scandal of some of the trustees allowing the paint to be removed from Smith's work.

Which Greenberg was sanctioning?

He was a trustee.

Was that officially the cause of your split?

Of course. I had to say who the trustees were in the piece I wrote about it in *Art in America*. The trustees were Clem and Robert Motherwell, and I just had to say that they obviously had given their permis-sion for stripping the paint off those sculptures. I remember meeting Betsy Baker for lunch at a Japanese restaurant; she had on a raincoat, out of which she pulled the slides of the stripped sculptures. It felt like, *Do you want to see dirty pictures?* It was great. And I told her of course I would write the piece, and Greenberg was furious. He never was able to appear in public again without artists saying, *How could you have done this?*

What do you think is so appealing or powerful about his criticism that it still figures so large, even if often as a straw man?

Greenberg was so incredibly lucid. He never said anything without giving an example, and he had this incredible sense of the specificity of the work in terms of the examples. I was confronted with this criticism by Tom Hess or criticism in *ARTnews* that was just breathlessly

276

effusive, that didn't make any real cogent sense or argument. For me, Greenberg was an incredible departure from that. In a way, I was sad that Greenberg and I had this split.

Leo Steinberg seems like such a luminous example of someone who came at these questions in a very different way. It seems like you were comfortable aligning yourself with him.

Absolutely. I don't remember exactly what the connection was, but he called me up when he was writing this essay "Other Criteria" [1972]. He gave it to me to read, and I said, *Leo, you cannot attack Greenberg if you misrepresent him*, because he was saying things about Greenberg that just simply weren't true. He was grateful that I helped make his argument stronger. We became very good friends. I used to have supper with him twice a year. We would have dinner at his house; he would order in either Indian or Chinese food, and he would smoke like a chimney. We would play Scrabble. Of course, he would always win.

What was it that Steinberg did that was different than the formalism of Fried or Greenberg?

Take the idea he developed of the flatbed picture plane—he found these terms for alternatives to the teleological modernist discourse. They always seemed so incredibly *apt*. One of Leo's favorite words was "diaphane." When he came to London from Germany, where his family immigrated after the establishment of the Soviet Union, he didn't speak English. He walked around London with a copy of *Ulysses* [1918–1920] in his pocket, and "diaphane" comes from the very first of chapter, where he's walking down the beach and looking out to the sea—the "ineluctable modality of the visible." That seemed to encapsulate Leo's sensibility as a writer, almost as a poet.

When you and Annette Michelson started *October*, what was your vision for it, as a way of writing and thinking about art?

When we left *Artforum*, in 1976, we decided to start our own magazine. The way we were able to do this was that Jaap Rietman had this wonderful bookstore in SoHo, and he agreed to buy out the first issue. That gave us the money to start.

The way we came up with the name *October*—John Coplans, the editor in chief of *Artforum* at the time, was interviewed by *The Village Voice* when we left, and he said, *We've purged the formalists.* When Eisenstein made the film *October: Ten Days That Shook the World* [1928], he was ordered to reedit it to remove Trotsky from the narrative. So he was purged too.

One of the things John Coplans was totally allergic to was art theory. At one point I wanted to publish Michel Foucault's *"Ceci n'est pas une pipe"* [1973]—*No, no!* He didn't want any of that. When we started *October*, our first idea was to publish the kinds of essays that had become anathema at *Artforum*, trying to characterize various movements in contemporary art. One of them for me was video, and that's why I wrote "Video: The Aesthetics of Narcissism" [1976]—*We can't just pretend this isn't happening!* So in that first issue we published Foucault's *"Ceci n'est pas une pipe"* and my essay on video.

How did you make the decisions around the format—that there would be no images, for example?

It comes from our horror at *Artforum.* One of the things that happened at *Artforum* was that the editorial space was shrinking because it was all taken up by images, advertising—you know, the way it is now. We thought, *We are not going to have that.* Our policy is to give writers as much space as they need.

The way the design of the magazine happened—we had to get the text to the publisher on a certain day, and we didn't have a design. I stayed up all night copying the design of this very beautiful magazine *Oppositions*, which was published by Peter Eisenman's Institute for Architecture and Urban Studies and designed by Massimo Vignelli. I just copied *everything* from Vignelli—the running heads, the width of the text, the footnotes, the whole thing is absolutely ripped off from him. Then we sent it in.

How did you meet your husband, Denis Hollier?

I was in Paris working on an essay for an exhibition at The Museum of Modern Art, *"Primitivism" in 20th Century Art* [1984]. I was writing about Giacometti, and my friend Yve-Alain Bois suggested that I read Hollier's book on Bataille, *La prise de la Concorde* [1974]. I read it and I thought it was *so brilliant*. Then a friend of mine, Leo Bersani, called me and I said, *Leo, I have to tell you, I've just read this book by your friend and I can't believe how brilliant it is!* He said, *You can tell him yourself, he is in Paris.* Then Denis called me and we arranged to have lunch—that's how we met.

In addition to your personal relationship with Hollier, your engagement with Bataille, especially around his journal *Documents,* really opened a new direction in your thought.

Absolutely.

How would you describe that change—what did it represent for you, what did you want to figure out there?

Well, as you pointed out, in my development within this whole modernist scope, I was becoming more and more disenchanted with the teleology of modernism, which moved toward some sort of formal perfection, which I thought was simply not true—it certainly was not true of Giacometti, where the whole idea of the movement from the vertical to horizontal was crucial. That's how the idea about Bataille entered what I was doing, with the whole notion of formlessness, which offered a different path through modernism.

The Optical Unconscious has an incredible structure that alternates between an italicized personal narrative and an art historical argument. How did you develop that way of writing?

That was really a decisive change in my writing. Since *The Optical Unconscious* was an attack on an idea of the history of modernism as teleological, I thought I had to abandon the teleological narrative at the level of writing. I thought of several examples where this abandonment worked. One of them was Denis Hollier's work on Bataille, which has these extraordinary digressions. And then also the writing of Roland Barthes, which is very important to me. Barthes has constant recourse to these little parenthetical emendations and enlargements, which I think came out of his engagement with Proust, who did endless editing to *À la recherche*. That was my first absolute self-conscious attempt to change the way my writing worked.

The other thing is on the level of form—I'm thinking about what you've described as the "paraliterary" in both Roland Barthes and

Derrida. How did Barthes influence this aspect your work?

In *Writing Degree Zero*, Barthes talks about his dislike of what he calls classical narrative, which he thinks of as omniscient narrative. The opposite, which he supports, is narrative of the first-person present— diary or journalism—writing that does not know what the ending is. Then the reader and the writer are on the same side of the page. Neither has more knowledge of the end than the other. That was for him the ideal of avant-garde writing, because it broke with classical narrative. The importance of what he called zero-degree writing remained very important for me, and I think that this drive to talk in the first person in some of my art criticism comes from that.

To write in the first person is also a question about authority, and a question of to whom the person is speaking.

I think only Leo Steinberg, in terms of art historians, really thought about who he was speaking to. Most art historians assume they're speaking to classical humanists; they don't really have anything beyond that to think about. I'm trying to think about who Roland Barthes thought he was speaking to—I think he was speaking to the students in his seminars, who had the same investment in the idea of the avant-garde as he did.

Is that who you're speaking to in your writing?

Always. I always am speaking to people who want to break with what Barthes would call the *doxa*, that which goes without saying. The drive to find new models has never let up with me.

One of the things that is useful about *Under Blue Cup* is the attempt to make sense of the "medium," which you say "exfoliates outward from the binary of *memory* opposed to *forgetting*." I found that immediately resonated as true. I'd love to understand more about how you came to that.

I lived through the whole of postmodernism, which I found endlessly depressing. This drive to forget the whole history of the medium and the idea of the medium itself—to sort of trash it. What was important for me were these artists for whom the idea of the medium remained crucial for their work. I thought, *Basically, what happens with these artists is that since their medium, like painting or sculpture, has been absolutely paralyzed by critique, they've had to invent a new medium.* Like Ed Ruscha inventing the car as his medium.

There's a way in which you have to give something a shape in order to remember it, so to talk about the medium as a foundation makes sense.

It's what Ruscha calls a rule.

I was fascinated by your book on de Kooning. I don't know if you experience it this way, but I felt like it was a return, in your writing, to the kind of close looking that characterizes your formalist period. What led you to write that book?

Well, I had written my senior thesis at Wellesley on de Kooning, which I didn't think was very good, frankly. The literature on de Kooning then was so prolix. I'm thinking about Tom Hess—just effusive. Then I was at Wellesley and floating into the art library came *Art and Culture* [1961], and there Greenberg laid it out for me in "'American-Type' Painting" [1955]. That was an absolute revelation.

When The Museum of Modern Art had its de Kooning exhibition in 2011, a close friend of mine asked me to take her through the exhibition, and I did. As we walked through it, I was giving her this running lecture, and all these people were following us and listening. Then I began to think, *Well, this is pretty good, what I'm saying. I should write a book.*

Looking at *October* in the eighties, there seems to have been a very clear antipainting position, and I wonder how you related to that at the time—obviously your major work was on photography and sculpture.

I have a sort of natural leverage on the issue of painting. Part of it is that my experience of twentieth-century art was grounded in the National Gallery of Art in Washington. I used to go there with my father, and one of the things I found so beautiful were the Georges Braques—which I thought were amazing in terms of the layering of the various forms of facture. Painting was for me a kind of anchor into what was new about *new art.* I never really felt this sort of denigration of painting that was part of the seventies' and eighties' relationship to modernism. For me that was simply not possible, because painting was so crucial.

The last question I have is about the role of Duchamp. It's almost like the story of postmodernism is a parable about one interpretation of Duchamp eclipsing another. It seems like even within your writing he functions differently in *The Optical Unconscious* than in *Under Blue Cup.*

I have to tell you, and this is not really answering your question, but I think anybody who really gets interested in Duchamp goes *crazy*—

I've noticed that. [Laughter.]

They flip out. Duchamp is the conduit to psychosis. I think this is true for Thierry de Duve, who cannot get out of this compulsion to relate everything to Duchamp. In *Under Blue Cup*, I'm not very charitable to Duchamp—I think he was a very malign influence on the history of modernism.

It's interesting to consider the multiplicity of someone's work, and that there is one vein of interpretation of Duchamp that might have a negative impact, but which doesn't retroactively invalidate the original work.

People who go insane think of Duchamp as creating a justification for jettisoning modernism—it's not that I think it's a wrong interpretation, just one we shouldn't pay much attention to.

As I wrote, I was trying to be sure that I hadn't done any of the things the patriarchy had always done, which was hard to avoid. It's the same thing with racism—it's almost impossible not to end up doing some of the things you've been conditioned to do, even if you are deeply conscious.

Lucy Lippard (b. 1937) is a writer, activist, and curator closely associated with feminist art. Her chronicle of the rise of conceptual art, *Six Years: The Dematerialization of the Art Object from 1966 to 1972* (1973), is an indispensable touchstone for the period. In the 1970s, she became the most prominent critical voice arguing for feminism within the art world, cofounding the collaborative journal *Heresies: A Feminist Publication on Art and Politics* in 1977. Her criticism is collected in the books *Changing: Essays in Art Criticism* (1971); *From the Center: Feminist Essays on Women's Art* (1976); and *Get the Message? A Decade of Art for Social Change* (1984). She has written the monographs *Eva Hesse* (1976) and *Ad Reinhardt* (1981), as well as the influential books *Overlay: Contemporary Art and the Art of Prehistory* (1983); *Mixed Blessings: New Art in a Multicultural America* (1990); *The Lure of the Local: Senses of Place in a Multicentered Society* (1998); and *On the Beaten Track: Tourism, Art, and Place* (1999).

Lucy Lippard

When did you first realize you wanted to be a writer?

When I was around twelve. Before that, I wanted to be a professional
rider—because I was horse crazy and worked at a stable. I didn't have a
horse, but I imagined I had a horse. Then I thought, *No, maybe I want to
be a writer, not a rider.* [Laughter.] My mother was a great reader, and there
were always books around. I read voraciously and unselectively. I read
Moby-Dick [1851] much too early and never really got it, but in eighth
grade I got the high school prize for a story. I bought a tennis racket
with the twenty-five bucks. It may have occurred to me then that I could
make a living at writing. Reading just *leads* to writing. Isn't that more or
less how you came to writing—by reading?

Yes. Reading a lot.

I think that's what does it. Then, if you're no good at it, you figure
that out eventually and do something else.

Did you study writing at Smith?

No, I never studied writing. I didn't want anybody telling me what
to do about what I liked best. I had an English teacher in high school
who was a classic New England "old maid"—and I hate that phrase, but
she was the prototype of it—and she was wonderful. She could tell I
loved to write, and she told my parents. In a funny way, her recognition
made me think, *Oh, yeah, I do love to write.* At Smith, I took one course
in creative writing with another wonderful woman named Evelyn
Page. She wrote detective stories under the pseudonym Roger Scarlett
with her partner Dorothy Blair. She limited us to one violent death per

semester—that was the easiest way to wrap up a story. But that's the only time I was ever in a writing class.

So then were you studying art history at Smith?

Yeah. Studio art and art history—you could do them together there. I had George Cohen as a teacher—not a well-known artist; vaguely a sort of social realist. He praised something I did. I got all excited and came home to my parents and laid my art out on the floor and told them, *Maybe I shouldn't be a writer, maybe I should be an artist.* And they looked at it and said—*Writer!* [Laughter.] That sealed it.

After you graduated and moved to New York City, were you still writing fiction?

Yes. I got another prize for a story when I graduated from college and thought I was hot shit. I'd get up really early and write for a while before going to work—basically awful, sarcastic love stories aimed at *Redbook, Cosmopolitan,* or *The New Yorker.* I thought I'd make a living at that and then do something "serious"—write the Great American Novel. Soon I got very involved in my own weird life on the Lower East Side and got to know some artists, mainly those who also worked flunky jobs at MoMA. I don't think I did much fiction after a while. I was having too much fun living on my own for the first time. And I was having no luck whatsoever publishing with the magazines, for *obvious* reasons. [Laughter.]

How did you start writing criticism?

Well, that was unintentional. I think almost every art critic is unintentional. Have you ever run into someone who said growing up they always wanted to be an art critic?

No!

Exactly. Once I'd gotten to New York, I immediately wrote some reviews and sent them to *Arts Magazine,* where Hilton Kramer was the editor. Mind you, I knew *nothing,* but I wrote these little reviews and he wrote me back. He was very sweet, one of the few things I'm fond of about Hilton, because we later went head-to-head. He said, *You're a good writer, but come back when you've been in the art world a little while.* In other words, *You know nothing,* and he was totally right. I felt so rejected that

286

I didn't send anything in again for three years. I wrote something for *Art Journal* on Max Ernst and Jean Dubuffet. By the time I *knew* what I was talking about, I ended up at *Art International*, which was the best magazine then.

What was the process of being edited like when you started writing for *Art International*?

I don't remember being "edited" much, since I *hate* being edited. Jim Fitzsimmons, who was the editor, was in Switzerland. I remember writing to him once to explain that I missed the Anthony Caro review I was supposed to do because I'd just had a baby, and he was horrified to realize I'd been going around pregnant to galleries representing *Art International*—apparently that is not what Fitzsimmons wanted his critics to look like! I'd only met him once. We had dinner one time when he was in New York. I lucked into that job because Max Kozloff recommended me. He and Barbara Rose did the "New York Letter," where you'd round up lots of shows, and you could sort of work it your own way, make the reviews into a more cohesive article. Barbara quit, and then Max quit, and I ended up with the "New York Letter," which was a real lucky move. I think that was probably the time I figured out I might as well do this art criticism thing.

Your early writing on Max Ernst is very interesting in retrospect, because collage plays such a large role in your later work. It seems like his way of collaging images into a kind of disjointed literary narrative was an important influence.

I wanted to write my master's thesis at the Institute of Fine Arts on fantastic landscapes from the seventeenth century to the present, but my professors discouraged that because it was such a huge subject. Ernst was going to be part of it, and then I got to work on his MoMA show, when I was freelancing for the museum after I left a job at the MoMA library, and it made sense to concentrate on him. You're right: collage has been an obsession and a medium for me. The Dada and surrealist idea of juxtaposition of unlikes as the source of a new reality probably underlies much of my work and even my cooking—stews being my favorite. I always say that collaboration is the social form of collage. So, in a way, is street activism, as we're often introducing a foreign, even hostile viewpoint into a public context—never so much as today.

When did you start feeling like you were a "critic," like you accepted that as an identity or a role?

I didn't call myself a critic for long. I always disliked the term, because I was an advocate for artists, not an adversary. I don't recall any particular model; I just read the art magazines and went to a million shows and got to know some artists. Dore Ashton was writing for the *Times* when I first got to New York, and she was something of a female role model. John Canaday fired her for "knowing" artists—*biblically*, I assumed. We were both married to artists. Similarly, I was always most influenced by the art and artists I hung out with. I didn't write about things I hated. Well, every now and then I did—Jules Olitski comes to mind. I kind of went after the Greenbergians, because they hated what I was involved with. I was called an art critic, but I always just called myself a writer. Now it's interesting because they call us "art writers"— they don't say "critics" as much anymore.

Your early essays, gathered in *Changing*, have a lot of close formal argument, which is different than your later work.

That was pretty common then. In a funny way, when you look back at it, it was like I was teaching myself how to look at art. But I don't think it was particularly original.

Do you think that kind of formal attention came into your writing because that was important to the artists, or was that just the critical discourse at the time? It sounds like you were taking cues from the artists more than what anyone was writing.

I was always pro-artist because I was well aware that what I knew about art I learned from artists—not from criticism. I got a certain amount from just sitting around with artists. I had a painter friend named Hank Pearson, who you probably never heard of, but who was fairly well known at that point and was an interesting guy—son of a haberdasher from North Carolina. He always wore a suit and tie. He helped me paint the ceiling of my loft one time, and he never took his suit jacket off. I remember going to the Met with him; he had one long fingernail and he'd point it at a detail in a Raphael or something: *See how that works, and see how the paint works here*, and so forth. Going to the Met with an artist was far better than anything I'd ever gotten in an art history class. I always pass the monographs I write by the artist for corrections first—before the publisher. I was recently accused by a catalogue editor of "kowtowing" because I quoted the artist so often. I've *always* done that. They know more about the work than I do, and this artist was exceptionally eloquent.

Could you tell me about meeting Ad Reinhardt and the process of writing the catalogue for his Jewish Museum exhibition in 1966?

I don't remember how I met him—it may actually have been in Paris—but he was an icon of the minimalist/conceptualist gang I hung out with. I guess I wrote a review and he liked it. I asked Rita, his wife, years later, after he died, why he chose me to do the Jewish Museum catalogue, and she said he just wanted to get away from the usual suspects and I seemed to be a fresh voice. We shared a certain iconoclasm, I suppose. And then he was just such a character—that's what I liked about him, aside from his art. He was constantly bitching and whining about the art world and about his colleagues, but with such wit.

Reinhardt was such a terrific writer, and I think his writing had a big influence on the minimalist and conceptualist generation as well. Like Robert Smithson's writing—what was your relationship with him?

Bob and I knew each other, we hung out with the same people, but I was never in any of those social scenes. I've never been good at that, or I didn't want it or need it or something. I mean, I'm *social*, but not into "scene" things. Bob went to Max's Kansas City every other night, and he'd bring a question to be discussed; he'd come ready to talk. I was there very rarely, but I love to argue, so I'd argue with him. I remember a ridiculous argument we had where I was for *infinity* and he was for *finity*. You know, I liked him, but I always said he was a more important writer than he was an artist, and that pissed him off—for good reason, I guess.

You told him that? I think it's true.

I think I wrote it. Though I do agree that *Spiral Jetty* [1970] is iconic, for many reasons.

One time at a party Bob said to me plaintively, *Why do you always argue with me?* And I said, *I thought you enjoyed it as much as I do!* [Laughter.] Who knew then that he was quite as important a figure as he's become. Then Sol LeWitt and I helped make Eva Hesse important after her death. I mean, she was as important as all those guys, but if we hadn't done that book on her work, we might have lost her—Sol made me do it.

Your monograph *Eva Hesse* was important also because it was the first major work you did on a woman artist, right?

She died in 1970, and I became a feminist a few months later. I always thought that she would have become more of a feminist than she was at the time, though she had read Simone de Beauvoir and recognized every minute of it. I mean, her experience was that she was *beautiful* and *vulnerable*—a very appealing combination—and smart and a great artist and so forth. Sometimes I'm not sure where we would have gone with our friendship after feminism. By the time I was writing that book, I was a total feminist, and I had written a lot of articles on women in the early seventies. I remember at that time I got into a real fight with my old and valued friend Max Kozloff while he was an editor at *Artforum*, because I wanted to write a series of monographs on women and he called them "featurettes." However, Max was open to change, and Joyce Kozloff, who he was married to, made sure of that!

One thing that is so impressive about the Hesse book is seeing all these aspects of your thought being worked out in their fullest form: the serious formal and conceptual intelligence joining with the feminist perspective. It's also interesting because you and she knew each other so well personally.

She even babysat for me. I say to my son, *Tell people Eva Hesse was your babysitter!* We were all really devastated by her death. Sol LeWitt was her dearest friend, and he immediately went to her sister and said, *We need to get a book done.* Her sister said, *Fine,* and we got the estate to pay me, because I couldn't afford to do it for free. It was difficult to write that closely about a friend, and I didn't want to write about her neuroses or her lovers or whatever—it had to be about her art. In the writing I was always having to move away from personal things I knew, which was hard sometimes.

Did you interview a lot of people about her for that book?

Yeah.

I'm interested in how after people die, you get these funhouse versions of them from other people— it's both sanitized and too dramatic at the same time. How did you experience that?

I was very aware of not making a Sylvia Plath–type mythology about Eva, as I think I said in the introduction. As a feminist, I was extremely sensitive to that. But then here was this beautiful young woman who was a great artist who died. I hope the pathos isn't too obvious.

What did feminism mean at that time in relation to writing about art?

It meant being pissed off at the way women artists were being and had been treated. I mean, there was a lot more to it than that, but in terms of writing, that is where I was at. As I wrote, I was trying to be sure that I hadn't done any of the things the patriarchy had always done, which was hard to avoid. It's the same thing with racism—it's almost impossible not to end up doing some of the things you've been conditioned to do, even if you are deeply conscious.

Your style as a critic is incredibly clear.

Hopefully—that's what it aims for.

But then there are moments where you do very experimental things—like the catalogue for the show _Information_ at MoMA in 1970, which begins with the long note: "The following instructions were sent to Kynaston McShine in lieu of an Index to the _Information_ catalogue, for which the necessary information did not arrive in time. When I realized it would not, I decided to substitute some absentee information arrived at by chance. I opened a paperback edition of Roget's Thesaurus to _absence_, hoping to get some ideas. The book had been given to me, second-hand, by a friend in December 1969; I had not opened it until this point (Wednesday, April 15, 1970, 3:30 PM, in Carboneras, Spain)."

I was so amazed MoMA let me do that. The same with the

experimental text for the Duchamp catalogue. It was Kynaston, who was at that point a dear friend—before politics got in the way—who asked me to do both of these. That was all coming out of conceptualism, which really gave me room to breathe. It was changing people's heads, and it was a group of people I could really play with.

How did you reconcile your extremely straightforward pieces with this more experimental stuff?

Well, the experimental stuff was "creative"—that was the part of me that was going to write fiction, and the other stuff was how I was making a living, and of course enthusiasm about the art, if not about the art world.

So the impulse you had to write fiction shifted into the experimental pieces?

You could say that. By 1970, I thought I should give fiction one more shot. I sold some prints I'd bought on time in the sixties and spent a few months in a Spanish village, in a house that belonged to the French critic Jean Clay, who I'd met when we juried a museum show together in Buenos Aires in 1968. Carboneras was then a tiny fishing village, and I lived there from March to June with Ethan, my five-year-old son, as I wrote the first version of my novel *I See/You Mean* [1979], along with that piece for *Information*—which gives you a sense of what I was up to. The experimental novel was an unreadable conceptual artwork—descriptions of photographs and an index with clues to the "plot." When I got back to New York it evolved into a more feminist novel—still pretty unreadable, but great fun to write. Trouble is, I really didn't enjoy *reading* experimental novels, and I finally decided that I didn't want to spend my life writing something I wouldn't want to read myself. *I See/You Mean* was published but never distributed by Chrysalis, a feminist press. Years later, it sold out at Printed Matter, and last year it was translated into Spanish as *Yo veo/Tú significas*.

I did write another novel in 1977, 1978—really more for the pleasure of writing than any expectations of publishing it—when I lived on a farm in Devon for a year, with my then twelve-year-old son. It was called *The First Stone* and was about the role of politics in the lives of three generations of women. My friend the novelist Esther Broner said the dialogue needed a lot of work, and I ended up putting it away, because I'd gone on to something else, though there was some interest in publishing it.

Charles Simonds and I did an artist's book called *Cracking* [1978] in the late seventies that has finally come out in English, after being published in German years ago. It was images of his Little People's dwellings and landscapes and my abstract erotic narrative about a woman archaeologist who falls for an earth spirit emerging from the land and the architecture and gets literally sucked in. Finally, around 1988, after a wild rafting trip on the San Juan, I started another novel—called *Upstream*, I think—but it was awful, and with that the fiction urge dried up.

In 1967, you wrote: "Formalism's specificity did a good deal to clear the air and to bring the critical method closer to the antisentimental approach of the art, though its major drawback was a tendency to eliminate from its evolutionary systems an increasing amount of the better art being done." I imagine that was directed not only at Clement Greenberg, but at the critics who were extending his project, such as Michael Fried. "Art and Objecthood" was published about five months before you wrote that. I'm interested in how you interacted with that group.

Once I went to a lecture Greenberg was giving at MoMA. I went with Donald Droll, who was a very close friend, a gay gallerist at Fischbach who was the reason I got to do *Eccentric Abstraction* [1966] there, as well as the reason Eva Hesse showed there. Anyway, at this talk, Greenberg was going on about his stuff, and he was a good speaker but very authoritarian, which always gets my back up. I raised my hand during the question period and asked, *Can you explain what you mean by "quality"?* And he said, *If I have to tell you that, I have to tell you the difference between red and green.* And I said, *Rosenberg and Greenberg?* And everybody laughed, because those were the two critical poles at that point. Phil Leider was sitting a few seats down from me, and later he wrote something to the effect of, *So embarrassed to be anywhere near that woman!* Anyway, I went

293

up afterward and I introduced myself to Greenberg, and I said, *I'm Lucy Lippard, and I'd still like to know what you mean by quality.* And he said, *Oh, you're Lucy Lippard; I thought you were a schoolteacher from Queens.* I said, *No, and I'd still like to know what quality is.* Greenberg said, *I can't talk to you now, but I'm heading to a party up at Larry Rubin's, if you'd like to come along.* Now, Donald wanted *nothing* to do with this—*I'm not going up into that snake pit!* Nobody wanted to go with me, so I went by myself to wait for the bus to head up to the party, because by that point I had the bit in my teeth—I thought, *It's time to get this Greenbergian monkey off my back.* I was standing at the bus stop, and Greenberg and his pals came out to get in a taxi, and he said I could ride with them. In the cab, *nobody* spoke to me. When I got to the party, *nobody* spoke to me. So I looked around Larry Rubin's house at all the paintings, and then I went home. I never got near him. That really freed me up on some psychological level, because he was an art-world god at that point—*Greenberg this and Greenberg that.* He had great scorn for minimalism and conceptualism; God knows what he thought about feminism. A friend of mine ran into him in Canada and Greenberg told him, *The art world is in such terrible shape that people like Lucy Lippard can be taken seriously.* So my friend rushes back to tell me, and I was *flattered!* [Laughter.] That group was something else. They were vicious face-to-face. Once Kenneth Noland told me I had mean little eyes and everything I wrote was beneath contempt. [Laughter.] This was all prefeminism, but when that came along I was ready . . . Later, Hilton Kramer wrote that at one point, I was going to be an important art historian, but then sadly I "fell victim to the radical whirlwind."

Were there other writers that you were not necessarily competitive with but felt an affinity for?

Not very many, except conceptual artists were all writers, and, in that sense, yes. I could play with them, and sometimes we'd do things together. But that's part of my authority problem: I've never had a mentor, or studied what I should have. Of course I read my colleagues and think, *Oh, that's great.* Certainly I read every art article and went to some thirty shows a week and endless openings for twenty-five years—

294

I was steeped in this stuff, paid my dues.

I'm interested in the formation of Printed Matter in 1976 from that minimal/conceptual/feminist scene, all of which entailed a lot of writing and documentation.

Well, Printed Matter was ten years after conceptualism really started. Again, it was Sol who was doing these artist's books that his dealers would use to promote his work. They were come-ons to spend big bucks on a sculpture, but he saw them as equal works of art. And we were seeing other artists doing similar stuff. Seth Siegelaub, who I had lived with for a while in the early seventies, had his publishing project International General, and he promoted artist's books too, so I was very into that, and Sol just said, *Let's do something.* We got Walter Robinson and Edit DeAk—she was a mess, but very smart and a good writer—they came over and we brought them in. Sol was seeing Pat Steir then, and she was an important participant; she had been a book designer. It was just a matter of finding a vehicle for these things. They weren't traditional art books, so bookstores wouldn't take them; they weren't art and they didn't sell, so dealers wouldn't take them. So, Printed Matter started in a one-room office on Hudson Street, in the same building as Artists Space and the New Museum. But Sol was the impetus, because he was the one making artist's books, and I was an advocate.

Around the same time, you helped found the collective Heresies, which, from 1977 to 1993, produced the journal *Heresies: A Feminist Publication on Art and Politics*. How did it help shape your work?

We all have different memories of Heresies's origins. My memory is that I was at Joyce Kozloff's kitchen table. I think we were alone, but other people remember being there too. Anyway, Joyce and I were talking—this was I think 1975—and we felt it was time for another move in feminist art discourse; that it needed to be more intellectual and more political. We thought there should be a voice and a space. The magazine was going to be the voice. And Mimi Schapiro was the advocate for the space—a school like the Woman's Building in LA. I was very close to Judy Chicago, but I never knew Mimi particularly.

When she got to New York, she took me aside and said, *We are the leaders.* And I said, *I'm not a leader—feminism means collaboration to me, and I love collaboration.* So she and I never really got along very well. Also, she had some kind of problem with lesbians, who were and are some of my best friends. Anyway, Joyce and I had a meeting, and this bunch of women got together, and for about a year we had endless open meetings about what we wanted to do. It finally formed into about twenty or so people. Out of that, nine of us were Aries—I'm one of them—which means bossy, noisy people. [Laughter.] I wanted to call it "Pink," but luckily I think it was Mary Miss who came up with *Heresies* after a Susan Sontag quote, and there turned out to be a British journal called *Pink.*

Heresies had a different audience than anything I had written up to that point. I don't think it changed the writing itself very much, but it made me a lot more relaxed—giving me a sympathetic, if contentious, base from which to take off. At *Heresies* I didn't have to worry about "mainstream" editing. By the late seventies, I knew I was a good writer—though I never had any illusions or even the urge to be a "great" one. The form wasn't much up for grabs, but the content was new, and that came from daily ongoing conversations and readings with other women whose experiences were different from mine. Of course, this started for me in 1970, but continued to be eye-opening through the decade. Some of the other "heretics" were more intellectually and politically advanced, and I learned a lot from them.

I've always thought of *Heresies* as having a strong lesbian presence.

It did. Harmony Hammond was a founding member, and she did the issue "Lesbian Art and Artists" in 1977 and *A Lesbian Show* at 112 Greene Street in 1978. Now we live across the creek from each other in New Mexico.

You said Miriam Schapiro was weird about lesbians, and I wonder if it was a point of contention within your feminist art world—I don't know how you identify, but I think most of your romantic partners are men.

They've all been men, for better for worse. I always thought it would be lovely to be a lesbian—didn't happen. [Laughter.] I've had friends who've tried to *convince* me. [Laughter.] And people always *thought* I

296

was a lesbian. Marcia Tucker and I both did this at least once: during feminist lectures some guy would jump up and say, *You must be a dyke!* and I'd say, *Damn right!* So I guess that got around.

One of the things you've done a better job of than most people is being straightforward about how your personal and romantic relationships relate to your work, as though it's just factual and not a big deal— which to me is the most intellectually honest position anyone could take.

There was a time I thought about making an art piece: a stack of transparent sheets mapping affairs and friendships and other relationships between everyone in the art world, all laid on top of each other, overlapping, so to speak. [Laughter.] Once someone said to me—and I think it's true—that you could always tell who I was with by my work. For instance, you had the Bob Ryman period, where I was writing about minimalism and painting. Then John Chandler, coauthor of "The Dematerialization of Art" [1968]—he was a student of analytic philosophy, and that part of the essay came from him. And Seth Siegelaub, which was conceptual art. Harmony Hammond jumped me at one point when *From the Center: Feminist Essays on Women's Art* came out, because one of my experimental fictions in the back of the book, which was sort of sexy and feminist, was dedicated "For Charles" because I was living with Charles Simonds, whose very sensual landscapes were definitely another influence on my work, especially *Overlay*. Harmony said, *It's a feminist book and you dedicated this thing to a man!* I think I fall for people because they know about things I'm interested in. For the past nineteen years, I've been with a lefty social anthropologist raised in New Mexico, and my last three books have been about the archaeology and history of New Mexico and land use.

I want to talk about *Mixed Blessings: New Art in a Multicultural America*, which is a book that describes itself as being about "the ways cross-cultural activity is reflected in the visual arts, what traces are left by movements into and out of the so-called centers and margins." Was it through the work you were doing with *Heresies* that you became interested in the problems of what was then called "multiculturalism"?

Not so much *Heresies* as the general climate in the 1980s, and the political work I was doing with Political Art Documentation/ Distribution and others. I asked friends from every ethnicity and gender whether I should do that book, and they all said yes—*Throw her to the wolves*. I'm glad I did it. Of course at times I put my foot in it—that's inevitable. My grandfather was the last white president of an all-black college in Mississippi and my mother worked in what they called "race relations" in Louisiana in the 1950s, so I was raised with an old-fashioned antiracism. Howardena Pindell, who was and still is a close friend—we have the same birthday—called me a racist at one point, and from then on I knew that if I was going to work on "multiculturalism," as it was then called, there'd be times that would happen and times I deserved it.

What was the process of doing the research for *Mixed Blessings* like? There are some well-known names, but many are interesting artists I'd never heard of, and they are from all over. It seems it took a lot of travel and primary research around the country.

Yes, but I was already doing that. When the book came out, a MoMA curator said to me, *How do you find all these people?* And I said, *Well, you know, there is the American Indian Community House. There is the Studio Museum. There is the Asian American Arts Centre. There is the Museum of Contemporary Hispanic Art and El Museo del Barrio—all in New York City— that's where you find all "these people."* They were everywhere; it's just that to most of the art world, they weren't on the radar. And because of my politics, I knew about all of them, and I was interested in what they were doing.

How did you start working on *Overlay: Contemporary Art and the Art of Prehistory*?

As I mentioned, I was living with Charles Simonds at the time, and originally we were going to come out to the Southwest for a year— we'd saved some money and we figured we could live very cheaply in northern Arizona or New Mexico, where we'd first come together in 1972. Anyway, Charles got a DAAD Fellowship in Berlin, but I wanted my son to go to school in English and I wanted to be out in the country, and there was none in Berlin in the days of the wall. Through a whole series of marvelous coincidences, I found a cottage on a farm in Devon. Then we went back and forth and spent vacations together, but Charles's work was definitely one of the reasons the megaliths in the English countryside made such an impression on me. Well, that and land art generally, because these prehistoric megaliths *were* earthworks. I wrote about outdoor art and public art from the early seventies on, so it was an interesting extension of that. An artist neighbor told me about them, and I wandered up onto the Dartmoor in the fog, and there was this line of stones going off into the distance. It was recognition, and love, at first sight.

Overlay also seems like an ingenious solution to the problem of your writing postfeminism, as it was about art that no one owned, art that had some collective or social function.

Right. It was also my "goddess" period. My present partner hated *Overlay*. When we first knew each other, he gave me a few off-prints of things he'd written, because we were both writing about Native Americans and photography when we met, and in one of them he talks about this crude and unfortunate book by Lucy Lippard called *Overlay*. I ran into him and said, *Remember this?* [Laughter.] Ever since, if somebody comes up to us and says, *I just love* Overlay, I nudge him. [Laughter].

Your parents must not have messed you up as a kid. You seem to have a healthy ego, for people to say such horrible stuff to you all the time and for you to just roll with it.

Actually, people don't often say horrible things to me—it's just that when they do, it's hard to forget. [Laughter.] I was an only child and a wanted child, and my parents were intellectually interesting and encouraging. My father was very proud of what I did, but sometimes just horrified—like when I was living on the Lower East Side and sharing a bathroom in the hall with a Puerto Rican seaman. Or the Bowery bum I brought up to Maine to meet my parents, or the risqué puns I used in a *Village Voice* piece about feminist sex workers.

You have a tough skin.

I'm eighty now—I've lived through all of this. I don't think I was that tough in the early days. I don't hang on to hurt feelings. I just get angry. Which has served me well.

In a way, *Overlay* seems like the opening of the whole later part of your writing life, which is much more concerned with landscape and the environment.

Yes. I wrote the book on place, *The Lure of the Local*, after spending time in the West and then moving to New Mexico. I thought I should practice what I preach, so I started doing the local stuff. *Overlay* was definitely the door to all of that. I was always trying to get *out* of the art world—escape this and escape that. I still give a lecture on conceptualism, feminism, and political activism, called "Escape Attempts." But I never really escaped except when I was backpacking, camping out, or wandering around the countryside and finding megaliths or petroglyphs. There was no art world there.

What does that tell you about what art is?

I love saying that we need to expand the definition of art, and certainly social practice and a lot of eco art has expanded it. *If an artist does it, then it's art*—that always made sense to me. But when someone says to me, *Your criticism is art*, I say, *No*. Anything a critic writes or a writer writes is *writing*. Because that's what I am. I'm not trying to be an artist. Art does keep expanding. I often quote Rick Bass, who said something like, *The activist is the artist's ashes*. And I say, *Out of those ashes rises a new definition of art*. I love the idea that art is all over the place. I originally wanted to call *The Lure of the Local* "All Over the Place," and my publisher said, *It's a little too close to the truth*. [Laughter.]

How do you see the environmental work you've been doing as related to your earlier art writing?

Frankly, unless I'm asked, I don't think much about my "earlier" or "later" work at all. I just do the work. I wrote a few odd little columns for *Studio International* in the early seventies, and in one of them I said something to the effect of, *No art has ever moved me as much as nature*. So that sensibility was always there. I've always loved being outdoors, mucking around in boats, and since the early seventies have hiked and camped. So the environmental was a thread all along.

300

After I started spending time in the West and finally moved to New Mexico twenty-five years ago, I got an entirely different take on "landscape" and am now more interested in "land use." Today, when I'm lecturing on my most recent book, *Undermining: A Wild Ride Through Land Use, Politics, and Art in the Changing West* [2014], I have to keep reminding myself that this is an art audience and to go easy on the seductive statistics. With my other books, I've lectured on them while they were in process—never after publication, when I was sick of them and off on a new tangent. But with this one, I'm still babbling about it, because the issues are continually evolving, and they are different in every geographic area, so I can almost write another chapter each time. I'm doing a talk in Missoula next week and found the recent special election there grimly fascinating, as well as the advent of Secretary of the Interior Ryan Zinke, who's from Montana, and his threats to public lands.

I was immediately interested in *this* place—Galisteo, New Mexico—when I first saw it in the late 1980s and came out to visit Harmony Hammond in the early nineties. I'd ask, *Where's the book about Galisteo?* It's a well-known place that nobody knows about—famous because all of the Pueblo ruins in the Galisteo Basin. Finally I got to Eric Blinman, an archaeologist and the director of the New Mexico Office of Archaeological Studies. He was writing a book on this area, but finally said, *You might as well go ahead and write it, because I'm never going to get time to finish this.* I'd been researching for years, and he became my mentor on the archaeological part of *Down Country: The Tano of the Galisteo Basin, 1250–1782* [2010]. He probably doesn't agree with some of what I said, but he really kept me from making a total fool of myself. I got two history prizes for it.

Just visually, it's a really beautiful book.

That is because of my friend Ed Ranney. He has photographed Peruvian archaeological sites for years—Inca ruins, beautiful stuff. He has a sensibility that makes something out of what looks like nothing in ordinary images. This landscape is hard to photograph, and archaeologically there are often just a few stones and earth mounds left.

I met Ed through César Paternosto, who wrote a wonderful book called *The Stone and the Thread: Andean Roots of Abstract Art* [1996]. He brought Ed to meet me in New York, and when I moved out here it turned out he lived right across the basin. Recently Ranney did a beautiful book of photographs with Yale called *The Lines* [2014], about the Nazca Lines in Peru, and I wrote the text. I like working with photographers. I wrote the text for another friend—Peter Goin—in a book on Chaco Canyon.

That connects again to your commitment to collaboration. There is an aspect of your work that is not just what you've written, but the interplay you've orchestrated in the images and texts in relation to each other.

It's nice that you saw that. I don't think most people do. It's so sad now with Powerpoint, because I used to really love putting two slides side by side for lectures—I redid them every time, and I could say something new with the juxtapositions. Two images look awful in Powerpoint—too small. Now I just have one image and it pisses me off.

You mean back when you had two slide projectors side by side?

Yes, with two images next to each other—*big*! It was such fun playing with the pairs, and what you could say that way.

Collage appears in different iterations throughout your work. You'll put together different kinds of texts—quotes, things you've written, different voices—and then add captions, extended captions, sidebars, marginalia. It's the same with images: there are images that are "art," and then images that are "not art," but these inform the art. So when you talk about collage, especially when you get to a book like *Mixed Blessings* or *Overlay*, it clicks into a holistic work—those books almost feel like image-text knots.

I've always liked what feels like the *impossibility* of writing about images, and I always welcome the chance to mess around with form in ways that try to address that. I used to think that I wrote differently when confronted with different kinds of art, though I'm not sure that's true anymore. In my experimental fiction, I was trying to make photographs act as "readable" paragraphs in a narrative, but I never figured that out. Writing parallel to the art, or collaborating with it, is what I've been trying to do, and it's certainly more fun than just acting alone.

What's interesting about your work as a whole is how much it covers and evolves while at the same time being remarkably consistent and coherent.

I always like change. I get bored easily. It doesn't bother me if someone says I'm illogical—so what? Long ago I wrote something about criticism called "Change and Criticism: Consistency and Small Minds" [1967]. Nor am I a theorist. I always say, *I like ideas, but theories are like ideas with hardening of the arteries*. I know that sounds pretty anti-intellectual. So be it. When I'm asked about my "methodology," I just say, *One thing leads to another.*

It's like that thing where if you get
up close enough to something, it
starts to blur. Now, our tendency
would be to back off a little bit to
refocus, and what I'm saying is,
Let's ride with the blur for a little while.

Fred Moten (b. 1962) is a poet and theorist whose
book *In the Break: The Aesthetics of the Black Radical
Tradition* (2003) explores the sonic and aural lineages
of the black radical tradition. *The Undercommons:
Fugitive Planning & Black Study* (2013), written
collaboratively with Stefano Harney, set the terms for
contemporary discussions on the fate of the university
and has become a key text in both art and pedagogy
circles. His book of essays *Black and Blur* (2017) charts
his sustained engagement with contemporary visual
art. Among his books of poetry are *Arkansas* (2000);
B Jenkins (2010); *The Little Edges* (2014); and *The Feel
Trio* (2014). He is a professor of performance studies at
Tisch School of the Arts, New York University.

Fred Moten

Maybe we should start with your early experiences of music and sound. When did they first enter your consciousness?

In early childhood. My mom really loved music, and my father did too. They both loved it, thought about it, and made all kinds of interesting critical formulations about it. I just grew up in a house like that, in a neighborhood and a general social milieu where music was important. Kids had their own well-developed musical tastes—we all bought records and talked about the music that we loved. I can't remember when it wasn't part of my consciousness.

Where was this?

Las Vegas.

What did your parents do?

My mom was a schoolteacher.

And your father?

When I was young, my father worked for the Las Vegas Convention Center—he was a laborer there, I guess he helped set up exhibits and cleaned. He always had two jobs. He was a really hard worker, worked as a bus driver and a porter in the casinos. My mom was the first of two people in her extended family to go to college. She became a schoolteacher, and I think she had a real calling for it, but it was also sort of a limit, a horizon, for black women in the midfifties. There was no one with much formal education in my father's family—he went up to the ninth grade. Because of the presence of the hotel casinos and also Nellis Air Force Base and the Nevada Test Site, and because Las Vegas was a union town, people who were so-called unskilled labor could still get decent jobs, enough to buy a house—maybe a better way to put it is, enough to *lose* a house. There were a lot of people who were recent migrants from the South, so even though I grew up in Las Vegas, the part I grew up in was like a transplanted town from Arkansas.

At what point did your intellectual and creative relationship with language emerge?

I think skill with language was very important in the community I grew up in. There were guys who could play basketball, and they got a certain kind of respect. There were guys who were *cool* in some general way. And then there were guys who could just *talk*, and, in particular, talk *about* people—you know, playing the dozens or whatever—and they got lots of respect. It was an extremely verbal youth culture. We would sit around and talk about each other all the time, make fun of each other, and mess with each other. That's not such an unusual thing, but I think what was particular to it was there was a recognition early on that some people were skilled at it, so in that sense recognizing linguistic skill was an early thing.

A lot of times I get annoyed at the way the term "privilege" is used in certain discourses, and part of it is because some take "privilege" to be an absolute term when it's a relative term. They usually just mean "money." I grew up in a working-class community—we didn't have a lot of money—but in terms of a preparation for a life of paying attention to language and music, it was extraordinarily privileged. There couldn't have been a better place to grow up to prepare me to do the kind of work that I do.

What did you study in college?

It was 1980 when I went to Harvard. I really grew up in the seventies—the Black Arts Movement and the Black Liberation struggle were part of the milieu and felt immediate for me in an intense way, and I went to college thinking I was preparing myself to become a part of that. I think I actually declared a double major in sociology and economics. I had to take one of the big required courses called Social Analysis 10, which was really just an introduction to macroeconomics, and it had a "radical" section where you'd read a little bit of Marx, along with Malthus and Smith and Ricardo and Mill. I took a class in agricultural economics, and I had this not fully developed sense of trying to prepare myself to join the third-world revolutionary struggle. But between playing football and all this other political stuff, I just didn't have time to go to class. So I flunked out, and I had to go home and work for a year, and that's when I got much more into literature. When I came back to school I decided I'd be an English major instead. One of the classes I flunked was an expository writing class, so I had to take it again in summer school. My teacher was a woman named Deborah Carlin. She was important for tipping me over the edge and into studying literature, because when I went back I didn't know quite what I was going to do.

When did you start writing poetry?

I had this friend in grade school called Robert Shearing. We used to take popular songs and make sort of adolescent dirty lyrics out of them—this was when I was maybe twelve. We actually had notebooks where we would write them out. So that was probably the first time. I think I came to Harvard with some poetry I'd written in high school. I wrote a lot the year I was working when I flunked out, too. When I got back my second year, I applied for *The Harvard Advocate*, which is a long-standing literary magazine, and I got on, and that was where I met Stefano Harney—he was on the magazine too. Also, I took a class that year called Modern American Poetry from Helen Vendler. I disagree with a lot of what she says about poetry, but that was a very important class for me, because I saw that aside from the initial difficulty, I could read it, and also because she set an example for what it is truly to love the poetry one loves. And then the other big thing is that Stefano, in his freshman year, had an expository writing teacher named William Corbett—

The poet! Right, I noticed he gets thanked in all your books.

Bill is a dear friend and mentor. And not just for me. If anyone ever really writes a genuine, authentic history of late twentieth-century American poetry, he would be at the center of it, not only because he's a great poet in his own right, but because he was at the center of the social world from which it emerged, both in New York and in Boston, where he lived for so long. I'm definitely one of his kids.

He published your book of poems *Arkansas* with his press, Pressed Wafer. Did you also study with him?

I met him at a bar in Cambridge with Steve Harney. He gave me a copy of this wonderful book of his called *Columbus Square Journal* [1976], which I still have. I never took a class with him, but I went to his house for dinner, a lot—like all the time. I met Michael Palmer at his house, and Lee Harwood—all these folks. All of a sudden this world of what they used to call postmodern American poetry was not just in a book for me, it was at Bill's house, and I became a part of that world.

You articulate the relationship between Amiri Baraka and Frank O'Hara in your book *In the Break*, which makes a lot more sense to me now, thinking of you emerging from that Bill Corbett context.

Well, I knew Baraka from the bookshelves of my house growing up, but I didn't know that he had such a fundamental and important place in this American experimental poetry tradition. I learned about that, and all of a sudden Baraka was this person who Bill knew and had stories about. So, it was like being introduced to him a second way, from a different perspective. Bill gave me my copy of *The Autobiography of LeRoi Jones* [1984]—a lot of stuff came back to me through Bill. So all these things started to converge, and I experienced them as part of the same general phenomenon, as opposed to separate phenomena.

Baraka occupies a central place in *In the Break* and your explication of the black radical aesthetic. What does he represent to you, and how did you approach the discourse around his work?

My original approach to him was to somebody who was just a fundamental part of what I would come to call, by way of Cedric Robinson, the black radical tradition—that is how I knew him. And then I became aware of how important Baraka was within the context of this experimental poetic tradition, which had become important to me by way of Bill Corbett and under Stefano's influence—it was a slightly postadolescent college thing, but we lined ourselves up with those poets. We were the Creeley-Duncan-Olson people, as opposed to the Lowell people, you know. I remember Vendler would give lectures about her contempt for Pound and the Poundlings, and we were the Poundlings—we made that move.

The Pound puppies!

And it was a move that Baraka turned out to have made himself. There's an amazing moment in his autobiography where he's in the air force reading *The New Yorker*, and he starts crying—*What the fuck does any of this have to do with me?* It was not long after that he discovered Allen Ginsberg and they began to correspond—Ginsberg was from Newark too, and offered another way of thinking about art that in certain ways was more akin to the kinds of political aspirations that were already there for Baraka.

There was another strain that I was interested in: my sophomore year at Harvard, Barbara Johnson, the great literary critic and theorist, came from Yale and was the person given the task of introducing literary theory, which had long been resisted in the English department at Harvard. There were other people doing theory there at the time, like Susan Suleiman, but Johnson had a certain force behind her because she worked so closely with Derrida and had translated *Dissemination* [1972], and all of that. She taught a course called Deconstruction the second semester of my sophomore year, and that was a very important class for me. It was the first time I'd read Derrida, de Man, Saussure, a little bit of Heidegger. Of course, it turned out Baraka had been intensely reading Western philosophy in the midsixties, particularly Heidegger and Wittgenstein. So again, Baraka was at the convergence of all these things that I had been interested in: music, experimental literature, radical black politics, philosophy, and literary theory—he was there for all of it, so he was the model for me. Also, what I admired about him was that he never stopped; he kept moving and changing and thinking through things. And then there were things that were problematic: anti-Semitic formulations, which he would later be the most critical reader of, the complications of his sexual politics, particularly around queer stuff—all of that for me was rich, interesting, and important.

When I developed in my own thinking it always felt like wherever I'd gotten, he'd already been there first.

So you had a very long and deep relationship with Amiri Baraka through his work, which you wrote about in *In the Break*, but you also must have met and interacted with him a number of times. I'm interested in what it means to write not just out of the knowledge of what someone has done, but from an experience of who they are.

I don't think I could go so far as to call it a "personal" relationship, but it got to the point that he knew who I was. I wish it would have been that. And if it wasn't that, I'm sure it was more a function of my reticence about that kind of stuff—you know, I have certain heroes, but it takes me a while to muster enough courage to actually try and talk to them. But I think I see what you're getting at. When you read someone very closely and carefully, really immersing yourself in their work, it's more than just a relationship with a book. That is a personal relationship too. There are certain writers that if you read them enough, you begin to feel a different kind of closeness. I never met Shakespeare or John Donne, but my relationship with them is more than merely literary. With Baraka it was that, too, but at a higher level of intensity.

***In the Break* charts a specific path through the black radical tradition that terminates with Adrian Piper, but there is nothing really "visual" in the book—aside from a luminous moment where you talk about Beauford Delaney. It is really a sonic and phonic argument. With *Black and Blur*, there is a lot more engagement with visual art, especially contemporary art. In fact, you mention an important early experience that you had at the Fogg Museum of Art with a Renoir. I'd like to understand the story of your relationship with visual art, and why that Renoir was important to you.**

I mean, I love visual art. And I also really love art history, as a discipline—when I say that, I mean to say that, like any other discipline, one has a love-hate relationship to it, because it's got all kinds of blindnesses and exclusions and brutalities. What I love about reading art historians is that they have real talent for looking at stuff closely, and I like to read them talking about what they're looking at closely. It's not like I have those skills—I don't. Those are skills people learn, and you do develop your own way of looking over the course of time, and a lot of that just comes out of repeated looking. With the Renoir . . . I mean, Harvard is an evil place. Part of the way that evil manifests itself is that they just own a tremendous amount of shit. It's unfair. And it should be broken up. But you're there, and you take advantage of it—sometimes against your own inclinations, and sometimes just by accident— they've just got so much. I wandered into the Fogg one day. Like a lot of nerdily inclined undergraduates, I had a period of being interested in Van Gogh self-portraits, and they have a good one there. But what killed me was a Renoir: *Gabrielle in a Red Dress* [1908]. I just decided to go there two or three times a week to see that painting. I started reading about it, to understand how he did it, and the thing I was fascinated by was the way Renoir used color—it wasn't that the first impulse was a representational one, or an impulse toward portraiture per se, but that it was a way of experimenting with color, with how a shape or form might be composed out of color. Not only was it the painting that I loved—the particular tones of her skin and the relation between her skin and the dress—but I loved that it gave me insight into *how* artists make art—something deeper than just wanting to make a picture of somebody.

You talk about the "irreducible phonic substance" of Beauford Delaney's paintings; when I look at those paintings, I'm pierced by the intensity of their color. It strikes me that a lot of what you describe as the "aurality" of these images, that part that exceeds language, correlates to color within the visual field. The essay you wrote on Chris Ofili moves in that direction.

This will be something of an impressionistic, jumping-around kind of answer: I remember watching a documentary on Elvin Jones, the drummer for John Coltrane's great quartet. It was later in his career, and at one point he's playing the drums and starts talking basically about his experience of synesthesia. He hits the ride cymbal and says, *See, for me that's yellow.* In the course of writing *In the Break*, I was reading a lot of stuff on synesthesia—there was a way that what I wanted to do was link up synesthetic experience with this other kind of cognitive experience I was fascinated with: what Wittgenstein calls "seeing aspects," when you see something and then it turns into something else. It's essentially just the duck/rabbit phenomenon. Of course, Wittgenstein would say that it doesn't turn into something else—it's the same thing, you just see a different aspect of it. So, I was thinking, *What if there was something within the general sensual field that operated in a similar way to this seeing aspects?* Instead of saying, *First it was a "duck" and then it was a "rabbit,"* you would say, *First it was a "duck" and then it was a sound.* The reason why I'm thinking of Elvin Jones in relation to Beauford Delaney is that I'm thinking about a very particular abstract painting by Delaney, which is a kind of study in yellow, and it's a very thick impastoed yellow—

He's the patron saint of yellow!

For me, Beauford Delaney is always connected with the sound of Elvin Jones's ride cymbal. And if I were to think about describing that effect in terms of a particular word, not only at the level of meaning but also phonically, it would be "shimmer." There is *shimmer* in Beauford Delaney's painting in the way that there is *shimmer* in Elvin Jones's playing. And for me that shimmer is totally bound up with what Samuel R. Delany calls "the motion of light in water." When I hear that phrase, "motion of light in water," it's connected to a sound. And also, because it's a *motion*, it becomes a question about movement. In a way, I feel like what I'm doing is a kind of reverse engineering, so to speak, of what immediately shows up as a synesthetic experience. You know, it requires a linking together of all these folks.

There are some people who have written about sound and visual art, and it usually manifests itself along two lines: as a representation of "sound" or representations of occasions in which sound is being made in some conscious way. Or they'll talk about it as a certain terminological overlap, with regard to questions about tone, et cetera. But what I was really trying to say is that when we experience something visually, the other senses are not turned off. And similarly, when we experience something aurally, the other senses are not turned off. That our experience is part of a general synesthetic—but I didn't want to call it "synesthetic"; I think I used the term "holosensual"—field. One way to think about it is as an earlier version of what I now call "blur"—and that does come back to the piece I wrote on Chris Ofili, in a way totally influenced by Glenn Ligon's writing about Chris Ofili.

To make sure that I'm clear, when you use the term "holosensual field"—that refers to the intermeshing of all of our perceptual faculties?

What I was trying to say in the book, and what I'm still trying to say, is that it's impossible to try and make a separation between what I was calling the "ensemble of the sense" and the "ensemble of the social"— and that notion of the ensemble of the social is directly out of early Marx, "Theses on Feuerbach" [1845]. I want to say that there's a sociality of the senses, which is a formulation Marx makes in the "Economic and Philosophic Manuscripts of 1844": *When the senses become theoreticians in their practice.* I was trying to talk about that, as something that is actually occurring in our encounters with art, and in particular with black art. That goes against the grain of a whole lot of commonplace formulations people make about aesthetic experience, and about the place of aesthetic experience in the formation of the subject.

The other part is that this is within the context of my attempts to work through Derrida, particularly in relation to Saussure. I was working against the grain of this movement that can be traced back to Enlightenment discourses on language and music and is present in a powerful way in Saussure, which is the notion that a universal science of language requires what Saussure calls the reduction of the phonic substance. Now, if you're interested in black art, there is no reduction of the phonic substance. That is not necessary and it's not possible. Or J. L. Austin talking about the necessity of bracketing out what he calls "mere accompaniments" of the utterance—well, I'm listening to James Brown, and the most interesting shit in James Brown is the "mere accompaniments" of utterance—and I want to be able to talk about them.

Bringing it back to contemporary art, you could have subtitled your recent book, in an almost Sontag-esque way, "Against Description." There is virtually no visual description, and I felt that carried an implicit

critique of the ways art is ordinarily written about.

It might seem like a contradiction, but I don't think it is. What I said before is true: I love art historians' capacity to describe, which for me is inseparable from their capacity to look closely. That's not something that I want to denigrate or disavow, but it's like that thing where if you get up close enough to something, it starts to blur. Now, our tendency would be to back off a little bit to refocus, and what I'm saying is, *Let's ride with the blur for a little while.* That's within the frame, so to speak, of the so-called individual artwork, but it also exists more generally within the structure of the kinds of aesthetic experiences galleries can produce, in which the works cannot maintain their separation from one another. What I experience is artworks reflecting other artworks within the space, and what I realize is that that phenomenon of blur happens all the time whenever I see a show. Riding with the blur goes against the commitment people have to the strict individuation of the work, which is a mirror, so to speak, of the strict individuation of the artist and, also, of the beholder, insofar as there is a kind of relay in those three things that are all meant, at the end of the day, to somehow buttress or enshrine a common, already given notion of individual subjectivity. What I am interested in is how all of this is constantly being messed up, even while we're constantly pretending that it isn't.

Is the blur not just between the works physically in the room, but also the existence of other artworks and objects that come to mind but are not physically present?

Oh, yeah.

So, it's a time-space blur?

Yeah. Everything is going on. There is an enigmatic line I always wondered about that Coltrane has in the poem that he wrote to accompany the third part of *A Love Supreme* [1965], something like, *It all has to do with it.*

In the chapter on Adrian Piper at the end of *In the Break,* you say, "Sound gives us back the visuality that ocularcentrism has repressed."

When you think that all you're doing is *seeing* something, you're not even really seeing. That is the thing. You attempt to reduce all the other sensual registers, it can't help but limit or restrain the sensual register that you want to be dominant or exclusive.

Do you think that when one is writing about art, there are ways to signify the limitations or the partiality of those descriptions? Often in criticism, the experience of looking can be presented as a narrative: the eye does *this*, then *this*, and *that*, which is a roadmap for how the object functions visually. That kind of "narrative" in your work is constantly resisted and undermined. But could we write a story that resists narrative?

The problem is just *how*. I don't want to be fundamentalist about it, like disavowing narrative as such, but I think what is important is imagining the possibility of a detachment of narrative from the individual subject to which narrative has traditionally been submitted. It's not that there is no story, it's just that there are *more* stories.

I'm both enamored of art historical description and at the same time concerned with its limitations, and most of those limitations have to do with the commitment that art historians have to the absolute singularity of the individual work, the individual artist, and the individual viewer—that what is at stake for them is the relay between those individual things. And in this respect it's very much a kind of Kantian project, as it emerges in Greenberg and his great students Krauss and Fried, but even the people who think of themselves violently disagreeing with those folks still agree on those basic fundaments.

So, music becomes a model of art where a group of people are listening and a group of people are making.

It's the ensemble. And it's the recognition that the solo is an emanation of the ensemble.

You often write poems about subjects that you also write essays on; I'm interested in what those two different forms offer you.

Poetry just lets you put stuff together in a different kind of way, in a way that does not immediately tie you down with certain kinds of diegetic or argumentational responsibilities. The criticism is the same thing, it's just that maybe you have to show more of the connective tissue that allows you to put these things together. In a poem, I can just put Thornton Dial together with with Sleater-Kinney, and I don't have to explain it. The other stuff, it's not just that you *have* to explain it, but you *want* to explain it—*How do these things connect?* You show the conduits through which there is commerce between these seemingly different things.

You reference a broad range of philosophers, from Adorno to Glissant to Deleuze, which positions your writing within a specialized academic context. How have you seen these things coming together with your other widely varied interests?

A lot of times, people just go by their first impressions. When I read Derrida the first time, it wasn't like I knew what was going on; it was just that I knew I wanted to read more. So I kept reading. It seemed clear to me that it had something to do with what I was interested in. What could be seen as a broad intellectual context is, for me, narrow but winding. One of my best friends from college is still one of my best friends, a guy named Alan Jackson, who's a cardiologist in Chicago, and another friend is named Errol Louis, who's on NY1 in New York—he's a journalist and political commentator. We were all reading Kropotkin together—we were interested in anarchism, and we picked that up from Noam Chomsky. It was part of our politics. We were black nationalist nerds. Al studied the history of science, and I'd go to his classes and listen to Everett Mendelsohn lecture. There was a group between Harvard and MIT called Science for the People. E. O. Wilson was inventing sociobiology, and James Q. Wilson was writing this evil book with Richard Herrnstein called *Crime & Human Nature* [1985], which was basically an argument for preventive detention—one of the origins of so-called super-predator theory—all that shit was going on, and we all took it personally as a fundamental assault on our lives. And we were very much influenced by an older student named Eugene Rivers, who was a brilliant autodidact, a working-class black Philadelphian. He was deeply embedded in these politics and in the notion of black working-class liberation and struggle, but he was very religious and embedded in the black Pentecostal church. I'm pretty much a heathen, but I still have an intense relationship with black liberation theology

316

as espoused by James Cone and others—liberation theology was totally important to us. We were reading Gustavo Gutiérrez and Leonardo Boff, because for us it was all connected to what we were doing. We would go hear Stephen Jay Gould lecture. We carried *The Mismeasure of Man* [1980] around like it was the Bible. We had another friend named Abner Mason, and he was the founding president of this group called the Karl Popper Society for the History and Philosophy of Science—and he carried around *Conjectures and Refutations* (1963) like a bible. That was a very strange and particular group, my friends in school. But, everything I'm doing goes through that, in the same way it goes through the neighborhood that I grew up in.

You know, when I would visit my grandmother in Arkansas, she used to wake me up in the morning reciting Paul Laurence Dunbar and John Keats—she loved poetry—and she cleaned up this white woman's house. If she were born today, she'd be who knows, but she was born in 1913, so she cleaned up white women's houses. This is where you come through; this is where you come from. It seems *broad* because it's all over the place, but it's really just *winding*. You know, it's like a river that winds through all these different terrains, and part of it winds through the history of science, and part of it winds through category theory and general topology, and part of it winds through Russian cinema—I'm just *interested*. Some people are like, *I don't want to read that!* I've always wanted to read everything! People got all these reasons for not reading stuff now. Shit *triggers* them. I always wanted to be triggered.

That clarifies so elegantly and simply your discussion of "study" in *Undercommons,* which is just that people want to know stuff, and then they find it out—that *is* "study." Sometimes universities are good for that, but most of the time it happens someplace else.

The university is job training, but without teaching you how to do the job. It's where they teach you how to suffer in order to do a job. That is what it's for. And at the same time they're teaching you that, they're tantalizing you with all these amazing intellectual resources, like, *Here's some superficial relationship to this thing. Not a deep one; we're not going to give you time to actually think about a fucking thing, we're just going to give you time enough so when you're at a cocktail party at your law firm, you can act like you've read an Edith Wharton novel.* People want to *know* shit, man. Just like you said: people do. You have to go to school to learn how to *not* want to know shit, and they do a really good job of that.

In New York, I helped run a free and open art school, and every night of the week people came from all over to talk about art—it was really poignant, seeing people dragging themselves there after work to be together and talk about something they love. I don't want to be overly dramatic, but I think we all should be having serious doubts about the continuation of the university in its current form.

I remember one time me and Stefano were invited to talk at a conference at UC Riverside by the Cultural Studies Association, and the theme of the conference was "Another University Is Possible" [2015]. I remember Stefano was like, *This university is not possible!* People got so mad. It was interesting, because I think what people were basically saying is that we're being cavalier with what still constitutes a fundamental conduit for upward mobility, and how could we say that from our positions as well-paid college professors. I love the university. Just like I love my mom. But, you know, five or six years before she died, I had to come to grips with the realization that she wasn't going to live forever. And she wasn't meant to live forever.

My favorite movie is called *Shoes of the Fisherman*. It was made in 1968. It has Anthony Quinn, Vittorio Di Sica, Leo McKern, John Gielgud, and Lawrence Olivier in it. It's about this Russian political prisoner who also happens to be a priest. At the beginning of the month, he's in the gulag, and through a series of incidents and accidents, by the end of the month, he becomes the pope. The big theological argument in the film has to do with the place and the function of a personal God. Oskar Werner plays a character named Father Telemond, basically modeled on Teilhard de Chardin. Eventually Telemond is called before an inquisition and they say, *We just need one clear statement of what you believe.* And he's like, *I believe in a personal God. I believe in the Resurrection, but in the final analysis, what I believe in is the world. I believe in the goodness of the world. I believe in the values of the world. And in my final hour, mastering all doubts, this will be the faith that I return to.* And there is this drumbeat, and the inquisition guys are like, *No, man.* He really doesn't believe in a personal God—he says he believes in it, but he believes more in something else and they know it. And the inquisition condemns him to silence. It's all great. I watch it like every three weeks. There is a moment where Telemond is like, *I love the Church, but I hate her. I can't live within her but still I can't leave her.* That is one possible way of describing my relation to the university. Look: it's *dying.* You know, there was a moment in which the university might have made a stand against online learning, against these for-profit models, but they decided to not go against them, but to emulate them; that what those places were doing was not against their most fundamental tenets, but that they were, in fact, doing their jobs better than they were. Still, there are a lot resources collected in the university, and we should try to get as much of it as we can.

When you start mapping out the people who've made a substantive impact on art discourse, far more than the race of the artists discussed or exhibited, the racial homogeneity of the people writing about art is shocking. I wonder if there is a connection between that and the way you've framed the black radical tradition as pitched in a distinctly nonvisual direction?

I mean, certainly in my house, growing up, music and, on a secondary level, literature were the dominant art forms. Then after that it would be dance and sports. But visual art wasn't a big deal. I remember reading this great essay by Baraka called "The Myth of a 'Negro Literature'" [1962], where he's actually saying, *There is nothing in this literary tradition that approaches the music, in terms of its complexity and depth.* This was a commonplace formulation that seemed empirically true, though there's a great new book by Brent Edwards called *Epistrophies: Jazz and the Literary Imagination* [2017], which calls that so-called empirical truth into severe question. Still, for many, the music is at the top. In a way, it's actually analogous to a similar hierarchization that happens in Western philosophical thinking, where music is conceived of as the highest art because in some ways it's the most abstract and therefore the most generalizable, and thus the most capable of transcending its own sensual base. Also, insofar as racism and race have generally been conceived of as primarily visual pathologies, that exacerbates this formulation.

But one of the artists whose work really opened up for me a whole new set of questions with regard to this is Thornton Dial. It's not just Thornton Dial, but particularly how his work was collected and exhibited by the Arnett family. The most important thing for me is basically what Bill Arnett has been saying, and it's the kind of thing that once you hear someone say it, it feels like it must be true: that there is in fact a powerful black visual tradition that was as intense and widespread as the music, and disruptive of normative conceptions of visual value, in the same way that the music is disruptive of normative conceptions of musical value—but it's really the yard art and bottle trees and things that are so beyond the pale of what people thought of as visual art that nobody looked at it that way. I remember driving through places in Arkansas with my grandfather—I wish I could go back in time as myself now and say, *Look at all that art*. But back then it was just, *So-and-so is crazy*. Or, *So-and-so likes to do shit like that*. You know, Rauschenberg was driving around the South, he saw all that stuff.

The bottom line is, there *is* a powerful and intense and rich tradition of black visual art that is analogous to the music, just as there is a rich and intense tradition of black movement that has its own relation to what some scholars more narrowly define as dance. And a black "verbal art" that harkens back to the way that Jakobson and the Russian formalists used that term—"verbal art"—in a way that they didn't use the term "literature." Sometimes my old mentor at Berkeley, Roy Thomas, would use the term "orature" to describe it. That stuff was always there. So, I think that on the one hand, it is possible and necessary to critique ocularcentrism, and on the other hand, it's also necessary and possible to recognize this rich tradition of black visual activity that has the same level of richness and complexity as everything else in black artistic and social life.

Do you think that the tools for properly approaching that tradition exist within the field of art criticism or history, or is a new language

needed? Where will that come from?

Everything always needs new language. We constantly have to renew the language of any mode of inquiry. Some of the tools for that are in art history, and some are in other places. If you've really got to do something, and it's really important, you don't give a shit where the tools come from. You get the tools wherever you can find them, and then you deal with the consequences that attend those tools as you work with them. You don't reject tools out of hand just because they come from this or that place. To me, that means you aren't serious about getting the job done—you're serious about something else, maybe about some bullshit notion of purity, but you're not serious about getting the job done.

There's just so much more to do as
a poet now, because I think what's
essential about poetry is so dispersible.
There's an openness right now between
art worlds that is just so exhilarating.

Eileen Myles (b. 1949) is a poet, novelist, and art journalist whose experimental first-person writing has become a touchstone for the identity-fluid Internet age. Their fiction includes *Chelsea Girls* (1994); *Cool for You* (2000); *Inferno (a poet's novel)* (2010); and *Afterglow* (2017). Their writing on art is gathered in the volume *The Importance of Being Iceland: Travel Essays in Art* (2009). Recent books of poetry include the book *I Must Be Living Twice: New and Selected Poems 1975–2014* (2015).

Eileen Myles

What was an experience that made you aware of language as a *thing*?

It's hard to say. I think starting at about ten, I first understood language as a place that was truly a place. If you didn't have enough room in your house, if you had to share a room with your sibling and never had space, you could have a notebook, you could have a diary, you could sit in the hall under the light and leave something there. Writing began like that. I went to Catholic school, and I knew I was funny when I wrote essays. In class the nun would say, *Whose essay do you want to hear,* and people would want to hear mine. I just think it was always part of how I got to take space. I guess also, in education, it just was a procession of, like, legalities: there was prayers, there was the Pledge of Allegiance, there was reciting a poem. There was always this *language obedience,* this language real estate that was part of saluting where you were.

In high school, we saw ourselves like the antijocks. We would go to sports events to drink and hoot—I guess we had friends on the team, but, basically, it was to yell funny things and be an antiforce. It just was always part of a thing of power growing up—to be funny, and to say things, and to gain attention that way. It was a long time before I realized that language or writing was something I could *do.* I didn't have ambitions about writing until college, I guess. But it always seemed like something I had access to and was good at. It was part of how I survived.

Those forms that you mentioned—the formal prayers and the pledge—those are not personal forms. As a kid, I always felt that kind

of language was coming down to me from somewhere else. Did you feel like you had to wrest it away for yourself?

Right. Say the poem was "To a Waterfowl" [1818] by William Cullen Bryant: "Whither, 'midst falling dew, / While glow the heavens with the last steps of day, / Far, through thy rosy depths, dost thou pursue / Thy solitary way?" It's nothing, except the fact that I know it. It got installed. We had a set of Collier's Junior Classics at my house, and the last volume was called *Poetry, Reading Guide, Indexes* [1958]. I found some poems that I used as spells against my brother—I would yell poems at him.

Parallel to that language experience, what was your consciousness of aesthetics, or what was an aesthetic experience that was important to you?

I think art films. I was lucky enough to grow up near Cambridge. There were always these little art theaters. I remember seeing my first Bergman movie, *The Passion of Anna* [1969]. At the very end the voice-over says, *This time his name was Andreas Winckelman*, and the guy is just walking around, turning, until it dissolves into a still. There was something about that turning, and that freeze, and "This time." It seemed like a secular hagiography—I remember it was so astonishing. I just became a follower of foreign films. Boston had this critic Stuart somebody in *The Real Paper* who turned me on to Fassbinder. I was heterosexual then, at least in my behavior, but in many ways boys were boats to culture—dating boys who were smart, who would know about something cool—*Let's see* Pink Flamingos [1972]. *The 400 Blows* [1959]— I was forever changed by Truffaut movies, because they proposed a seriality that wasn't television. He would make the next movie, and the next, and he would tell us the story of a life. *Chelsea Girls* was so much affected by that.

I was of the TV generation, and all those shows were so great. I grew up in such a collective way. Everybody got *Rubber Soul* [1965] for Christmas, everybody got *Revolver* [1966]—all those Beatles albums. One of my first memories was being four or five and seeing Elvis Presley on TV. There were so many experiences that were collective, but there

was also this winnowing and starting to understand coterie, that only
a few of us would get on the bus to Cambridge and go do certain things.

**It seems in a way that collective cultural experience was really useful
as an armature against which to articulate this other kind of experience.**

Yeah, the *irony*. There was an anthology that is so great to look
at now called *Coming Attractions: An Anthology of American Poets in Their
Twenties* [1980], and Dennis Cooper and Tim Dlugos were the editors
of it. They made us be a group with this book. It was very pop—like,
Gilligan's Island would be a perfectly good subject for a poem. Or *The
Flintstones*. People loved to make poetry out of that. I didn't do that
though—I started to try to make my own life into a TV show, that was
more my impulse. To *be* pop.

**When you got to New York in the 1970s, what was the landscape
like for you, socially and artistically?**

Coming to New York, it was hard to understand that the people you
were living around were people you had heard of. Really, the biggest
thing I realized was that the *big*, the *out there*, the *prominent* was now
close. My neighbors are artists, and it's not crazy to think that I am too—the
cultural swarm was intimate. Not the future, it was the present. That
was just really hard to get at first, that *you did stuff*. You weren't some
fraud driving a cab who was writing a novel. I think a lot of it was *class*.
Artists? Yeah, bullshit artists!

Then finding the real vein of what I was excited by, like in the
poetry world, finding St. Mark's Church, as opposed to all the other
little scenes. There were a million scenes, and even though they didn't
look that different, some of them were connected to things that were
exciting. At St. Mark's Church, once I figured out that that was the
poetry I loved, I understood that it connected to dance and art and that
these people all knew each other. And yet it limited me for ten years,
too, because if it didn't come through the doors of St. Mark's Church,
I didn't trust it entirely.

How did you start writing about art?

It was just like, *How does a poet make a living?* Being an art writer was
a way. People older than us had done that. Alice Notley would teach

325

workshops at St. Mark's and she would be like, *We're going to look at this Jim Dine thing,* or, *Everybody has to go to the de Kooning show and write poems.* But it seemed *old.* It was like, *I don't want to do what Frank O' Hara did— write a poem about de Kooning.*

When I moved into this apartment, there was a pile of mimeo books just sitting on the floor, so I think the person who lived here before me went to workshops at St. Mark's Church—some guy who went to Brown. There was a book by Patti Smith, there was a book by Peter Schjeldahl. I knew Peter from anthologies, because we were all students of the second generation of New York School poets. I knew Peter lived in the neighborhood, so I wrote him a fan letter. I *loved* his poetry. He wrote me back and said, *Call us.* Peter was having a "comeback"—*I'm a poet again and I'm not an art writer, I'm through with that.* I became his young poet friend who was reconnecting him to the poet life.

He was of a generation in their thirties always looking over at each other, seeing how everyone else was doing. Ted Berrigan had been their teacher. When they were twenty-two or twenty-three, Ted was twenty-eight, and he lorded it over them. Then he went away for a long while, and now he had come to New York and still lived kind of like a kid and was friends with the kids, and they were broke. Everybody else had found a place for themselves—Ron Padgett taught poetry to kids in schools, and Peter was an art writer. When Ted died, Lynne Tillman and I sat down and had this conversation. She wanted to sit shiva and talk about Ted, because she had known him in London in the sixties and said that back then Ted fully believed he was going to be as big as Bob Dylan or the Beatles. That's who he felt like. By the time he was in New York in the seventies, he didn't think that. But he was the one giving us the lore. It was great for poets to have someone who talked about our whole art life as being true. We didn't have to be something else. His house was accessible to us, he was our friend, he was our teacher, and he was our Fagin—telling us how to sell books and get invited to dinner. He wanted gossip. He was the teacher of the life and a total advocate.

Peter was like, *Don't be a bum like Ted, be an art writer.* We would meet at One U and have a drink, and we'd meet Lynda Benglis or Betsy Baker, and he would introduce me—*This is Eileen, she's a great poet*. He was very generous and championing. It was all set up for me, but I did not want to go through that door. It wasn't until Rene Ricard did a performance at the Guggenheim and was like, *Now you must write about this for* Art in America—*you know Betsy Baker, you can do it. You're a genius. Blah blah blah.* So, Rene made me do it, and I did it. When it came out in print, people were like, *Oh*. I was just one of the little poets, but suddenly people seemed impressed that I could actually write for *Art in America*—which wasn't even that cool then—and so was I, and that you could get a hundred dollars to write four hundred words.

Also, I ran the Poetry Project at St. Mark's Church in the eighties. That was a big deal for me. I think the NEA cut us in 1986—we lost like fifty thousand dollars, and I was the director. We had an art auction with all these artist friends—Elizabeth Murray, David Wojnarowicz— everybody was happy to give art to the Poetry Project. When the art world stepped into the sanctuary, it was just like seeing, *Oh, this is a whole other kind of energy*.

There was a period where Chris Kraus worked at the Poetry Project —was that with Bernadette Mayer or was that with you?

Me.

How did you meet her?

She lived in the neighborhood and went to all the Poetry Project stuff. There were all these little theater companies in the East Village— you know, Club 57, Poetry Project, Mudd Club, the Pyramid—all those different forms of nightclub theater. There was a theater company right across from Mogador, a basement theater that Chris was involved with.

The Wednesday night series was the big-deal older poet series. The Monday night series was the younger poet/first-reading series and performance art stuff—it was definitely the pipeline to other things. There were very few venues for performance art in the eighties; the Poetry Project was one of them. Chris did this amazing striptease in the Monday night series—she was up on a table in a G-string spouting theory. It was so great. It wasn't, like, conventionally *hot*, she was just this skinny girl with a bad complexion gyrating and spouting Derrida or whatever. It was life-changing. She dated a poet and she eventually ran that series, but when I first met her, she was just performing.

Right after I ran the Poetry Project I just cast myself into the art world, into performance art, into theater, anything but poetry, but I was still writing poems. I couldn't get my poetry book published. Then Chris, who was my friend, had started doing this series Native Agents, and she was like, *Let us publish it*. It was so great for me to be published in that context, which meant people in the art world and a whole other theory world were reading this East Village dyke's poetry. I mean, it was more complicated than that. It was transformative for me.

In the opening poem of that book, *Not Me* [1991], you admit that you're *actually a Kennedy*. It's funny because you're so *not* a Kennedy— your background is in fact the opposite of that—so it needs the "Eileen Myles" persona for traction as part of what makes it go. "Eileen Myles" as a character, who is also sometimes just called "the poet," has developed in different ways across your work—how did you start constructing that within the writing?

I *am* a Kennedy. We're not that different. Yeah, but it goes back to Truffaut. I'm like, *Why is there no female Antoine Doinel? Why is there no female Dobie Gillis? The Many Loves of Dobie Gillis* was my favorite show when I was a kid. *Chelsea Girls* is *Dobie Gillis*—*What can I tell you about Thalia Menninger?* he would say, and then he would go off on the story about Tuesday Weld.

What I consider my first "Eileen" poem is called "The Nude Bombadier" [1976], and I even spelled it wrong, like in a Boston accent. I remember I woke up with some guy and was hungover, and it was like I could *see* myself. I was watching a video. That weird desire to be able to watch yourself living that you would have particularly before there was social media. Anyway, I wrote this poem. The last line is, *The nude bombadier, she weighs in at 126*. And it was like, *This time his name was Andreas Winkelmann*, except it was me. I said how much I weighed—that was when I felt sufficiently skinny; I was doing enough speed. I had arrived. The Kennedy was not much of a stretch.

So the influence of art films was about a different way of telling a

story that's not linear necessarily, but it still progresses in time the way a poem does.

Absolutely. I feel like all that watching television was about learning narrative in a short visual way. When you think about early TV being a straight line from vaudeville and radio—which is what performance art in the eighties was too; McDermott & McGough did that New Wave Vaudeville—everybody knew exactly what they were doing. "Vaudeville" actually means "the voice of the city." With the Eileen character, I constructed somebody on stage that was *me* and was *not me*.

It seems like the solution you came up with for writing about art, but also for writing about all aspects of life, is to create a voice that functions like an all-terrain vehicle.

Yes, it's like I'm a camera. I'm not the subject matter; I'm the device.

The question is then about the relationship between the language experience and the thing that it's describing on the other side of the language experience. In an art context, this is the work of art, but in a life experience it could be something else.

In a way I would say that art writing taught me how to write fiction.

How so?

I felt like I really was having a hard time transitioning from poetry to prose, and I didn't really have a prose rhythm. The first thing I wrote became the chapter in *Chelsea Girls* called "Bread and Water." I was living with my girlfriend in this very desperate way, and I thought, *Oh, God, what if I just write a story that just copies exactly what we're doing in real time and doesn't use quotes and includes all the sounds in the room, and the sirens out in the street, and everything that's in my head, and everything that we're saying.* It's like, *Turn the camera on and listen and take it all in.* I think that story was my breakthrough: *Oh, I can write this.* Writing art reviews meant that I was working with editors, which was not necessarily a pleasant experience—challenging me sentence by sentence. Around that same time I started to write long pieces for *The Village Voice.* Again, forcibly moving whole hunks of prose around. As a poet, very rarely would anybody ever fuck with your writing. I never really learned to write prose in my actual education. I didn't go to a good school where they made you write introductory sentences or whatever—that was not my education. Thank God. But writing about art and, you know, just doing journalism made me have a sense of how malleable prose is. Plus I felt the rhythm once I was doing it.

I remember I wrote a story in *Chelsea Girls* where there's a painting in the bedroom of the person I was having sex with, and I described it using the chops I had from writing about art. It was a little joke for myself, and every art review I ever wrote was a private joke with myself like—*If I can do* this *in an art review, it would be really fun to write. Art in America* would tell me what they wanted me to see, and I'd tell them what I wanted to see, and somehow what I wrote about was a compromise. I was writing a lot of reviews in the eighties and the nineties. I just remember going in to a show of Sylvia Plimack Mangold that *Art in America* sent me to and thinking, *No, I hate this.* As I was going out the door I was like, *Wait, I love trees.* And I thought, *If I could start the piece with that line, I'd write it*—and that's what I did. Brooks Adams got the joke, and it made me love him; he said, *You started a review with "I love trees"!* It was always something like that that would make me pull the review together.

Do you know that women's art group from the 1990s—Women's Action Coalition?

Yes.

I always felt that I started WAC, because I pissed off this painter with one of my reviews. I'd known her forever as one of the few dykes in the art world. I would see her at the Duchess, which was this women's bar. We just knew each other on the scene, we were friendly and everything. I liked her. She had great parties. I didn't really know her work, and then I saw a painting, which had these dicks with cartoon cum that were like speech bubbles—she aligned the cartoon space of a comment with an orgasm. *That's great.* I knew she had a show coming up, and it was time for me to write a feature, not just a review, and I told her I wanted to write about her, and she was excited. Though, weirdly, she did not invite me to her studio. I think I told *Art in America* I wanted to write a feature and they were open to it. Then I saw the show—and I didn't like it. *Uh-oh.* I told the magazine, *I don't think this is the show I can write a feature on*, so they said, *Review it.* The review was . . . *mixed.* She totally shit. In fact, I did everything wrong—I think I might have even showed her the review before I sent it to the magazine, and she was like, *You can't do this. You're criticizing my work in an art magazine! Don't you understand? This is my career!*

When I turned it in to Betsy, she asked, *Is this person a friend of yours?* And I was like, *Yes.* And Betsy goes, *Well, my question is, can you write a negative review of a friend?* Again, it was, like, a parade of naiveté, because I thought that was a challenge—I didn't think it was a question! I was like, *Yes!* And this artist just hated me forever. To this day, she'll just see me and point this wizened finger at me across the room.

When I got a job at UC San Diego, I remember her saying, *I heard you left New York for a teaching job*—it was like there was somebody excitedly waiting for my every unsuccessful moment, and it was that artist. And I think when she got that bad review, it was just simultaneous with her wanting her work to become more *political.* She needed to flex her power in some other way, and so I think she organized the first WAC meeting.

[Laughter.]

I swear to God, it was right at the same moment that it was like, *Fuck Eileen. Fuck that review.* But I helped her!

You live by the sword, you die by the sword. Do you feel there were times someone was critical of your work in print, and you were totally cool with it and stayed friends?

Actually, I think I'm not very good at it. Recently I realized I was still mad at Steve Abbott—his daughter Alysia Abbott wrote that book *Fairyland: A Memoir of My Father* [2014]. Steve Abbott was a guy in our scene who died of AIDS. He was a poet, a journalist, and once he wrote a review in *Poetry Flash* where he referred to me as *a Cooper-identified younger poet.*

What does that mean?

That I was some younger poet who was influenced by Dennis Cooper. I thought, *That's weird.* I mean, Dennis and I are friends, and I'm even a few years older than him. We have lots of the same influences, but we did really different things with them. It was just the *sexism* of it, that the female had to be derivative from the male. The guy's the original. Always. Still to this day, if Steve Abbott's name comes up, I will compulsively tell you the shitty stupid thing that he said. He was a very sweet man, we were friends, and we always made time for each other when I was in the Bay Area. Steve was kind. He took me to the Zendo where Philip Whalen was abbot. If Steve were alive I would probably remind him of it, but I would never not hang out with him or not be friendly with him because of it. So it's different, I think.

How do you think getting sober and being in therapy have affected your writing voice?

Well, drinking and not drinking are radically different experiences of living. I think through getting sober I've been thrown into contexts where I've learned how to speak intimately publicly. One of the big things I've learned is how to manage public silence. I think it's so interesting to be saying something and then suddenly not know where you're going and to be able to stop and presume that nobody's going to interrupt you or take the mic away. I had this idea in the eighties that in part was about Russian poets, but also performance art, that you would change the game and survive by memorizing your poems; suddenly, they became more monologues than poems. When you don't hold a piece of paper, people don't make the poetry association; they listen, and they were already used to listening to Spalding Gray or Karen Finley. Then I experimented for a while with "talking performances," where I would improvise. At one point, I was invited to speak to a women's theater company in the East Village called WOW. They were having their tenth anniversary, and there was a big event at PS122. I thought, *I know who I'm speaking to; what is the story I can tell these people that I wouldn't forget in a tornado?* There are stories that are *your stories*, right? I was gang-raped when I was eighteen, and of course it was horrendous. I had a room full of women there, so I just got up and I started talking about driving to Cape Cod with my friends in college and slowly it became that story. It was amazing, because I was watching the faces in the room as I was telling it. It was such a politicizing feeling.

332

Then, in response to George Bush running for president, I just thought about how much fun it was to perform "An American Poem" [1991], the Kennedy poem, and to have that room in my hands. I thought, *What if I actually ran for president?* That's where the two really linked. I would write speeches for a speaker who was me, which was what I was always already doing writing poems. I think all these learning experiences—learning to speak, learning to talk, learning to actually be in the room—changed some of my sense of what writing was. Which in some ways is always an improvisational experience. I'm always amazed: if I'm writing a novel and I wake up and I get coffee and I stay in bed to write, it always seems like because it's Tuesday, I write it *this* way, but if it were Wednesday, I would write it *that* way—and those accidents happen to be what becomes the book.

I don't know if you still identify as a lesbian, but I think in a large part of your writing life, your character could be described as one. How did that affect the way you developed your writing voice?

I think it was part of the motivation, that danger and discomfort and excitement about being queer, about being a lesbian, just saying it. My work went *whoosh*—when I described the "nude bombadier," *she weighs in at 126*, it was a revelatory experience that I could write this way about myself and my own existence, but I had these thoughts and conflicts around sex and sexuality. It was confusing—like, *Am I a lesbian?* Yes. But I'm also a boy and a man, and a trans person.

Did you ever interact with Jill Johnston?

Yes.

She's such a hero for me as a writer; I wish I'd known her. Could you talk about how you knew her or what her work was for you?

I'm part of the generation—there were so many of us who read *The Village Voice* around America. Here was a lesbian column in a newspaper. We came to New York to be Jill Johnston, with that Stein-like prose, talking about her art life. Her book *Lesbian Nation* [1973] was a bible for all of us—I think my girlfriend and I had "Lesbian Nation" painted on this wall. It's incredible how unknown she is today. By the time I got to New York, Jill was not here. I think she had a big nervous

333

breakdown in the late seventies. Maybe she was still here, but the column stopped.

I remember going out and wandering the streets in the late seventies in the West Village one night and taking amphetamines, still wearing my work shirt, and being in a café in the West Village, and some older guy leaned forward and he was like, *Who are you?*

First of all, I love that. Just a stranger asking, *Who are you?*

I said, *Eileen.* He said, *You look like Jill in the old days.* It was the most amazing compliment I ever could have gotten.

Mission accomplished.

She was just legend. I read *Gullibles Travels* [1974], I read everything. But what happened, Kathy Bradford—do you know this painter?

Of course, yes.

I wrote about her work, and we became friendly. Her girlfriend Jane had been lovers with Jill in the old days. I became friends with the two of them, and they introduced me to Jill. She seemed quiet, but also like she was quietly laughing—she had that air of somebody who's in on a tremendous joke. Part of me thought, *She's a little mentally ill.* Then when she and Ingrid Nyeboe got married in Denmark, she got in touch and suggested that I write about their marriage for *The Village Voice.* I was like, *Absolutely.* They had gotten married in Denmark in 1993 and then had another wedding here, at Geoffrey Hendricks's loft. It was really interesting because gay marriage was so not yet here. Jill and I just became friends; they would come to my parties and so on. It ended— apparently this was the Jill way. The New-York Historical Society decided in '96 or '97 to have Jill and I have a public conversation on Gay Pride weekend. They wanted a title for the talk, and Jill wasn't going to give one, and I came up with "Lesbian Pirates of the Avant Garde," which I heard she *really* didn't like—I think because it suggested that she and I were equals, and I didn't understand to what extent we were not. She came completely trashed. I mean, the story was that she had been to the dentist that day and she was on prescription drugs, but she was loaded, and when we got on stage it was clear. It was that laughing Jill with a secret attack joke—she was not going to participate. Then

I did what I knew to do, which was kind of to bottom to her: *Of course, you are a great hero of mine . . .* And she just sat there. Then she said, *I get it about you—you're a good girl.* She would only participate on that level of shitting on me. It was such a painful travesty, and the room was *packed.* It was just one of the worst experiences of my life.

Part of what this speaks to is the complex and layered dynamic that exists intergenerationally between artists. You had the experience as a really young poet of having relationships with older people, and now that you are famous and in a certain position, what has it been like having these connections with younger artists and writers?

I mean, it can be *strange.* I've have always had younger friends, and even, problematically, probably overidentify with younger friends, but I do know how long I have lived, and I know where I have been. When I did the anthology *The New Fuck You* [1995] in the nineties, I brought some people together who felt they were becoming a scene. It was the first time I felt older, because I remember being at a party and they were in a tight circle, and they were so excited about each other that they kind of wouldn't let me in. Who hasn't had that experience, right, when you come crashing off your pedestal—which you thought was reality, but you were just their last cultural crush.

I want to loop back to what you started to say about having an art benefit at St. Mark's Poetry Project and seeing the art-world people come in, and the difference between the poetry-world and the art-world people. How have you seen that dynamic evolve?

It's completely reversed in a weird way now. I almost think to the extent that poets care to live it and enact it, the art world is beholden to poets at this point in time. I think part of the reason I did not want to participate in the art world when I was a young poet was because I wanted to be a *poet.* And it seemed the whole way of relating to the art world then was *me* writing about *you.*

I think at this point in time, it's almost like waking up to the condition of being loved or something—the art world is now more than happy to have you write a poem for a catalogue text, and the poem does not even have to be about the art. *Just park next to me.* I think there's so much room for poets *as poets* in the art world right now. The art world wants these new objects, and I think we're it. When I watch parts of the poetry world have "movements," I'm like, *Wait, this is the moment to be strewn. Do anything but consolidate with other poets. Write a TV show.* There's just so much more to do as a poet now, because I think what's essential about poetry is so dispersible. There's an openness right now between art worlds that is just so exhilarating.

It would be an incredible time to be a young poet. Or *this* poet. I have to remind myself that being sixty-eight does not mean that certain parts of the art world are closed to me, including film. It's like, *Just make the work.* I mean, certainly sexism and ageism and homophobia and transphobia are everywhere. I also think it absolutely behooves us to make art in the total absence of those things—the only idea I have ever had was to act like they don't exist. To write not so much a "lesbian poem," but write a poem in which the lesbian is a free agent in the world. It's not *incidental*, but I deal with being queer incidentally, just as if, *This is my oyster!*

How do you define art for yourself?

I don't know why the word "adjudicated" comes to mind at this moment, but I feel like it is sort of an adjudicated, sensuous pile of things. I mean, that's what a poem is. It's like, *How did you make that? —I just put some stuff together.* That's the thing, to be a law unto yourself, right? It's almost like the payoff. It's the prepayoff. I'm making reality here.

The first role of someone who writes about the past is simple: to try to bring the past forward into the present with more complexity, so that at some basic level the historian takes on the role of the storyteller.

Molly Nesbit (b. 1952) is a historian known for charting the late nineteenth- and early twentieth-century French avant-garde in two books: *Atget's Seven Albums* (1992) and *Their Common Sense* (2000). She also writes about contemporary art, publishing in *October* and as a contributing editor in *Artforum*. Nesbit has contributed to many artists' catalogues, including publications on Gabriel Orozco and Rachel Whiteread, and cofounded the collaborative project Utopia Station with Hans Ulrich Obrist and Rirkrit Tiravanija in 2003, which has proliferated texts, performances, and discussions around the world. She has been collecting her writings in a series called *Pre-Occupations*, which so far includes *The Pragmatism in the History of Art* (2013) and *Midnight: The Tempest Essays* (2017). She is a professor of art history at Vassar College.

Molly Nesbit

When we were talking earlier and you said that *art history is the study of a work of art in real time*, does that mean you're looking at a historical object in relation to the needs and realities of our present, or are you looking at the work of art in relation to the moment it was made? Or is it the oscillation between the two?

The first role of someone who writes about the past is simple: to try to bring the past forward into the present with more complexity, so that at some basic level the historian takes on the role of the storyteller—someone able to tell all different kinds of stories. You choose your stories, try to enlarge the past and make it strange, so it can open up and be responsive to its own particularities. You're also always cognizant of the fact that you feel this story, this history, will have some meaning for the present—though the questions the present brings to it are always *implied*, they don't need to be there outright. The best history is subtle.

How did you start writing on contemporary art, and how do you see it related to the task of bringing forward the complexity of the past?

Well, it really was Hilton Als who literally opened the door for me when he took me to meet Jack Bankowsky in 1992. Jack had become the new editor of *Artforum*, and he had liked an article I'd written for *October*, my very first article about Duchamp. It's in *Midnight: The Tempest Essays* under its original title, "The Copy" [1986].

As for the bridge between contemporary art and the past? The bridge can be crossed from either side. And how to explain that? Let's

339

see. The other piece of the historian's mission is to try to recuperate wisdom. I suppose you could say—this is something I absorbed long ago from Hilton's way of working—that the work of the writer, be it fiction or nonfiction, is also all about pulling that kind of deep experience, that thing called wisdom, forward. Wisdom doesn't come in a package. Wisdom doesn't have a brand. Wisdom is much more fluid and incandescent. One of the reasons you find me speaking this way today is that I'm in the middle of my lecture zone in the introductory survey course at Vassar, which goes from the caves to Pierre Huyghe, Yang Fudong, and David Hammons—in other words, pretty close to the minute-time of the absolute present. It makes you think about history from a very high elevation point, because when you cover this much material at once, when you try to understand the substance of change, you have to make sense of great swathes of time. Any generalizations need to be tested. Normally in the contemporary art world, we don't think about things in quite this way.

Eventually, it became clear to me that as the complexity of a situation unfolds, one needs to understand that artists, past and present, are people, working in situations that they cannot completely control. That was one of the most important lessons learned from immersing myself in the world of living artists. It was a lesson Teeny Duchamp taught me by example—"The Copy" also opened the door to her. In the course of human events, I found myself meeting Teeny and then becoming friends—I saw her a fair amount whenever I was in France. She would invite me to stay, and we'd talk about all kinds of things, from chocolates to Wittgenstein. We had fun. When we talked about her late husband, the one thing that she insisted on, although she never said it outright, was that he was a person, he wasn't a myth. The more that simple fact sunk in, the more radical it sounded to me, because most art historians, and art critics especially, treat the artist as some kind of chess piece, or an integer in a problem, rather than a person with existential needs, someone facing existential challenges.

"The Copy" was written for a symposium, right, "Multiples without Originals: The Challenge to Art History of the 'Copy'" [1986]?

Yes. In 1986, Rosalind Krauss had been asked if she would do a special session at the College Art Association; the Getty was sponsoring a group of special sessions as a way of confronting—let's call it the "soft revolution" that was taking place in art history, in which the theoretical work of the Europeans, particularly the French, was being brought in and used to reset the terms of our most basic questions. For those in the discipline who weren't reading Althusser or Foucault or Barthes and weren't interested in new literary theory or structuralism or psychoanalysis, this was hugely upsetting, because it seemed to fly in the face of all the German scholarly protocols that had been brought here by the émigré art historians in the thirties. The émigré art historians, mainly from Germany and Austria, had set up a new chapter in the study of art history in American universities. It was much admired, itself very important, and produced a new stage in American art history, but once installed it didn't want to make room for other points of view, and this led to a culture war within art history itself that was pretty vicious, in the eighties especially. It became political, too, so that if your work was at all understood to be involved with ideas that supported the left, whether it was overtly Marxist or not, you could pretty much expect to be condemned, and if you were a junior faculty member, you definitely weren't going to get tenure at an Ivy League university. The most famous instance involved Tom Crow, who did not get tenure at Princeton. All this wasn't some kind of polite disagreement: it had to do with how art could be talked about and understood. The stakes were real.

You went to Vassar and studied art history, and then you went to Yale. What was the terrain like there? How did you navigate it?

At Vassar, I was lucky, because the split in art history was already opening up there in the seventies, thanks to Linda Nochlin and Dick Pommer, so I understood that there was a counterculture building. Then, in the midseventies, I went to Yale. Anyone admitted into the Yale art history program was given permission to do their work in the way they wanted as they went forward. There was a big group of us that wanted to study French art and architecture, and after our coursework we went to Paris to do our thesis research. We were interested in social questions, urban issues, and the way in which abstraction could be understood as a machine aesthetic—the work of Meyer Schapiro was fundamental to our thinking about modern art. Most of us were students of Robert Herbert.

Once arrived in Paris, we met everyone else who was working in the Parisian libraries from the other American universities. We also met people coming from England, Germany, Italy, and Greece. People from other disciplines were also working in the Bibliothèque nationale, so there was this much bigger and richer collective conversation that developed over the years. My own education expanded at Yale and expanded again in the Bibliothèque nationale. It was there, in the late seventies, that I met Adrian Rifkin, who was at that point very much involved with the work being done around Jacques Rancière—that was just naturally part of the conversation, as was what was going on with Félix Guattari and the journal *Recherches*. My conversations mostly had to do with Marxist and social history, so I went and spent a year in England in order to understand the British work there better, and then I came back to the States. *Atget's Seven Albums*, my first book, was born from that world of exchange—in many ways, it participates more in the debates going on in England than in those setting the terms for the discussion of photography in the United States.

After I returned, happily I got a visiting job at Berkeley for two years in the early eighties—Foucault came while I was there. An interdisciplinary group in the humanities had formed and founded a magazine called *Representations*. There was just a ton of energy around this bigger historical and philosophical way of thinking about things, and it was hugely challenging to be walking into those worlds of mind at Berkeley. Two years later, there was a chance to work in New York City, and I took it, mainly because I wanted to be closer to Europe and I missed the East Coast. I was offered a job at Barnard. The Barnard/Columbia situation that I entered was completely split by this culture war in art history that I've described. I had a real sense that if you wanted to think along certain lines, you had to be prepared to defend

342

yourself. Nothing could be taken for granted.

In the eighties I moved between New York and Paris, doing research on mechanical drawing and finishing my Atget book. It was then that I met Rosalind Krauss, who was going to Paris all the time, too, and was involved with thinking about photography and the ways Foucault's questions could be used to modulate Greenbergian ones. And so we developed a conversation and friendship. We were not really thinking along exactly the same lines—Rosalind was not a Marxist, to put it mildly. I once joked with her that I was base and that she was superstructure. She was a little taken aback, but she got it. She laughed too. But she did not support *Their Common Sense*, the book that laid out my research on mechanical drawing and the new orders of modern language.

Moving forward, since you want the big picture and the frames do change with time, what really launched me into the *Pragmatism* book was seeing that the philosophers I have most admired—Foucault and Deleuze and Guattari—were actually using historical techniques to do their philosophy. They needed the research. They needed the empiricism. They needed to move things out of one place—meaning field—and into another. They were setting up philosophies of practice. And that, too, was theoretical work. It also meant that this new activity called theory could actually be grounded in something that was bigger, deeper, older, and philosophically more profound. The mix of things coming together in New York City in the eighties and nineties in many ways follows from the mix of things I found in Paris. The idea was to keep it alive and to bring all that to my writing about art. And that would not just deepen our understanding of how Marcel Duchamp jumped ship in 1912, but also deepen our understanding of the way artists work now. So when I met Jack, and he asked me to write for *Artforum*—he was very permissive, God bless him—that is when I began to get more involved with thinking about how to put these ideas into play, to bring them out of the Bibliothèque nationale and onto the street.

How do you know Hilton Als?

When I first arrived at Columbia, Hilton was a student who walked into my seminar. But things knit together in ways one couldn't have imagined. Hilton had taken Ken Silver's seminar on Warhol. Ken, a friend from Yale, was leaving to go to NYU, but he told Hilton about me and to take my seminar on the readymade, which Hilton did. When he finished at Columbia that spring, it turned out that we needed a new office assistant at Barnard. The new chair, David Freedberg, had this idea that we should find an artist who needed a job, and I said, *Hilton needs a job—he's a young writer, how about it?* David was enthralled, and that was that. Hilton took this job extremely seriously, and he was there with us for a few years, and as you can imagine, it was great. He put up a photo of Pina Bausch next to his desk. He was already writing and curating and fully inserted in the downtown New York art world. He was beginning to write for *The Village Voice* and would go off to work at the New Museum. Anyway, we would stay in touch, and from all this, we developed a fine, old friendship.

Another one of my old students is the gallerist David Maupin. He had taken a class with me at Berkeley. When he found out I was back in New York, we remet, and he also introduced me to a lot of people; it was through him, for example, that I met Rem Koolhaas. All these conversations, you see, build and grow. We went off to Documenta X [1997]—and it turned out to be the place where all those ways of thinking that I was describing in the seventies and eighties came to fruition as an exhibition. That made me realize that all this really did go together in the present, that it was perfectly possible to write in the bigger philosophical, historical way, and to do so in the context of the art being made right now.

Your description of that insight of working with Teeny Duchamp and realizing, *This is a human being* strikes me. We tend to forget that intellectual history is just a bunch of people with very complex interpersonal dynamics, and the more you know about it, the more you see that the human parts are the secret structure of the story. How do you understand the role of the interpersonal in intellectual development?

Nobody thinks all by themselves. Nobody makes art all by

themselves, either. The way in which an idea can move in the world has something to do with conversation, and it also has to do with the friction it encounters in terms of material conditions and limitations in knowledge itself. When you write, you normally write to be read, though you may not be writing in order to be understood *easily*; you may be writing a little ahead of the people involved, because you're trying to see if you can make your idea grow into a new idea. But the way in which ideas can go out and live in the world is similar to the way works of art go out and live in the world—they have to exist. So what kind of an existence will it be?

We should take the story here forward a few more years. By the time of Documenta X, I had come to know Benjamin Buchloh, who also moves across the social circles of artists and writers and thinkers in his own political, philosophical way, and he introduced me to Gabriel Orozco. I had understood that all these ideas expanded to many other continents, and that kind of expansion struck me mightily, between the eyes, when I saw Chris Marker's *Sans Soleil* [1983] for the first time. In order to see *Sans Soleil*, I had had to order it for a film screening for one of my classes at Barnard. I spent a decade trying to catch up with what I saw in *Sans Soleil*. In the late nineties I met Chris, and I was also beginning to meet the people who would come together in Utopia Station, which started as a collaboration with Hans Ulrich Obrist and Rirkrit Tiravanija for the Venice Biennale of 2003.

Utopia Station becomes the new iteration of the Bibliothèque nationale, with that kind of richness and wealth and growth—intellectual, personal, social growth. It was like literally walking into an expanded version of things, happening at another scale and absolutely *actual*. It was really something extraordinary in 2003—brought into a kind of new focus because of 9/11, but more importantly because of the onset of the wars in Afghanistan and Iraq and the effort to try and stop them, to produce a peace movement that could actually stop a war, which we know is not easy to do. We were also focused on the emerging World Social Forum as it was convening in Porto Alegre and Mumbai. *Utopia Station* involved a whole new, loose community of artists and writers and architects who wanted to come together, to be together, and do things together and be truly self-organized. It produced a set of friendships that remain alive to this day. We keep looking for ways to do things together again. We do so informally all the time.

So personal relationships are definitely a piece of all this—a piece that's got forward momentum. The only reason to tell my story here is that it allows me to give the momentum its detail, to show you the way in which the lives of minds mutate and occupy spaces at different times. Nobody's biography settles down into one story. We circle back to the art history question: the work of an artist is not one thing or attached to one idea; it's attached to a timeline and a space program that involves living a life. The work of art may express that life somehow, or it may just be along for the ride, but it's not going to completely sum it up.

In *Pragmatism*, you write about George Kubler's *The Shape of Time* [1962], which I'm very interested in. I recently taught it, along with Henri Focillon's *The Life of Forms in Art* [1934], to artists in Miami. They strike me as books that have had more influence on artists than on scholars— their work didn't really get picked up in subsequent art history.

Actually, Kubler shut Focillon's thinking down a little bit, because he didn't let Focillon's politics come forward.

The way you explicate that in *The Pragmatism in the History of Art* was a revelation to me—there is nowhere else I've seen that dynamic articulated. Neither of them developed a "model" that you could apply.

Well, that's it. You've just said it. There's no model. And what people search for, especially at the beginning of their studies, is some map that can explain everything. If you're really going to tell the truth about what we're doing, *there is no map*. There are questions—*What is actuality?*—but there is no map. Some people can cope with that, but it means you have to go forward in the dark. In life we go forward in the dark, too, and one of the problems now in early 2017 is that we are in fact going forward in a dark that doesn't seem even to take the shape of a tunnel.

George Kubler wrote *The Shape of Time* when he thought he was about to die. And then he didn't die. And so he returned to his work

346

without those metaphysical problems looming in the foreground. When I arrived at Yale in the 1970s, we all had to take a methods class our first term. The syllabus of that course varied from year to year, but generally each member of the department came forward and talked about the kind of methods of inquiry that they used in their area of the field and each week we read something in relation to their work. Sheldon Nodelman came and spoke about Alois Riegl, for example. We read *The Shape of Time*, but Kubler himself did not come because he just wasn't intellectually in the same place as he had been when he wrote it. I would also bet that he didn't want to see his work as a method. In fact, it is kind of unusable as a method, though you could perhaps adapt it to some of the formalist thinking in the 1970s—it was involved in morphologies. The real strength of the book was the actuality question and thinking about the temporalities of history, while keeping the wonder of the stars and the rainbow.

But Kubler's book begins from the work that Focillon had left unfinished. And so part of what one feels as one reads *The Shape of Time* is the loving effort on Kubler's part to bring Focillon's work and wisdom forward without really saying so, to bring it forward as a greater truth. It's a book written out of filial duty but goes beyond the filial part; Kubler is really trying to ask the biggest questions possible, of art and everything else. It's hugely inspiring, because intuitively you grasp that those are the stakes for what we do. We really ought to be asking history and art history, and ourselves, to step up in that way. You don't get that sense of mission very often right now, except through the forward trajectories of the civil rights movement. As a result, the idea that one should try to be an "intellectual" is foreign to our culture. We have instead inculcated a culture of professionalism, which is why the "skilling and deskilling" debate has become so intense.

You've developed a specific way of writing, closer to experimental narrative than academic prose; it's very unusual. As I was reading *Midnight: The Tempest Essays*, I was wondering how much you reworked those essays from how they originally appeared over the past thirty years.

I didn't.

So you were writing that way from the jump? Have you always been engaged in experimental form?

The essay "What Was an Author?" [1987] is where I started, and that's the first essay in the collection. I think most writers will tell you that it's like singing: you have a voice, and you have to figure out what you're going to do with it. A singer cannot sing in every register. Also remember: that historical and philosophical world that I walked into in the seventies and eighties allowed for truly experimental writing. Especially if you think of Deleuze and Guattari, with their unfettered Nietzschean permissiveness. Rosalind Krauss herself was interested in that dimension of the project, even more so after she met Denis Hollier. Experimental writing was one of the things that the two of us often talked about. I also think that is one of the reasons Hilton and I became friends, because of our mutual interest in making words do things; it was he who egged me on.

My book *Their Common Sense* basically went beyond the pale in terms of art historical form and voice. It's full of conviction about how to tell a story, and if things are not mannerly, then why should we try to keep them neat? These days I've often laughed with my art history friends that it was not exactly a "career move" to write that book. It took a few years to find a publisher for it, and that publisher, Black Dog Publishing, was, not coincidentally, based in England. The experience taught me that there are real consequences—that if you want to really do your work in a way that performs the extreme experiment, you have to take responsibility for it not fitting in, maybe never fitting in. And for people not wanting to follow along. Not everything is suited for mass culture.

It appears to me today that art history is a stagnant field—there doesn't seem to be any energy or pressure coming from within the discipline. The only real energy I see is coming from other directions— like African American studies. Do you see that?

No, and here's why not: you're looking at a transformation of the American university into a STEM-centered and STEM-heavy operation.

348

The humanities disciplines are being squeezed, and it's not at all clear that the liberal arts departments, with their chairs of expertise, are going to survive structurally. Already there are people who say the early twentieth century may not be a field that will be taught intact in fifteen years' time. The nineteenth century has to argue for its reason for being. Linda Nochlin was not replaced at the Institute of Fine Arts—feminism was not seen as something that needed to endure there, as such, in the curriculum. But the idea that any of these field designations is going to survive even the next decade is an open question—it seems crazy to say that, but on the other hand, I'm looking at my own school, Vassar, where we have long had a historically strong and well-known art history department: every time someone leaves or retires, we have had to prostrate ourselves to try and save the line, and more often than not, we have failed.

That said, art history itself is fine and ready for the future. It's as interdisciplinary a field as you can imagine: you can think about anything you want as an art historian. It's got the metaphysics intact; it's got all the big philosophical questions waiting to be raised; it can go toward material science or the issues of social justice. But if it only presents itself as some little field from which professional curators can come—it's doomed. If it becomes a breeding ground for polite conversation and investment strategies—it's doomed. Focillon once told his students that *art appreciation is not knowledge*—and he was right.

I'm inspired by those late nineteenth- and early twentieth-century art historians who created the discipline, and I'm wondering what tools you see as unique to art history, as opposed to every other discipline that it intersects and overlaps with.

The German art historians you admire from the late nineteenth and early twentieth centuries produced a generation of students that included Erwin Panofsky and Alexander Dorner, but they also created outliers who were not, strictly speaking, art historians, like Walter Benjamin. Benjamin couldn't get a job in the university, so he was obliged to apply his intellectual gifts elsewhere, but he certainly did not stop writing or thinking. It's not as though the lines of succession flow easily, ever. In our time, art history is nevertheless a place from which we can think about the transformations of cultures, about the role of visuality and objects in spaces and images in the public sphere, about the way in which the older forms are transmuted through new technologies—that is a problem that comes up through the centuries, it's not a new problem.

As the new digital platforms come to define the public sphere and give artists new places and fields though which to explore and work, the old maps cease to function. One way to get your bearings is to measure this morphing present against the past—not that the past is the "dead other" or the "bad father" or the opposite of the present; it's that there are elements from the past that are still active inside this present. You need the past to think the present. Just take the early twentieth-century avant-gardes, which in many ways show us a situation comparable to the one we are living in now, where everything seemed to be turning upside down. There was no secure place for the work of art to be. And there certainly weren't secure forms of representation that people could count on surviving time. The classical tradition, and everything that went with it, was crashing, and what was coming forward was a set of elements, new rhetorics, that people could work with. In many ways the initial problem was to figure out what spaces painting and architecture could occupy, so that new decorative arts collectives could form. Little magazines came to be extremely important spaces for people to work in. Eventually the art galleries were going to pick up steam and become a third way, and we know what happened. But remember, in the middle of it all, there is confusion, rampant confusion—the lights are out. That is precisely when you have these new energies coming though, thinking philosophically about change, the blowing up of modern literature, or the proliferation of voices—there is a very productive explosion that takes place at the beginning of the twentieth century. To understand that you can have those periods of explosion and everything doesn't end is psychically useful for us a hundred years later. Benjamin is such an important thinker because he's willing to look this explosion in the face, to try and think about it, but his way of thinking about it was to go back to Baudelaire, in the nineteenth century, to find an indirect, historical way to help articulate the problem of extreme upheaval.

Where did you first experience the sense of having a special relationship with language or with telling a story?

I learned to write and speak about the past from teaching. Art history, as you know, is taught in the dark—lecturing in front of luminous images. I think what you're really hearing in my writing is a spoken voice. It's not the voice of the radio broadcaster; rather, it's been adapted to presenting things in this situation with other people there in the shadows, listening. The scene is genuinely collective. That way of lecturing was something I learned from my own teachers; the Yale lecturers were particularly gifted, Bob Herbert and Vincent Scully especially.

Did you want to be a writer as a child? When did it become clear that you wanted to be an art historian?

Well, there's nothing too dramatic in this plot. I grew up in upstate New York, outside Rochester. I went to public school with a lot of smart people. Everyone was good at stuff, I was not special, and, like many of my friends, I liked writing, and at that point I also liked making art. My mother was an art librarian, and as a result I knew what art history was. I was also strangely practical and I thought, *I like literature and history and I love to make art and I like studying French, and I could combine all that as an art historian.* For those reasons, I just jumped into it. As for writing, it's not like I heard a voice in the night—I knew that I had a voice that was there, and I used it.

How has your deepening relationship with contemporary art changed the way you write?

It hasn't. The basic way of laying things out was there before I really started writing about contemporary art. I didn't write at length about people who were alive and with whom I was in conversation as I wrote about their work until I wrote the essays about Rachel Whiteread and Gabriel Orozco. *Their Common Sense* was done by then. I would count my conversations with Hilton to be art conversations. In my own circles, Hilton was opening up the way writing could approach truth, and

Rosalind was writing *The Optical Unconscious* [1993]. I don't know if you remember that the chapter on the *Rotoreliefs* [1935/1953] opens with me asking a Marxist question. It wasn't always a gift to be cast in *The Optical Unconscious*, but at least I had a good speaking part.

Their Common Sense, Pragmatism, and Midnight—a reader needs to be very sophisticated to understand the kinds of interventions you're making in those books; there are not explicit arguments. If the reader knows the stakes of the intellectual histories, they can begin to understand what you're putting forward, which could be otherwise missed.

You might say that ideas are not being allowed to dominate experience or historical conditions, and that's because ideas are just participants in these larger perspectives or sagas. There's a fair amount of intellectual history being written in between the lines: if you start with my Atget book or *Their Common Sense*, you see that I have studied the kind of knowledge that is not officially intellectual—instead, it's technical, public, and popular. Over time, I was interested that I had repeatedly gotten myself into those problems, since they are not ever going to be fashionable. I am now committed to the idea that one can and should think about art and historical material from the bottom up. I work on contemporary artists from the same kind of bottom-up perspective. The idea that philosophical ideas function to illuminate the world from the bottom up is slightly destabilizing for many academics, but it's just how I understand things. I don't have a good feeling for the abiding importance of hierarchy—I really don't. I'm impressed by accomplishment, but I'm not particularly impressed by power in and of itself. It follows from the fact that Duchamp was a person, that everyone is a person, so we should all be able to talk together—hierarchy shouldn't get in the way of that.

There are very few times in your writing where you say, So-and-so said to me. You do not make yourself a feature in the writing, although in many cases the writing feels that it can only be held together by the gravity of a single person.

The decision to use the first person is often temperamental. Also,

I suppose it's a set of attitudes inculcated from the very reality of writing about the past. Obviously you don't walk around as yourself saying "I" when you're recounting the past. It's not as though I'm seeking to say, *So-and-so said to me*, but on the other hand, you learn things through conversation, and there is no reason why knowledge that comes in conversation shouldn't be communicated. But you have to reference it somehow. The line of Leon Golub's that I used as an epigraph for *Midnight*—"Life is wild"—was said in conversation at the end of his life. We were talking, as we did in those days, about utopia.

A really compelling critique is a
critique that's grounded in love—
in the love of an art form and all its
possibilities. And love is not a science!
That's where it gets complicated.

Jed Perl (b. 1951) has been a surprising, thoughtful, and
often dissident voice in the New York art world since the
1970s. He began writing for *The New Criterion* shortly
after its founding in 1982 and contributed to many other
magazines before becoming the art critic for *The New
Republic* in 1994, a post he held for twenty years. His
historical books include *Paris Without End* (1988);
New Art City: Manhattan at Mid-Century (2005); and
Antoine's Alphabet: Watteau and His World (2008).
He's also published three collections of criticism—
Gallery Going (1991); *Eyewitness* (2000); and
Magicians & Charlatans (2012). Recently, he brought
out the first installment of his two-volume biography of
Alexander Calder, *Calder: The Conquest of Time: The
Early Years: 1898–1940* (2017). He publishes regularly
in *The New York Review of Books*.

Jed Perl

Let's start by talking about your early childhood. What was the culture like in your house growing up?

My parents were New Yorkers. I was born here when my father was in graduate school at Columbia, working on a PhD in physics. They were artistically and intellectually inclined—I have some of my mother's Museum of Modern Art books with her maiden name written in them. I grew up in a family where going to museums, concerts, and talking about ideas was the air we breathed. We always got *The New Yorker* and *The New Republic*, and we started getting *The New York Review of Books* when it first appeared in the sixties. I remember my parents coming home from a dinner party talking about Susan Sontag's "Notes on Camp" [1964]. Obviously, there's little distance between the world I grew up in and where I am now.

From the very beginning I was interested in the intense experiences that the arts can provide—that all the arts provide, whether visual, literary, musical, or theatrical. These experiences are very mysterious—they're both immediate and lasting, peremptory and penetrating. As a critic, I've wanted to describe these experiences. But I've also wanted to try to understand them—and understand how they help shape the world we live in. What I've come to believe is that the arts—all the arts—are powered by a dramatic interaction between the authority of tradition and the freedom of the individual. Art is an expression of one's uniqueness, but an expression that depends on forms and values—visual, literary, musical, and so forth—that have a history, a genealogy. It's the tension between authority and freedom that gives the arts their life-giving impact. I believe that holds true for all art in all periods—whether the carvings done by an anonymous craftsman on a medieval cathedral or the work done by a modern giant like Matisse, Stravinsky, or Colette.

What are some early aesthetic experiences that were important to you?

I always drew and painted. I was also fascinated by the lives of artists—I had that book *The Private World of Pablo Picasso* [1958], with David Douglas Duncan's photographs of Picasso, which were taken in the fifties, when Picasso was living in South of France. I *loved* going to museums at a very early age. In my early teens, we lived in California, and I would come back to New York to stay with my grandparents in Brooklyn—that was back when you got on the subway by yourself at a fairly early age and nobody thought anything of it. I would go up to The Metropolitan Museum of Art or The Museum of Modern Art by myself and just take everything in. At the same time, in my teens, I got really interested in criticism. *The New Yorker* had incredibly exciting critics— Pauline Kael in particular.

And you were drawing and painting. In your teens, were you primarily interested in being an artist, or were you writing, too?

I stopped drawing and painting for a number of years at around thirteen. I wrote movie reviews for the high school paper and then went to Columbia for college, though I really didn't know what I was going to do. By then I hadn't painted in four or so years. After taking some art history, I found myself wanting to try a drawing course; then I got very involved in painting again. One of the men I studied with at Columbia, Leon Goldin—a very good painter—said, *You should go to Skowhegan,* the summer art school in Maine, which I did. I hadn't been in an art school environment before, and at Skowhegan, almost everybody was from an art school. I'd also begun writing art criticism for the *Columbia Daily Spectator,* the school paper. I met my wife, the painter Deborah Rosenthal, at Columbia—we've been married a long time. She had been a printmaker and then was working on a degree in English. She went back to printmaking and then to graduate school at Pratt. She became an abstract painter and has been showing in New York for thirty years; she's been an influential teacher of painting and also written a good deal, often about the modernist painters who've meant the most to her, among them Paul Klee and André Masson.

By the time I graduated, I wanted to be a painter, and for a number of years I was painting and writing—for *Arts*, *Art in America*, and a couple of other places. Then sometime in the eighties, when I was in my early thirties, I came to a fork in the road and decided to focus on writing.

When you were studying art history at Columbia, what were you studying and who were you working with?

I was into a whole range of things. There was this amazing course on Venetian painting given by David Rosand—a formidable teacher and scholar. I took the last undergraduate course Meyer Schapiro taught on the sociology of art. I was just kind of into everything, though I was never really interested in studying contemporary or modern art in an academic setting.

You edited the terrific collection *Art in America 1945–1970: Writings from the Age of Abstract Expressionism, Pop Art, and Minimalism* [2014] for the Library of America. It's such a loving celebration of the complexities of art writing. It's also a kind of revisionist history of that period—it includes a lot of idiosyncratic and minor writers from obscure places. When you started writing criticism, who were your models?

Criticism for me has never meant just art criticism—it's always been about criticism *in general*. Edmund Wilson is one of my great heroes— I don't quite know why he became my hero when I was in my teens, but he did. I've read everything he's written, even his poems and plays. Among the critics who've been important for me are the dance critics Edwin Denby and Arlene Croce. Pauline Kael, who I read for years and who became a friend, was very important. What spurred me to write about art in college was finding myself in a specific community of artists. I never painted abstractly, I painted representationally; I saw myself as part of a cohort of people, some of whom were much older, whose work I felt hadn't been seen to the degree it should be, or whose voices hadn't been heard in the way that they deserved. I began writing to advocate for and celebrate those artists. One of the first pieces I wrote for *Arts Magazine* was about contemporary still-life painting—it's called "The Life of the Object" [1977]. I don't have the article in front of me now, but as best as I can recall the dozen or so artists I discussed included Gabriel Laderman, Louisa Matthíasdottír, and Fairfield Porter. As I shifted from being a "painter who writes" to being just a writer, my perspective started to broaden. I remember thinking, *I want to be able to deal with all different kinds of things—to test my sensibility against a wide range of stuff—to understand the whole range of what's going on in art.*

I came into the scene with my passions. For example, I was very interested in Balthus. My first book, *Paris Without End*, was about trying to trace a different lineage in French art since World War I, emphasizing people who *didn't* move into abstraction. Eventually I ended up at *The New Criterion*, and then at *The New Republic* for twenty years, where I had this wonderful mandate to cover the scene however I wanted to. I began to feel that it was really important for me to understand where other people were coming from. I remember when Rosalind Krauss did a book and a show about surrealist photography, *L'Amour fou* [1985]; it was a whole world of thinking—the theory of language—that I'd never looked at before. I was skeptical about a lot of what Krauss was saying, but I had to get up to speed before I could articulate my qualms. It was wonderful and exciting to learn on the job. At some point I remember thinking, *I really do have to understand Michael Fried, not because I want to engage with him directly*—his arguments are so interwoven and inbred that it's finally impossible to really engage with them, at least in a critical way—but I did want to try to place Fried in a broader context. I've always wanted to react to things in my own way—as *me*—but you can't do that until you understand where the other person is coming from. I don't feel an obligation to engage with a lot of the "theory" around the art—that doesn't interest me. But I do feel an obligation to understand enough about the theory such that I'm aware of what's going on around me. I want to know what the issues are. I want to have a sense of what people might say in response to my arguments, so that

I can take all that into account as I'm articulating my own position.

I've just finished writing a piece for *The New York Review of Books* about Donald Judd's collected writings, published last year. Judd is someone whose work I love—especially the hundred aluminum boxes in Marfa. And I love his writing. I don't *agree* with a lot of it, and I don't agree with a lot of his taste, but I find the vigor of the writing, the vision of it, incredibly exciting. It's fun to interact with that sensibility, that voice.

When I first read Judd's criticism, in art school, it was like jumping into a clean mountain stream—*Oh! This is description!* Judd seemed to offer a way of describing that was itself analysis. Of course, he was writing from this particular perspective as an artist. When you started out as a "painter-advocate" for a group of representational painters in the 1970s, did you see that as a reactionary position?

We didn't feel we were reactionary. If anything, we felt we were revolutionaries—that we were reasserting fundamental, foundational values. But it's also important to remember that the art world was smaller then, and so we didn't feel balkanized. There was still a sense that we were all in it together—that artists who were working in many different ways were part of the same great adventure. Maybe younger artists and critics still feel that way today; I'm not sure. In any event, one of the things I wanted to do in the *Art in America* anthology—this was also part of the impulse behind my book *New Art City*—was to knit together different strands of the story. I wanted to find a way to tell the story of art in New York that brought together what are regarded as the so-called major and minor players. There's a mainstream history—Pollock, de Kooning, Judd, Warhol, whatever—but there are always other voices. History as it's happening is much richer and messier than many historians later want to admit. Most people writing about art focus on what they regard as the major players and act as if the rest of the voices are off in some other room—way over there. Or else they focus on what they regard as the minor players and treat them as if they were operating on a totally different wavelength. One of the things I try to do—whether I'm writing about the present or the past—is remind people that the situation is always complicated, interwoven. I try to suggest that some of the artists who haven't gotten the lion's share of the attention are much more important, or of more profound quality, than they are given credit for; and maybe some of the people who, for one reason or another, are seen as the "key figures" are really not quite as satisfactory as we've been told. I've always liked the idea of trying to knit together these stories in new ways.

In *Calder: The Conquest of Time*, one of the things I wanted to do was bring in a lot of the people who were important to Calder but are overlooked, so that he can be seen in a broad context, so that it's not just always Calder-and-Miró. It's difficult to write that kind of history—history in which you have a lot of variegated strands woven together. Part of the reason people write either about the mainstream artists or what are now called the "outsiders" is because it's simpler to do one or the other. When I put together the anthology for the Library of America, I wanted to include critics from very different "camps"—both the painter-poets who tended to write for *ARTnews* and include John Ashbery and James Schuyler and the critics who took what many have described as a more theoretical approach to art, including Michael Fried in his long essay "Art and Objecthood" [1967]. What I wanted to show is that all these writers are part of a larger story. When you open your eyes and your mind, you can begin to see that artists whose work looks very different are often reacting to the same things. Lots of abstract artists have credited de Kooning as a key influence, but there are many representational artists for whom de Kooning was important, too. People tend to think things connect in straight lines, but the reality is much more complicated. A single artist or idea can impact different people in radically different—and equally valuable—ways.

Another problem that many people have when they try to understand the visual arts is that they fail to look at influences and impacts that may lie beyond the visual arts. One of the really interesting things about Calder is that he was close to a lot of literary people—Malcolm Cowley, the important critic, was a very close friend. Calder and Cowley had political connections and interests in common, and all too often

360

the art historians fail to examine that kind of relationship. Another too often overlooked aspect of Calder's career is his lifelong fascination and engagement with theater. I'll give one example. Much too little focus has been put on Calder's collaboration with Virgil Thomson on a 1936 production of Satie's *Socrate* [1919], a work for voice and orchestra. This was one of the most important things Calder did in the 1930s, but to get into it means you need to get into who Virgil Thomson was and Satie's critical place in modern and contemporary music. I suspect that many art historians are put off by all those connections. I love following them wherever they lead—it helps to enlarge the picture.

You have these panoramic historical chronicles in *New Art City* and *Paris Without End*. Now you've written this Calder biography. I'm interested in the differences between those forms and their attending intellectual questions; how did you approach writing a biography of an artist?

I find the challenge of writing different kinds of books fun— exciting. I'd never written a biography before, and I don't have a plan to again—not that I haven't had a totally fabulous time working on this. I've always read biographies, and one of the things I found myself asking at the beginning was, *What are the biographies that are really wonderful? And why do they work?* In the very early phases of working on Calder, I read Richard Ellmann's *James Joyce* [1959] and *Oscar Wilde* [1969], which are both phenomenal biographies. One of the interesting things about these two biographies written by the same man is that they're totally different. That's because they're about very different people— and Ellmann responds completely to the needs of his subject. The Wilde is incredibly social and includes all these secondary figures, while the Joyce, which is the story of a rather solitary man, is much more monolithic. Leon Edel, who wrote the great biography of Henry James, published a series of lectures called *Literary Biography* [1957]. I found them unbelievably useful. He addresses questions such as, *What do you do with a secondary character who appears at three different chronological points in the story?* What he says is, *You decide on the most important point in the story where this person appears, and you bring them in then, get us up-to-date on*

361

where they were before and where they're going to go—you do that all right there. Writing about Calder got me interested in the *techniques* of biography.

I'm curious about how you ended up at *The New Republic*. Can you describe the process of getting out of college and starting to write?

I came of age in the late sixties, when nobody thought about how they were ever going to earn a living or have money when they were old. We were very idealistic—which somehow involved being somewhat impractical. I went to graduate school—I got an MFA in painting from Brooklyn College. I had weird part-time jobs, like working for a company that did fundraising auctions for Jewish organizations— mostly selling schlock paintings and Salvador Dalí prints. They were really nice people. I started writing criticism—you don't make much money writing short reviews. I got involved with *Aperture* magazine a little bit. Then I started writing for *The New Criterion*. I hated the politics. Hilton Kramer was the founding editor, and we almost came to blows about his crazy right-wing politics, which got crazier as the years went by. Then I was approached by an agent. She got me connected with *Vogue* around '83, and I started writing things for them. That was when Alexander Liberman was still the creative director of Condé Nast. Another book I had loved as a kid—do you know it?—was Liberman's book *The Artist in His Studio* [1960].

Of course!

I never owned a copy, but I took it out from the public library a lot. Early in my time writing for *Vogue*, I went to the *Vogue* Christmas party. Alex was there, and I told him how much I loved *The Artist in His Studio*. He had been reading my work in *The New Criterion*; he read everything. He took me out to lunch, and we talked about a great many things— and the long and short of it was, I ended up with a Condé Nast contract. I was writing about six or eight pieces a year and was suddenly making an amount of money that you could kind of live on. I was also teaching part-time, some at Pratt, some at Parsons.

Leon Wieseltier was the literary editor at *The New Republic* from 1983 until a couple of years after Chris Hughes, a man with a Facebook fortune, bought the magazine. I went to college with Leon—we actually met in Meyer Schapiro's seminar and stayed in touch. I had been writing a little bit for the magazine, and eventually Leon asked me to be the art critic, which evolved into a full-time job. For much of the twenty years I was at *The New Republic*, I was a full-time staff member, with full salary, benefits, an expense account—although I lived in New York and the magazine's offices were in Washington. As somebody who is interested in nonfiction writing in general, I loved publishing my essays in *The New Republic*, where a piece about a visual artist could be right next to an essay about a novel or a political or philosophical idea. For me, criticism has always been about engaging with that larger world.

Much has been said and written lately about the culture of *The New Republic*. Leon Wieseltier has been accused of sexual harassment and inappropriate advances toward colleagues, for which he has apologized. I will only say that Leon could be a visionary editor and gave writers of many different ages and sensibilities a chance to develop their ideas in public; that was true for me, as it was true for Paul Berman, Ruth Franklin, Adam Kirsch, Cynthia Ozick, and James Wood. I shaped the art coverage—I just said what we were going to do, and we did it. I would sometimes go to fifty or more gallery shows a week, just walking around. After a couple of months I'd think, *I have a theme here.* Leon didn't always know what I was going to do. I'd say, *We'll do this big show at MoMA this month, but I'm going to do a piece about contemporary galleries next month. I've got enough to make a story.* It was an incredible privilege to be able to do that.

I worked with many tremendous editors over the years—both at publishing houses and magazines. It was a great honor to work with Bob Silvers at *The New York Review of Books* in the last couple of years of his life; the first thing he asked me to do was a review of the Jeff Koons retrospective at the Whitney, and he enthusiastically embraced the long, highly critical essay that I handed in. My first book, *Paris Without End,* was published by Jack Shoemaker, who founded North Point Press. And I was brought to Knopf by the extraordinary Carol Brown Janeway, who is well known not only as an editor, but also as a translator, and who became a very close friend. Carol published not only *New Art City* but also *Antoine's Alphabet*, which is my most personal book. We worked together on *Calder* until her untimely death; the Calder biography is dedicated to her.

How did you get to know Hilton Kramer?

That connection came through a friend of my parents, a woman named Anita Ventura Mosley, who'd been with Hilton at *Arts Magazine*. My father was a physicist, and she married a colleague of my father's. What people don't understand about Hilton is that at heart he was an old New York bohemian; his eventual rejection of liberalism, however misconceived, was grounded in a belief that liberals had somehow betrayed the arts. Most of Hilton's old friends eventually found that they couldn't talk with him about politics. I'd met him when he was still at the *Times*, and when he started *The New Criterion*, he asked me to write. I didn't really know what the orientation of the magazine was going to be. In the first issue he presented a virulent attack on the sixties and the student movement, and I wrote him a letter that said, *Look, I just I can't work with you!* Then a year later we crossed paths, and I did begin to write for him on a regular basis. However far apart we were politically—and we were very far apart—we did have kindred sensibilities when it came to the arts. And he liked the idea that I was going out and writing about art other people weren't writing about. He never second-guessed anything I did—even when I attacked people who were his friends. If you notice, a lot of Judd's criticism was written for *Arts Magazine* when Hilton was the editor. In the introduction to Judd's *Complete Writings 1959-1975* [1975], there is a laconic line where Judd says something like, *People ask me what it was like working for Hilton Kramer—he was fine.*

For Hilton, I came to represent in the magazine the values of an artists' world, which had always been important to him but which he was stepping away from as he became more engaged in political matters. By the third year or so of the magazine I was writing all the time. Hilton had some of the quality of a broken-hearted lover when it came to the art world; he couldn't face what Warholism had done to the New York bohemia that he loved. He said to me one day over lunch, after he

364

had been meeting with some students at Parsons, *It was so great to just sit with a bunch of painting students*—and he meant it! The tragedy of Hilton was that he couldn't accept that his own taste and sensibility hadn't prevailed. *The Age of the Avant-Garde* [1973] and *The Revenge of the Philistines* [1985] are remarkable chronicles of their times. If you look at them, you see that a lot of the things he believed in didn't triumph, and a lot of the things he disparaged did. It's hard to face that. To write finely thought-through essays, as Hilton did, and then to realize that in the end they haven't made all that much difference—that can be very hard. You have to face the fact that the world just goes on, that the artist you thought was a fool may well have a retrospective at The Museum of Modern Art, while many of the artists you admired are still largely unknown. I think all this broke his heart. Eventually—unfortunately—he looked for simplistic explanations. I remember he once said to me, *Warholism is the thing that brought everything down*. I remember thinking, *Yeah, Warholism is a problem, but what about Reaganomics? That's a problem too!*

When the Robert Mapplethorpe controversy blew up, the comment that I've always liked the best was Helen Frankenthaler's. She said, *This is not the thing that I would have voted for, but once a committee of our peers has voted for it, I support it. Because I support the whole enterprise of the NEA*. But Hilton started acting like a kid who hadn't gotten the party favor he wanted. Okay, he didn't agree with the panel's decision, I understand that. What I don't understand is why he wasn't uncomfortable when he found himself in league with Jesse Helms and the philistines. Maybe he was uncomfortable. But he certainly didn't act as if he was.

If you look at a lot of the really great journalistic critics—figures like Edwin Denby, Clement Greenberg, Randall Jarrell, and James Agee—you realize that most of them only wrote on a very regular basis for a relatively brief period of years. They did it for five or ten years, but then they stepped away a little bit, kept writing, but less frequently. Greenberg never stopped writing completely, but he stopped writing regularly. The same is true with Denby. I think they felt they had said what they could. They came to criticism with a particular sensibility, a particular vantage point. They put in their oar; they surveyed the scene; they helped shape taste, at least to some degree; and then they withdrew. The thing about Hilton was that he could never bear to withdraw. He loved the hurly-burly, the controversy, the drama. He couldn't do without that.

How have you dealt with that: advocating for the things you believe in that remain disregarded by the culture, while watching the things that you hate being celebrated?

When you've done a couple of hit jobs that people have talked about, one of the dangers is that people want you to keep doing them. At *The New Republic* Leon would say, *Are you going to do a "job" on so-and-so? I'd say, No. I can't just do that all the time.* Partly, you have to be engaged in the craft of what you're doing in a way that stays interesting for you. Criticism doesn't have all that much to do with going thumbs-up or thumbs-down—although that's often what people talk about. Criticism is about articulating a set of values—a sensibility, a philosophy—as you explore works of art. If you're going to attack something, you're obliged to explain on what basis you're attacking it. You can't just say that you don't like such and such; implicit in your argument must be an affirmation, a sense of what you value. Something I'm always concerned about when I write an attack on an artist is that I understand where the artist's supporters are coming from. I don't want to just blindly lob grenades. You want your readers to feel that you're fully engaged in what you're seeing and feeling. I was very pleased, sometime after I published a takedown of Gerhard Richter, to see Peter Schjeldahl in *The New Yorker* say something like, *Now, you can't deal with Richter without considering Jed Perl's essay somewhere in there.* For me, that's saying that we're all engaged in a conversation. However tough a critic gets, it's got to be a conversation, not a shouting match. People like it when a piece of tough criticism is done with a bit of wit—sometimes, when you're describing a depressing situation in the arts, it's good to have a few jokes.

Your books focus on the first half of the twentieth century. What's the difference between writing from a historical and a contemporary perspective?

366

I think the "me" has a different place in criticism. What we want in criticism is a *particular* person confronting things. And, over a period of time, as you read that critic, you begin to have a sense of where that person is coming from. I've had people say insightful things to me about my sensibility, which they've deduced not from knowing me personally but from reading me over the years. When I'm sitting down to write a piece of criticism, the first question is, *What did I think and feel about it?* Even if it's something like that Judd review—though the writing is fifty years old, what I'm writing about is my engagement with the book right now. People do write whole books that way, but for me the book writing—the historical writing—tends to submerge the "me" into some larger or different kind of movement.

How have you dealt with writing about people you know personally?

It's hard. When I write about somebody I don't know, I almost try to imagine I know them. And when I write about somebody I do know, I try to forget them. Truly. Inevitably you end up knowing people you write about, to one degree or another. When I started out, I didn't know if any of it mattered—I couldn't imagine that I actually had an audience—so I felt completely free to say whatever I wanted. When you start writing, you don't know if people are reading, and you don't know if anybody is going to care. And then, after a while, you realize people *do* care. One of the things that's amazed me over the years is that sometimes I'll write something I think is really tough about someone I know and I'll think, *Oh, God. This is going to be awful.* And then they turn out to be fine with it. A person will say, *I really thought it was interesting what you said; I don't totally agree, but* ... Basically, I've always felt my job as a critic is to try to be *me* and figure out who I am. Your obligation as a critic is to yourself, and to the craft of writing. No matter how sophisticated you are as a critic—no matter how much you know about the intricacies of the arts and the complexities of the art world—you need to retain some fundamental simplicity. It's those basic, immediate reactions that fuel your thinking and your writing. When you've lost that, you've lost the core, the source.

People in the art world—I suppose it's true of any professional world—can get so obsessed with their "insider" knowledge that they lose track of the big picture. There's a danger of overcomplicating things. In New York, everybody's always trying to figure out the backstory. Sometimes the explanations that people come up with are much more complicated than the reality. For example, when I was starting out as a critic, I was friends with the painter-critic Sidney Tillim. Sidney was a wonderful critic, but he did have a tendency to overintellectualize things. I would go and have coffee with him—this was before I really knew any of the players at the magazines—and he would be saying, *Jed, they cut two paragraphs from my article. And it was because of this editor and this critic and this artist and this* . . . And once I got to know some of the people at the magazines he was talking about, I realized they cut it because there wasn't space on the page. It was much simpler than he imagined. You know what I mean?

I do! But what is it in particular about criticism that brings out these conspiracy theories?

Well, criticism is about our passions. From a critic you want clarity, you want clear thinking, but mostly, I think you want huge passion. One of the great things about loving the arts is those moments when you lose yourself in them, like, *Yes. This is it!*

All my favorite critics are lovers at the core.

Yes.

Especially when they're mad!

Exactly! A really compelling critique is a critique that's grounded in love—in the love of an art form and all its possibilities. And love is not a science! That's where it gets complicated. There are many different reasons to respond to a work of art. Not everything we respond to strongly is necessarily a masterpiece. It can be a work of art that expresses certain feelings, certain emotions, certain sensations. The critic Thomas B. Hess, in his writings about de Kooning, was very good at picking out striking qualities in works that I suspect he didn't think were masterpieces. In some of the things he wrote about de Kooning in the 1960s, Hess found ways to talk about the work—in relation to the experience of the city or of Long Island—without insisting on a strict valuation of the work. That is something you can do as a critic—you can highlight particular qualities or characteristics. In other words, you can say, *I don't really feel like grading this—I'm not into giving it a B minus or a B plus. Instead I want to talk about what interests me about it.* One of the things I've realized as I've followed artists for a couple decades is that often really interesting artists will have a show that doesn't knock your socks off the way an earlier one did, but that doesn't necessarily mean all that much. It may mean that they're in a transitional phase—and for a critic, that may be a moment to think, *I'm going to hold off a little.* Is it then dishonest to not run to your word processor and write, *This show is not as good as the last one?* Maybe. But now I'm more inclined to think, *I'm going to let this be and see where this artist goes from here.*

There is a lot of sensitivity in your writing about the layers we experience in an artwork. Particularly in your Watteau book, *Antoine's Alphabet*, there's a beautiful parsing of the simultaneous, ambiguous, emotional situations latent in those paintings.

I couldn't live without the arts. I mean—I couldn't live without my friends and family, but I also I really couldn't live without the pleasure of paintings and books and music. And those pleasures are multilayered. That's why any simplistic political litmus test for art really drives me crazy—from any side. I'm thinking of people who are tempted to say, *Ezra Pound was an anti-Semite, therefore we shouldn't read the* Cantos [1915–1962]. Believe me, I understand who Pound was, but that doesn't change the fact there are pages of ravishing beauty in the *Cantos.*

I'm especially interested in the "fictional" qualities of your Watteau book—you imaginatively inhabit the inner lives of historical figures and write from their perspectives. That is a real departure for you, and something that few art critics would do. I think Dave Hickey does it in a fanciful way, and of course something like it happens in Diderot too.

Facts can become very oppressive. I've spent so much of my life dealing with and worrying about facts. *Is this true? Is this how you'd describe that color?* Or, if you're talking about someone else's responses, *Is that fair? Is that measured? Is that exaggerating their opinions?* It was just a tremendous liberation to try to imagine situations and tell stories. An example in *Antoine's Alphabet* is the section in which I describe Cézanne painting his son dressed as a harlequin. I jumped off from little bits of what was known; then I took off with it, I imagined this loving relationship between a father and a son. I did actually get a scholar of Watteau to look at the book. He pointed out places where I hadn't been aware of certain situations. The playfulness of *Antoine's Alphabet* gave me wonderful opportunities to experiment with my writing—and that goes back to the fact that writing itself is what I'm passionate about. I look back at pieces I wrote a long time ago and I will agree down to the ground with every opinion stated—thank God—but I will see things in the writing that I'd like to do differently.

What do you think the function of criticism is today?

I think criticism is a fundamental human impulse. Styles of criticism may change, but something essential remains. When people walk out of a movie theater, the first thing they say is, *What did you think?* Criticism is not some weird esoteric activity. It's a natural outgrowth of our concern for the world around us. My vision of criticism today is still based on what the work of certain critics meant to me in my teens and twenties. As a reader, I found myself interacting with writers who cared about the same things I did. With the critics I loved then—again, I go back to Edmund Wilson and Pauline Kael—I was engaged in an exchange of ideas and feelings about the world. I got to see things the way somebody else saw them. They guided me, excited me, turned me on to things. They sharpened and deepened my responses.

Something I think *New Art City* shows perfectly is that there were a number of structural factors after World War II that produced this exceptional thing that we call cultural life in New York City, and that the economic, social, and intellectual forces that fostered serious criticism no longer exist. Mid to late twentieth-century art criticism is actually a very specific and historically bounded entity.

Look, the first thing I'll say is, you and your generation—how old are you?

Thirty.

I think it's up to your generation to find the way forward. I'm not planning to stop writing, but I do think the ball is literally in your court. The art of criticism has never been an easy one to practice; like any serious creative endeavor, it's a struggle. But the circumstances are especially challenging now. There are fewer outlets for serious criticism, at least in the print media. And the scale of the art world—and the outrageous amounts of money now involved—has become oppressive; it's a weight that threatens to flatten all of us. If you want to take a dark view of things, you can argue that a great period of cultural expansion and enlightenment may be ending. There was a dream that began in the nineteenth century that the audience for "serious things"—whether scientific knowledge or artistic experience—was going to continuously expand in democratic societies. There was an idea that as education expanded, more and more people were going to be able to embrace the arts and the sciences. It's possible that the mid-twentieth century was the climax of that kind of expansion, at least in Western Europe and the United States. In the early to mid-twentieth century, more and more people were being exposed to complicated artistic, literary, musical, theatrical, scientific, intellectual experiences. Those were relatively pure experiences; they weren't being dumbed down, at least not to the extent that a lot of experiences are dumbed down and diluted today. By now the scale may have tipped in the other direction. The desire for an ever-expanding audience for the arts may be diluting the power of the arts.

When I say that the weight of the art world—the weight of the blue-chip galleries, the art fairs, the gonzo auction prices—oppresses all of us, I don't mean to say that people don't go on doing what they do, or that there isn't a lot of really good work being done. There is. But we're living in a new Gilded Age. And there's a lot of stress involved in trying to keep our bearings. A poet friend recently sent me this from Wendell Berry: "To be sane in a mad time / is bad for the brain, worse / for the heart." That's how the art world often leaves me feeling. The art world used to be a smaller world. People could map the whole thing. When I walk around Chelsea today, I often feel I'm not an art critic so much as I'm a sociologist. I'm not looking at the art; I'm looking at the size of the space and calculating the cost of running it. Of course, all of that can be interesting; I've certainly written about that kind of thing from time to time. But in the end there shouldn't be any difference between how one responds to art in a big gallery or a smaller gallery. You know what I'm saying?

Yes.

When you go back and look at *ARTnews* in the fifties and sixties, you find that by and large the criticism reflected a sense that everybody was here because they had complicated, passionate feelings about the nature and possibilities of art. Of course, there were art-world politics back then, too. There was lots of it. But now we're in a situation where the art-world politics threaten to overtake the art. It's not just the art world; the book world is that way too. I think it does have to do with scale—the scale of success right now is downright crazy. De Kooning and Pollock were still living quite modestly in the postwar years, despite having developed major critical reputations. Alexander Calder had a retrospective at The Museum of Modern Art in 1943. It was a huge success—it was extended and it was a turning point for him. He went at that moment from being an artist enormously admired among a vanguard audience to being known to a wider public. But even in the late forties, he and his wife were still living month to month; they had very little money. My point is: there's a crazy scale of success today that has nothing to do with the things we really care about. No matter how much we may understand this intellectually, I think it's really affecting us.

One of the things that upsets me now is that when there's a big show of a contemporary artist at one of the New York museums, you read reviews in *New York*, *The New Yorker*, and the *Times*—and basically everybody's on the same page. It would be very good for that mythical "general public" everybody is always talking about if somebody would come out with a different point of view—then people could go to the show and work things out for themselves, thinking, *Okay, the person at* The New Yorker *really loved it, but the* Times *thought there were a lot of problems*. Then you would have some options—you could begin to navigate it for yourself. I think I've sometimes provided that alternate view. Until my review of the Koons retrospective at the Whitney came out in *The New York Review of Books*, there had pretty much been lockstep critical praise—at *New York*, *The New Yorker*, and the *Times*.

Do you feel like people *expect* contrary views from you?

I think people expect me to call it however I see it. People who read me are not always sure where I'll come out on things, which is probably the way it should be. I'm not sorry that people remember some of my takedowns—of Richter and Koons and Rauschenberg. But I also hope people remember how enthusiastic I've been about artists including Joan Snyder, Bill Jensen, Louisa Matthíasdottír, Barbara Goodstein, Robert Gober, Duane Michals, Douglas Blau, and Jean Hélion. I carry a torch for Balthus's late work, and some people have mocked me for that. But generally I think people are disappointed when they feel like I'm just saying what is more a generally accepted view. They expect me to walk my own path—whatever that may be.

That must be an expectation for a critic in general.

Well, it should be.

When I look at something, first I try
and figure out what it is. Then I see
if the little quality bell rings. Henry
Geldzahler, who was also a very close
friend of mine, used to say that seeing
something new and important made
him want to vomit. That's *right*.
I think you have a visceral response
that you don't necessarily know how
to communicate, or understand.

Barbara Rose (b. 1938) is a critic, curator, and historian
who helped define the zeitgeist of the sixties and
seventies with essays like "ABC Art" (1965). She wrote
for *Artforum* (1965–1973), *Art in America* (1965–1971),
Vogue (1966–1988), *New York* magazine (1971–1977),
and *Partisan Review* (1975–1996) and was the founder
and editor of *The Journal of Art* (1988–1991). Her books
include *American Art Since 1900* (1967); *The Golden
Age of Dutch Painting* (1969); *Art-as-Art: The Selected
Writings of Ad Reinhardt* (editor, 1975); *Lee Krasner*
(1983); and *Autocritique: Essays on Art and Anti-
Art, 1963–1987* (1988). She was senior curator at the
Museum of Fine Arts, Houston, from 1981 to 1985 and
recently curated the traveling exhibition *Painting after
Postmodernism* (2016).

Barbara Rose

In the introduction to your collection of art criticism, *Autocritique*, you say your first act of criticism was quitting the piano, and your second was quitting painting. I want to know more about that.

That's right. I am a child of immigrants; my parents were not born in this country. My father was an illegal alien who was born in Warsaw and arrived in the US in 1926 as an illiterate thirteen-year-old stowaway. My grandfather—who was Austro-Hungarian, as we used to say—had the Metropolitan Opera on all the time when I was a child. Music was considered a proper cultural activity worth pursuing. I was a very good pianist—I won national scholarships for free lessons. It was something that my parents applauded. My Canadian cousins were also concert pianists, so there was that gene in the family. I used to practice four hours a day. Then they put the television next to my Steinway, and that was the end of that. [Laughter.]

I had a talent for drawing, and maybe I could have been an artist, but I studied with the wrong people. I went to Smith because it was the only good school where you could major in studio art. Unfortunately, my teacher was Leonard Baskin, and I knew that all those big owls with funny eyes—*This is not art*. But then I thought, *I don't know what art is, because I come from some terrible suburban milieu*. So I took the Pyramids to Picasso course at Smith. My teachers were the greatest experts.

I came to New York and spent senior year at Barnard and immediately went right across the street to Columbia to the PhD program. I was one of two girls in my class—the other one was Margit Rowell's older sister Luisa, and they managed to harass her into leaving to get a PhD in anthropology with Margaret Mead. She looked like Veruschka. The macho professors drooled. But no matter what they did to me, I was not going to leave. And so there was a lot of persecution—shall I say "harassment"? I read about Harvey Weinstein now and I think, *Isn't that the experience of every woman in the world? Like, doesn't that happen to everybody?* Of course it happened. Like, *Miss Rroose, wouldn't you like to carry my slide case?* I said, *No, I wanted my own slide case.*

It was very overt, and in one or two cases punitive, and it took me a long time to finish my doctorate because I had men who were my enemies. Actually more like my *admirers*. Because there were no full-time women on the grad faculty, I minored in archaeology; there were women in archaeology.

When you got to Columbia's art history department, what was the intellectual terrain?

My professors were all Europeans. Even though Meyer Schapiro was an American, he was born in Lithuania and had studied with Germans. I studied with Rudolf Wittkower, Julius Held, Charles de Tolnay, Philip Pouncey, but I did most of my work with Meyer Schapiro. He was my hero. Meyer gave one seminar on the New York School, and that was barely acceptable to the faculty. I was not interested in studying modern art. I thought, *I'm a modern person, I understand my age, what do I need this for?* I wanted to study things that I didn't understand and that would be a new kind of knowledge for me—I studied old masters, connoisseurship, and especially medieval art and archaeology. It was a very specific kind of art history. This was strictly *Kunstgeschichte*. We used to talk in hallowed terms about "our discipline." By the time you got out of there your mind was formed in a certain way.

How does that scholarly work parallel your writing criticism?

Like most of the things in my life, it was an accident. I got a Fulbright to Spain to do research on sixteenth-century painters in Navarre, which was my dissertation. Walter W. S. Cook, a great man, was the founder of the Institute of Fine Arts, where I was also taking classes, and he became my mentor because he taught Spanish art history.

My artist husband and I both applied for Fulbrights, with the idea that whoever got it would take the other person—and I got mine. He didn't. In Spain I realized that because of censorship, nothing was known about twentieth-century art. It was a funny thing: cubism was invented by two Spaniards—Picasso and Gris—and modern sculpture was invented by another Spaniard—González—but in Paris. And in Spain they didn't know anything that was happening in American art. So I started writing, in Spanish, the "Crónica de Nueva York" for a magazine called *Goya*, which was essentially an old master magazine, because I wanted them to see images of Franz Kline and de Kooning and pop art and things that they'd never seen. So that was the first criticism I ever wrote.

In the beginning of his collection of criticism *Art and Objecthood* [1998], Michael Fried says his real introduction to the New York art world was coming to stay with you and Frank Stella in New York. It sounds like your place was a kind of a salon.

I became part of the art world when I was very young, just because of where I lived. I had no plan. I intended to be a professor of old master Spanish painting. For a while I lived above the Hansa Gallery, and I just met *everybody*—again an accident. It was easy. I'm a very sociable person, so yeah, Frank's and my place was like an open house. People used to drift in and out. Frank had graduated from Princeton, and he had all his Princeton professors who were still his friends—Bobby Rosenblum and Bill Seitz and Stephen Greene—who would all come around. And then Frank knew Carl Andre and Hollis Frampton from Andover. I met Don Judd and Lucas Samaras at Columbia—they were getting master's degrees in art history. Don was taking the most difficult courses on old masters—his specialty was iconography, although he did study with Schapiro. We met in a seminar on Venetian painting, and he became my best friend at Columbia. He was a great intellectual—no question. So we knew these people from school. We'd always have people come around and I had my "guest chef" program—because I can't cook.

So how did you experience the scene around criticism when you started writing?

First, you have to understand that we didn't like *ARTnews*—it was the house organ of abstract expressionism, and we were against that.

But, didn't you work at *ARTnews* for a time, early on?

I was an editorial assistant. It was my day job when I was a student at Columbia. It was really a joke. Thomas B. Hess, the editor, later became my best friend, but when we started out, he insulted me—I was this little girl, and I remember him saying, *This isn't a school for creative writing.* My revenge was to hire Carl Andre to be our proofreader, knowing Carl would drive Tom crazy—which he did. Later I split my job as the art critic for *New York* magazine with Tom in the seventies.

But, simply, we were against *ARTnews* because we were the new kids on the block and we wanted to do something *new.* It was the sixties and we had a different kind of music and clothing and we were going to start all over. It was the youth culture, and we were the beginning of it.

At the same time, while Hess was holding down the fort for ab-ex at *ARTnews*, he was also publishing Gene Swenson's "What Is Pop Art?" interviews [1963–1964] and Allan Kaprow's essays in the magazine, so there was a kind of intergenerational complexity that it never gets credit for.

ARTnews didn't have complexity, Tom Hess had complexity. He really was a genius—and he certainly died too young. He was very intellectually curious, open-minded. You have to understand that the editors of art magazines at that time were very special people. I know Tom went to Deerfield, and then Yale, and he had this whole coterie of Yalies—Milton Gendel and all these people who were really seriously smart. And Phil Leider was the editor of *Artforum*, and he was incredibly smart. These were brilliant educated people, and they were real editors. They knew the difference between what's an idea and what's not an idea, who's a writer and who's not a writer. There was selectivity. This does not go on anymore. The problem is not that the emperor has no clothes. The problem is that there is no emperor. There is no authority. It's all global goulash in the blogosphere, and writers earn nothing.

You also worked at Leo Castelli's gallery around that time?

I was the receptionist. I was so poor. Frank Stella was my best friend and was showing at the gallery. He said, *Maybe Leo will give you a job.*

My parents had disowned me. My father would say, *Do you know what a phudnik is?—A nudnik with a PhD!* They just stopped talking to me. Then when I married Frank, in 1961, it was truly hopeless. I didn't see my family for a while, which was really my mother's doing. They rejected the idea that I would be an art historian. My father said, *Art history is useless and pointless. You will never get a job or meet a decent guy. I want you to change your field and meet a better class of people.* So, anyway, I worked for Leo because I was so poor. And he didn't have very much money to pay a receptionist—maybe he paid me six dollars an hour.

That must have been a real education.

I saw so much art going in and out. Ivan Karp would schlep in all this art. Ivan was amazing—he loved pop art, and he would bring all this stuff into Leo's at a time when Leo basically wanted to show the New York School. He had *Scent* [1955], Pollock's last painting, over his desk. And over my desk was the first lithograph Jasper Johns did at Tatyana Grosman's, *Coat Hanger I* [1960]. It wasn't like a gallery, it was more like a family. We took care of each other. There was Sal Scarpitta, and Friedel Dzubas, and Frederick Kiesler—they were the old guys, but they liked us and we liked them. It was a hangout.

One of the earliest pieces you wrote was about how Johns and Rauschenberg were not neo-Dada, which also must have come out of the fact that you knew them and were in the scene around Castelli's. How did that essay come about?

Michael Fried was a very close friend of Frank's, and a close friend of mine, and Michael was writing the "New York Letter" for *Art International*. Michael persuaded me that this article I'd been working on called "Dada Then and Now" [1963] should be published—I wanted to dispel this idea that Rauschenberg and Johns were Dada artists, because I didn't see them that way. I thought, *Nobody in this country is going to print this*, but Jim Fitzsimmons was over there in Lugano, Switzerland, publishing *Art International*. He printed it and then said, *Why don't you do a "New York Letter"?* That was it.

My other friend at Columbia was Max Kozloff. I really esteem him a great deal—I think he's brilliant. He called me up one day and said,

Do you want to write for this new magazine? They're in California, they don't really know what they're doing, but you and I can be the contributing editors. I said, *I guess so.* And that is how I started writing for *Artforum.* But they were still in San Francisco and it was a very small-time publication.

It seems like Clement Greenberg was a model for you as a critic. How did you first encounter his writing?

When I was an art history student at Columbia, suddenly everyone was abuzz—*Have you seen David's magazine?* "David" was David Rosand, who was a Renaissance scholar, who put out a magazine called *The Second Coming.* In this magazine he published an article by Greenberg, "How Art Writing Earns Its Bad Name" [1962]. At this moment art criticism was all total subjective junk—all Rosenberg and pseudo-existentialism that just meant *nothing.* Then all of a sudden, there was this very concrete, in English, focused method that Greenberg laid out, and he just seemed like such a hero—a giant in an arena of dwarves. Immediately, and as a result of *that* article, he became the person you wanted to read. When he published *Art and Culture* in 1961, we all read it—we ate it up. *Oh my God, this man really knows what he's talking about!* That essay "Collage" [1958]—nobody ever explained it like that before! It was with that book that Clem created his image as *the* dominant personality and authority.

How did your relationships with Michael Fried and Clement Greenberg interact with your being married to Frank Stella?

Michael was our mutual best friend and was the witness at our wedding. Our son is named after him. Personally, I think he had to choose between Clem and Frank, and he chose Clem, because Frank did not fit into that Greenbergian dogma—he just didn't. Frank doesn't have the kind of personality where you tell him what to do and he does it. His persona just did not fit into the disciple mold. The same is true of me: I rebel against authority—that's just my personality.

Also, as I say, I was friends with Don Judd, who made much more sense to me than Clem. You have to remember we were friends with Rauschenberg and Johns, who were "out" as far as Greenberg was concerned. I don't recall what he called Bob, but he said Jasper was *a genuine minor master*, and I didn't see him that way—I saw him as much more important than any of the color-field painters. So, that was the end for me and Clem, who hated pop art. That show he did, *Post-Painterly Abstraction* [1964], was awful, and the essay was awful. I thought, *He's trying to create a school of painting under his direction, and I don't believe any of it.*

However, it seemed like Greenberg provoked a level of rigor and intensity in writing about art—

There's no question. There was a clarity, and also a philosophical basis, which was English analytic philosophy, for better or worse. He wrote in a very concrete manner and it was not full of flourishes—he was not continental philosophy. It was not this kind of abstruse theorizing, it was really very empirical.

In your essay "Pop in Perspective" from 1963, you conclude: "Pop art is not only art, most of the time it is not even bad art, judged by the same standards which one judges abstract art. If the level of formal invention is not great, it is scarcely worse than that of most of the abstract art shown today, nor is the content more vacuous. And sometimes, it is distinctly better." That's something that happens throughout your criticism—it seems like you're never setting into a final stance.

I don't have any final positions. You just go by intuition—I strictly work in terms of intuition and experience. I have no theories.

I found that exciting: *This is a critic who is not ideological, it doesn't add up to a system—I don't know what she's going to say about any given thing*. You seem comfortable letting things sit in contraction as you move from one part of an essay to the next.

Well, things are often in contradiction. And not to see both sides of a question is a kind of ignorance that I don't adhere to. I think you have to look at a global situation and see how you feel about it.

However, there is something you stated earlier, which is that criticism is about values and making judgments—"The rest is art writing," I think you wrote. I would like to understand now how your thoughts on judgment have evolved.

I still believe that. It only evolves by looking at things. Art criticism is a visual experience. I've had very rich visual experiences, grounded in great painting. I've looked at a lot of great painting, and I ask myself, *Why is this Velázquez great? And why is this one not as good? Or, Why is the school of Velázquez not good?* These are judgments I've spent my life making. So when I look at something, first I try and figure out what it is. Then I see if the little quality bell rings. Henry Geldzahler, who was also a very close friend of mine, used to say that seeing something new and important made him want to vomit. That's *right*. I think you have a visceral response that you don't necessarily know how to communicate, or understand, when you see something new and important. I miss that feeling.

Aside from Greenberg and Fried, as you were developing your critical voice, who were the critics you were in dialogue with—or against?

Well, the newspaper critics were ridiculous. I thought Hilton Kramer's taste was particularly ridiculous. But I studied Hilton's style to learn how to write, because it was a good literary style. I also studied the way Clem and Meyer Schapiro wrote, because I wanted the same kind of clarity and specificity, and that is really how I taught myself to write art criticism. I am not a natural writer.

How did you come to write "ABC Art" for *Art in America*?

I wrote that article and I think Phil didn't like it, so I gave it to Jean Lipman at *Art in America*. "ABC"—God knows was not my title. Also, the term "minimal art" was not my invention—which I make very clear. I said I found the term in a book by Richard Wollheim. People ask, *Why did you write that article?* The truth is I wrote it so that my friends who weren't selling anything would sell some art. That is the only reason I wrote it. It was also a kind of diary about my life—the things I was reading and the plays I was seeing. It was a nexus of music and theater and literature and art that came together in a certain sensibility that people started to call "minimal."

What I like about that piece is its form. In the beginning you state: "Though my end is simply the isolation of the old-fashioned *Zeitgeist*, I want to go about it impressionistically rather than methodically. I will take up notions now in the air that strike me as relevant to the work.

As often as possible I will quote directly from texts that I feel have helped to shape the new sensibility."

Completely. It was just my life. What I was drawn to, what I cared about, the things that I was involved with. To a degree there was a general interest in logical positivism as a philosophy and in the plays of Samuel Beckett and the thought of John Cage. John was terribly important to me, as well. I dedicated my first book to Meyer Schapiro and John Cage—they were the two people who ruled my life and my thought. Because John was an enormous influence, Asian thought became very important to all of us—we all studied Buddhism. I think Richard Serra and Philip Glass are still tantric Buddhists.

How did it come about that you ended up editing the book of Reinhardt's selected writing, *Art-as-Art*?

I just loved Ad. I thought that what he said made sense. I used to go up to Columbia to class, and when I came back downtown—we lived on Union Square—I would stop by Ad's studio while he was painting the black paintings and talk to him. He was very open to younger artists— he and Barnett Newman were the only two of the New York School who cared about the younger generation. Again, it was that sensibility, very much a minimal, drone music sensibility, that I understood.

I was interested in Ad's work and I thought the book needed to be done. The terrible thing that happened was that while I was doing it, Ad died—it was very sudden, a heart attack—*boom*. I continued to work with his wife, Rita, because the documents were all there. There are many more writings than I included, and I feel guilty because it should be redone and expanded. Although, he repeated himself; I said, *Ad, why did you keep publishing the same article?* He said, *They didn't understand it the first time.* He took a position. It was a difficult position, and it was a position I believed in. I still believe art is art and life is life, and I don't think that they have anything to do with each other. All of these terrible shows that try to make politics into art are just iconographic illustrations. Ad was very active politically, as is Mark di Suvero, but they did not compromise their art by turning it into propaganda or illustration.

I adore your essay "Diane Arbus: The Art of Extreme Situations" [1972]. This is partly how it ends: "To have understood that *human nature itself has been deformed*, to have seen that the most banal subject has its layers of personal kinkiness and traumatic alienation, is an esthetic discovery of the first order. That a woman came to this understanding is not coincidental at this point in history, when the art and literature as well as the lives of women reflect the extremity of their current existential situation."

Yeah, but I could write something like that and still be called antifeminist because I wouldn't join up with the "movement." I don't *do* movements. I'm a professional nonjoiner. I'm not joining *anything!* [Laughter.]

Of course, Lucy Lippard wrote the essay for Ad Reinhardt's Jewish Museum catalogue in 1966.

Lucy was always a friend. And remember that Lucy was married to Bob Ryman, and I was married to Frank Stella, so naturally Ad was terribly important to both of us. At one point she told me, *You'll see, one day you're going to fall, and when you fall you're going to fall hard.* I said, *I don't think so.*

She meant you were going to fall for feminism?

Yes, feminism. *No, Lucy, I really don't think so.* It never occurred to me if the person I was writing about was a man or woman or gay or straight or black or white or whatever—*it didn't occur to me.* Then I went back and I looked at what I had done, and three major monographs were on women—Helen Frankenthaler, Magdalena Abakanowicz, and Lee Krasner. I curated Lee's retrospective at MoMA in 1983 and pulled her out of the shadows, because at the time people just referred to her as "the widow Pollock." I was revolted by that.

You were one of the editors who left *Artforum* in 1974 because of the controversy surrounding Lynda Benglis's dildo advertisement, along with Rosalind Krauss and Annette Michelson, who went on to found *October.*

The Lynda Benglis ad—that was the end. Also John Coplans, who was the editor at the time, was hopeless—bringing out cock rings at lunch. *This was not good.* John was a card-carrying misogynist—a nightmare—but we put up with him. And the time came when we just didn't want to put up with him anymore. So Annette and Ros came over to my house to talk about what we would do after *Artforum*. I wanted to do essentially "The New York Review of Art." They said, *We're going to do* October. And I asked, *But what are we going to do in November?* [Laughter.] I knew very well what they were thinking, because Annette was deeply engaged with the revolution and came out of that literary and philosophical milieu in Paris. The format they wanted was *Tel Quel*. Well, I had been to those *Tel Quel* meetings in Paris—no way was I going to do that. I thought it was deliberate obscurantism, and I didn't want to be involved. So they went their way and I went mine; they did *October* and I did *The Journal of Art*.

You once wrote, "For art criticism is no science; very little that can be said about an art work is verifiable. Very little that is verifiable is relevant to a discussion of art."

I think that's true. I gave up on logical positivism at a certain point. If you do that, then what are you left with? Instinct, experience, values based on comparative judgments. That's *all* you're left with. Here's what I think: the artist has an intention. Now, the first question is, *Can they communicate that intention?* If they can't communicate it, it doesn't matter what they intended. If you believe they *can* communicate, then you're into the *message*—which is how I deal with art at this point. It has a message, but what is it? You're trying to decode that communication. That is what I think "criticism" or art writing can do. Because the people writing it have more experience doing that than the people reading it—presuming there is someone reading it. The relative importance of criticism now is minimal. Nobody cares. They figure, *If I'm that rich I must be smart. Who needs experience or years of study?* Criticism is not how values are formed today. There is a great deal of propaganda—the museums are owned by their trustees, who are not collectors, but *investors*. And when you get to a situation where you cannot expect the museums to be truthful or honest—who is the authority?

How did you start making films about art?

Michael Blackwood called me up in 1968 and said, *I want you to write these movies*. He was a German filmmaker. His brother was named Christian, and they came to this country after surviving the war in terrible circumstances. Their father had been involved in the German film industry, and Michael set up a company in New York. He was a good businessman, and he would get German money to finance movies, but he didn't know anything about art, so he called me because I knew all the artists. Lana Jokel was editing his films at that point. Michael would disappear to Germany to find money, and somehow Lana and I were alone making these documentaries. We worked together a long time, until she went off to make movies herself, and I went off to make my own movies.

Did you see that as an alternative to writing criticism?

Well, because of my friendship with Annette Michelson, I became very involved in film history. I started reading it and I wrote a number of articles about film history in *Artforum* and other places, and I taught film history at UC Irvine. But I was not going to make avant-garde films myself—I'm not an artist and I don't make art films. I decided that I needed to make these documentaries because we were going into a new dark age and no one would be able to read, and these would be like the manuscripts in Saint Gallen—people would find my videos in a thousand years and discover that something had actually happened. I saw very clearly that we were going into a dark age. And now, here we are.

Also, in a film, you get all this complexity: you have words and sequences of images that you can play off of each other. One of the things you write is that "there are no literary equivalents for visual experience, and this is the heart of our dilemma as art critics."

There isn't.

And it seems like turning toward filmmaking was a way of trying to address that problem inherent to writing about art in a different way.

That is true. Seeing these people make these works, listening to them about why they made them, how they made them, and then actually seeing the images would be a more direct way to teach about art. Because it's really pedagogical project. I have no pretensions about my documentaries; they're nice.

At the end of your introduction to *Autocritique* you essentially say, *This is the record of my disillusionment with, and alienation from, art criticism.*

Yeah, I gave up.

How would you describe the factors that made you decide you didn't want to write about contemporary art anymore?

It just wasn't compelling. It wasn't interesting enough for me to stay involved. In 1988, I started *The Journal of Art* with Italian partners, which is a whole other story—they bankrupted me and closed my magazine, which was making money, and it was a nightmare. But when I started it, I thought I could do a magazine to get my point of view across, a magazine that covered archaeology to the present—all of art history, which was probably insane. I used to write reports from a different city every month, about what the art world was like in that city. At that point, I still believed that you could communicate important ideas, or you could have discussions or dialogue, in that format. I don't see that as a possibility in what is now called the art world. Everything is for sale. My magazine was not. I refused ads if I thought they were for lousy or commercial art. My editors were highly educated. Okay, I'll admit it: I only hired Ivy League graduates. They've all gone on to do great things. And I paid the writers all the money that came from the ads. I insisted on paying the maximum available for first-class writing. Now the writers are treated as slaves, unpaid serfs, faceless bloggers. Peter Brant still owes me a thousand dollars for a piece that was published last September in *ARTnews*. Robert Mnuchin published a text of mine without a contract or agreement—a piece on Morris Louis I think now is wrong and would *never* agree to have republished.

Seriously, this is a sick, disgusting situation. But it's all the same— the .000001 percent are sucking all the money out of the economy so they can jet around to art fairs and biennales on yachts and private planes, gorging themselves on tax-free parties and feeling like geniuses because they are not just having fun, they're making a pile in speculation. Workers are replaceable in the gig economy. Well, we are now in gig criticism. Just slot in the "gray matter" between the art for sale. Nobody reads it anyway, but it gives those gallery catalogues "a touch of class."

One day I got out of a truck and was at some party and someone asked, *What do you do?* And instead of giving a long story, I said, *I'm an art critic.* And the person just said, *Cool.* I was one just because I was saying it, and that's still true in New York.

Jerry Saltz (b. 1951) is an art critic who has marshaled his outsize persona and immense popularity into a unique role he sometimes refers to as that of "folk critic." He entered the New York art world in the eighties, editing the books *Beyond Boundaries: New York's New Art* (1986) and *Sketchbook with Voices* (with Eric Fischl, 1986). Soon he was contributing to *Art in America, Flash Art,* and *frieze.* Throughout the late nineties and early aughts, he was the senior art critic at *The Village Voice.* His criticism has been collected in the books *Seeing Out Loud: Village Voice Art Columns Fall 1998–Winter 2003* (2003) and *Seeing Out Louder* (2009). Since 2006, he has been the senior art critic for *New York* magazine. He received the Pulitzer Prize for Criticism in 2018.

Jerry Saltz

For various reasons, some of which you're responsible for and some of which you aren't, you often get talked about as a cartoon character. I would like to get more of a sense of you as a person. Perhaps we should start with your early life: When did you first become conscious of art and decide that you wanted to be an artist?

I hated art as a kid. It was for sissies. I grew up in the inner city of Chicago. Then my father invented something called the Dexter handheld sewing machine—you may have seen it late at night on cheap-o commercials—and made enough money to move to the suburbs. Art was not part of my life in any way, shape, or form. It wasn't anything we thought of or talked about. One day, when I was ten years old, my mother brought me to the Art Institute of Chicago and kind of parked me there—it was a real mystery to me, I didn't really understand it. I walked around there, and at one point got stuck looking at two paintings. In one a guy was in a prison cell with people visiting him outside. In the next his head was on the ground, and his neck was spouting blood through the cell. I remember looking back and forth, and it suddenly hit me that these two paintings were a narrative, they were telling a story. My mind was blown. I looked around and thought, *Everything here is telling a story, everything here has a code, has a language—and I'm going to learn this whole language and I'm going to know the story.*

Shortly after that, my mother committed suicide. We were never told about it, so what sounds like a traumatic event never, in my life, actually happened. I came home and was only told my mother had gone to visit the angels, and that was it. She was never spoken of again in our house, never, not once. And I never went back to a museum and long forgot about that episode, until many years later I realized my favorite artist was Giovanni di Paolo, the fifteenth-century painter who made those two paintings I had seen. Later, when I saw his work, I went completely wild inside—the Met has two. I did not know why at first, but now it's obvious.

So your mother, out of the blue, took you to the museum? Was she artistic?

She was a housewife. I had two other brothers . . . This is so boring. Do you know where I begin when I read biographies? I skip to the chapter that starts, *And then she arrived in New York City*, or, *And then he came to Paris*, or, *And then they got to Moscow*. I have no interest in people's early lives. I always assume the author will say, *There is some connection . . .* Duh! I just want to read about what happened once you got there, but that's me.

So you have an aversion to me asking about your childhood?

Yes! [Laughter.] I can analyze anyone else's. I almost think it all goes without saying, so I'm not that interested in biography doing that.

But that story about the paintings was really terrific.

Okay, well, Giovanni di Paolo—look at the stuff I love: I love narrative, I love small scale, I love local color. Don't forget, if you know his style—he's painting during the Renaissance, but he's still in a late medieval mode. He's an individual, and I'm totally interested in that.

You say you're not a reader, so when you saw those paintings and realized they were stories, what was your context for narrative—from TV or movies or comic books?

I think it came from growing up in a house where nothing was spoken about, so I had to grow invisible antennae. Looking back, I suspect that in this fine middle-class suburb, I was treated differently as a child of a suicide, that the people around me, people's parents, would have changed. There would have been a dark cloud over me. I suspect that that's how I grew these antennae. I have a great sense of the pheromones and the kind of group mind around me, and I'm constantly making giant stories out of that.

Of course, I watched TV, but mainly I was a kid who watched sports and whatever sitcoms were on at that time. I wasn't a film student, and certainly I didn't read. Never occurred to me to read. It was out of the question. To this day, I pick one gigantic book each year and spend the whole year reading it. I'm a slow reader, but I'm going back to get the whole canon. I started with the *Iliad* and proceeded from there; if you name a big epic, I've been there.

Without trying to bog you down in more biographical tedium: Chekhov's gun is placed on the mantle at age ten in the Art Institute of Chicago. When does it finally go off? When did you decide to be an artist?

In high school, I was not good with girls, and I looked around and saw that the theater people were having sex and the art people were having sex. The theater people were a bit, you know, *demonstrative*—I wasn't reading the codes. So I picked art, and thought I'd try to go into the art world. I somehow ending up thinking of myself as an artist—I don't think I knew a thing about art. Art to me was Michelangelo, Salvador Dalí, Gustav Klimt, Vincent van Gogh, M. C. Escher, and Norman Rockwell—that's probably my canon. It's a nightmare canon, it's a disaster, but that's the suburban middle-class kid in me who didn't know, and who was too stupid and too smart-alecky to learn. So I tried to go to some school—didn't work. Tried to go to the Art Institute, and just started hanging out in the cafeteria, going to protest marches, trying to meet girls, saying I was an artist.

What is interesting to me about that story is that I don't recognize any artist I know as having had that experience. It's almost always something they know very early on. It never seems like a decision they drifted into.

They're like ventriloquists or gay people: apparently you know when you're very young if you're going to be a ventriloquist. Like, *very* young. Then you go through phases of denying, accepting, or trying it out. Artists usually know when they're very young without going through the "hiding" part of the narrative. I did not know. I had no vision of my life.

What you said about developing antennae to piece together larger narratives makes a lot of sense, because that is something that has run through your writing career. For instance, those two early books you did in the eighties, *Beyond Boundaries: New York's New Art* and *Sketchbook with Voices*.

I tried to throw all the copies of *Beyond Boundaries* out, but some survive.

I got them both online, easily. They're really interesting as documents surveying New York at that time. You'd been in New York for five or six years then, and you did these books attempting to make a big picture of what the art world was like. How did you start working on them?

There is another phase I haven't written about: it was the last phase of making art. Another portfolio of my very last work just surfaced, and I'm about to get it back. These are portfolios that I thought I had thrown out, that were lost along the way, and out of nowhere it looks like about seven hundred drawings surfaced.

Anyway: I tried to keep making art in New York; it didn't work. I got a job as a long-distance truck driver, and I was miserable. Just in agony. I would romanticize it to people—*Oh yeah, I'm going down to Texas again,* the whole thing. Eric Fischl, who I knew from Chicago, asked if I'd like to help him with a book he was doing called *Sketchbook with Voices*— would I be the one to interview artists and find out what problems they would assign to the art world? He paid me with a drawing, which I lost or a girlfriend got along the way, so that was irrelevant. It reintroduced me to wanting to be in the art world. The artists in that book were famous—I would have nervous breakdowns doing them. I remember standing at Alex Katz's doorbell and thinking, *I've got to get out of here, I can't do this.* I don't know how you've done it as a young guy, meeting all these really famous people, because I have a fear of really famous people to this day.

I kept making art, and I got this assignment with Eric Fischl and thought, *Oh gee, I could be an art critic—that must be easy! You know, maybe I could meet women that way, maybe I could be in the art world that way. Maybe I could get back into the family of art that way.* It's not like I didn't know what was going on in art, either. In that period, if you asked me any eighties artist, I could tell you who they were, in Germany or here, didn't matter, I knew. Then the people who did Eric's book offered *Beyond Boundaries* to me, and it was the exact moment that the early eighties were segueing into the much bigger thing of the late eighties—commodity art, neoconceptualism, all of that theory-inflected work that would grow into multiculturalism. I happened to put enough of them in the book not to look back and be totally horrified that I missed them.

Why do you have such a bad feeling toward that book?

I wasn't grounded enough. I shouldn't have been the one to do a book like that. Again, it wasn't paid, I've never been paid for any of the books I've done. I've done five and never got one dime for it. But I think most people on our side of the aisle, in criticism, just want to be in print—I do. I'm not ashamed of them, but I've never looked at them again.

When you first started writing criticism, was it for *Arts Magazine*?

I wanted to be an art critic, and as I drove around the trucks, I would fantasize about what I would do. I thought, *I've got to be different somehow.* I came up with this idea that I wanted to write about one work of art, as opposed to a show. I would start writing columns on single artworks: "Notes on a Painting," "Notes on a Sculpture." So I floated my crush on *Arts Magazine* around the high school that was the art world—*Oh, I sure would like to write for Richard Martin.* One day, he called up and said, *Hello, I'm Richard Martin, would you like to write for* Arts? And I told him my idea, and he said, *Sure.* It took me the full month to do it—I look back now and that's sort of unbelievable. I've never had the luxury of that much time again. And that is how I started.

That was the late eighties?

I was born in 1951, and I'm sixty-seven during this interview, and I think that my first piece probably appeared in '89. Just so everyone reading this knows: *Late! Bloomer!* I am a *very* late bloomer, and you can be too! I was thirty-eight years old before I wrote my first word. Mozart

395

was dead by then. Michelangelo made the *David* [1501–1504] at twenty-nine. I really started late. And I've never gone back to read that work, either; I tend not to look at the early stuff.

You started to write for *Art in America* in the early 1990s.

Arts closed, and Betsy Baker of *Art in America* asked if I wanted to write for her, and I said yes.

Do you remember how that happened?

I have to assume that I would hang out as much as I could back then and hope that I could maybe get a job somewhere. Roberta and Betsy knew each other. I always assumed at that phase of my life I was getting things because I was with Roberta. I'm aware of that.

By the time *Beyond Boundaries* comes out, which Roberta wrote an essay for, she had just started writing for *The New York Times*?

When we started working together, she had been fired from the *Voice* and had no job at all. It was a short period, maybe a year. She was single, I was single, she was a freelancer, and we got together. We celebrated her first column for the *Times* together as a couple.

That's a great relationship marker!

I'll say.

So how did you start learning to write criticism?

Everything I learned about criticism I probably learned from Roberta. Before Roberta, I thought, *I guess you talk to the artist and you get the inside scoop there, then maybe you read all these smarty-pants theory people and you throw a bunch of that in, and that will be what criticism is.* In very short order, I saw Roberta was doing it another way, and I loved what she was doing. I had never read her once before the *Times*, because again, I was a lazy, smart-alecky guy, and because I thought, *Oh, she's a former* Village Voice *critic—she was famous once, and now she's in the wilderness. I'll rescue her!* [Laughter.]

I learned to look at the art myself from Roberta. I learned not to talk to the artist from Roberta. And then from myself and necessity, I learned that I have to tell the truth. As deadlines came faster and I took what I was doing more seriously, rather than just as a device to be in the art world somehow, or to be liked, I started realizing that I was hearing all sorts of things in my head that I hadn't been writing but now wanted to write. In order to be as honest as I could in my criticism, I had to say the positive but also the negative. I became horrified by criticism that was all positive all the time. Sometimes there seemed to be a squirrelly opinion buried deep in an *Artforum* review, where in the second-to-last graph, they'd say, *Such and such* problematizes *the art*... Then you never really knew where they stood. When I read things like that, I always felt like the critic wasn't putting herself or himself on the line, that they were hiding behind something. I hated it. I'd say, *There's no juice here, there is nothing vulnerable, there's nothing real*. And so I tried to write in my real voice, so that people could say, *Well, Jerry is a dope*, or, *Jerry is on to something*. Or, *There is a grain of truth to what he's saying*. And that is what I was trying to do when I started writing criticism.

It seems like one of the ways you started creating an identity for yourself as a critic was in the big pieces you wrote for *Art in America* in the early nineties. They were these epic, marathon pieces, beginning with one called "May Day" in 1993.

It's detailing everything that happened on one day in the art world in 1993. Something like forty shows opened that day, and I wanted to create a sense of how much was in play, maybe how much is *always* in play in art.

And it was a really long piece.

It was a hinge moment, and we're in one now—an extended one, let me tell you. Then I did "A Year in the Life: Tropic of Painting"—

Right, in 1994. You created categories to talk about everything that was happening in painting, my favorite being "Our Bodies, Our Selves, You Asshole" to discuss painters like Nicole Eisenman and Lisa Yuskavage. How did you conceive of doing these pieces? They have a pretty unusual form.

I always think the "form" of criticism is really worth plumbing and playing around with to see what can be done. I don't think I invented this. I give you Oscar Wilde's "The Critic as Artist" [1891] as an example, or my favorite, Alexander Pope, "An Essay on Criticism" [1711], and that is written in rhyming fucking couplets.

Well, he was just deliciously the smartest—*The Rape of the Lock* [1712]? Story of my life.

I know. [Laughter.] And he writes, by the way, my favorite translation—

Of the *Iliad*. Mine too. And it's deeply out of fashion. Every time I try to get someone to read it, they say, *No thank you!* They want something that sounds more modern and raw and thus somehow more ancient.

It's totally accessible because it's in rhyming couplets—you read two lines and catch your breath, and it's all there again.

But back to those long articles: I thought, *Play with this form. Make this alive.* Criticism should be interesting, and I thought maybe I could make it more than just about the show, and I could frankly cover my weakness in an open way without shame. I'm very prejudiced, but I think Roberta is unsurpassed at examining a work of art—really looking at it. Maybe my attention span isn't long enough or my eye isn't sharp enough, but I needed, out of necessity, to find other things to do in criticism.

What is interesting to me about those long pieces is that they seemed like the beginning of you using yourself as a persona within the writing, as a character.

I'd say that is true, too. I started to locate myself in it: *I'm at dinner, I went here, I felt bad about having to invite myself there.* I liked doing that a lot, obviously.

The other thing about those pieces, which relates to something we started talking about earlier, is that they're almost panoramic views of the art world as a whole system. The thing that is so charming about the "Tropic of Painting" essay is that you talk about noting it all on sheets of colored graph paper, all the painting shows of the year, and doing the percentages. It seems that grappling with this bigger, quantifiable art world was part of what your persona was—

I think that's very perceptive, and it goes all the way back to me wanting to grow antennae. To see if I could understand this thing that I don't understand. Because we don't understand Mozart. We don't understand art. And yet I'm always looking for gigantic systems—like

Dante. I've read all of Proust. All of Whitman. Every epic. I'm rereading *Paradise Lost* [1674]. If I could develop a system to understand the whole world, then I'd know more than I could know. These are obviously juvenile ways of trying to have control of a life I had no control over as a kid. Confronting this thing you can never know—art—this great, subjective mystery where every painting is different every time, and yet somehow you have to say what you think.

What role do obsession and hyperbole play in all this? For instance, in the cover story you wrote on Matthew Barney for *Art in America*, it said that the article was "by a critic who has watched *Cremaster 4* over seventy-five times." Viewing a forty-five-minute video seventy-five times is well over a workweek of just watching. Why did you have to do that, and what solicited that kind of relationship to Matthew Barney's work?

When I first saw Matthew Barney's work, I saw it as Giovanni di Paolo. I saw it as Dante's *Divine Comedy* [ca. 1306–1321]. I saw it as *Paradise Lost*. I saw it as the Tibetan Book of the Dead—these things I've read and fallen in love with. Do I actually know about these things? Of course not. Like all people who read them, I think I know, but only much later realize that I don't. When I first saw Barney, within one second, in his studio, I went, *I understand this entire thing*. I've had this with a few artists that I've seen before they've shown—Kara Walker, Matthew Ritchie— these complicated, gigantic systems. So when Barney made his first film, every single person wrote, *This makes no sense, this is just surrealism and fantastical*, and I thought, *No, it's pretty easy. If I just watch this carefully, then I will understand it.* That's the only way I could access it. I could not approach it the way all those other brilliant critics did, by seeing half of the film. My genius friend Peter Schjeldahl has probably never seen all five of the *Cremasters* [1994–2002] in full. He doesn't have to in order to write brilliantly on them. He's that good. And yet I have to sit through all the motherfuckers over and over and over, because that's me.

That early childhood experience with a beheading painting is interesting because of your continued engagement with medieval images of torture on your Instagram. But I also want to ask—you wrote recently

that your father would hit you with a strap fashioned in the shape of his hand. That was so strange and shocking to me. Did he make that himself?

That is shocking to people, but it is a part of my childhood story in the way yours would be shocking to me. I was never hit early in my life, but when we moved to the suburbs, my mother killed herself, and my father remarried a Polish Catholic woman who brought in her sons, one my own age, so I became a twin. They were what were then called greasers, or, really, juvenile delinquents. Their hair was slicked back and they wore tight jeans—they were cool. The first night I was with my new brother in the same bedroom, he woke me up and said, *We're going out*. I said, *What do you mean?* He said, *We're sneaking out the window*. And we crawled out of our house and wandered around our suburb. He brought tools, and we took down all the street signs and brought some home and put them under the mattress. My father eventually found them and was furious, and as I was about to confess, my new stepbrother said, *We don't know how those got there, maybe Charley*—our older brother—*put them there*. And I saw another way of life right away, a more outlaw life, and I thought, *This is cool, you can lie, you can sneak out of the house, I don't have to be a normal kid anymore. I will compete with him for the crown of being outlaw*—which was a hard crown to wear in that house. It meant beating each other up severely. Then my father started spanking us. And my stepmother had this belt, about eighteen inches long, four inches wide, that she brought from Chicago, which she and her ex-husband used to use to strap their boys, and she had it fashioned into the shape of my father's hand. As he'd hit me, I remember I'd just stare him down. I'd think to myself, *You are not going to see me react*. My brothers eventually started beating my father up. It never occurred to me to do that.

So you have this very stately suburban home, very large—if you drove past it today in what is now River Forest, you'd say, *This guy grew up with a lot of privilege*—two separate entrances, two dining rooms, three floors of bedrooms. But as in all houses, hell had broken loose. That is why as a kid I used to crawl through the bushes and stare at what I did not know were Frank Lloyd Wright homes. They were right next to me, about sixteen of them. I kissed a girl in one of them. These houses became really important to me.

What did they represent to you?

An ideal existence. These really beautiful homes, I thought they were Japanese or something—his earliest work is there, and I highly recommend taking the tour. He was an American genius. Busby Berkeley, Fred and Ginger, and Frank Lloyd Wright were the three early American popular geniuses. I was witnessing American genius without knowing what I was seeing.

Of course, Frank Lloyd Wright is another one of those totalizing visions for how to live.

A way of living. So: giant systems, idealized lives, other peoples' lives that I would learn about through my super antennae, that I would assimilate without having to read about or really know their language, because I was too scared and lazy. So I would invent my own system.

Do you think that is why you've said the art world is "an all-volunteer army, and we all come here naked. We all have similar needs."? Is that why you value the art world, as a kind of bohemian family?

I see that—this was the family that none of us had. Your generation comes from slightly better families, but I still think that people have to individuate within this new art family. It is all volunteer; you can get in just by saying it, as I did. One day I got out of a truck and was at some party and someone asked, *What do you do?* And instead of giving a long story, I said, *I'm an art critic.* And the person just said, *Cool.* I was one just because I was saying it, and that's still true in New York.

Something I noticed by reading your writing from the 1990s and your two collections of writing from the *Voice*, which goes up until about 2008, is that your persona as a critic has evolved. I'm not sure if it tracks specifically with your engagement with social media, but that seems to have something to do with it. How do you understand that trajectory?

I understand it as a trajectory, that "I" somehow got in my work, against the rules a little. I didn't mean to be getting into my work as much as I did, but I liked it, because it allowed me to say more things. Then came social media; that made me understand, finally, that I didn't have to be only speaking down or from on high to other people, but I could be speaking *with* other people. Back and forth. That I could be myself, but as a character, a second self, because my real self doesn't go out—it has never gone out. But this second self goes out all the time, it goes to openings. I want to show everybody they can get into this family much easier than they think. If I can, of all people, at such a late age, you can. *You can do this!*

When did you start thinking about your "second self" self-consciously, as a tool for your criticism?

That is social media, for sure. I was in a bar when, finally, I couldn't be in bars before—it's too loud for me, it's too late for me, it involves too much flesh-on-flesh. I do have a hard time when people are super high, because of my antennae—I can't locate them, so it's like I'm getting a false positive all the time, and that is hard for me. Online was like the bars and backrooms I always wanted to be in. It felt like when Quentin Crisp said he had one great moment at the end of his life where these sailors were openly flirting with him and there was no problem—he wasn't going to be beaten, they were not going to take him home; it was just a beautiful flirtation where everybody understood what was going on. I felt that way online. I thought, *We can all talk to each other. Critics can stop being at the top of the pyramid and be wrong in real time and be right in real time.* Fighting with people, having arguments, and having the ability to change your mind in real time—I love that. I just love it.

It also has gone hand in hand with you assuming your own kind of celebrity, which was why it sounded so strange to me earlier when you said you're frightened of famous people. It seems to be a fascination of yours. How do you understand that dynamic?

I'm super lucky, and I'm aware of it. When I go out, I'm often recognized. Imagine: An art critic being recognized? I think I have to understand that gift, and to keep myself as open in public as my second self is online, with the half a million followers. I go to twenty or thirty shows a week; seeing art is really my whole life outside of writing

402

about art. Every person who says hi to me, I tell myself, *Stop, talk to them, tell them what you're really thinking and talk to them until they bullshit you, and when they do that, tell them, You're doing your sales pitch on me, stop, let's just keep talking.* I'm trying to do a Vito Acconci thing, under the floor, masturbating in public, but still having this private self that is constructing it, making myself have an involuntary spasm. And I see that people treat me as a cartoon character in writing—*Of course Jerry Saltz was off in a corner doing whatever.* I have to accept that. But I don't want it to erase the greatness or horribleness of my work. I grant that, for many people, I've made it very easy to put that in front of my work.

You created this character for yourself, and it seems like other people have adapted it for their own purposes too. It reminds me a bit of how people talk about Dave Hickey—art-world people love to hate him like a cartoon villain, but it doesn't really have anything to do with his writing, which is gorgeous, or as a man, who is a cowboy sweetheart.

Well, at least when you get people to read his work, they kind of grunt and admit, *He's a beautiful writer.* When they get to me, it's just, *He's the one who was on TV.*

To the question of the celebrity: When you did that really long interview with James Franco in *New York*, I have to admit that I rolled my eyes and thought, *Really, Jerry?* Why did you want to do that?

I had written very negatively on Franco. Twice, I think. Turns out Roberta had too. It was like this guy had been pounded. Franco had written terrible things about me too; he made fun of me a few times on social media. I, for whatever reason, have elephant skin. You can say whatever you want about me and I seem to be absolutely okay with it. It's bizarre, but I can do it, because to me there is a grain of truth in whatever you say about me, because I have to ask, *What did I do to allow you to say it? How am I responsible?* Because, ultimately, I *believe* in criticism.

New York magazine asked me to do the interview. I said, *Are you insane? I've only seen* Spring Breakers *[2012], which I'm in love with, and the movie where he cuts off his arm.* I think he's a great actor. Then I said, *I can't be around a famous person,* but they insisted. I went nuts, and I loved doing it once it started. Why? I think he was one of the most honest "quote, unquote" artists I've ever met in my life. When you ask artists to name another name, or talk about their dealer, or about a big fight they had with a collector, they say they *can't*—they have to protect their domain. Franco was not like this; he would go right at it. He would say, *You hated this about my work*—he would challenge me on it. I found it incredibly refreshing.

It's one of the only interviews you've ever done. Why is that?

I'm a bad listener, as you can see. I get off on my own tangent in order to understand things. And I don't care. I don't want to hear about artists' lives that much. I don't like interviews that recap a person's career. I would be most interested in interviews that told me exactly how you made something. If somebody paid me to do my own set of interviews, I would just say to an artist, *Let's look at one painting, I want to walk through second by second how you made it*. Just technical shit. I do not want to know what it means. Because it doesn't. Whatever you say it means, it doesn't.

I was at Tanya Bonakdar Gallery, and some famous artist had a show of clouds. I was looking at the clouds and a person said to me, *Those are clouds above Ferguson, Missouri*, and I said, *They are fucking not that. Do not say that to me! It's not in the work. It has to be in the work!* I'm pretty old-school on that.

Even when you used the metaphor of Acconci's *Seedbed* [1972] as a way of describing what you're doing as a critic—what's the sex thing for you? There was period where people were coming after you for the sexual pictures on your Instagram, and I want to know how you've understood that.

Of the images that I was posting that people didn't like, ninety-nine percent of them were works of art. One-half of one percent might have been nonart photos. One photo in particular that I happened to post without thinking about what it could mean got people really upset. Ninety-nine percent are works of art—I'd say works of overlooked genius that have only come to light because of the miracles of digital photography and image sharing online. If I have an idea while I'm

404

writing, if it's a beheading, I will then go to Google and hyperlink my ass off until I find some incredible site of pictures from the end of the Roman Empire to the very beginning of the hegemony of Christianity—that is the period I love, this estuary where these two worlds are absolutely overlapped. I would post these sick images of incredible things: demons fucking people, beatings, breasts being cut off, balls being opened up, and write ridiculous captions like, *I'm going to do this to you at your crit today at Columbia*. That is the wise guy in me. I will grant that those images would not have disturbed people without the captions, that I did prompt them, didn't realize that they were making people *that* upset. But people were really upset. And I didn't know it. I was so horrified.

It's complex with you, because you are the self-styled "folk critic" who speaks to people outside the art world, more than any other critic does. So when you were saying that artists won't talk trash about their dealers or other artists, it's maybe not necessarily because of middle-class values, but because we're protecting our little gang from the harsher culture of the outside world.

I've said this before: I think criticism is a form of showing respect. I do not think it hurts the art family to say things that you've actually thought and considered. The people who were objecting to those images were not the outer-world people, they were art-world people, and it was then I understood something that I see more of now. A certain conservatism in the art world is afoot again, a desire to police other people's pleasure. I understand that; I have it too. And I speak up when I see it, and I guess people have to speak up when I do it.

The last thing I want to ask you about is how you said earlier that we're living in a "hinge moment." I'd like to understand a bit more how you see it.

We had such a luxury these last eight years, and really we were correcting history; black lives were mattering, and more women were and are finding their way into the canon. The prices kept going up, and going up for women, too, and artists from South America and Asia, and it felt like the art world did open up. The system seems broken to me and played out. I don't have suggestions for what's next. A handful of artists hit the lottery and made a lot of money; good for them. I like to think they provide cover for the rest of us who are trying to do our work, while all the attention is on the eleven auction prices, fifteen zombies, or the five megagalleries, or on what Marina, Jeff, or Klaus are doing—sometimes Jerry gets thrown in there—but that gives cover for other things to happen.

So, the emergency we are living in—we will see if people will adapt. Even the people just painting abstract stripes, the deep content of "now" is in them—they watch the same idiot news things that everybody is watching, and we'll see if that feels like it's part of their work, or if the art world is hiding in its belly button. Or, if the art world is just an ongoing system because it has momentum. But I really see galleries closing in the next year or so. The prices are too high for young artists. Collectors always say to me, *Jerry, you always knew about new art, now when we go see a young artist it might cost twenty thousand dollars.* What I tell them is that if they don't have crazy money, and they have children, they would be an irresponsible ass to be spending twenty thousand dollars a pop on artists for whom the odds are very high that they will not be around in a few years. They'll have given them temporary life, and that's all.

When people lament that after their MFA they had to stop making art, I usually say, *Good.* **The tragedy is if they had to go into debt for it, but I think if you can stop making art, you should.**

That is the last word: don't be an artist unless you really have to be one. Because ninety-nine percent of the people reading this are going to be poor. One percent will make big bucks, and that is not the definition of success. It never was. Nobody ever thought it was. There was an illusion of it for a while, and it was fun because half of them were pretty great artists, but you know, this new phase is here. It's already happened.

But aren't feelings the only things in the universe that we can really know? They're the *actual* us. Thoughts are lawyers for our feelings. Memory is a pile of stories determined by feelings and continually revised to fit new feelings.

Peter Schjeldahl

How did you begin thinking of language as a *thing*—as material you could do something with?

Thinking didn't have much to do with it. I was one of those kids who are crazy about words. There's a great Paul Valéry line I wrote down decades ago and just came across again: "All our language is composed of brief little dreams." I love that. Every dictionary should be subtitled "The Interpretation of Dreams."

Let's see, the first poem I ever wrote: I was in sixth grade in a little town in Minnesota. The last day of school, we had a picnic. I was lying in the grass, looking up, and saw a hawk flying around, which wasn't unusual, but it gave me a funny feeling. I turned over and wrote a poem—I knew it was a poem because it looked like one. I don't remember anything about it except the chorus: "Winged avenger from the skies!" I'm not sure I quite knew what "avenger" meant, but the sound of it appealed to me. When I finished I was dazed, and I took it to my teacher. She looked at it and said, *That's nice, Peter, but what's this about a "winged avenger"—that's very unpleasant.* It was four or five years before I wrote another poem.

What is interesting about that story is that it starts with seeing, then feeling, and then come the words. I admire how your criticism foregrounds the way you feel in front of the work; in some ways it seems like that is your subject as much as the artwork itself.

Katy Siegel has called me the "feeler" among art critics, which sounds kind of creepy. But aren't feelings the only things in the universe that we can really know? They're the *actual* us. Thoughts are lawyers for our feelings. Memory is a pile of stories determined by feelings and continually revised to fit new feelings. Anyhow, the emphasis in my writing was born of necessity. I was never educated in art. I saw and loved it before I knew much of anything. I thereby lucked out of the problem of learning about art before you see it—because you will always be dealing with that information at the expense of what affects you at firsthand. Ignorant as I was in the sixties, I discovered very quickly that I was the world's leading expert in my own experience. I got praised for making the most of that. I think Jasper Johns said one of my favorite lines, which I remember vaguely as, *Personal style is only common sense. You figure out what people like about you, and you exaggerate it.*

The artists you were paying a lot of attention to in the eighties were painters like David Salle and Anselm Kiefer, but you were always writing on older art, too. The thing that was so vital about your writing on an artist like Manet was that it was with eyes trained on contemporary painting.

If I'm functioning properly, that should always be the case. Anyone with a live sensibility, an open mind, and an interest will be like that. I define contemporary art as every work of art that exists at the present moment—five thousand years or five minutes old. We look with contemporary eyes. What other eyes are there? And we are alert to beauty, which, as Baudelaire pointed out, happens when something temporary sparks with something timeless.

One of my mottoes is, *Anything has a value if you know what it is.* If you can say what the thing is, the value becomes apparent. It may be a very small value. It may be a negative one. I also swear by Gertrude Stein's wisdom: "Description is explanation."

Something you once wrote about sculpture: "The best modern sculpture always expresses some sort of existential gawkiness, capitalizing on the same intimacy of shared space that makes most sculpture irritating." I think that is insightful; I've always thought there aren't as many critics who can write about sculpture as well as painting.

Sculpture is a learned taste for me. It is far and away the hardest art.

The demands on it are crushing, especially since it came off pedestals. A painting is an imaginary world, and it hangs on the wall out of our way. There is room in the real world for an infinity of imaginary worlds, which you can deal with or not. The conditions that apply to anything actually in the world apply to sculpture, with the added challenge of blatant uselessness. Three questions we might ask of a sculpture that we unexpectedly encounter are, *What is that? Why is it there? When will it go away?* If those questions take hold, the sculpture is sunk. There has to be some immediate response that skates past them. It can be dislike. The sculpture has to excite your feelings immediately to have a chance of working for you.

From your writing, it seems like the domain of art helps us understand our sensations of being in a shared world.

The arts are a great laboratory of absolutely free play of ideas and emotions that normal social life can't accommodate. You can play war, and nobody dies; play love, and nobody has their heart broken. It's also an education in physiology: the mechanisms and functioning and limits of consciousness.

When did that interest start?

In the sixties—drugs had a role. I dropped acid maybe five times. The first time was kind of great, the second was iffy, the other times were nightmares. That wasn't a good enough excuse not to do it, because if you had a bad trip, that was a character flaw—you had failed the drug. But it gave me a lot of information. It's hard to describe, of course. It's as if every bit of the mind is vividly active and being monitored, but by nobody—phenomena without a witness. Which may freak a person seriously out.

In my everyday life, I have so many feelings that sometimes I think, *Come on! Get over it!*

Me too. I had my last drink in 1992. I had the usual mode of help. One of our watchwords is *feelings aren't facts.*

Feelings are *not* facts?

They're realities. But a fact is a reality with consequences. If you act on a feeling, that's not the feeling's fault. It's a choice—maybe a compulsive one, if you credit the spectacularly stupid thought that you need the drug, or the behavior. You may never stop having that thought when you get sober. But you pat it on the head—*So cute, so dumb*—and proceed sensibly.

In those terms, is an artwork a fact or a feeling?

A fact. It has consequences, however trivial. At best, it detaches from whoever made it and can somewhat change the world. There are so many ways for art to fail. One of them is for the maker to enjoy it too much. That's treason. I compare it to a chef eating his own cooking and then proudly handing you an empty plate. The proper chef merely samples the food, then gives it all to you.

Which explains why you've written relatively few profiles of art-world personalities.

I can't. It's horrible. In twenty years at *The New Yorker*, I've attempted half a dozen profiles and completed three—Marian Goodman, Rachel Harrison, and Laura Owens—with a lot of handholding help from my great editors Virginia Cannon and, lately, Cressida Leyshon. People won't shut up and they won't stand still. I can't get any distance on them. I'm hopeless with anything animate, including pigeons and squirrels.

I'm committed to dealing with artwork formally, but in a profound way, it only matters to me because a human being made it, and there is great complexity to that.

One of us did that—that's a constant point of identification. There's a certain resemblance to sports fandom, which Roger Angell called "insatiable vicariousness." It's like entering into the mind and heart of whoever made a thing, within the ambit of your knowledge and experience. This pretty much limits me to certain strains of Western art. I may be excited by other cultures, but I can't know how they feel from the inside. I believe that I can comprehend some impulses in Western art even far back in time. I've had moments of connection with classical Greek art, less so the Romans, because I don't like them. And Christian art of most varieties.

I think it is fair to say that dealing with someone's artwork will get

you closer to their intentions than talking with them about it.

Looking at art is like, *Here are the answers. What were the questions?* I think of it like espionage, "walking the cat back"—*Why did that happen, and that?*—and eventually you come to a point of irreducible mystery. With ninety percent of work, the inquiry breaks down very quickly. You reach an explanation that is comprehensive and boring. Bad art, as any good artist will tell you, is the most instructive, because it's naked in its decisions. Even adorably so. When something falls apart, you can see what it's made of. Whereas with a great artist, say Manet or Shakespeare, you're left gawking like a fool.

One thing you've done rhetorically over the course of years is a descriptive one-two punch: "I find Freud's work hard to like and almost impossible not to admire"; or something like, *At first glance I thought it was junk, on the second I was in heaven*—two seemingly opposed sensations put side by side.

Serial impressions. I think that's how learning from experience works, on the way to knowing that, finally, we don't know anything. One thing I say in my sometime talk with regular folks who say they hate some art is, *That's good, it's an authentic response. But maybe linger a little. Have another response. You might hate it even more, but you'll have learned something about yourself.* Resisting a new experience is really a sign of physiological health: we are whole from moment to moment, and then we encounter something contradictory, and the proper first instinct is to feel threatened and to fight it. That's a crucial moment—when we probably see most deeply into the nature of the thing. Fear vivifies. *All hands on deck. Red alert.* If the thing is good and we stick with it, our resistance breaks down, we integrate the new fact, and we are whole again. But the moment of threat is where the action is, and where I like to focus.

I would like to get a better sense of the evolution of your facility with language. When you briefly were in college, and for years afterward, you were seriously engaged with poetry. What was your poetry like then?

Whatever I'd just read. I would go from Robert Frost to Rimbaud to Allen Ginsberg to Pablo Neruda. I was completely knocked out when I discovered John Ashbery, at a time when I was into surrealism and I thought he was a surrealist—I was wrong. I discovered the possibility of making enchanting poetry that is incomprehensible—what a liberation that was! It didn't have to make sense. I won the poetry prize at my college with a very long imitation of Ashbery. It was reviewed in the college paper, which said, *Its fault is trying to fit epic form to a lyrical impulse.* Which was acute.

You said to me once that the only class that impacted you was on baroque poetry. What was it about that?

It was about the professor, this old mousy, tweedy guy, Philip Sheridan, who was very kind, very sweet, married to a fairly racy French woman who taught French. He had long ago given up on trying to interest students, but he loved the material. He went back to late medieval poetry, starting with John Skelton. I wrote a paper in Skeltonics. He said it conclusively proved that that couldn't be done. Then I wrote a paper on Richard Crashaw's "A Hymn to the Name and Honour of the Admirable Saint Teresa" [ca. 1648–1649], which he said was the best-written student paper he'd ever seen. He had learned that I was flunking some of my other classes and said I had an A from him already—*So please drop this course and pay attention.* I became indignant: *How dare he even suggest that!* I kept punishing him with my loyalty. It was a little chance at self-esteem—mixed with narcissistic grandiosity, but a rehearsal of seriousness.

Were you also looking at art, or was it just poetry at that point?

Poetry, literature, sports—basketball, drinking, chasing girls. Being weird. Not wanting to be weird. I wanted to be normal. But I was attracted to art. I knew nothing about it but was subject to epiphanies. A big one, I remember, came between my junior and senior years in high school, when I worked at a daily newspaper in a small city, Mankato, in Minnesota. At lunch hour I'd go down to the drugstore and read books that were in racks. There was one little book on impressionism. I was looking at the color illustrations, and a Pissarro street scene just absolutely nailed me. I think that the effect was like, *Somebody made this for me to look at.* My looking, beyond only seeing, was anticipated. The picture had been waiting for me! I didn't buy the book. I was broke. But I returned to it repeatedly.

I know that you lived in Paris for a year and then came back and started working for a newspaper.

No, I was a reporter first. In 1962, after my sophomore year of college, I was an intern at the *Des Moines Register*, in Iowa. I didn't want to go back to college, and I wanted out of the Midwest. I applied to papers in small cities next to big cities, three on each coast.

That's a plan! Why did you wanted to leave school?

First of all, to get out of town—I was still in the town where I went to high school. My parents lived there. It was time for adventure. Also, I was doing badly in school—I hated school. I yearned for a big city. I was just smart enough to know that I couldn't get a job in one, but at that time every town in the country had a daily newspaper. It was a roll of the dice. I heard back from only one, *The Jersey Journal*, in Jersey City. I guess it was an offer for an interview. I packed what I had into my little sports car—an Austin-Healey Sprite, a rare gift from my parents—and drove through the day and night straight to Jersey City and went into the office. The editor I talked to said, after a while, *You don't have a place to stay, do you?* I said, *No.* He said, *Oh, hell, take a desk.* [Laughter.] Utter happenstance! I always remember a line by E. B. White: "No one should come to New York to live unless he is willing to be lucky." I didn't have a lot going for me, but I made myself a target for strokes of luck.

When you started working for *The Jersey Journal*, what were you doing there?

I was a reporter. I started on obituaries. Mostly just some phone calls or clippings. Then longer ones, talking to people about the deceased. I was such an innocent. Once I talked with a guy right next to the body of his grandmother. He said, *I know you'll do a good job*, and he shook my hand—and there was a bill. That's how things were done in Jersey City, a place marinated in corruption. I learned lots of things there, including how to write readably.

The copy editors were these fat, burned-out reporters with stubby cigars, sitting around the city desk. They'd take your story and use number-one pencils—practically black crayons—to mark it up, then throw it back at you. You had to figure out what was wrong. You kept rewriting and handing it over, and getting it back. They never looked at you. Finally, they'd send you with it downstairs to the guy at the Linotype—big rackety, smelly machine turning molten lead into type. That was like winning the lottery. Ten Iowa Writers' Workshops couldn't have taught me more in a year than I learned in any given week at that paper. I got once and for all how to make sentences.

How long did you work there?

I worked there for a full year, '62 to '63. Then in '63, I went back to Carleton for what would have been my senior year, but it was my junior year. Then I dropped out for good, came to New York, and worked at the paper that summer before heading off to be a starving poet in Paris.

Okay. You went to Paris in '64?

Yes.

One of your collections of poems is called *Since 1964* [1978]—what was it about that date? Did you start focusing on poetry in a different way?

I just felt it was the first time I wrote something worth keeping. During the previous year in Jersey City, 1963, I'd seen that Kenneth Koch was teaching a poetry workshop at The New School for Social Research—I knew of him from *The New American Poetry, 1945–1960* [1960], a great Grove Press anthology of beats and Black Mountain poets and New York Schoolers—and I took it and met all the poets on the Lower East Side, where I moved, commuting to work by the Holland Tunnel. When I came back, in '65, I lived on Avenue B and went to The New School again, with a feeble ambition to complete my BA—which I never did. Meanwhile, I freelanced. I worked for a while for *Avant-Garde* magazine, which was edited by Ralph Ginzburg, a shady left-libertarian semipornographer. I was the only writer in offices full of technical and promotion people. So I'd write one article an issue in my name and others with pseudonyms.

Like on what?

416

I wrote profiles of Amiri Baraka, Phil Ochs, and Jerry Rubin—counterculture figures. I wrote a "new translation" of the racy parts of Petronius's *Satyricon* [ca. 54–68 CE]. What I did was, I went out and bought three different translations, propped them up on my desk, and wrote something as unlike any of them as they were unlike each other, but juicing up the sex. I can't remember the name I used, but he was identified in the magazine as "America's foremost Latin scholar." Rag-tag adventures and misadventures were normal then—it was a *bohemian* city.

But when you came back from Paris, you became more involved in the downtown poetry scene—how did that affect the kind of poems that you were writing or the kind of language that you were interested in?

I remember wanting to bring back the occasional poem, addressing worldly matters. I loved Alexander Pope and John Dryden and the eighteenth century, when poems were for sale at the newsstand. That led *nowhere*. I remember my friend Dick Gallup, a poet who, like me, was a little dubious of having to make a social revolution, one night proposing a new ideology to be called psychedelic Republicanism— which would rhyme our drug regimen with our lurking conservatism.

Once you told me that in retrospect your relationship to rhyme was wrecked by the prevailing attitudes of the poetry world.

Yeah, rhyme and meter. I was picking it up from Auden, trying to write in traditional forms. I remember one of the first poems I handed to Kenneth Koch, he wrote on it, *Wow, you write like Matthew Arnold!* I took that as a put-down, though I don't think he meant it that way. I thought, *So that's out, we're not doing that anymore. Free verse from now on.*

In the poets you mentioned, whether it's Crashaw or the eighteenth-century poets, there's a rhetorical voice that it seems like you continued developing outside of a rhyming structure.

Yeah. Rhetorical voice, which I felt ashamed about. I was haunted by Verlaine's line, "Take rhetoric and wring its neck!" I thought, *I have to do that! But how?*

In the lineage of New York School poets, there is a strong art critic tradition; they were famously close to artists. Did you see being an art

critic as just another aspect of being a poet?

It was a milieu. You would hang out in studios. You went to parties, like at the Park Avenue digs of Lita Hornick, the publisher of *Kulchur* magazine, with pre-Baraka LeRoi Jones. She'd have live music by, like, Steve Reich or Charlemagne Palestine, and there'd be the hot painters. Park Avenue beat-meets-elite. You'd go to Max's Kansas City at a time when the minimalists drank in the front and the Warholians were in the back—walking back, as I would, was like passing through heavy metal to get to strawberry shortcake. There were around-the-clock scenes. Amphetamine helped, until it backfired.

At that point, did you see your criticism and poetry complementing each other?

Never. I thought the criticism was what I was doing to support myself as a poet.

Right, which is what John Ashbery says.

I remember Ashbery at one point saying sarcastically, *Peter, you really want to be an art critic? I mean, like Roger Fry?* [Laughter.] I felt that it was a squalid thing to do. When I met Brooke in 1973, she was making money acting. I thought, *Fuck art criticism, I'll be only a poet*. But at that point, I was becoming more and more alienated from the poetry scene and confused about poetry: I didn't know what a poem was any longer. Then we needed income from me, and I discovered that art criticism was all I could do that they pay you for. After our wedding, I wrote a long poem, "Dear Profession of Art Writing" [1976], taking care to insult everyone in the field by name. I remember David Bourdon, who I referred to in the poem as a "cub reporter," wrote me a card saying, *Kindly keep me out of your future verbiage*.

But I received stunning shots of encouragement. When I wrote a review in the *Times* of Bob Dylan's double album *Self-Portrait* [1970], I got a postcard from Ashbery calling my piece, as I recall, *a ravishment of the senses*. Meanwhile, in the early seventies, when I was first with Brooke, I was senior editor at *Art in America* under the inspiring Betsy Baker. That was a job I split with Scott Burton.

How did you split it?

Morning and afternoon.

What was that like?

Editing, copyediting, rewriting articles. From my newspaper days, I'm a crack copy editor—I can make anybody sound like they can write. I was writing pieces, too. I had friendships with lots of artists. I was friends with James Rosenquist for a time. He did a cover for a book of my poems called *Dreams* [1973]. And, of course, Joe Brainard and George Schneeman and Larry Rivers and Alex Katz. I was becoming sophisticated by osmosis. I was learning as I went along, writing for the *Times* and other places. For a long time, everything I knew about a subject went into the piece. Nothing left over. My knowledge of art history is a quilt of patches, most of them acquired on deadlines.

How did you come to terms with the different forms of art criticism, the varying lengths and purposes of reviews, features, profiles?

The genres. The first things I did for *ARTnews* were one-sentence reviews at a time when *ARTnews* reviewed every show in town—that was part of the business model, and the number of galleries was a fraction of what it became. I would do twenty or thirty of those a month at three bucks a pop. It was great exercise. I remember someone pointing out that when Jimmy Schuyler wrote them, he would put one good word in every sentence—some unexpected, perfect American word like, say, "bonus." It was about writing sentences that pack in a maximum amount of information but that *float*.

A lot of those single-line reviews at the end of *ARTnews* felt like they had a kind of irony to them. Like, *So-and-so exhibits tasteful watercolors of Maine sunsets, prices unquoted*.

There could be an amused, sometimes sarcastic, sometimes wondering tone. You had no room to *state* an opinion because you were describing. So your attitude was a shadow, in dappled light. Even when I couldn't write poems that were sufficiently refined, or sufficiently manly, or whatever seemed *de rigueur,* I could do that. I could write better sentences than anybody.

Now and then, I did Dadaistically rebellious things. There was a symposium in *Art in America* with different art-world people responding to a Cézanne show. I wrote that I hated Cézanne and I explained why. An absolute pan of Cézanne! I remember thinking, *Okay, that'll do it. I am out of the art world forever.* Then I got a note from Robert Rosenblum, whom I had never met, and who seemed to me an Olympian figure, saying how thrilled he had been by my piece. He loved every word of it—and if I told anyone that he had said so, he would have to kill me. [Laughter.] We became friends. It seemed like the world wasn't going to let me not write art criticism.

The seventies were a transitional time in art criticism, with people scrambling out from under these towering, polemic figures like Greenberg. How did you see what you were doing in relation to the larger scene?

I had no weight. I bounced around. I had no presence. I was impersonating a critic, often with a weirdly elderly tone. I didn't have any critical aim. But that served me in the long run. Something I say to students is: *You come into a scene and you're a nobody. I know how painful it is to be a nobody, but you'll look back at this as the most important period of your life. Because, particularly in New York, if you're a nobody, no one will bother to lie to you. You are getting absolutely authentic, real knowledge everywhere you go and everywhere you are. The moment you're a somebody, everyone will try to spin you, as they should, because they've got careers to tend.*

I was a nobody for quite a few years. I hung out with artists, drank with artists, slept with artists. I was Peter the poet. *The New York Times* was held in contempt. Uptown was held in contempt. You'd get nausea if you went above Fourteenth Street. I had no idea how useful that was for what I became, that scalding immersion. Luck again. Never a plan.

The other interesting thing is that, having been in the art world consistently for as long as you have, so many of the same artists have stuck around with you. I marvel at the expanse of your writing and that you find new things to think about the same people over the years. Do you think that's why most critics can't sustain it for more than a certain period of time?

I don't know. I believe that you can't look at the same artwork twice. It doesn't change, but you do. Saying certain things about it disposes of those things. They sink into the sand of yourself, and you're no longer engaged by them. The work is fresh again, if it's any good. You mustn't be persuaded by your own writing. You mustn't buy your own patter.

Every time you start from scratch?

From fundamental doubt. At times, I've made the best possible case for something that I didn't really like very much. At other times, I'll write about, say, Picasso, whom I'm in awe of but without being rock-bottom *sure* that he is even a good artist. What would it feel like to be sure? The guy spent his life dirtying up canvases and fucking women and that matters to anybody *why*? I think that may have to do with my noneducated, up-from-the-streets newspaper formation—basic reporter's cynicism. The feeling, *I've seen it all*. Of course, that's just part of the mindset. Auden talks about a poet needing a censorate in his head: "a sensitive only child, a practical housewife . . . and a brutal, foul-mouthed drill sergeant who considers all poetry rubbish." One thing I value in myself, though it torments me, is the impulse to think the nihilistic thought, that what anybody does is stupid and that what I do about them is stupid. *But damn it, they did their best, and I'll do my best too, and we'll see how it goes.* Also it's Scheherazade: tell a story to survive the night, every night.

What is it about painting that has continued to hold a special place for you?

The succinctness of it. The rectangle. The organization of everything at a glance. The *speed*. First of all, *Why do we like pictures?* The optic nerve is equipped for a lot of hard work in dealing with reality, as with binocular perception. Pictures eliminate the effort. You can perceive depth without refocusing your eyes. The efficiency is pleasurable, and an engine of *cultivation*. For cultivating your senses and sensibility, you can't beat painting, because of the *nuance*. It engages our strongest sense, the eye, and our finest physical aptitude, that of the hand—*it's about the hand and the eye in concert*. It physically delivers the represented, the imagined, the conceived, the transposed, whatever. *Bang!* Right there. By the way, why do 3-D movies disappoint? Because they're not 3-D, they're 2-D.

It took me years to become really accepting of photography, because it has a less complex relation to reality. I like photography now. As a graphic art, it has a direct vector from eye to brain—it's bodiless— and thus is conducive to thinking. But it is limited expressively. And sculptures because they take time. You have to walk around them, and walking is tiring. But with a painting, if the painter knows what he or she is doing, every square millimeter of the surface is what it is *on purpose*, infused with consciousness and choice. Looking at it is like putting on a virtual-reality helmet where you're seeing with somebody else's eyes, thinking with somebody else's brain, feeling with somebody else's heart. It's a vacation from yourself.

The other thing about what you are describing is that painting is there all at once and it unfolds in time, but it doesn't do that in a linear way.

The time is *yours*. Every other art—and I mean *every one*—entails some imposed or required time, from a start to a finish. The time of looking at a painting is all yours. When you start or end is up to you. So is how you go about it.

One big thing I realized is that you're actually one of our great writers on public sculpture; the very idea of public space is important to you. To me, the ones that really stand out are your celebration of Saint-Gauden's *William Tecumseh Sherman* [1902], in Central Park, and your condemnation of Richard Serra's *Tilted Arc* [1981].

Public sculpture is both political and aesthetic by definition: the two words are yoked together. It has to succeed both ways to succeed at all. It's an intellectual luxury to bring aesthetic speculation to bear on something that is inherently public and political, you can take it in so many directions. But of course it's a rat's nest of problems, with so many pitfalls. It raises, and usually disappoints, our general hopes for society. We want the world to be better. I sure do. I'm a liberal. I want the best for everybody, God help me.

Well, you're wearing socks with images of Abraham Lincoln on them right now. I'm interested in the way that your writing about public sculpture is an occasion for your thoughts on democracy.

422

I buy the American story. I buy the American myth. I'm a patriot.
I see plenty wrong with America, and I respect people who address the
wrongnesses. But you have to belong to something. I'm always thinking
about democracy, which is a wildly chaotic way of organizing the world.
Popular versus elite. One line I like from my old friend Christopher
Knight is, *In a democracy, anybody gets to be an elitist*. But the imbroglio
never goes away.

**Your stance on the removal of *Tilted Arc* was roughly, *Why does this
one asshole get to dictate how these people experience their everyday
lives, based on what authority?* However, I think you were the lone,
serious art-world voice making that case.**

I was. And I caught hell. I don't enjoy catching hell. But I guess I
promised myself that if I think I'm right, and it's important—and
it's not just me being contrary—then I should do that. Happily, you
discover that when everybody hates you for a couple of weeks you
don't die.

**When the art market swept back up in the eighties, how did the
landscape then change in terms of writing about art or the kind of art
being discussed?**

Money was able to talk again. In the seventies, the power people
were curators. Critics were squeezed out. In the 1980s, there was room
for a critic again. There was public conversation, and controversy, that
anybody got to weigh in on. I remember a big hostile question for critics
was, *How does it feel to have power?* Everyone asked that. Because for the
sixties generation, power was evil. Richard Nixon had power. At first,
I denied that I had any. Then I got to the point of saying, *It's great, I want
more*. But "power" isn't the right word, because it means nothing unless
you do something with it. You can have electricity, but if you don't plug
anything in, it's kinda moot. If I boost an artist's market, fine, but no
investor can come whimpering to me if it's a bad bet. I don't work for
them.

**Often I think of the artist and the critic creating a dyad, or com-
pleting each other at a certain moment—like Ruskin and Turner, or
Baudelaire and Manet. I'm wondering if you ever felt that with a certain**

artist, at a certain moment, you were the one who totally *got it*.

I think that every time I write, or I try for it. And I try to hit a balance between what I'm confident about and what I'm not confident about. When I'm ambivalent about some art I think, *What would I like about this if I liked it?* Then it's sort of like becoming a lawyer for the artist, with myself as the jury. If that fails, I think, *What must the people who like this be like?* It becomes sociological. Like when I write about Damien Hirst, whom I despise—but the ways in which some people enjoy him intrigue me. Liking him doesn't make them bad people.

There is an aspect of your writing where you get worked up into penning love letters. That feels like almost a primary mode for you: head over heels.

It's how I want to feel all the time. I want to be in love with everybody. I know not to expect that. When it happens, it's always just a glimpse. But when something seems life enhancing, then yeah, *pull out the stops.* I don't want to go to my grave with a stock of unused superlatives.

In an obvious way you were much influenced by Oscar Wilde's "The Critic as Artist" [1891], but I know you're interested in late Wilde too, especially *De Profundis* [1897].

What a fabulous essay—it's just, I don't know if I can believe him. *De Profundis* is so profound and so moving, but it's almost like he's writing it from a projected Saint Oscar perched on his shoulder. Well, it might be the sublime of the rhetorical—where rhetoric breaks free of an argument it wants to win and speaks from where its heart would be, if it had a heart.

I'm interested in *De Profundis*'s rhetorical use of Christ as the embodiment of the artist's personality, the one who suffers.

I'd totally buy it, but then I can buy other ideas about Christ that are not commensurable. Christ is *very handy*. And we haven't been able to replace him, have we? You don't get great Western art or much of great Western anything, postantiquity, without him.

We share an interest in religion, but also morality—how do you see those things touching or inflecting art?

424

I think moral values are *way* more important than artistic values, and both get twisted when you try to make something happen between them. A person obsessed with morality can make a work of art that conveys it, but it's not the morality that pulls the work off as art. I think it's important that people believe what they're saying—believe that there's a use in saying it. But that's neither here nor there, aesthetically. There's no right or wrong in art, only good or bad. I know that's hard to admit, because conscience claws at us.

Speaking on the idea of someone believing what they're saying, which would be *conviction,* and that conviction being somehow palpable in the experience of the work—is that through form, or something else?

It needs the form. The form does the work, sometimes to sickening effect. Hard cases have always fascinated me, such as Leni Riefenstahl's *Triumph of the Will* [1935]. I remember the first time I saw it. Halfway through, I had the thought, *We can't beat these people!* But guess what? The film is shattering because it's good art. There is nothing more hapless than trying to square artistic quality with political virtue. Some of the best art ever came out of the Counter-Reformation. Same with the peak of the Inquisition, which was similarly motivated.

The Counter-Reformation, especially Caravaggio, looms heavy in my mind lately.

Me too. More and more, really.

Why do you think that is?

The idea of a reaction co-opting progress. There's something horrible about Caravaggio. The insight that stays with me from when I was in Rome last year seeing Caravaggios: he's a nearly exact contemporary of Shakespeare. They both have fantastic psychological penetration, but Caravaggio has it with *no sympathy*. Shakespeare is vastly sympathetic—unillusioned but sensitive. People who are unsympathetic generally have very crude ideas of what other people are like. Not Caravaggio. He's a criminal angel.

There is also an overwhelming orchestration of *belief.*

Oh sure, that's the chassis—you don't get anywhere without the stability of belief. That's how you connect with the people as characters, full of meaning—mythic. It's similar with Rembrandt, who takes people off the street and makes myths of them, matter-of-factly. Or when he did Bible stories. He doesn't argue with them, he just as much says, *Okay, that happened—what was it like? What was it like to be Abraham— you're about to slaughter your son, and then you're interrupted by a delicate angel who is physically stronger than you are, when nobody has been stronger than you in your whole life?* You don't generally get Rembrandt when you're young. I didn't. You have to have lived enough. Some other artists are slow burns in different ways. It took me a long time, but I did come around to Cézanne.

Yeah, I'm still not there.

You have to slow your looking way, way down.

The other piece of this is your Lutheran childhood. I am interested in its influence on you as a thinker and writer.

Lutheranism was iconoclastic. The Catholic church had all the images. Lutheranism is cold churches on cold mornings with weak sunlight leaking in. It's the loneliness and starkness of being alone with God. *Every man his own priest,* Luther said. That'll fuck you up when you're twelve. But then later, I actually read Luther and realized what a genius he was, despite his flaws, notably the unforgivable anti-Semitism. His is a theology of freedom—which, however, sounds better than trying to live by it turns out to be.

I don't know that this is accurate, but it seems to me that the early piece of yours that feels like a totally new sensibility and made its own complete contribution was the long piece "Edvard Munch: The Missing Master" from _Art in America_ in 1979.

Well, that may have been the first where I felt, *If I don't say this, no one will.* My Norwegian ancestry entered in, and I fancied that I kind of looked like Munch. It was a romantic identification, but grounded in an idea of the resourceful rebel who is driven to tell truths. That's an ego ideal that I could reach out and touch. Then came the chance to bring Munch in from the cold. He had been left out of modernism. Boy, does he hold up. It's like every year we lose another reason for not

426

respecting him. If you try to keep him out, he comes in under the door. But chances of revaluing artists aren't limited to neglected ones. I guess it goes as well for my essay "Edouard Manet" [1983]— as much as with the Munch, there I went all in with personal uses that I have for art, and I was dazed by how well that seemed to work. I almost had to stare at the byline to believe I'd done it.

I always want to know any critic's personal uses for art. I've *got* to have a sense of who is talking to me. If it isn't present in a first paragraph, I stop reading.

Do you think that a degree of narcissism is essential for being a critic?

Absolutely. It's basic operating equipment. But as with any complicated machinery, you have to be careful—keep it engaged with the task at hand, not let it run amok. You are giving someone who is utterly not you something to read.

I think it's really important to remember
that when you're writing criticism, or
just simply being an engaged viewer
or member of the public, you're not
passively receiving something—you're
actively contributing something that
wasn't there until you came and gave it.

Barry Schwabsky (b. 1957) is a poet and art critic.
He began writing criticism for *Arts* and *Flash Art* in the
1980s and contributes regularly to *New Left Review*
and *Artforum*, where he coedits international reviews.
His books of criticism include *The Widening Circle:
Consequences of Modernism in Contemporary Art*
(1997); *Words for Art: Criticism, History, Theory,
Practice* (2013); and *The Perpetual Guest: Art in the
Unfinished Present* (2016). He has written catalogues
and monographs on artists such as Dana Schutz,
Howardena Pindell, Alex Katz, and Sue Williams, and
edited the popular Phaidon anthologies *Vitamin P:
New Perspectives in Painting* (2002) and *Vitamin P2*
(2011). His books of poetry include *Book Left Open in
the Rain* (2008); *Opera: Poems 1981–2002* (2003);
Trembling Hand Equilibrium (2015); and *Heretics of
Language* (2018). He has been the art critic for *The
Nation* since 2005.

Barry Schwabsky

How old were you when you first became aware of poetry?

I guess I was really little. In the apartment where I grew up, there was an anthology of English poetry from Chaucer to Yeats, or something like that. It had been my mother's, from her one year at Brooklyn College before she had to leave to work. She took an English course, and this was the textbook from it. It was just there, and I used to pick it up and read it. It didn't seem different from the lyrics of songs I heard on the radio. It seemed natural to be curious about it.

I grew up in Paterson, New Jersey, and when I became aware that someone had written a book-length poem about Paterson, I was flabbergasted that anyone would want to do that. So I went to the library and got William Carlos Williams's *Paterson* [1946–1958], and that is when I started reading modernist poetry. Because it was published by New Directions, I looked for other books they published and was then reading Ezra Pound, Denise Levertov, and so on.

The other thing is that somehow poetry is just an idea that is in circulation that everybody is exposed to. I think every lovelorn teenager writes a poem. It's really more a question of why most people stop, or become convinced that it doesn't have anything to do with them, or they with it.

If poetry is an idea in the air for everybody, then what is that idea?

It's not one idea. It's many ideas. But maybe it's just something like articulating a relation to reality through words.

At what point did you start writing poetry yourself?

Like I say, I don't think it's a question of starting, I think it's a question of not stopping.

Then, rather, at what point did you adopt being a "poet" as part of your identity?

Well, that's a different thing. Maybe in college. I don't think I had a sense of an identity as a poet until then.

Were you ever a musician?

I always wanted to be, but I never had any talent.

So what is the distinction between *Everyone writes poetry, we all grow up with nursery rhymes, et cetera* and *I always wanted to be a musician but I didn't have the talent*? Music has to be just as "natural" to our experience of the world as poetry. At what point does the "talent" peel people off from poetry or direct them toward it?

I think it's a little bit different, because in music there are actual physical requirements for success. I started to learn music theory, and I could understand it and so on, but there was a limit to how well I could play any instrument, and that was the end of it. Maybe if I had thought about singing, which I never did, I could have found a way to go further with it.

One of the things that is striking in your criticism is that it feels like its primary relationship is to language, but language in the sense that it relates to sound, as opposed to the visual world.

Yeah, I think my sense of where I can find the poetry in the language has much more to do with the resonant than the imagistic side of it.

When you invoke music as an example or as a metaphor, it has a clarity and power unusual in art writing. How do you see your relationship to music?

It's hard to encapsulate, but it's very important. For instance, I think one of the things that has been important to me in writing poetry, as a sort of model or influence, is a particular experience that you probably know, because I think it's a very familiar one: when you listen to songs, particularly in rock music, which is where I come from, sometimes as you are listening the words come in and out of understandability. In other words, sometimes you just hear the voice and you can't really make out the lyrics, and other times, it is very clear what they are singing. To me, that very fact of going back and forth and having those transitions between clarity and incomprehensibility, or the materiality of the voice on the one hand and what it wants to communicate on the other, really touches me. I always thought it would be great to create that effect without the music, just with the words. *How do you do that?* It's not as if I've invented some technique; it is just one of those big things always in the back of my head.

An example is that song by the Crystals, "Da Doo Ron Ron" [1963]: "I met him on a Monday and my heart stood still / Da doo ron ron ron, da doo ron ron / Somebody told me that his name was Bill / Da doo ron ron ron, da doo ron ron." Who knows what "da doo ron ron ron" actually means, but we all have some emotional sense of what it's saying within the song. But is that something different from what you're describing?

It's funny, because one of my really, really old poems had "da doo ron ron ron, da doo ron ron" in it! I'm trying to say, *How can I have the "da doo ron ron" feeling while having words you think you can read?*

I thought the most dazzling piece in *The Perpetual Guest* is your review of the exhibition *Blues for Smoke* at the Whitney [2013]. The way you examined not just the formal and experiential implications of jazz, but also the cultural and existential ones, showing how those open onto the specific experiences of African American abstraction, was really superb.

That was something very personal for me, because even though I write about all kinds of contemporary art, in whatever medium, my basic analytical model comes from painting. If I look at a piece of conceptual art or a video, of course I'm looking at it as what it is and not pretending that it's a painting, but there is a kind of framework for formally understanding that thing and the relation of its parts that I developed from looking at and trying to figure out paintings. In a way, what *Blues for Smoke* did was make me think, *Well, wait a second, I don't necessarily have to have painting as a model, maybe music can be the model for painting and all the rest*. How you do that, I don't know yet. It's a long row to hoe, as they say.

So I was grateful, on the one hand, to the makers of that exhibition for really making me think about that, but at the same time they evaded trying to grapple with it as much as they could have done. Of course, there is an idea about music that has always been important in painting; think about Kandinsky and so forth. But for me personally, that lineage that treats music as the emblem of the "abstract" in Western art never really touched the thing that gets to me about music or about that art. Suddenly I realized that maybe this other tradition, the way these African American painters were coming to abstract form *through* their lives, *does* touch on it in a different way. I'm not any more sure than were the curators of *Blues for Smoke* of where that leads, but I have the feeling it leads somewhere.

That article was searingly insightful about Jack Whitten's paintings, and you did that without *visually describing* a Whitten painting. So what is there? There are Jack Whitten's words and an analysis of the conceptual structures you extrapolated out of his paintings. What I'm trying to say is that a lot of writing on art rests on rigorous visual description as a form of analysis, but you do something different.

In a way, maybe it goes back to what one has a talent for. I've never felt that I had a talent as a describer in that sense. I've tried to push myself to be better, because you need to do it sometimes, and I think giving a reader a sense that what you're saying is anchored in the actual experience of the thing is crucial. But at a certain point, I realized there are ways to bypass parts of that. For instance, if you read Clement Greenberg's criticism, he doesn't describe a great deal. He tried to get to the point of what's significant about this thing, and he supplied the minimal amount of description necessary to make that clear. I saw that I could go that way and function better. Whereas if you read a critic like Max Kozloff, in his writing in the sixties on painting, he is a very luscious describer—almost in the way of a food critic describing the specific tastes of the cauliflower or whatever it is, and when I read it I think, *I can never do that the way that he does*. I'm not making a hierarchy of value within critical writing; I'm saying you just have to come to terms with where *your* value is. If you're built for basketball, don't try and make it as a jockey.

Something that runs through a lot of your reviews on visual artists is your engagement with their *language*, so whether it's Jack Whitten or Jimmie Durham or Boetti, you bring in what they've said and written. How do you approach incorporating an artist's words into an argument?

That is something you have to be careful about. First of all, artists, like everyone else, use lots of words: *Which are the ones that really count?* You're editing them—without permission. You're imposing choices that somebody else might not find to be the right choices. Just like when you're giving a visual description—you can't actually describe every mark in a painting; you have to pick the ones you think offer the greatest clarity about the intentions with which this thing was made. It's the same with words. Of course, you don't want to put the words in the way or in the place of the visual thing; you want them to be something that points toward seeing what's there. I think for artists in our time, writing and talking have become an important part of what they do. Because it's not like we're in the sixteenth century, where the church tells us what the subjects of the art are and theology tells us how it's interpreted. The subject matter and its relation to other circles of discourse in the world have to be somewhat supplied by artists.

You open your review of Peter Schjeldahl's book *Let's See: Writings on Art from* The New Yorker [2008] by saying that he is the art writer you are most envious of on the level of style. How has style in your writing evolved?

It's definitely evolved; I've never really thought of trying to look back and recapitulate what that development was. I think there was a certain point when I really wanted to go toward hardcore, formally descriptive language that would be very much inside the development of the artwork. When I look back on things I wrote then, I find them almost unreadable. And yet, it seemed important at the time, because I was aware of a lot of people who were doing the opposite, which was looking for a topical hook to hang the work from, to display it as an emblem of what a particular micromoment of contemporaneity represented. That always felt false, so I wanted to go the opposite way—but then that opposite way wasn't really right for me either.

Since then, I've tried to do something with a more permeable membrane between the inside and outside of the work. A somewhat conversational tone seems to allow for quick shifts in and out without trying to underline too emphatically the points where artistic things go toward social things or political things or everyday things, and yet have those entries and exits there.

How did you start writing criticism?

I arrived in New York in 1982. I was writing poetry—

In the vein of?

I was much influenced by John Ashbery. I was very interested in the New York School in general. I got to know some slightly older poets who were here in New York, and they were writing for art magazines—

Including who?

Most importantly John Yau, who recommended me to Richard Martin, who was at that time the editor of *Arts Magazine*. That was in 1984. That is when I started to write for art magazines.

How long had you been looking at paintings before that?

I got quite interested in painting in high school, I think partly because of poetry. I started to read people like O'Hara, and I was curious about who these painters were that he was talking about. I remember going on a school field trip to The Museum of Modern Art and immediately loving Rothko. From '79 to '81 I was in graduate school in English at Yale. I thought I was going to get a PhD in English and be a professor, which didn't happen.

What were you going to work on?

My initial thought was to work on English Renaissance poetry—Wyatt, Shakespeare, Sidney, all that. When I got there, I realized that the most interesting work that was going on was actually in romanticism; if I had stayed I would probably have gone that direction. I had a girlfriend who was studying art history. Through her, I got to know some other people studying art history and also in the art school, and it just became a normal thing to talk about art. After two years, it was clear

434

that I should leave academia. My girlfriend got a grant to go to Italy to do research for her dissertation. I thought, *I'll go to Italy too*. I found a job teaching English, and we'd go every weekend to every church and little museum and look at all this medieval and Renaissance and baroque art.

Where were you living?

We were in Milan, but we traveled all over northern and central Italy. That was a real experience of seeing painting and sculpture in the place it had been made for, so you get a different sense of the relationship of art to its environment than you get at The Museum of Modern Art, which had been my thing up until then.

When you started writing at *Arts*, what were you reading as models for how to write about art?

Well, for one thing, I started reading other things in art magazines—*Arts Magazine* and *Artforum*—and after a little while I started writing for *Flash Art* and *Artscribe*, which existed in London then. In terms of other influences, I think that Roland Barthes's 1979 essay on Cy Twombly was really my holy grail.

Why?

Because it was so sensitive and inventive, and because it was so clear to me how emotional it was. He was able to take his feelings and make an intellectual construct out of those feelings so that anyone else could enter into it without having the feeling imposed on them. Feeling became a way of knowing and vice versa.

Your book *Words for Art* is a very impressive volume on art writing, and one of the most impressive things about it is that I can't really figure out your agenda. You're talking about a number of different approaches to art with greatly varying methodological commitments and intellectual stakes, and you're very fair with each of them on their own terms. When you put them together, what did you notice about that group of essays?

In a way, I could wish more of an agenda had emerged from it. But it's true that I didn't enter into that project with an agenda. When I say "project," the earlier things in the book are things I wrote just as separate book reviews because I was interested in a particular writer or book. Then, after I had done a number of them, I thought, *I'm interested*

435

in this idea of writing about art writers, so I'm going to look for opportunities to keep doing it, and maybe I'll have enough of them to make them into a book, and eventually I did. As a book, they should add up to more than the sum of their parts. If it's the case that they do, it's not because it makes an argument for a certain way of writing about art to be the right one, or for certain qualities of art writing to be key ones. It's simply that as a fellow practitioner I was curious how different people went about it— whether as critics, or philosophers, or artists, or whatever.

What do you think of the role of "taste" or "opinion" in criticism?

I think those are two different things. "Taste" seems to be almost corporeal—*Does it taste good or not?* Whereas "opinion" would be more of a reflected judgment, or at least that is what it implies to me. I think taste is really a great tool, because it's something that happens when your tongue comes into contact with something that is not "you." Taste is where you and the world meet. What is the flavor of it? Is it sweet or sour or bitter or salty? I think taste means a primary way of getting acquainted with the world and interacting with it. And it can be very immediate, but I don't think it's interesting to stick to that immediate feeling. There are things that you once tasted and spat out because you didn't like them, and later you find out that you do. Taste seems so physiological that it's easy to forget that it changes, and that you can cultivate and educate it—it can become wider or narrower. I think the interesting thing about taste is to not accept it as it is, but to keep working on it and see where it takes you and where you take it.

So it's not about rejecting taste, just about not accepting it as final?

Absolutely.

Then how would you describe "opinion"?

I think that is also something that needs to be relativized. You need to understand how tactical or temporary or contingent it is. I don't think it's as important for criticism as taste. But I think it's always there.

In reading your criticism, it doesn't feel like it's driven by your opinions. But there are critics who feel that their opinions are the name of the game.

In the sense of their judgment, like, *This is good or not good?* I think that judgment is something different than opinion. For me, anyway, judgment is a horizon. *Is it good or not?* is really fundamental in art, but the answer tends to be somewhere far out in front of you—you're not really there yet. Whereas maybe opinions are something you have along the way to judgment.

In your life as an editor and critic, how do you understand the ways art criticism functions now and how it is different than when you first got involved in the mideighties?

I remember very distinctly, sometime fairly early on, I had written something about a group show and had critical things to say about the work of one of the painters in it. Later, I met the artist, and he said, *I thought about what you said in that piece and I decided that you're right.* That freaked me out, because that was the first moment I realized that I'm not just writing for myself, but that someone might actually take seriously what I was saying. Now I needed to take that into account. I had to realize that this thing I was doing basically for my own pleasure had consequences for other people and that I had a responsibility. But how much weight should I give to that? I don't want to get into the *pose* of responsibility. I don't like it in other people, and I don't like it in myself.

How would you articulate that pose of responsibility? I think it's something palpable and also ineffable. How do you understand what your "responsibilities" are?

It's to the reader and to the artist. On the one hand, I think it's really important to remember that when you're writing criticism, or just simply being an engaged viewer or member of the public, you're not passively receiving something—you're actively contributing something that wasn't there until you came and gave it. That thing that you're giving, in the very nature of it, is something without a foundation— you're making a leap, the leap of interpretation. And yet in making that leap and giving up that foundation, you're not just doing any old thing. You have to be as serious about it as the person inviting you to participate. I think one way of ensuring that, and this may seem like a contradiction, is to be serious in that way that's not *too* serious—not to make too much of what you're contributing. In a way, that goes back to my private apprenticeship to the poets of the New York School, because that was always part of their implicit critique of what had seemed to be the dominant American poetry when they came on the scene in the 1950s: that it was too self-serious and too overt in rhetoricizing its own literariness. They realized it could be more serious to be witty in a certain way, or more answerable to reality to be frivolous—I think I've really taken that to heart. Not that I ever write things that are frivolous, because that is not my style—

But the sense of the conversational is there in your writing. Your reviews for *The Nation* are longer than a standard column but shorter than an article. There is something about their form that's a perfectly balanced and conversational length. How have you approached writing in different formats?

Partly it's just good luck that I got a chance to write at a magazine that gives me a substantial but not unlimited amount of space to work with. It's like somebody making a painting; they stretch a canvas of a certain size, and the marks put on the canvas are going to be made in relation to that scale. I know when I'm writing for *The Nation* I've got about twenty-eight hundred words, and I've got to make something that works at that scale. If I write a review for *Artforum*, I know it's going to be about six hundred words, and I approach it with that in mind.

How do you navigate your personal relationships with artists as relevant to writing you've done about them?

It's not necessarily easy, because I was writing early on in order to become more involved with art, and that really meant being with artists in order to understand what they were trying to do. Having those conversations has always been really important to me, but at the same time, I'm not the spokesperson of the artist, I'm doing my own thing. It's almost like something two-year-olds do called parallel play: there's a stage where children play in the same space next to one another, but they are playing individually; only later do they get to the stage where they are really playing together. So in a certain sense it's like that, where I'm playing and kind of looking over and seeing what they're doing, and maybe they are looking over and seeing what I'm doing, but we each have our own thing. Sometimes you get into slightly uncomfortable situations, for all sorts of reasons, because people that you have these informal personal relationships with don't like it that at a certain point you seem to be exercising judgment over them. Or, that you're not exercising the judgment that they thought you should have had.

In that little piece you wrote on Schjeldahl, you quote something he said to you: "Your criticism is about the studio; mine is about the opening." I'm wondering how you see that as positioning your criticism.

I don't think that has anything to do with being more on the side of the artist, because the artist is at the opening, just like they are in their studio. But it does have to do with my emphasis on, *Why did this person do this?* Whereas maybe for Schjeldahl it's, *What effect did it have that this person did this?*

Do you think there are any persistent misunderstandings about art criticism or what it should be?

I would say there is a lot of confusion or mystification about it. One question has to do with that idea I mentioned of whether the writer is the spokesman for the artist or for the art world in some broader sense. We all want to say, *I'm just speaking on behalf of myself, this is me,* but it's also right to remember that when you're speaking as yourself in public, you are still positing some circle of agreement around yourself, so who is the real or imaginary group that the "I" is representative of? That is one question. And the other, in many people's minds, is the relationship of all this to the art market, and that is something we haven't really talked about.

Do you *want* to talk about it?

I don't *want* to, but I don't know if you can avoid it. I don't think any of us writing today, with the possible exception of Roberta Smith, can imagine that we have a direct effect on what happens in the art market, the way we imagine maybe Greenberg did in his day. And yet, criticism more broadly is certainly one of the things that keeps the market running and makes an atmosphere of interest around art in general.

So even though the individual critic may not have any measurable weight in terms of what goes on in the market, the broader sense of critical interest might, and the activity of art magazines is part of that system. The question is, *Can we be more precise in our understanding of how that happens? What's the good of it and what's the bad of it?*

Do you conceive of the kind of writing you do as having any relationship with the market? The way you write and what you write about, I don't see how it does.

Simply the fact that you are writing about this artist and not that artist is somehow part of the cloud of information surrounding their art. But how? I'd like it if I thought my writing could help those artists whose art I appreciate. I'd like them to have an easier time earning a living and more peace of mind, but from what I can see, what I write doesn't seem to have much of an effect on that.

I think it's a pretty accessible thought that when we've rained down "Tomahawk" missiles on fifteen countries in the last thirty years and called the South Bronx "Fort Apache" in the seventies, these are not unimportant psychological elements of the country that are worth investigating, without instantly becoming about manifest destiny or white supremacy. How do we avoid that trap?

Paul Chaat Smith (b. 1954) is a major voice in contemporary Native art and culture—creative, funny, and searingly humane. With Robert Warrior, he coauthored the magisterial *Like a Hurricane: The Indian Movement from Alcatraz to Wounded Knee* (1996), now a standard text in both Native and American studies. A selection from two decades of his writing was published as *Everything You Know about Indians Is Wrong* (2009). Since 2001, he's been an associate curator at the National Museum of the American Indian in Washington, DC, staging the exhibitions *James Luna: Emendatio* (originally developed for the 51st Venice Bienniale; both installations 2005); *Fritz Scholder: Indian/Not Indian* (2008–2009); *Brian Jungen: Strange Comfort* (2009–2010); and *Americans* (2018).

Paul Chaat Smith

What was an early important aesthetic experience you had?

My family went to the 1964 World's Fair in New York, which has always been a captivating thing for me—ideas about what the future might be, how *amazing* it's going to be, and how it almost never works out that way. You want it to be so beautiful, and maybe even back in 1964 I thought, *It's not going to be like that.* But it's still really a delicious thing to consider, and then to watch what actually happens. I remember walking underneath a mock-up of a Saturn V rocket—it was unbelievable how large it was. I was taken by the cheesy plastic-fantastic sensibility of it all.

How would you describe your relationship to language growing up? I know your grandfather was a pastor in Oklahoma who'd hold services in Comanche, and that you grew up outside of DC.

When I went to visit my mom's side of the family in Lawton, Oklahoma, they had a complete set of *National Geographic*. In mid-twentieth-century Oklahoma, that's an education. I'm not sure I thought about it at the time, but my grandfather on that side made his living *speaking*, as a minister, which must have been an influence. Both my parents were educators, but they were not particularly worldly or sophisticated. I have an indelible memory of watching my dad write a book—this would have been the midsixties—in the backyard of our house in College Park with his shirt off, typing on a manual typewriter. It was called *Rural Recreation for Profit* [1966]. He did another called *Planning and Paying Your Way to College* [1968]—so he was always doing multiple things, and within that was writing. He was never a gifted writer, but he felt that language was really important. So, I think watching him type, and watching it become a book, was a big deal.

I remember after that, I learned how to type—one of the few things I really did on my own. I got a book where you learned how to touch-type, and I learned how to do it at home using a manual typewriter. Being a writer was sort of in the *ether*—my grandfather giving sermons, my dad writing a book. But no one ever said, *Oh, you should be a writer*.

My dad went to a one-room schoolhouse in Dibble, Oklahoma. Even though he was good in school, his education was so poor that when he went to the University of Oklahoma he had to transfer. Anyway, both my parents had limited educations, but they really valued education. It drove them nuts that I was a terrible student. They just knew it was really important and we had to get ahead, but they didn't really know how to help us in school, or how to think about stuff like, *What do you really want to be?*

You went to Antioch College in 1973, and as part of a college internship you volunteered to work for the American Indian Movement, or AIM, in South Dakota—what was it like when you arrived?

It was a little scary, because I was really on my own. But I embraced it right away. In the years before, I'd gone to the big mobilizations in Washington, DC—like the antiwar moratoriums. The idea of being part of the revolution was very comfortable for me. It certainly tied in well with my sense of self-righteousness, of being on the side of the angels, and all of that.

I was aware very early what a privilege it was to have a front-row seat to the Indian movement in the seventies. Being linked to Antioch meant that I had some legitimacy, so that when someone would ask, *Who's that guy, what is he doing?* I could be identified—*He's the one in this program.* I didn't have any particular skills—most of the people were lawyers or legal investigators, paralegals, who had very particular things to do for the trials. I didn't have any of that. I don't think I would have been particularly good at learning it, either. In that sense it was a great setup to just be there.

What really made an impression on me was the chaos of the mass trials that began in 1974, when hundreds of people were indicted for every conceivable charge, including cattle rustling, which was a brilliant way for the government to put the ordinary people of the movement on trial. But it wasn't a big story nationally—in fact, it was hardly covered by the press. The only things that got covered then were the Russell Means and Dennis Banks trial. I was always fascinated with that disconnect—that arguably the largest mass political trial in US history doesn't get any news coverage.

I met Dennis Banks pretty soon after I arrived in South Dakota. Russell Means wasn't there a lot, but I ended up in the Russell Means clique. These guys were in their thirties. They didn't come out of student activism. Most of them had been in jail. Dennis Banks had been an executive with the Honeywell Corporation—they'd had these rich lives that were not necessarily what you would have thought.

How did you first meet Jimmie Durham?

It was a few days after I arrived in South Dakota. He looked like Abraham Lincoln then because he had this beard. I'm not sure what I thought of him at first, actually. He makes a big impression on people. He explained he had lived in Switzerland and was an artist who had come back to help AIM. He was one of the leaders of the legal defense committee—I don't know what his relationship was with Russell Means at that point, but he was already a significant person there. When we talked, I think he was vetting me to see what use I would be. I think I got identified as a smart Indian who could be helpful, even without any skills.

Jimmie had contacts in Geneva, and he persuaded Russell Means that we needed to be a liberation movement working with the World Council of Churches in Geneva. A Methodist women's committee arranged for the AIM offices to be right across the street from the UN—Jimmie had all these contacts that nobody else in AIM possibly had.

I became somebody who was helping Jimmie—at the UN office and with a newsletter AIM put out in San Francisco. This again was the Russell Means faction—basically, if I was Jimmie's lieutenant, he was

Russell's lieutenant. Obviously I learned a great deal from talking with him. He just had a very clear-eyed sense of AIM and its flaws—he was very realistic about things.

Something brilliant in your writing is your engagement with the long history of representations of Indians—the complexity of their presence in all forms of media since the beginning of film. Does that come out of the ways AIM was thinking about the media?

I remember weeks after I arrived, there was a trial for a riot at the Custer County Courthouse in South Dakota. Wesley Bad Heart Bull was killed by white people, and justice was not coming. So his mother, Sarah Bad Heart Bull, participated in this riot—everything is so fucking overdetermined with Indians, of course, it's got to be "Custer County Courthouse," "Bad Heart Bull," all of those things. So, this is the mom of some guy who was killed; she gets arrested, and then she's on trial in Sioux Falls, South Dakota. I can't remember what our side did, stood up or made some kind of demonstration, but a SWAT team came in and cleared the courtroom. I remember meeting this Irish dude who had ties to the IRA who bragged about being interviewed about the riot on the *Today* show. That way I became aware of how AIM was being portrayed. But in terms of what I wrote later, which was what you're riffing on—that a lot of the representations were rooted in deliberate staging that went back to Edward S. Curtis's photographs and Thomas Edison's films, in sometimes brilliant, sometimes stupid ways—I don't know how much I thought about that back then. Maybe I was just taking it all in. When I was writing *Like a Hurricane*, it was really clear that people like Russell in particular really understood what it would take for the movement to be heard. And some of what it would take was playing on those tropes and repurposing stereotypes in different ways.

After you and Jimmie both resigned from AIM in 1979, you moved to New York. When did it feel like being a writer was on the horizon as a serious possibility for you?

I would say it was writing the first book, *Like a Hurricane*. I guess I had written a few small pieces by then. The book became this *thing*—it was basically like taking everything that's dear to you and throwing it over a very high fence so you have no choice but to do it. At that point in my life, the idea of writing the "truth about AIM" book, which nobody else was going to write except me and Robert Warrior, was a big part of my identity. The very first book proposal we did said it would be a collection of essays by different people involved with AIM, and this smart agent said, *No, you guys should just write the book*. It seemed too audacious at first, given that we'd never written a book before. Robert at least had published a big piece in *The Village Voice*, so he'd written more than me. We took that advice and got a really good publisher, New Press. It was through the ordeal of writing that book that I forced myself to write—failure was not an option.

In your essay "Radio Free Europe" for the recent catalogue *Jimmie Durham: At the Center of the World* [2017], there is an anecdote about you going to see him in Mexico when you started working on *Like a Hurricane*. The advice he gives you is, *Write it for people smarter than you are*. How did you approach writing that book?

Robert and I had a lot of agreement on what the book should be. Before he became an academic, he had this brief life as a journalist, so we both had a journalist's sensibility—we weren't going to start with the 1868 treaty, and we weren't going to do the ponderous things a lot of people do. It turned out I had a flair for writing stuff set in the moment, trying to draw out the elements that are most interesting to me, and that made it more readable. Also, I found that I couldn't write unless I really cared about it, which sounds cool, but that's a huge problem in many ways, because there's an awful lot of stuff I'll never write because I can't become interested in it enough to do it. We decided the book was going to focus on three key moments, which all happened before I become part of the AIM. That advice from Jimmie Durham is very helpful—*Make it for smart people*. I took that as saying, *Take all the issues you have with AIM, and instead of deciding what the right political line is, explore them through the book.*

People would say, *Oh, you're going to really write about AIM and tell the truth, you'll probably get killed*—which was silly, but there was an idea that it was dangerous to do. The major thing that shaped the book was that we really cared about our Indian readership, who already knew these things about AIM. If you are just writing for a white, left audience, one might focus on the FBI and the whole *Feel bad about the 1868 treaty* stuff. But if I'm writing for Indian people, most of whom felt a great affinity for AIM and then were disenchanted by it—if I want *that* audience— I have to be straight up about it.

At many stretches, it feels almost cinematic—there are really precise stylistic decisions about the structure. How did you get to that?

I picked certain things that resonated with me and built it from that. I knew I was going to use an account of Buddy Lamont's funeral. One account mentions a hundred-gun salute—I knew that was a perfect chapter title, "Hundred Gun Salute." It's an amazing moment, he's the local hero, the Oglala guy killed at Wounded Knee—most of the people were not from there, they were from outside—and he's buried in his military uniform. That's so powerful—those were things I felt I could write about.

At first I thought, *Okay, there's this meeting in which the elders decided to call in AIM. We have to reconstruct that meeting in every possible way*. I start trying to do it half-heartedly, but I'm not a very good researcher. I'd get bored with it, and you realize you don't trust the information that much anyway. There are things that you think you *must* have to nail it. What you discover is, actually, you don't have to do that. You know this meeting happened, you can rely on a few accounts, you don't have to be the definitive encyclopedic account of every single thing—that's just not possible to do.

What I was fascinated by was that after the occupation, people would find the fabric from parachutes on the ground. Or that people who'd lived there their entire lives found their homes completely destroyed. And if I feel engaged in details like that, my talent as a writer is that I can make it work, as long as I'm really invested. It was like assembling the things that I really cared about, and then making the narrative fit around them.

Your writing is often a meditation on the complexities of history— how it's written, communicated, and constructed for different people

and at different times. How has your relationship to writing history developed over time?

Lately I just feel like history is not a friend. I'm not even sure if it's a *frenemy*. History is a big mess. In retrospect, based on what we know now that we didn't know about AIM when we wrote *Like a Hurricane*, it's a soft book in certain ways. I don't think Robert and I ever made decisions to be untruthful about AIM's nature. What we've learned since then is almost half of AIM's major leadership was involved in an order to kill Anna Mae Aquash, who they suspected of being an FBI informant. It wasn't really part of our book—you could have that excuse. In many ways the book portrays these guys as lovable rogues who at their worst just might beat the shit out of people once in a while. Not killers. And they've accused each other, right? It's incontrovertible that some people in AIM were involved in calling for the execution of this person they thought was an informant. Which means there was a darker side to AIM than what we explored. I guess a harder question for me is, *If I had known all those things at the time, would I have gone there?* That would have been a very difficult choice, because I wanted to show AIM as deeply flawed but heroic. I think you could still argue it was. But it really changes when you have to account for some of these things that go way beyond what a lovable rogue does.

I was personally invested in the narrative of AIM, too. The book was really trying to be tough and truthful while saying, *This was important.* Whatever you think about AIM, when you look at the scope of the twentieth century, that period of activism, the most overlooked thing about AIM was that thousands and thousands of people participated in the occupation—in terms of raising money, food, crossing those lines, over months. It was a mass activity in a way that doesn't get enough attention. That's true regardless of whether the movement was more screwed up than our book accounted for.

I was watching this Martin Scorsese film called *The 50 Year Argument* [2014], about *The New York Review of Books*, the other day. There was this story that really resonated with me, about Frances FitzGerald, one of their journalists covering the Vietnam War. She was a hero to their liberal readers. Then she started reporting on all the horrible things that the National Liberation Front did and was vilified—people turned on her in an instant. I feel like that's what we're living at this present moment. You choose your team, and you want to hear what you want to hear. The complexity is understanding that the NLF was a legitimate anti-imperialist, anticolonialist outfit that did all kinds of wonderful things, *and* it's absolutely guilty of atrocious war crimes. The one doesn't mean the other thing isn't also true. Humans are flawed, the world is flawed, and more and more it's not like there's good guys and bad guys in the way that some of us hope for. I was very fascinated in that film to see that the same journalist, the same person you thought was amazing, you could so easily say is either a liar or that you don't want to know the truth of what she's saying.

You gave a talk at the Walker Art Center during the height of the controversy around Jimmie Durham and his identity as a Cherokee. Your take was so "grown-up." I loved this part: "I love doubt. I love confusion. Sometimes I even love being wrong. Anything's possible, right? If Jimmie Durham is a fraud, it would rank somewhere between two poles for me. The first would be finding out my parents were actually KGB officers. The second would be a colleague that you've known for decades, whose house you visited, who shared stories of their childhood and their siblings, you met their spouse and have friends in common, and you find one day every single thing they told you about their past was a lie. Hard to imagine what that would feel like, but I'm sure it would make me feel dumber than a box of rocks, which in a way would be deeply interesting."

I was really surprised to see an art critic recant her glowing review of his retrospective once the controversy erupted. What do you make of all that?

I remember the rock critic Ellen Willis saying something like, *The Rolling Stones are sexist and they're really awesome, and, so, deal with it*. That's like, Harvey Weinstein made some amazing movies. Right? That doesn't mean the movies are now awful. He's obviously this terrible person. It's so interesting that artists and people who follow art would have so much trouble with that, because we just know that a lot of great artists have been terrible people. That's part of it. What I decided with AIM is that you can't just pull out this or that aspect that you want—because all of its problems, all its contradictions stem from its brilliance. I think with a lot of artists it's the same.

When you started writing criticism, who were your models?

The *Voice* was pretty influential, the idea of critics who could write in really different ways with their own style. Early on I was reading people like Hunter S. Thompson. I had this book by Oscar Zeta Acosta, *The Autobiography of a Brown Buffalo* [1972], in the early seventies—that made a big impression on me, that somebody could have this outsider Chicano activist thing and be writing in a first-person voice. When I was in New York, there was access to a lot of great criticism. I followed Stanley Crouch, for example—somebody coming from a very different perspective. I liked the fact that criticism could express a worldview— basically a critic is imprinting their worldview on you. I also liked the free-ranging nature of it, where you could talk about music and politics at the same time—both activism and art. That really suited me.

Many of the essays in *Everything You Know about Indians Is Wrong* are in the first person, and in many of your essays you've deployed this hyperstylized first-person character. What's the relationship between the "Paul" character in the writing and in the world?

I think the character came from writing *Hurricane*. The book was in large part me figuring out what I thought about AIM—*as* I was writing the book. Not before. It then seemed only natural to be more explicit about the texts being PCS deciding what he thinks about the topic at hand, in real time. Though I think the PCS character is a lot more fun than I am.

How did you start writing on visual artists?

My stock answer, which I think is really mostly true, is that politics got boring and artists were having more fun. I would say that's it. By the end of AIM, there were all these different factions. Jimmie and I always liked that movie *Life of Brian* [1979] because they have this funny riff about the "People's Front of Judea"—all these little factions set in Jesus's time. All of that kind of absurdity of the New Left was manifesting itself in AIM until it was tedious and irrelevant. Then I saw that artists were actually engaging some of these larger questions I was thinking about.

One thesis of *Like a Hurricane* is that AIM never had a political agenda—there was never something coherent like *land to the tiller*. It was reacting to things in an extraordinary way and understood invisibility as a huge thing that all Native people could relate to, and was asking, *How do we change that?* A lot of Native art was about the same kinds of things—*How do you overcome how most people see Indians? How do we create a space to be seen and understood differently? How do we make work relevant to our lives?* And the ways the artists were asking all this was more interesting. Once I got past the idea that I had to know about painting and art history to describe the work and what it means, it just made sense to write about it. And I got gigs writing about art—hopefully because my stuff is good, but also because there are very few people writing about Indian art. The best writers tended to be people like Jimmie, or Jolene Rickard, who are themselves artists—and that's a different thing.

My art writing evolved over time. Mainly I liked getting published, and I could get published writing about art and I could still talk about politics. Everyone who asked me to write about art usually knew *Like a Hurricane*, and they were somehow interested in me bringing an activist's understanding.

You write, in the broadest sense, about contemporary Native art—is that fair to say?

Yes.

Though it is weird to put it that way, because it's such a vast array of things that you write about. How do you conceptualize the diversity of that group of artists?

I think I generally avoided that. Kathleen Ash-Milby, my colleague in New York, has done us all done a great favor by saying, *"Native art" simply means art done by a person who says they're Native.* I think what I've really tried to do is figure out how the work of, say, James Luna is asking the right questions, the larger questions, and then I get to riff on almost whatever I want.

What has been most successful is when it's an artist for whom I can do real service by enlarging the conversation around them—by talking about the contemporary moment, or by contextualizing their work in relation to AIM, which you can do to some degree with both James Luna and Fritz Scholder. Those are the more ambitious things where I wasn't worried, *Do I have enough art history to do this?* I had confidence that this would be of interest to the field.

Both Fritz Scholder and Jimmie Durham have an interestingly ambivalent relationship to claiming Native heritage. In things you've written about both of them, you've described the function of their work and personas in the world as "ultimately an Indian project." I was interested to hear more about what that means, not just in the case of those two, but in a broader sense.

There are probably better examples, but there was this great line from a Springsteen interview: *There's an empty concert arena, then there's a band, then the arena is full of people—what happens each time is a unique new experience: it's something that's created together.* To me, the work of art and the reception of the work are new every time, and that's instructive to look at.

For the Scholder exhibition, I think a lot of curators would have said, *Okay, now there's this whole issue about his identity, and we'll deal with it over there.* But I'm always looking for that third rail, and for Scholder it's his fellow students at the Institute of American Indian Arts in Santa Fe, most of whom still hate his guts to this day. They went to school with him and say, *When he came here, he was an abstract painter—he ripped off our work.* They're furious even now. That's where the energy is, so go with that, instead of saying, *Don't pay attention.* I wanted to front-load it so we might see what's actually going on. And maybe this controversy is the key to understanding his work—that story of him saying, *I will never paint Indians—okay, I'll paint Indians, but I'm not painting Indians anymore— wait, I need money, so I'll paint Indians again.* To me, it's an irresistible narrative. And something that I'm qualified to talk about.

Well, what does it mean to then say that he, as a cultural figure,

is an "Indian project"?

I guess it's probably trying to get at, *What is the usefulness of Fritz Scholder?* You have an Indian-consciousness constituency saying, *Here's this guy, this weirdo, who has a fancy dog and drives a Rolls-Royce or whatever. He doesn't seem to care about us much, and he buys all these stupid ads in New York art magazines to get famous. What do we do with this guy?* The idea would be that we can put him to different uses. My mom hated Fritz Scholder—she wouldn't even come to the opening of that show, she dislikes his work so much. She doesn't care about art in general, she just thinks he made us look ugly. What I love about his work is it captures who we were before this mandatory retraditionalization thing. The fact that we hang on to him means that he's still significant—that these paintings and images have some use for the Indian world.

I see a lot of your writing about art as advocacy more than criticism per se. How do you see that, and what do you think is important to address in writing about contemporary art made by a Native American artist, as opposed to anyone else?

I think that's true. There's a certain low-key, triumphalist, pro-Native-art slant, and in the field we talk lots about someday having enough going on that a Native artist is slammed by a Native critic, which never happens. Also, I'm not sure my art writing has a larger critical point of view. Probably not. I would say from the perspective of 2018, I wish both of these art scenes had greater ambition to reach larger audiences. It feels like we've given up and no longer dream of contemporary artists being as significant, as famous, and as discussed as celebrities or athletes.

How do you understand the relationship between politics and art—between what artists are doing and other forms of pop-cultural representation?

I remember talking with Steve McQueen and other panelists about an event that was part of an Edgar Heap of Birds exhibition in Venice in 2007. He laughed at the idea that artists today are more or less political than they were centuries ago. I've always been close to that perspective: it's all political. I have felt disenchanted with the art

world in recent years, in large part because the artists I'm supposed
to like the most, Indian and others, make preachy, didactic work that
reaches an audience who already agrees with them. And that becomes
less appealing to me given the political economy of the contemporary
art world these days, how much of it is based on the extreme wealth
so many of these artists condemn. I understand the contradiction is
complex, and this doesn't make the artists hypocrites necessarily; I just
want it to be acknowledged more than it is.

**Your essay "The Big Movie" [1992] is a radical expansion of the role
of visuality in Native American history—you argue for very canny and
complex dynamics at play in these representations, in which Indians are
active participants.**

In a way, writing *Like a Hurricane* was saying, *How about a book where
Indians are at the center of it, and not just as the victims?* I started thinking
the same things about photography and films. I developed sort of a
novelist's sensibility about it. Like, you look at the famous Edward
Curtis photographs, and you know the Indians sitting there are not
stuffed. They got up in the morning, they did different things, they
were told to take their watches off so they wouldn't be in the photos.
I'm interested in what these people were thinking about while they
were doing their part to make these photographs. The thing that
motivated me to write the book about AIM was to counterbalance
the narratives out there, which were really about white people doing
things to AIM, as opposed to dealing with the vital lives of the people
actually involved.

In a similar way, a lot of very trite writing about Indians and
photography is really about the white imaginary of Indians and not
about the actual agency Indian people had. That they, in fact, could
be very intelligent human beings who were doing all these things for
strategic reasons, or not.

I'm having a real issue at the moment with a lot of the messaging
from the museum around a veterans memorial that we're doing.
They've made a central element of it this question, which is a
completely white-person question: *Why would Indians serve in the US*

military given how they've been treated? I understand why people would ask that, and I would not say it's a stupid question, or that at some point you wouldn't want to engage it—it's just not remotely a question that has anything to do with why most Indians are in the military, historically or in the present day. People don't wake up and think, *Oh, I'm an Indian and I'm oppressed. Somehow I've joined the army, but wait a minute, they screwed us over!* Most Indians who join the military do it for the same reasons other Americans join the military. I had uncles on my mom's side who were in World War II, and they are very patriotic. They wanted to fight for their country. They don't say, *I'm going to do this, but it's really ironic because . . .*

It's partly because you're talking about it so generally. What I try to do is look at really specific moments, details, individuals—then you can get at who people actually are. What you end up finding is that they are basically as smart as you are in that moment. They're not puppets, and they're not without any choices. My work is always trying to unlock that.

I see your new exhibition at the National Museum of the American Indian, *Americans* [2018], as a summation of a lot of the ideas you've worked on for a long time. How do you see them taking shape in this particular exhibition?

When we were first starting to plan this show, we held an important symposium with some of the smartest people in Native studies, called "You Can't Teach American History without Teaching Indian History." The punchline is, *Of course you can, because it's done all the time.* The level of Indian scholarship now is just extraordinary—it's like a golden age. Despite that, when these people teach undergraduates, it's like it's still 1970. The needle hasn't moved. Despite all of the public campaigns and great scholarship, in terms of an average American's knowledge of Indians, it's still almost at zero. What that tells me is, *It's not about more information, and it's not about correcting false ideas about history or stereotypes— because we've been doing that forever, and it hasn't move the needle.* The radical notion of the *Americans* exhibition is that we're telling visitors, *You're part of the Indian experience by virtue of being an American—Indians are so embedded in American national identity, in visual culture, that this really is about you.* With this show we're trying to say, *You are part of this construct.*

I think in 2004, it would have been a fair criticism to say you could come to our museum and learn about the Northern Cheyenne, and that's cool and interesting—they had great art and ideas about the universe—but then you could leave and it asked nothing of you. Because it had nothing to do with you—I mean, atomized exhibitions are constructed that way. Instead, with this show, we're saying, *There is no you without us: everything about this country is entangled with Indian consciousness, identity, history, continuing up to this day—it's in all our heads.* That's risky, because it's giving the audience a lot of power.

When I was researching *Hurricane*, I saw that throughout history, there is this recurring thread of feeling sorry for Indians. Back to the very beginning—*Lo, the poor Indian!* You get people writing in the mid-nineteenth century lamenting, *We're screwing over the poor Indians—it's so sad,* so we made this funny slogan: *Lo, the poor Indian!* Guilt about Indians has produced disastrous results quite often. The famous thing about the Carlisle school, where Indians were sent off the reservations—when it's discussed, they often show a cemetery full of dead Indian children. *Very subtle.* It wasn't a great place, but what people leave out is that, first, many Indians sent their kids there because it was much better than schools on the reservation; second, private boarding schools all over the world were fucking horrible—think about rich, upper-class English boarding schools and what goes on there. But most important to me is that the guy who ran it, who famously said "Kill the Indian to save the man," was a radical Republican antiracist. For his time, he was the most militant *Nation*-reading Bernie bro you could find. Because these were *radical* ideas, to take Indians and educate them. Most of the Indian world at that time *wanted* assimilation—it was just a question of on whose terms, and how much. When Indians today say, *We wanted to stay the way we were*—that's against reality, which is really hard to admit.

How has your conception of the audience shifted with this show?

This show will get a million plus visitors a year—all kinds of people, ninety percent of whom are non-Indian. If I'm interested in reaching that kind of mass audience, if it really works, it'll be something they think about the next day. It'll be something like, Trump says "Pocahontas" and they'll say, *Oh, I learned these cool things about Pocahontas at that exhibition.* Noticing the place names and the images will reinforce the idea that Indians are part of your life, whether you're white or South Asian or whatever. That this is part of the experience of living in this country.

I think it's a pretty accessible thought that when we've rained down "Tomahawk" missiles on fifteen countries in the last thirty years and called the South Bronx "Fort Apache" in the seventies, these are not unimportant psychological elements of the country that are worth investigating, without instantly becoming about manifest destiny or white supremacy. How do we avoid that trap? That's what I'm trying to get to. A lot of it is helping people feel that it's just kind of cool to think about. Museums are organized around didactics and messaging and all of that—I just think humans are so complicated. I never want to be *proscriptive.* If I get people with the spectacle, and they're thinking about how Indian experience is part of their own individual life in a different way—that's success.

I think the shift is thinking more deeply about who the audience actually is and what's the most impactful thing we can do. To do that turns out to be sailing against the zeitgeist and saying to the people wearing those red "Make America Great Again" baseball caps, *Come on in. Learn about this. Be part of it*—without irony, without, *We're going to show you how bad you are, how wrong you are.* I think that's what's radical about it.

I'm humbled by art, by its persistence and its unpredictability, and I'm always learning from it. It is just amazing to me how hard it is to see, and how little you see. As you grow older, you do see more and more, but you're still missing things.

Roberta Smith (b. 1947) is widely considered one of most influential critics in New York. Her early friendship with artist and writer Donald Judd provided a model for rigorous and clear aesthetic argument, which was further honed by writing on postminimal and conceptual art of the 1970s. She began writing for *Artforum* and *Art in America* in the 1970s before moving to *The Village Voice* (in 1981) and then to *The New York Times* (in 1991), where she is currently cochief art critic.

Roberta Smith

I'm interested in the longer articles you wrote for *Art in America* in the
1970s, when you were splitting an editorial job with Scott Burton—

In *theory.*

What does that mean?

It means I couldn't edit—I didn't know a thing about editing. Betsy
Baker basically hired me so I would write for her. She gave me a job,
which meant I could leave *Artforum*, which I was really happy to do—

Why?

I had just been savaged in the magazine by Jeff Perrone. He reviewed
a big Donald Judd show at the National Gallery of Canada in 1975.
I'd contributed a catalogue essay that was a rewrite of my college thesis,
which traced Judd's transition from two to three dimensions, basically
from 1952 to 1962. When Jeff reviewed the show, he called me, in effect,
a groupie, a flatterer, and a stooge. I've come to really like Jeff, and
by now I tend to view that Judd piece as juvenilia. But as might be
expected, you don't forget that kind of thing, especially one as rhythmic
as that. Jeff came into the art world writing nervy, negative pieces about
big names. He was very smart, some takedowns were probably in order,
but it was also a very efficient way to achieve power and visibility. The
Artforum article came out just as Betsy offered me that job, so I had no
problem leaving. Another thing was that I had been hired by Robert
Pincus-Witten, who was easy to work with. Then he left and I was being
edited by Max Kozloff, who one day accused me of being a formalist.
Or at least informed me that I was one. At that point, I didn't know

quite what it meant, but he didn't seem to be on my side!

When you moved from *Artforum* to *Art in America* in 1976, were you able to write differently?

Art in America was very different, easier, looser. I had written only one little article for *Artforum*, on Jared Bark; otherwise, I'd done nothing but reviews. I was terrified of going from the reviews section to the front. At *Art in America*, I was getting much more support—and all of a sudden was writing long pieces that Betsy put on the cover. I guess Betsy saw a potential in me that hadn't been recognized at *Artforum*. In addition, she was a great, sympathetic editor with no agenda who taught me a lot, as many editors do.

Obviously it helped tremendously that she was a woman, which, unbelievably, I wasn't quite conscious of at the time. In many ways I'm a late bloomer. It probably took the arrival of the first woman to head the culture department at the *Times* for me to gain absolute clarity about it. I've worked under about a dozen culture chiefs, all men, several of whom were wonderful. But having Danielle Mattoon in that job changed everything. It transformed the atmosphere and enabled me to relax at the *Times* in a way that I never quite had. When I was first there, and for a long time, it felt like being on a football team and they hadn't given you the playbook.

In 1978, you wrote an article about Scott Burton, "Scott Burton: Designs on Minimalism," for *Art in America*; I thought this line was lovely: "It seems safe to say that Burton wants his objects to have charisma—a physical, quasi-erotic magnetism that is both fascinating and a little repellent due to the extent to which it is abstracted and purified (and withheld) by being presented in such formal, material terms."

I don't remember what I've written. You could have written that yourself and I'd take your word for it. So what is your question?

It's a lovely description, but it also seems like something that might come out of a personal relationship, from knowing the artist as a person. I wanted to know about your transition from being embedded with the artist and writing from their perspective to your present

position, in which you have to stay critically aloof from personal involvement with artists.

What changed that was going to *The Village Voice* and realizing that I wasn't writing for the artist or the artist's approval, that artists don't control the meaning of their work. I remember being tormented writing a feature for *Art in America* on Philip Guston, wondering, *What is Philip Guston going to think about this?* And realizing in the end that he probably didn't think much of it. The *Voice* gave me this important thing that is hard to have, writing in the art world: a readership. Or it was then, before everything could be instantly put online. Around this time, a writer friend said to me, *If you really want to be a critic for life, you have to get out of the art world and get a readership.* And that is when I went to the *Voice* and asked for a job, which I eventually got. When you have a broader—and a weekly—readership, everything becomes more immediate, pressured, and also pleasurable. Your sense of responsibility and loyalty instantly switches to the readers—at least it did for me. It's hard to describe, but suddenly you're in conversation with a much larger, more varied audience. The weekly appearance makes it feel like you never stop talking. And you get the idea, delusional or not, that the readers want to hear from you. It encourages a condition that I think is basic to writing criticism: *disinterestedness.* You have to be disinterested in your own responses, no matter what they are. You can't have either an agenda or fear of what some artist or friend will think. You learn to shut all that out more; you learn to go deeper into yourself. Mainly you're faced with the task of simply being *honest.* So you want to edit things like the artist out.

Does that mean you don't do studio visits?

During my first decade in New York, while writing for art magazines, I had gone to artists' studios all the time; they were part of my DIY graduate school. At the *Voice*, I felt that if I went to one artist's studio, I'd have to go to all artists' studios—it wouldn't be fair. These days, I have studio visits with close friends who I don't write about, or do little more than mention in passing. Carroll Dunham is a friend, and a couple of years back we filmed a short studio visit with Michael

Blackwood as a kind of substitute. I'm kind of cameraphobic and still haven't watched it.

But you've reviewed Carroll Dunham.

My, my, you have been deep in the archives! Obviously I'd suppressed that for the moment. I reviewed a show of his at Sonnabend in the late 1980s, when I was relatively new to the *Times* and still a stringer. I think I was naively testing the waters of writing for a much larger publication. I got some backlash from friends and others, which quickly and rather painfully clarified the ethical situation.

What was interesting to me about that particular *Times* piece on Carroll Dunham is that it's one of the most Judd-like of your reviews, in tone as well as approach. It starts: "Each work features one shape rendered in one bright color on a rectangular surface composed of one or more 40-by-60-inch sheets of paper mounted on panels. As this eight-painting series progresses, the surfaces enlarge. . . . The first three paintings—respectively red, green and brown—are on one panel each. In other works, the ground doubles, then triples and so forth, culminating in the largest work, 'Purple Shape,' which occupies a 9-by-12-foot surface of five panels." Do you think you wrote it like that because you were so personally close?

I don't know. It could have been that. It may also have been an attempt to emphasize the formal progression, the systemic nature of such seemingly spontaneous, superficially childlike work. Also, I was still finding my voice at the *Times*, which felt so different from the *Voice*. And in addition I was still at the stage where every deadline was a kind of trauma.

You write these things and file and edit them, and then you sort of want to kill yourself. I don't think that is unusual. Especially for weekly writers, there's often this incredible regret—you think of all the stuff that is *not* in it, and that it's badly written. You can't see it. Then all the things you've shut out in order to write—like, *This is going to hurt some feelings*—rush back in. I still can have a mini breakdown on Thursday nights before the paper comes out, but it's become more comedic. Jerry usually ridicules me out of it, basically saying, *If you're down about your writing, it must be Thursday night.*

Something I love about art criticism: ethical agreements that are actually articulated and hashed out in other forms of journalism are completely amorphous and opaque in art writing—there is no set standard for what constitutes the ethical boundaries between artists and critics, socially and professionally. It sounds like when you moved to the *Times* you had to work that out for yourself.

I had to work that out a bit, partly because I was a stringer for five years and wasn't given the same time and attention as staff writers, so I was a bit more on my own. It's not that hard, in a way. You don't go to gallery dinners; you don't pursue new friendships with artists; also, you ask dealers to stop talking if they are giving you a spiel about an artist. You try to keep the situation as uncontaminated as possible. And let's face it, the main person you want to hear from is yourself. But seriously, as an art critic, you have to remember: all you really have is a certain kind of integrity and credibility based both on what you write and how you behave. Not that it's limited to art critics or the art world. I guess reputation is all, everywhere. But it always seemed kind of stark to me, like the thing that kept the wolf from the door almost. Of course, that's rather laughable these days, when critics can earn thousands of dollars writing catalogue essays for art galleries. I tried that twice when I was between the *Voice* and the *Times*—the wolf was approaching the door—and wasn't comfortable with it.

So it was a kind of progression from publication to publication.

Definitely. The thing I'm just realizing right now, which was implied in your earlier question, is: I wrote an article about Scott Burton, a colleague of mine at the magazine that published it. *Jesus* I'll bet you were waiting for me to realize that, and I just did. [Laughter.] I wouldn't say that Scott was a friend of mine—but still, thinking about it today, it's a total conflict of interest. But that is the way those things were back then.

Art and criticism are born from those conflicting interests.

Absolutely, but that doesn't necessarily involve contact—or conflict—with the artist. There's enough going on inside yourself!

465

Art is the best art criticism, I think Jasper Johns said. Every reaction to it, consciously or not, is also some form of criticism, no matter how rudimentary. My particular job is to write about my reactions. I hopefully develop maybe sharper skills of looking at art and listening to myself in an attempt to produce something that is readable, that has some style and a point of view. It's not that I don't like artists. I love them, but they can get in the way.

I went through the *Times* archive from when you started publishing there in 1986 up to today, and it's interesting to watch names enter into the stream and stay there for thirty years, as the art world changes around and with them. It's even more interesting to see who disappears.

Totally fascinating. I was in the Whitney Independent Study Program when I wrote my Judd paper—my first experience of living in New York, and I moved five times in four months. At one point, I was living with four guys who were all in the program on the top floor of a brownstone on East Tenth Street. I was the last person to move in, so I didn't get a room, and built one out of orange crates in the dining room. You can imagine I often felt like I had no place to go, so I'd spend a lot of time in the library after hours, until ten or eleven at night, reading the reviews in the backs of bound volumes of art magazines. This was 1968; the fifties were only *just* over, but they felt like a century ago to me because I was so young, and because there was so much change in the early sixties.

Reading through those reviews was very educational. There were all kinds of artists who were emerging, but weren't in the art world as I got to know it. Artists like Lester Johnson or George Ortman, whom Mitchell Algus resurrected. I remember Ronald Bladen being reviewed as a painter, then as a sculptor, and then later he was embraced by younger artists like Bill Jensen. It was very sobering. It gave me an archive of neglected names and a daunting sense of how *fluid* everything is. The way attention comes and goes. Artists rise to the surface and sink again. How an artist endures that, how they keep making a living and developing during all that, when the art world isn't looking, is a major psychological effort.

Given the fact that your first serious engagement with art criticism was compiling all of Donald Judd's reviews for publication as a book, it's interesting that you've never collected your writing—is that not interesting to you, or do you believe that the review has a life in the daily paper that is not served by being in a book?

Yes in both cases. Nobody has thrown themselves at my feet and said, *I want to do this more than anything.* I'm certainly not going to do it. With a weekly deadline, you're always going forward anyway. The idea of rereading everything gives me the willies. I write for a *newspaper.* Until digitalization, I saw reviews as very ephemeral, written to be read quickly and tossed. You try to make your words as durable as possible, but newspaper criticism is fleeting. And I'm not crazy about collections of critics' writings, which may say more about me than them. I've read Jerry's two books, Peter Schjeldahl's *The 7 Days Art Columns*, and quite a bit of Greenberg from the four-volume complete writings. Otherwise a lot of those books just sit on my shelf. I don't want to put this thing out into the world that is just going to sit on people's shelves.

When you said Max Kozloff called you a formalist—that is something I'm really interested in. What makes Judd such a terrific critic is that he's extraordinarily opinionated, and yet it's grounded in form— there is this thing out there you are talking about *specifically*; it isn't "just an opinion." I think you've adopted that strategy: your reviews are driven by opinion, which is one of the reasons they are so important to the public, but they are grounded in form, which gives them weight and stability.

I'm not so sure of that. Form is grounded in specificity, but people still have different opinions about it. Michael Fried certainly did when it came to minimalism. Nonetheless, I do think form is the ultimate; it is what is really speaking to us in art. And form can be achieved in absolutely any way, in any medium, social practice included, but now it's neglected and people look down on it. I always wanted to write an article on content and how it has been completely confused with subject matter. I've heard people say, *Judd has no content.* You can't say that! Everything has content, certainly all art. Also, to a great degree, content is beyond the artist's control; mostly it's what they can't keep out of their art. It's the nonverbal part of it; even art that is completely made of words has to have it. Obviously novels and poetry have it. To me, form and content are together, not opposed to each other. Subject matter is outside them, it may contribute to them in some way, but it's really different. I think Dorothea Rockburne said, *Subject matter is what an artwork is about, content is what it does*—i.e., what it does to you. And form is how it does it.

What was your first awareness of form?

We were visiting my aunt in Hastings-on-Hudson, New York; she was a real estate agent and had a Mercedes-Benz. When I got in that car, it was intense: *Oh my God, some things really are a lot better than others of their kind*. I just knew that it was *quality*—incredibly made and thought through. I guess you could say it was rigorous, which is probably the least you can expect from luxury goods.

I wrote down something in a review of yours from the *Times* in 1988: "'If an artist says it's art, it's art' is an attitude prevalent since at least the 60's (the actual words, if I remember correctly, are Donald Judd's). I cut my art-critical eye teeth on this concept, and it has always seemed to clarify, focus and dignify the critic's task. It implies that the critic's job is not so much to dither around with the definition of art but rather to pass judgment on the quality of a body of work as precisely and convincingly as possible." I thought it was interesting the way "quality" functions in light of this conversation, and wanted to see how you feel about that as a definition for what a critic does, over thirty years later.

I still agree with that. Quality—however you define it—is what we're looking for on all fronts, not just art. You have to be open to it occurring in anything an artist calls art. I'm not interested in saying something is *not art*. One way I get around it in my head, which is completely chicken, is that sometimes I think people just aren't really artists.

I think that a lot.

I think a lot of people who've misplaced their talent or interests, for whatever reason, are attracted to the glamour of the art world, or

find a kind of safety there. With a lot of social practice, I think, *This
is great—now go out in the world and actually do something with it, actually
change something . . . and how about not calling it art?* Just kidding! But if
you make a pronouncement like, *This is not art,* you will eventually have
an experience that will assert itself as art and prove you wrong. Tino
Sehgal did that for me; it was this feeling of control and precision,
of form.

**It seems like you took the tools for addressing perception that were
called formal analysis—which were really honed, visually and bodily,
in Judd—and then directed them away from the Judd program and
applied them to everything.**

Art made me do it. I emerged from my time with Judd as a total
Juddite: painting was dead; illusion on a two-dimensional surface
was anathema. Then I encountered Philip Guston's late paintings and
conceptual art. Art teaches you and changes you. With luck, it broadens
your perspectives. Another part of my DIY graduate school is that after
working for Judd, I worked at Paula Cooper Gallery for two and a half
years in the early 1970s. It was full of artists looking for ways through
minimalism that involved objects and weren't overtly conceptual. These
included Alan Shields, Elizabeth Murray, Joel Shapiro, Jennifer Bartlett,
Robert Grosvenor, Jackie Winsor, Joel Fisher, and Jonathan Borofsky.
Being around them and their work was definitely broadening.

**The articles you wrote in the seventies on Scott Burton and Richard
Artschwager showed that evolution: you're bringing Judd's formal
intelligence to bear on somewhat opposed work, so that the illusion of
the Formica and the reality of the chair bring you to different ends.**

That's very flattering, but I think you have to remember the
diversity and physicality of the work he wrote about enthusiastically:
Oldenburg, John Wesley, Samaras, which all had subject matter and
was figurative in a way that his own work wasn't. But I do think art is
more engaged these days in subject matter, and it's a postconceptual
phenomenon. Conceptual art was a shock to the whole system, a lot like
cubism. Everything got rearranged. It made artists more interested in
subject matter, and many then and since have been trying to figure out

how to find form within it. I think most of the artists at Paula's were doing that. A lot of figurative paintings throughout history had already figured out form plus subject matter pretty well, and after conceptual art, artists have been figuring it out again, in a new way. This also applies to so-called abstract art.

This might sound like a tangent, but I heard that you grew up Quaker.

I am from a Quaker family, a birthright Quaker. My parents called each other "thee" and "thou." They were actually third cousins, from a few generations of related Smiths who all started out in a hamlet in Loudon County, Virginia, that renamed itself Lincoln—it was called Goose Creek previously—after the Civil War. Then just after I was born, we moved to Lawrence, Kansas, and we didn't go to meeting there. My mother went once and never went back. Basically, I think she had never been to a meeting where she wasn't related more or less to nearly everyone there: they were all mostly Browns, Smiths, Janneys, Taylors, and probably one or two other names. Gorky painted on one of the Taylors' farms right around there. I later learned they had some Gorky watercolors. That's Lincoln's little tie to art history. We went back there every summer until I was about eight, but then close relatives started dying and farms were sold. It all changed.

Still, even in Kansas, my mother maintained some kind of Quaker ethos or mythology. I loved the fact that, as a religion, it is egalitarian, there are no ministers or preachers, the education of women is valued. I also had some sense of plainness, although a complicated one. I remember my mother telling me about gray Quaker bonnets lined with silk and fitted with lots of tiny, perfect tucks.

This might sound hokey, but my experience of Quaker meeting houses, like the beautiful building over on Stuyvesant Square, is that they put you in a mood of perception or contemplation that seems like good preparation for Judd and minimalism—the testimony of simplicity, for instance. Do you think you were predisposed to respond to those kinds of aesthetics because of this Quaker background?

I might have been. When I met Judd and encountered his environment, I understood that everything in it was carefully selected and that everything in it attracted me. It brought up something already present in me and very important to me. To the best of my financial ability, I tried to buy things he and his wife, Julie Finch, had—Arabia tableware from Design Research on Fifty-Seventh Street; those Wearever cooking pots, with their wonderful straight sides. I went to Tiffany's to see the black basalt Wedgwood coffee cups, but decided I couldn't afford them. It was like being inside the Mercedes-Benz, but it was a *life*. And it was a life that I could, in small ways, aspire to. Of course, it then turned out that I'm a bit of a pack rat and that I live with someone who likes to arrange or "curate" all kinds of stuff all over the house.

You emphasize integrity as a critic. In another interview, you said, "I think sincerity and integrity are the primary value in art, and these result from making something as good as you can make it so that it reflects your ideas, interests, and your passions as clearly as possible." Something about your work as a critic relates to a strong ethic, so it didn't surprise me when I found out that you grew up Quaker.

That's interesting. I know it's definitely in there. Probably the thing I love most is that Quakers, or at least Hicksite, or nonorthodox, Quakers, which I sort of am, don't think Jesus was holy. He was a wise teacher, but a human one. I learned that when someone informed my mother that because of that little loophole, she wasn't Christian. She was a little taken aback, but it was fine with me.

Even so, what I find attractive about Quakerism, taken as an extreme form of Protestantism, is that it puts all the onus on you—you've got to follow *your* light. I feel that is potentially also our relation to form: form has to communicate to you directly, and there really shouldn't be an authority that overrides that. But people are so often disempowered from believing that feeling.

That feeling is really all you have when looking at art. Disempowerment comes from being instructed to look in only one way. The art world is in an interesting place right now, because it's wide open. I'm leery of what art students learn in graduate school; I think their ideas often get narrowed down. I'm just not interested in anything that verges on the ideological. I think it always trips things up. Even

Hicksite and orthodox Quakers weren't exactly tolerant of each other.

One thing we've learned in postwar art history is that pretty much every kind of art is going on all the time, at the same time, but usually only a strand or two gets attention at any one time. You have to be open to everything. Quality doesn't come from the carefully prescribed places or kinds of people that it used to. Everybody has aesthetic inclinations, and a certain percentage of them are visual and acted upon. Some people are at Creative Growth; some are in graduate school at Yale; some majored in English in undergrad, can't afford grad school, and are out on their own, working day jobs to have studios that might be in Bushwick or Detroit. And others are just out there doing it on their own in their backyards, garages, or living rooms, making things that might be discovered in the attic after they're gone. There is so much more art than we know about, whether past or present.

Clement Greenberg, too, if you look at his personal collection— his early writing was obviously much more open and eccentric than what was collected in *Art and Culture*. His career is almost a lesson in learning to unsee.

I know. I loved his early short reviews, when he was open. I think the intoxication of discovering Jackson Pollock—or thinking he had— made him kind of power-mad. Everything he did after a certain point seems to be just about power.

Power wants to consolidate more and more power.

And one form it takes is making other people wrong. *Art should be this, not that. Critics should do this, not that.* It's interesting to try at least to not tell other people what to do—which is hard. I'm not interested in reprimanding other critics in my writing—although I love arguing with them on panels. I just want to make whatever case for the art I'm writing about.

As a critic, how do you understand what it means to have an opinion?

Opinion is what you *do*, your process and your product, the thing that makes criticism exciting to read. I realized this from Judd, of course, but perhaps more from reading the reviews of lifelong critics like Pauline Kael and Edmund Wilson. Criticism is an evaluation more of pros and cons, not so often raves. I like to write negative reviews, but sometimes they're hard to justify when you've got as little space for galleries as we do at the *Times*. But sometimes not. Lately, I've been trying to do capsule reviews on Instagram, because space is so tight at the *Times*. I don't think these can be negative. It just doesn't feel right. But we'll see. Truth be told, I'd like to review just about everything I see.

There is a lot that is buoyant and optimistic about this conversation, but I heard you once say that you don't think Judd would be writing if he were starting out now. Why is that? What does that say about the climate of writing now that would not be amenable to him?

There is so much against what he believed in. His position was, *If you discover electricity, you don't go back to candles.* Judd would think a lot of painting now was going back to candles. But there are whole different groups of people making art. There are more women painting than ever before. Artists of color are in an interesting position. They've got a subject—African American experience in America—and some are finding forms for it. It reminds me of the German artists who arrived in the early eighties; you're looking at their work and thinking, *Wow, they've got the weight of German history sitting on top of them—that is really something to work with.* Art is not just pure form and space; there is more to it than that now.

I don't think it ever was pure form or space. That is why people think they hate "formalism." A lot of abstraction is predicated on the illusion of that purity.

You're totally right. I was being simplistic. As for abstraction, the most recent kind seems predicated on showing up that illusion as a fallacy. I wrote recently about the lack of a Philip Taaffe painting from the 1980s in the Whitney's collection and its show *Fast Forward: Paintings from the 1980s* [2017]. He made a kind of conceptual yet sensuous painting that he perfectly poised between the two main factions of the eighties, neo-expressionism and the Pictures Generation. I think most people don't even know those paintings, the op-art ones.

I don't.

Someone should do a show of them. He invented this great collaged surface by covering the entire canvas with prints on thin paper that added up to, for example, the waves of one of Bridget Riley's well-known op-art motifs, but a strangely disembodied and semitranslucent version. Then he would stain these new Rileys so that the waves softened or shimmered, becoming visually more complex, more naturalistic or decorative. He took a tall Vasarely painting that had three squares with lines intersecting at the center of each, tinted them red, yellow, and blue, and renamed it *Trinity* [1985]. Basically Taaffe was probably the first around then to show that abstract painting could appropriate—which many painters do today—while also demonstrating once more that most painters physically reinvent their medium in some way. So did Julian Schnabel, Jean-Michel Basquiat, and Elizabeth Murray.

Is that what you meant earlier when you said you were looking for personal form?

Yes. I don't think pure abstraction ever existed, but it hasn't got a chance now, because you can't do a monochrome without it being a comment on, or development from, a century of monochromes. Also, a lot of the figurative painting now is interesting because it incorporates abstraction in complicated ways. Going back to why I brought up Taaffe, he once said in an interview about the op-art paintings he used that he didn't think they were finished. It could be taken as a criticism of Riley—which is fine with me, because I don't like much of her work. But it is also positive: *There is more still to be done with this, and I'm going to do it.* There is a lot of that going on right now. There is more to be done with the entire twentieth century—it's open to being expanded upon. A lot of people will call that retro, but I think that is not the case. I guess the question is, *What amount of difference is enough difference so it feels like our time?*

As opposed to Judd looking for "new form."

Or a more subtle form of it.

What ways have you found to disentangle your self from writing about art? How are you aware of what you're bringing into the experience?

474

Again, you learn to listen to yourself, deal with your ideas, your musings, and whatever your unconscious churns up and interrogate them all. That could be a definition of writing criticism. Criticism is a process of trying to be honest, and I'm not sure you can ever achieve it absolutely. Saying exactly what you think is really hard. There is a way you just let your eye *be*, and you follow it. I agree with Greenberg in a way, that you could walk into a gallery and do a three-sixty turn in the middle and pick the best painting in the room. I think you would pick the best painting for *you*. When I say what the best painting is for *me*, some people will agree with me, some won't.

Is it like a representative democracy of taste—you've been elected because you have opinions other people can agree with?

That's one way to put it. I prefer to think that you establish a point of view and voice that people come to trust. Critics get positions because one or two specific people—i.e., editors—believe in their work enough to give it a try. Then it's up to you to prove yourself. You establish this credibility, this integrity, and then you get another thing, which comes from where you write but also from your own work: power. Power is given to you by your readers, you earn it—and you can lose it or have it taken away. All they have to do is stop reading you.

The thing that I'm interested in is use value. If people read you repeatedly, it is a measure of usefulness. When Jerry was first writing, he'd write a few paragraphs and get stuck. I would ask, *What does the reader need to know next?* The main thing I'm trying to do is get people out of the house to look at art, to open themselves to it, so they can learn things about themselves and about the world. Art is a mirror, and a sustenance, a food—very essential. It would be a tragedy if the NEA gets cut, not just for the money, but the symbolism: *You don't have to bother with art*—when you should bother with it like you bother with learning to read.

In 1989, you wrote a little piece about the effects of minimalism: "Similarly, it is not the nihilism of Minimalism that comes across but a kind of innocence and a complete faith in the eye's ability to see, and in seeing, to provoke critical thought. Needless to say, these are

important lessons for a nation as visually illiterate as our own." I loved that way of framing it.

Basically, I think opinionated art criticism helps the reader find pleasure and also develop a criticality that can be applied elsewhere. It spills over into other aspects of a person's life, like thinking critically about architecture or society or what it means to be a citizen.

I'm humbled by art, by its persistence and its unpredictability, and I'm always learning from it. It is just amazing to me how hard it is to see, and how little you see. As you grow older, you do see more and more, but you're still missing things.

I realized by the mideighties that
the ideas you impose on art, ideas
of what you think should be there,
are not smart or meaningful. Maybe
it assures one of one's own identity
or sets up limits, makes life and
looking easier, gives one a sense of
knowingness.

Lynne Tillman (b. 1947) is a novelist and cultural critic often associated with the downtown New York avant-garde of the eighties and nineties. She entered art criticism in the 1980s with her character Madame Realism, whose first mainstream appearance was in the pages of *Art in America*, offering stream-of-consciousness reflections on Renoir; subsequent exploits were collected as *The Madame Realism Complex* (1992) and *The Complete Madame Realism and Other Stories* (2016). Her novels include *Haunted Houses* (1987); *Motion Sickness* (1991); *Cast in Doubt* (1992); *No Lease on Life* (1998); *American Genius, A Comedy* (2006); and *Men and Apparitions* (2018). Her essays are collected in the volumes *The Broad Picture: Essays 1987–1996* (1997) and *What Would Lynne Tillman Do?* (2014). She is a professor and writer-in-residence in the Department of English at the University at Albany, and teaches in the School of Visual Arts's MFA in Art Writing Program. She writes a bimonthly column, "In These Intemperate Times," for *frieze* magazine.

Lynne Tillman

How was Madame Realism born? From what I understand, Craig Owens brought Madame Realism into art criticism in *Art in America* while he was an editor there, but she existed before that.

There was the first Madame Realism—I think it was 1983. Someone phoned me—so many phone calls, so little time—and asked if I wanted to contribute to a magazine on surrealism. I said no, but I began to think about Meret Oppenheim, who was the first person I ever interviewed and a female surrealist. After college I was living in Europe; she was in Paris, and I went to meet her. I began to think about the position of women in surrealism, which was not great. Then I thought, *Sir* Realism, and that's how *Madame* Realism happened, as a joke. I wrote the eponymous story just to write it; then I showed it to Kiki Smith, with whom I'd been friends since 1978. She was drawing severed hands and limbs then—and I thought, *That will work.* She read my story very closely and responded to the text. She drew sperm for the first time. In 1984, that story with Kiki's drawings became a self-published chapbook.

I had met Craig Owens in 1981 through Barbara Kruger. In 1986, when he was a senior editor at *Art in America*, Craig called and said, *We're doing a symposium on Renoir for an exhibition in Boston, and we'd like you to contribute.* I immediately thought I would bring Madame Realism back. I'm not crazy about Renoir, but it was a very popular show, so I decided to deal with it on those terms. I recorded people's responses as they stood in front of various Renoir paintings and then incorporated them into my essay, or story.

Fashioning the "I" within art criticism is something that rarely gets talked about, which is one reason Madame Realism is so great—she gets you off the hook for the things she thinks; she's roving around recording what she hears people saying during the exhibition. How did you first start developing that as a way of writing *in relation* to art?

It doesn't entirely get me off the hook, because people think Madame Realism is my alter ego or some such. She's not. Writing that way came out of necessity, out of my own ignorance—though I actually studied studio painting and had taken an art history course. Even if one doubts authority, I knew I didn't have that kind of information, I didn't have the sort of discipline an art historian has. If there is a version of political correctness that I understood in the eighties, it was a way of thinking about how to write "others" or "to others." *Thinking* about it, rather than simple, thoughtless replication. That is what I try to teach to students: *You are creating a character. Who is that character?* That is so important. I was thinking about how I could write sensitively about art and realized there is a way to use fiction for that—to think about why certain forms come about as they do. Or, why somebody would want to be making this. Or just to describe what it looks like. And not to be afraid to use metaphors sometimes. After Susan Sontag's *Against Interpretation* [1966], there was a real fear of *interpreting*. But in writing a story, you can have a character who is responding to something, and the character's identity is revealed through how he or she experiences the object. Identity's fluidity is partly in how we respond to things as they happen. People talk about not having a fixed identity—that doesn't mean you're protean and you're going to shape-shift, but it does mean that you're going to respond to different objects and different people differently. You don't have the same conversation with everybody. Hopefully.

I find your writing to be very psychological, but not emotional. It does seem like a hallmark of postmodernism to evade emotion or deny sentiment, because it's "manipulative."

I don't mind some good old-fashioned manipulation, if it's in the service of keeping my interest. It was a very dirty word in the seventies and eighties, a part of the antinarrative campaign I never was part of, because I like narrative, and using it is complex. I was writing narratives in the aftermath of structuralist film, which I had been involved with in Europe, where I had watched film grain for hours and hours, and one day I thought, *What am I doing? Yeah, film is light, film is material, and there is the grain of the celluloid—okay. What now?* Obviously I have feelings, and my characters do too, but the fear of sentimentality has always held my hand. I want the reader to experience emotions as much through what a character doesn't do or say as through what they do. Maybe more. If the character usually delineates her or his emotional states, where does the emotion of the reader lie? Further, what is meant by identification with a character? Wholesale or partial or what? What about disidentification?

When I've spoken to your former students, they say that, more than anything, they learned a precise and rigorous attitude toward writing as a craft. How did you begin thinking about language like that?

There were a lot of words in my family, not necessarily good ones, and they had material effects—material in the sense of emotional, psychological, and dramatic. Words were important and words could hurt you. I wanted to be a writer from the age of eight; maybe it was a question of having my own time and space to talk, and to be in control of what got said. I remember loving writing, sitting down, being alone, and I felt I was good at it; actually, I felt I knew it, and it was what I wanted to do. But as for teaching it as a craft, questions around word choice and syntax—if you are writing and not focusing on these, you are not dealing with your medium. It has its demands. Many people can tell a good story; few can write one.

You've created a unique position as a fiction writer in the art world. When you went to Hunter College, you took painting classes with Ron Gorchov and Doug Ohlson; was that the beginning of your involvement with visual art?

My father was a textile designer, so there was always an interest in color, design, material, texture. He had his own business with his brother, and they made their own fabrics, innovating threads. When I went to his office, I loved looking at the bolts of fabric, all different

481

colors and patterns. At Hunter, I was an English major and American history minor, and an acquaintance in my sociology class saw how miserable I was and suggested I take electives in studio art. Somehow, as weirdly out of place as I was, I thrived in that atmosphere. I was wacky, in my own way, and Gorchov and Ohlson both liked me. But I could never finish a drawing. I remember once we went to Central Park and we were supposed to draw something from life. I started drawing a building and only got half of it on a large sheet of drawing paper. Ohlson was so disgusted with me. One day in class he took my pencil away and gave me a stick and some ink, and I made a drawing. When he came back to me, he said, *What am I going to do with you? You don't finish a single thing all year and now you make the best drawing in class!* I said, *You'll give me an A?* It was interesting being freed from the pencil. I could also never get an entire figure on the page in life-drawing class. I had no sense of proportion. I couldn't get the whole body on. The head would be gone. It was hilarious, psychologically.

I don't know if you'd agree with this, but when I was reading your fiction I felt that it was so grounded in language, in words, that there was almost no visual description.

I don't often describe things, yet many readers feel my writing's visual. They see mental pictures. [Laughter.] I think it's because I allow so much space for projection. I remember an art critic telling me what she thought Madame Realism looked like. There had been one instance, in the second story, where I wrote, *She rested her hand on her own broad hip.* I was writing about the Renoir exhibition, and thought it was funny to have a broad-hipped woman looking at his abundant nudes. I never did that again, because I really didn't want to make a specific picture out of her.

I noticed the frequency with which the interview or dialogue form comes up in your writing. One of the reasons I'm interested in interviews is that I can be totally surprised by what someone else will say—they'll say things I couldn't make up.

I write what I'd like people to say. I remember a friend saying to me, *Your dialogue is so strange, have you ever heard anyone talk that way?* I said, *No, but I'd like to hear them talk that way.* It's an influence from Jane Bowles, whose dialogue is unique in literature.

How have you engaged with the problems of "identity" in your fiction?

I wrote *Cast in Doubt* as a riposte to identity politics. I'd finished *Motion Sickness* by the end of 1989, it came out in 1991, and I went right into writing *Cast in Doubt*. I wanted to question the idea of who can write what in terms of sexual orientation or gender. Many lesbians at the time loved it, as did some gay men, but some of the men I knew had problems with it. I was writing the voice of a gay man, writing in the first person, and one man said to me, *But that is not you, that is not how you talk.* I said, *This is a character, Horace, and he has a very definite way of thinking. He's not me.* Oddly though, it is sort of like *Madame Bovary* [1856]—*Horace, c'est moi.* I felt closer to Horace than to any other character I had written before him. In part, maybe you can put more emotion into something that is so very not you than something closer to you.

I wrote Horace as a unique individual, which is what I hope to do with all my characters. Craig Owens had AIDS; he died in 1990—this was before protease inhibitors—and I thought, *How can you think about this population having a future?* I realized the only way to do that was to go back to the past, so I set it in the seventies. I decided Horace would become very curious about a young woman named Helen. If he were heterosexual, the reader would keep thinking that he wanted to have sex with her. I think Horace does get kind of interested in Helen sexually, but the reader is not thinking, *When is this going to happen?* So his being a gay man suited a lot of narrative purposes. My other idea was that they would embody the differences between modern and the postmodern. Horace is my modernist, and Helen is my born-into-postmodernism postmodernist. Weirdly, it had more plot than any of the other novels I'd written until then, because when she disappears, he goes mad not knowing why. This gave him a reason to try to find her. Plot is so ridiculous—*That happens, X causes Y.* The thing that is most interesting to me about life is that you really don't know why things happen, why you do things, and you can't know what will be consequential. But in a plot, the reader is supposed to know why something is happening or supposed to know that something will happen, so as to keep reading, stay engaged.

Although he is a character, I noticed he also resembles certain aspects of your life. It made me curious to hear more about how that identification works for you.

That is a tough question, because it doesn't work in a simple way. It wasn't so much that I was making Horace like me; it was more that I became interested in creating a character like Horace who shared some of my interests. When the book was done, and I was writing the last chapter, Horace's letter to the reader, I was weeping. It had to do with looking back and having regrets and thinking, *I'm going to change this now*. There are things in my life like that. I stopped taking piano lessons from my wonderful piano teacher during my freshman year in high school. It doesn't occur to you then, when you're very young, that you'll never see this person again. Actually, she was a lesbian, and I knew she was a lesbian when I started lessons with her, at the age of eight, but my parents didn't.

How did you know?

For one thing, her partner was a woman who wore gray "mannish" suits and had short gray hair, while my teacher, Miss Matesky, wore flowery blouses and full skirts, and I put it together—I don't know how I knew the word "lesbian" at the time. My parents were naive about many things. I put that loss, losing her, into my first novel, *Haunted Houses*. Miss Matesky was also a Republican, and that was really upsetting to me, not her sexuality. Anyway, you don't realize when you're a kid that you're going to have regrets, because there is no reality to the past yet. I'm sure she's dead by now, but I have tried to find her. So, Horace has his regrets.

Your collection of essays *What Would Lynne Tillman Do?* has an interesting title; it acknowledges "Lynne Tillman" as a character. How did you think about that in putting that book together, or about doing something as "Lynne Tillman"?

I know what you're asking. Because the Lynne Tillman who writes is not the Lynne Tillman who is sitting here now. Lynne Tillman the writer has a series of questions she's asking herself, and approaches, and is focused on writing—and writing is just not the same thing as living. You're living, or you're alive for your writing, but, you know, I'm not going to put in all the slop involved in my little life. I filter a lot. When I'm writing, the idea is the writing, and it is not about *me*. I'm not engaging in old fights. When I write, I am not depressed. I can't write then. We can be better or worse than our characters.

The way you describe the relationship between living and writing— that has been on my mind all summer, because I was planning on driving around having adventures and writing, but I'm finding it impossible to do both at the same time. But the dream is to push them together. So I've been thinking about the endless displacement of writing, wondering if it *must* essentially be its own thing—done alone in a room after the fact.

You transform experience into words on the page. It's different from the experience. I could use the word "mediation," but it doesn't have the charge that it should. You don't put your life on the page; you put a reaction, a deciphering. When writing, you are conscious of using words, and you are conscious of the need to make them "good." When you're having a great experience, you're not thinking about that. There are people who write their experiences in a way that is close to them, so you can feel their presence in the writing, but that's just not something I am interested in—certainly not in my fiction. If anything, I am interested in moving as far away from myself as possible when I use my own experience. That is your *material*—it's a writer's material, even if you write the opposite of it. Horace, for instance, thinks the opposite of many things I think, but I have a lot of compassion for him.

How about writing about art: How do you approach apprehending works of art as experiences through words?

It is the only way one can talk about them, so you're trying to find the *right words*. Currently, I'm writing an essay on Carroll Dunham's paintings and doing very close readings, looking at every element, every detail in them.

What are the elements you're looking at?

Shapes. Figures. Where and how things are placed. Colors. How my eyes respond. Corners. Lines. I'm just looking at the whole, trying to separate interpretation from description, though description itself is biased because you are using these words, not others. You're always making choices, it's impossible not to, so how do you make choices that seem accurate to the art? Or apposite to it, which is what I try to do in writing fiction.

Words make images, but they are not pictures, like, say, a photograph. They have their own limits. There is a way in which you can look at something like a photograph, and try to translate it—which is why I began writing a character called the Translation Artist, though he's very hard to write. Going along with the idea that everything is translation: I once had a dream before the first reading I ever gave—I was in terror. In the dream, I get to the podium, which was similar to where Freud would have delivered a lecture in a medical college, and I take out my pages, but instead of words on them there are objects, tiny little objects about as big as your teeth, and each one is different. I have to translate those into words, instantly. So there you are. How do you do that? That's writing.

I've been fantasizing about pure description, which would still end up being an interpretation, although probably a very good one.

That is sort of exactly how I start an essay, imaging how to write it. There's no way around it. And what's wrong with that?

I guess it depends on how you feel about aspects of experience that cannot enter into language, or if you believe those exist.

Well, incomplete comprehensibility or excess might indeed be part of what makes an artwork, which is really what I'm getting at in this essay, because Carroll Dunham has made paintings of the Big Bang— how does anyone comprehend the Big Bang?

That is true *abstraction*: imagine the moment before the Big Bang, where all matter was infinitely compressed into a single point— contemplating that is really *abstract*, not what gets called "abstraction" in painting, which is usually just literal colors and shapes.

486

Are we the same person? Separated by years? Language has connotations, denotations, associations—but to go back to the question: *What is* wrong *with that?* An artwork is, yes, different from the words that might describe it and exceeds or is less than those words. People can get very bombastic about art too. I'm not an art historian—

Neither is Madame Realism, right?

I don't think she is, but Lord knows what she's been doing.

What would *you* like to be writing about art?

I'd like to write about a character driving around the South reading Simone Weil and Nathalie Sarraute, going to rural gay bars to describe the lighting. That character is just me.

Well, it can't be *you*, because you're not something on a page. And you are not lighting in a rural gay bar.

How do you distinguish between fiction and nonfiction?

I don't, not as writing.

So you've doubled down on saying that everything you write is fiction?

Basically. Because fiction is about making up something. Nonfiction is also making up something. How to tell it, in what order. These are aesthetic decisions, narrative decisions.

Taking this conversation as an example—I think it is intellectually dishonest to maintain that a direct transcription of an interview more honestly represents our conversation than a highly edited text would do. There is so much weird communication that happens in person that isn't caught by the recorded words. What I mean to say is that we have to edit this to sound more natural as written language than a straight transcript ever could.

Have you read Andy Warhol's *a: A novel* [1968]?

Yes.

Realism—whatever that is—Warhol tried to come as close to it, reality, as possible.

And it reads very differently than "reality" in literature. Flaubert's "A Simple Heart" [1877] feels more real to me than Ondine's transcribed life in *a: A novel*.

I have to say, not to me. Because realism is a genre. What we consider to be reality, or how we imitate reality, follows an established form. Writers, filmmakers, playwrights use the genre to establish what an audience believes or has been used to seeing as "real life." Of course it is not; it's a representation only. Warhol wanted to get at that specific issue in a way that very few artists ever have. Mostly, people are not interested in challenging that. It's not right or wrong to be uninterested, it just shows the extent to which we get at "reality" through unquestioned codes.

It's heavily filtered, and it's a lot of work to try and get to a sense of reality of a painting, or a person.

You know what Walter Benjamin says: *In order to love somebody you have to love without hope.* That is, without expectations.

What do you mean?

For instance, if you want a person to fulfill some fantasy you have of a lover, you will see that for as long as you can, until the reality of who he is comes through, and then you'll say, *Oh, he's not the guy I thought he was.* That is a very hard moment, and in fact you don't get to that point, even with a friend, for a very long time.

You've been with your partner for a very long time?
Yes.

How do you think having that long-term intimate relationship has affected your writing, or your understanding of yourself?

I think that writers want a certain calm, so they can write. Having a solid relationship at home has made it easier to do what I do. He's a musician, he wants to go to his gigs and rehearsals; he wants to practice. If we created a lot of drama for each other, like the drama I had before I was with him, we wouldn't get any work done. Most people have dinner together most nights, say. Often they have children, something that neither of us ever wanted. Some of my friends have never met David. I'm not hiding him. He's terrific. But we don't operate as a couple. It's a social convention I wish were less common. In the beginning of *Cast in Doubt*, there is a quote I've lived with and think is incredibly important: *It's not what someone gives you, it's what they don't take away.*

If you're in a relationship in which you are troubled all the time, then it's debilitating. I don't recommend it.

Are there any artists that you were really down on when you first saw their work but you've since changed your mind?

At a certain moment, and not really down on him, but very dubious: Jeff Koons. He's a complicated figure, but now I don't doubt his need to do what he does. Oh, I remember thinking I'd never look at another figurative painting again. That no one would ever paint one again.

When was that?

College, mid to late sixties. I thought figurative art was *over*. But I realized by the mideighties that the ideas you impose on art, ideas of what you think should be there, are not smart or meaningful. Maybe it assures one of one's own identity or sets up limits, makes life and looking easier, or gives one a sense of knowingness. Now my taste is catholic. I like different kinds of art, and writing also. I'm frankly interested in thinking, in seeing that in writing. I'm drawn to noncomplacency or anticomplacency in style and subject, and don't want to hear and read the same kinds of ideas over and over, written in the same ways. Mostly people want stability in their lives, but never doubt the structures that support it. I'm disturbed by, maybe in a bit of a war with, many social, cultural, and aesthetic conventions, and I think a lot of my work as an essayist and as a fiction writer is about questioning systems and beliefs.

What is that mysterious thing that makes some people, like you, doubt authority, even as a child, when other people didn't or don't?

In me, probably a deep insecurity. I don't really trust that I know, or what I know, or how I know it. And I don't trust what I know or think is true is true. When I had just turned six and was starting first grade, the night before I asked my father, *How do you know I can learn?* Then I doubted what I was learning. I really disliked the roteness of memorizing after fourth grade. I had doubts. I'm interested in what is at stake in believing as one does and interested in what I don't know and why I don't know it. How do we forget something or not think about it? Your absences and mistakes are more interesting than what

489

you remember and tell yourself about yourself and your achievements, and more important.

Thinking about your first novel, *Haunted Houses*, did you associate that insecurity with a gendered position?

I did. I do. Writing *Haunted Houses*, I was thinking that girls' lives are very harsh, that becoming a girl is just so harsh, and that harshness wasn't represented in what I had read. Not that it isn't in Jane Austen, but in a different way and of a different time, with different exigencies. Being a girl, for instance, you're meant to feel that you should not assert yourself, not be too aggressive, be seen more than heard. How do you make use of that education?

How has that changed over your life as a writer?

On certain days, the more I write, the more I know, *I can do this*. But that doesn't necessarily mean I feel much less doubt. I keep questioning what I do, the way I do it, and why. If I had to generalize about male writers—always tricky—I'd say that many don't doubt themselves enough. Everyone had a mother, and they are very easy to blame. Mothering is such a hard gig. Women identify more, in some ways, with their mothers, but men can disidentify. If more male writers stopped to consider, *Maybe the way I think needs work*, we'd have much better writing from them. I think younger male writers, overall, are less hindered by the sexual prejudices of their predecessors, gay and straight.

What is your sense of the purpose of criticism, for what you have written or what you like to read?

Sometimes writers can find words for moments and experiences that people who are not writers, who do other things, can't. Writers do that, often formatively, for writers-to-be, and may be why other people become writers. A thoughtful writer can sometimes be helpful in that way. That is one way of thinking about it—that a writer devotes herself to articulating states of existence. Also, I think that responding to the world, being in relation to aspects of living, finding forms and modes in writing to present emotions and ideas, is being in a specific relationship to life. You're thinking about it for the page. You write because you are ardent about an idea, a character, an injustice, a story, a symptom, and your passion could be important to another person. It's always surprising to me, Jarrett, when a person tells me that he or she feels something from my writing, or what it does for them. I can't experience that at all.

Does it make you uncomfortable?

I find it hard—actually, impossible—to experience it in any way at all. I can hear it, but I can't take it in. I'm the person who wrote these things, and the writing is different from the person. I think many writers and artists who are not total narcissists feel that way. There's all this romanticism about Baudelaire, Rimbaud, et al.—in certain moments of their lives, they wrote with great passion and clarity and made some wonderful poetry. Much of their lives was hell.

Trying to understand that relationship between the artist and the artwork is one of the central mysteries of art for me. Very different, but essentially linked.

This returns, in a sense, to identity politics, where the person and the thing are taken to be the same. That a person can or should only write about what she was born into or has experienced. It's not that way. Not to me. There's imagination, the unconscious, there are wishes, people are amazingly weird in how variously they see their lives. And there's empathy. It is hard to understand how someone who is a monster can make something beautiful—how does that happen? We want to make it coherent, make it agree, and turn people and life into something manageable. But we can't.

My part of black feminism—which nobody else has ever claimed—is black women being angry at black men for not being supportive. And nobody wants that, nobody wants to own that.

Michele Wallace (b. 1952) is a critic and historian writing on art, film, and black visual culture. She became a public figure at the age of twenty-seven with the belles lettres polemic *Black Macho and the Myth of the Superwoman* (1978). Her widely published criticism has appeared in *The Village Voice*, *TDR/The Drama Review*, *Cinema Journal*, and on her blogs, notably *Soul Pictures*. In 1991, she organized the watershed conference "Black Popular Culture" at the Studio Museum in Harlem and the Dia Center for the Arts, documented in the book *Black Popular Culture*, edited by Gina Dent (1992). Her writing on art and culture is collected in *Invisibility Blues: From Pop to Theory* (1990); *Dark Designs and Visual Culture* (2004); and *American People, Black Light: Faith Ringgold's Paintings of the 1960s* (2010). She is a professor emeritus of English at the City College of New York and the Graduate Center, CUNY.

Michele Wallace

What was your childhood relationship with language and writing?

My mother, Faith Ringgold, was a wonderful speaker, and everybody around me was a great storyteller. It was one of those things where in order to say anything at all, you had to be able to time it exactly to when someone took a breath, then you say something *devastating*, to put a curve on whatever they were saying. Of course, you can't do that until you are an adult—I can do that now, but it took me fifty years to learn how. Back then, I couldn't, so it was my grandmother, aunt, and all of these brilliant yarn-spinning people. Riotously funny. Like Chekhov and Albee combined. I couldn't talk, so I used to write things down. I used to keep diaries and was always trying to write a play, or a book, but it was very internal and I didn't necessarily show other people. At some point my mother said, *I always knew that you would be a writer*. I said, *Why?* She said, *Because you were always writing*.

I began to write seriously in college—that is, to write and show it to people. I had two disabilities. One was, I was very shy. I became very shy when I was about twelve. I couldn't talk. I would lose my train of thought, and I couldn't say anything. The other disability was that I was left-handed. I couldn't write well, I would skip words. There was a perception I had some learning issues that actually I didn't have. It's just that I had more to say than I was able to write with my hands. What completely cured that was learning how to type, because then I could write fluently and comprehensively, and ever since, I've typed everything. All that started coming together when I was in college.

Through all of that, I still couldn't talk. I was very afraid to talk. Most of my life I have been very afraid to talk. I can write it down and read it. As a matter of fact, there was a film that I was in about Billie Holiday, and what I say in it I actually read. Filmmakers never want you to read anything, they want you to spill it. I couldn't do that. Whenever I did talks, I had notes. That contributed to a lot of writing. I was lost in any situation like this, in which I had to speak in an impromptu way. Still, I think that when I talk, it's like I'm writing in my head. I'm doing it right now. When I talk, I'm writing, because I came to the writing first, and then the talk came out of it.

What about your early relationship to art and aesthetics? Obviously, you grew up with a mother who is a great artist.

I grew up with her going to art school. I was born in 1952. She went to college in 1948. She married my father, who was a pianist—classical and jazz—in 1950. My sister and I were both born in 1952. Mom and Dad broke up in 1954, whereupon we went to live with my grandmother. Mom was an undergraduate in art school when I was a little girl. Then I was a somewhat bigger girl while she was in graduate school, from '55 to '59. By that time, I can remember her doing these pastel self-portraits using a mirror on a bureau drawer. There is a collection of them. Just the whole business of her as an art student was very much a part of my childhood. I mean, I read all the books, even when I couldn't actually read. I would take a book to school in first grade and pretend that I could read it. The way to pretend you could read was to underline things. When I got a little bit older and could actually read, she always had all the art magazines, and I read everything she read. All I wanted to know was what was in my mother's head. *What was she thinking?* That provided me with my initial art education. Plus, she took us to museums all the time. I had a very extensive art education. There was good art training and education at the private school I went to, New Lincoln, in Harlem. By the time I graduated from high school, I would go to galleries and museums because they were a place where I felt comfortable.

We went to Europe in 1961 for the first time. I was nine, my sister

Barbara was eight, and my grandmother and mother took us. Mother was going to make her decision as to whether she would be an artist by seeing all the masterpieces of European art. We went to Notre-Dame, Sainte-Chapelle, and the Louvre. I believe on that first trip to France we also went to Versailles. We went to the Uffizi in Florence and the Vatican in Rome. This was when I recall falling in love with art. The more I saw and knew, the more I loved it. To me, traveling is, you go to the hotel and you find out what museums there are, and you go look at art.

One recurring aspect of your work is keeping an emphasis on the specific realities of the visual. When you were first going to Europe or first looking at art, what was it that hit you about that?

I don't know that I've separated art in museums or galleries from the rest of the visual world that I've existed in, because my grandmother was a designer. I'll never forget how strikingly beautifully dressed everybody seemed to be in Paris. These women in these fabulous suits, which they would frequently wear day in and day out. The way my mother would dress also—she would make herself something and wear it again and again. It was like it was a work of art. And you used it like a work of art, I guess. I don't go around changing the art on my walls every day. They didn't change their clothes every day, but what they wore was magnificent, and *built*. I grew up in Harlem in this fashion world of my grandmother and her friends and associates. Everything was beautiful. The clothes were beautiful. The people were beautiful. Their hair was beautiful. The music was beautiful. Their houses were beautiful, and the art was beautiful. There was art on our walls always, and then there were places you went to see *more* art. A museum was a place where you didn't have all these other distractions, and you could just look at the art. Then again, the people who were in the museum looking at the art had great clothes on too.

To me, beautiful people, beautiful art, beautiful clothes, beautiful furniture—it's all consistent, and actually, that was one of the things that always made a lot of sense to me about The Museum of Modern Art—which would be my ur-museum—because it did have furniture, design in general, photography, film. That modern canon made complete sense to me. I didn't really think about art and nationalism until much later, that there were aspects of American art that had a particular history, like in the nineteenth and eighteenth century, that I needed to consider. Didn't really think about that. Or how that related to African Americans, or Africans.

My mother really got into African art in the seventies. She went by herself in '76 and traveled north and south of both Nigeria and Ghana looking for art-making practices there, and came back with much news of that. It really influenced her work in the seventies—that's something I would really want to write about. Then she went back in '77 for FESTAC '77, the Second World Black and African Festival of Arts and Culture. One of the eeriest things about that is FESTAC had an exhibition that included some of my mother's work, which was mask work influenced by African art. The Americans hung it up in a corner designated as "craft." There's always this tension between what is craft, what is the "primitive," untutored, raw material of the art versus the sophistication of modernism. When we went to Europe, we also went to African art museums. I remember my mother saying that you could see more African art in Europe than you could in Africa. There was a sense that in many ways Africans had been divested of their work. I do tend to see it all as art.

When you were a teenager, how did you get involved with the art world, especially through your and your mother's group WSABAL— Women Students and Artists for Black Art Liberation?

I went to Mexico the summer I graduated from high school— they had great art in Mexico too. It was beautiful there. I joined this commune, and I wanted to stay. I mean, I was seventeen. Probably the marijuana I was smoking all day and the tequila I was drinking all night might have influenced my decision, since I had never done anything like that before. My thing was, *I'm good. I'll stay where I am. There's this cute guy. He's Guatemalan. He loves me. I love him. I'll just stay here. I'll go to school here. I'll get on with things.* My mother and I were not getting along well, so, *Hey, I'm out.*

Of course, she went crazy, which is good that she did. She says that she was hoping that letting me go to Mexico in the first place would feed my desire for independence. I guess, in her scenario, I would go to Mexico, spend the summer taking flamenco classes and studying Spanish at the university, and when it came to be August, I would pack up and come back and go to Howard University, like somebody with some sense, instead of getting lost in the marijuana and the tequila and the great food and the great sex and whatever—*the fun of it*—which is what I did. She dragged me back and put me in a juvenile home— a really nice place that no longer exists run by the Sisters of the Good Shepherd, an order of nuns devoted to the care of girls who have lost their way. Then the weekend before I was to go to Howard, she took me out, went shopping, got me clothes, packed me up. She took me to Howard University and deposited me in the dorm there. She told me, *Now, look, if you decide to go back to Mexico, I will not even know you're going, and I will not come and get you again. You do whatever you think is best.*

Well, I guess I didn't have the pot or the tequila to help me think this through, but the way I saw it was, *In January, I'm going to be eighteen. I tried it once. It felt a little calamitous. I don't think I'm going to do this right now. I think I'm going to stay where I am, try to do the college thing, and act like somebody.*

Her reaction to it was very extreme. She called the President of the United States and everybody. [Laughter.] And she came very close to having all the people in the commune arrested. For all I know, maybe they all were arrested. I felt like I had narrowly escaped some real craziness.

Anyway, I stayed at Howard. But Mother only allowed me to stay there for one semester—they decided that I was there partying. I loved Howard University. She pulled me out and I had to come back to New York. Then I found myself in the midst of the Art Workers' Coalition through Mother and Tom Lloyd, and also in the midst of a feminist revolution. I was converted into a feminist by my experience in the juvenile home run by the sisters, because I saw that the girls there were the mules of the earth, really. And I was doing the same thing they were doing. They were running away with the pimp around the corner, and their parents would go to the police and have them arrested. They would have babies—I mean, their lives were fucked. I was fucking my life too, except that I went to Mexico, it was a little bit *grander*, but it really came down to the same thing. Except, at my commune, we had birth control pills—that's a significant difference.

The home had an intimacy to it. And it was the first time in my life that I had been in an entirely female environment. It touched me deeply.

What year did you become a feminist?

1970.

You know, Lucy Lippard also became a feminist in 1970.

Yes. She would have become one at the same time as us, because we were right before her. Lucy's group Ad Hoc Women Artists' Committee was organized in 1970 to protest the Whitney Annual because it didn't include any women or artists of color. There was a lot of division between the women and the men, because the men were saying they wanted to keep the crap out of the Whitney. I think at that point Lucy and the other women realized that by "crap" they meant art by women. Period.

I'll never forget that one of the issues my mother got us involved with was that this art up at the Whitney was not the *best art*. This was epitomized for us by Andy Warhol's soup can. I remember us going down there and taking soup cans with us, and some other ways of deriding or making fun. I didn't know what I was doing. Remember, I'm eighteen—this is a choice between Andy Warhol and my mother. My mother's got all this art, and she can't get a gallery, and she can't get shown. That was priority number one for me. Priority number one for her. If you look at the WSABAL manifesto [1970], that's the way I read it today.

You wrote the WSABAL manifesto; were you publishing anything else?

With WSABAL, there was a lot of letter writing—actually, there's a letter in the Whitney exhibition *An Incomplete History of Protest* [2017] that I wrote to Marcia Tucker while she was a curator there, listing all the black women artists she should include in their shows. That was the beginning of my being a writer. I also wrote for *The East Village Other* and for the school newspaper, called *The Paper*, at City College. I was a fledgling, beginning writer, starting to publish. There was underground journalism, and I wrote about art. There were a lot of people in the art world who wanted to publish whatever I wrote. I think primarily because I was black and I was young. I could say that I was talented, but it doesn't seem like that was the reason.

Why do you say that?

I don't know how many people would say this, but when it came to the women's movement—we had protests and demonstrations and marches, and it was a lot of marching and photo-op type of stuff. A lot of women were self-conscious about the idea that feminists were not good-looking and that they were all over the hill, and then of course you had people like Kate Millett with her big overalls on—they weren't the *lookers*. Meanwhile, I was wearing my grandmother's fashions and all kinds of heels and makeup. The point is, I was trying to look as good as I possibly could, and this was greatly appreciated by the feminist circles in which I traveled. Their thing was, *Push Michele out front so that they can see that we're young and beautiful*. There was a great emphasis on youth at that time—it was the *youth movement*. It was a time to be young, and I was young. That meant I was smart, I knew things that other people didn't know. I guess I was being objectified, but I didn't see it that way. I saw it as an opportunity, and I understood that if I was going to be a writer, I needed chances to write, even if my writing wasn't that good. That's what I got.

At this point, were you interested in writing criticism or fiction?

First of all, I wanted to write about art, and I wanted to do art history at City College, but I quickly changed my mind about that because there was no way to study anything having to do with African or black art at the time. Then I decided to major in English, creative writing.

There's a reference in some of your autobiographical writing that you were involved with a writers' group at Alice Walker's house.

Yes. It was called the Sisterhood.

What were you working on then, and what was the nature of it?

I was working on *Black Macho*. It was about '77, but there was some tension between different constituencies within the group about what we were meeting for. The people who started the group were June Jordan and Alice Walker. Toni Morrison would come—she wasn't the queen yet, but she had every sign of becoming *the queen*. Everybody wanted to party and smoke pot and have fun, as was appropriate to their generation, and I wanted everybody to sit down and talk about politics and help each other. I'll never forget Toni Morrison saying, *You don't need anybody to help you with your writing. You need to* do *your writing. Everybody just needs to do their work!* I had some idea that we should all get together and work collectively—I was in the feminist consciousness-raising mode—*let's bare our souls*—and I was trying to find myself. In '77 I was twenty-five.

I've always been enormously good at getting myself in the presence of prominent people—because I'm from New York, and they were all there too. And then once you're there, you realize, *Well, I'm just like them. Now, how do I make this happen? What do I do with this? What's the opportunity here for me?* It always boiled down to writing something. It's all about how good you are and how much you know. I was many times at the very limits of my knowledge, and I was aware of the fact that I needed to live more, to have more life.

How did *Black Macho* come about? It's incendiary and very stylishly written.

I had an editor by the name of Joyce Johnson, and we spent two years working on it, page by page, chapter by chapter. My original proposal was for a book with ten chapters. The first one was supposed to be about black men, and that was *Black Macho*. Once I wrote that, she wanted me to publish it on its own. I said, *But this is supposed to be a book about women!* So she said, *Write one other essay on women, and then we'll go with that.* In my mind, I wanted to do *Sexual Politics* [1970]. From the beginning, her idea was that it was belles lettres—no index, no bibliography, none of that, just proclamations—and if I managed to destroy the women's movement in the process, so much the better. I realized we had different ideas once we got into a big argument about the press material saying that I was a black feminist, because somehow I had managed to write this book that she thought didn't say that. As far as the publisher was concerned, the women's movement was over—nobody wanted that, so why say you're a black feminist? But I insisted upon it.

So you publish this book at age twenty-seven. It's extremely provocative.

Intentionally so. I wrote a piece for *Woman's World* called "Black Women and White Women" in 1971. It was the same kind of thing about black men and black women at each other's throats—it was more crude, but the same kind of formulation, and I knew that I had something that wasn't getting said. My part of black feminism—which nobody else has ever claimed—is black women being angry at black men for not being supportive. And nobody wants that, nobody wants to own that. [Laughter.]

Where do you think the strongest backlash to that book came from?

The most intense backlash was from my own mother. She wrote a book about it, *A Letter to my Daughter, Michele* [2015]. It really has been unbearable, because it can never be undone or fixed. I'm still at a loss to explain how I ever got caught in it. For example, the book was classified as sociology. People thought I was trying to be a sociologist, and I saw myself as someone who wrote about art and culture. I had some things to say about society, but I never meant that to be the primary focus. I feel like everything that I have written since then, and even before then, is much more representative of who I am, particularly in regard to including my mother's work and activism among my influences.

In one of your essays, you say that growing up you wanted to be a black Lucy Lippard, but that you didn't understand all the things that were stacked up against being that.

Yes, and most particularly now. In looking at what she did, there isn't anybody like her. Her career is absolutely unique—*This is not a thing, you can't go to school to do it, ain't nobody looking for any more of it*. The only person who wanted Lucy Lippard to be "Lucy Lippard" was Lucy

Lippard, and the way it's looking right now, there isn't going to be another one.

What did that mean to you? Was it about being a writer in the art world who was functioning almost like an artist?

A writer. She's really a writer. She writes criticism. I didn't see it as being artistic. I saw it as being smart and doing what needed to be done—she was a big role model for me.

After *Black Macho*, you started writing a lot of cultural criticism, much of which is gathered in the collection *Invisibility Blues: From Pop to Theory*. How did your thinking or writing evolve over the 1980s?

I don't know about what happened in the eighties; they were a hard time for me. I had a breakdown in 1981. I had another one in 1984. I had another one in 1988. The years I had breakdowns, I didn't do any writing for the entire year. The writing was done in between, and much of it had to do with what I was asked to do. I was one of these writers who works for hire. If you asked me to do something and you paid me, I would do it. I was also trying to build a teaching career. I wanted to be a novelist, but nobody would publish my novel. If you're going to teach writing, you have to have some writing to anchor the fact that you're teaching. So I had to shift my focus, to not count on being a novelist.

What was the novel?

It's called *Former Friends*. It's a great big thing.

Did you write that at the same time as *Black Macho*?

I wrote it after *Black Macho*. All through the beginning of eighties I was writing and revising that book. I had a contract for it. Then I lost my editor for it. I lost my agent.

Was that because of the pushback against *Black Macho*?

I think so, partly. I was dead for a lot of people. There were getting to be black feminists like Audre Lorde and the circles around her, and bell hooks, and from what I could see, they *hated* me. They wanted me dead and gone. It was working. A lot of what happened to me at that time is explained by the fact that my mother made a kick head: a head that was supposed to represent me, and she used to kick it around as a way of venting her hostility for me. Meanwhile, I don't know how I

502

didn't understand that my mother needed me. I was so hurt by what I saw as her rejection, and she was hurt by what she saw as my rejection. That's the way the eighties felt to me. I couldn't get straight. I couldn't get right. There was no medication. I mean, all there was was Thorazine and lithium, but I was allergic to all of that.

When you were writing the novel, what were the models for what you were doing?

I didn't have a model for what I was trying to do with the novel—that was part of the problem. I felt as though black women were writing from a kind of a folksy, rural place in black culture that I didn't come from. I was urban and sophisticated. Of course, there's many more models of writing now. I felt very lonely and isolated in doing that. I would publish this book, but I just can't stand to read it—and you can't publish a book you can't read. But it's in my papers at the Schomburg Center for Research in Black Culture. It's very autobiographical in some ways, but I tried to disguise that. It's about a young woman who I thought was like me: feminist—kick ass and take names. Then another girl who was the other side of me, a dancer—shy and humble and kind of a masochist. It was me splitting myself into two. I couldn't resolve those tensions. Nobody liked the book well enough to publish it, and I was losing ground. So, I decided to switch careers to becoming an academic when I was in Oklahoma. First of all, I saw being a critic as being someone who could say what was wrong with a novel. *Okay, I have a novel, and people say there's something wrong with it. Let me figure out what it is. Then, in this process, I'll turn myself into an academic.* I was still in that mode when *Invisibility Blues* came out. Through that process and doing the "Black Popular Culture" conference, I realized the niche I really could carve for myself would be writing about visual culture, because I had a knowledge of it, and I had a love for it and a desire to do it.

How did you meet James Baldwin?

I was writing a profile of him for *Viva*, a short-lived women's magazine that was the female version of *Penthouse*. I was told to meet him when he got off the plane from Paris, at the international terminal. He came wandering off the plane. I introduced myself, and it was love at first sight.

What year was this?

1978. *Black Macho* was written but not out. Actually, he liked me, and he liked the book. He was *fearless*—truly fearless. From the moment he got off the plane, we hung out together for a week. He was up all night; I would stay up with him all night at Mikell's, where his brother was the bartender. I was trying to interview him like you're interviewing me, but Jimmy was hard to interview because there were other people talking. He'd say, *Oh no, I can't tell that. You need to tell that.* He was surrounded by family and friends the whole time—I didn't want to hear anything they had to say, I wanted to hear what Jimmy had to say. I was trying to conduct a proper interview, but that was impossible.

One of the days, I took my sister with me to meet him, and I remember him saying that he didn't care anything about being a celebrity or being famous: *All I know is that I love some people and they love me, and that's what matters.* My sister said, *But you're the most famous black writer in the world.* He basically said that was not going to help him sleep at night, or make him feel right with himself. I guess the point is that fame can turn on a dime. It turns on you. You need to be in the world with people.

He lived in a house with all of his family. It was a small apartment building. When he stayed in New York, he was in the top-floor apartment with his mother. I would visit him there every day. Every night, he and his friends would continue to talk until the sun came up, and then Jimmy would go home. I'd get in the cab and go back to my house. I lived in NYU housing because I was teaching in the school of journalism there then. As soon as I woke up, I would go back to his house. I was to bring fresh-squeezed orange juice. The day would go on, and we'd be talking. He'd greet me in his underpants. He was a tiny little thing, just a doll. I was crazy about him. That was the first time that I can remember really falling in love with a gay man. He was exquisitely open. I talked to him about gay rights, but he didn't want to have labels for things. Now, in retrospect, I can see much more clearly that he didn't believe in fracturing the community in these ways—not because he was afraid of being known or seen as gay; he didn't have a problem with that at all. Another part of it was he just was trying to figure out how to stay alive, because sometimes he would say, *Medgar, Martin, Malcolm, and me. I could be next. I need to stay alive for my family.*

When you look at the generation of art critics like Lucy Lippard and Rosalind Krauss—they're all white. There is real racial homogeneity in the public voices discussing visual art. It seems like most serious black thought was focusing on music and literature. How did you experience that?

I experienced it as increasingly upsetting. It has taken me a long time to accept an idea my mother taught me, which is that people often don't regard visual art with the same awe and respect that they show for the other arts.

I just have always felt that the thing that's being ignored is the thing I need to focus on. Why devote my energy to stuff that's being done and done and done? There's a cultural matrix that involves all of this, but if you take out the visual part, it's in no way complete. I don't know how you talk about black music without images. *Really.* For instance, Billie Holiday was all about the way she looked. I can hear black people all day talking about the sound of her voice and the drugs and a million different other things, but they don't feel safe talking about the way she looked. They don't know how to talk about it. They can get you some pictures. Of course, a photograph is *only* about the way she looks— that's all a photograph is. It makes them uncomfortable. I think it has something to do with being black and that seeing blackness as a look creates a general discomfort with any discussion of how things look, or how people look. I think we've been disenfranchised by that.

Is that one of the reasons that you started working on silent films, because they're *all look*?

I love silent films. I found them to be the key to race and looking for me. When I did my PhD in cinema studies, I was looking to find out where stereotypes or problems with black visuality had originated. What was the originary moment? The art historical perspective was to look back at art history, but I wanted to take cinema as a case study for the way images worked within the culture. My dissertation was called

"Passing, Lynching, and Jim Crow: A Genealogy of Race and Gender in U.S. Visual Culture, 1895–1929" [1999]. I was trying to do a genealogy of the problematics of the visualization of black bodies. I felt as though I'd really located something very to the point about the translation of the stereotypes of race into film, and all the ways in which it was constructed—blackface and the laughing and the watermelons. Because there were a lot of experiments done in silent film, and, I think, because race was much less of a completely circumscribed notion at that point, you can watch it being formulated. You get a chance to see that people were not in complete agreement about what race meant. There is just wonderful writing about this by my friend Jacqueline Stewart, as well as by other members of the Oscar Micheaux Society.

I think everywhere you look in visual culture, you see that—a culture war going on between the white people who liked black people and Asians and Mexicans and the ones who didn't. It was like this war between white people, about who was cool, about what was beautiful, about what was good, and it went on in the cities. It really dates from the end of slavery, because that's when you needed to construct these separate spaces. It's all about urbanization. It's all about transportation. It's all about ways in which we want to exert control over the lived space that we really didn't need before, when there was no question about, *Your status is not our status*.

I want to know how you came to do the "Black Popular Culture" conference, which was hosted jointly at the Studio Museum in Harlem and the Dia Center for the Arts in 1991.

The reason I was inspired to do "Black Popular Culture" is that I met Stuart Hall and the black British crew—Isaac Julien, Kobena Mercer, John Akomfrah, Paul Gilroy. I went to a cultural studies conference in Birmingham and met Stuart. I was very excited about these black scholars who were not essentialist, who were not consistent with the essentialist apparatus that I was used to in my home country. I thought that this was very much needed as a way to talk about our intellectual and visual lives. Because it was cultural studies, it seemed very oriented to the twentieth century and therefore to the technologies of vision.

506

They themselves were somewhat more inclined to talk about music, but I thought that they were more interested in the visual than people around here. The main thing I wanted to do was to bring them into conversation with intellectuals here in this country. Dia had done a number of other conferences with people like Hal Foster and Phil Mariani. Word got around that they were interested in doing something black. I managed to propose the conference at the same time that we were all trying to be anti-essentialists—that should've cancelled itself out, you know; as Stuart said, *There's no "black" in black popular culture*. It was still important to do because there was still racism in the art world against blackness.

The presentation you gave to close out the conference was titled "Why Have There Been No Great Black Artists?"

Yes, I was taking off from Linda Nochlin's essay. When I delivered that address at the end, I hadn't slept for three days. I was completely out of my mind. But I had written what I was going to say, so I was able to say it. Now I can look at the tape and see what I look like while also knowing how I was feeling inside at the time. I look very serene, but I just absolutely am not. I was expressing a sense of disappointment. Okay, I wanted to bring American and British black intellectuals together. But also I was trying to bring black people together with Dia. I felt a sense of disappointment to see how the Dia people were essentially unchanged in their notions of what the canon was, which was there all around you—Walter De Maria, Joseph Beuys, and the rest. They had the money, the collection, and the scholarship. Nothing we had said or done had in any real way altered their notions of the greater value of their material compared with what we were producing. Nobody had challenged them on their own ground. There was not ever real discussion of the visual, except Margo Jefferson, who talked about the movie *Cabin in the Sky* [1943], and Judith Wilson, who talked about pornography in Romare Bearden—and none of us had really succeeded in bringing the challenge to the visual itself, as part of the permanent record.

When I gave that speech, "Why Have There Been No Great Black

Artists?," I thought I was saying something ironic. And I was trying to draw a distinction that maybe Linda wasn't between being *famous* and being *great*.

Part of the argument at the end of *Invisibility Blues,* which was your master's thesis, was about the cultural forces that conspire to silence black intellectual women. I just wanted to know if you could speak to that, and how it's shifted, changed, or regrouped.

Disappearing black women. Well, Ralph Ellison came up with this paradigm of invisibility, and it does seem to me that after Jim Crow, and the unregenerate racism of a slavery period, and then Reconstruction and post-Reconstruction, that the paradigm of invisibility remains with us still. It's very difficult to contend with because, in some ways, there's a sense in which being invisible is the ideal—as in, *You don't need to be thinking about my race.* You and I don't need to be thinking of ourselves as, *You're white and I'm black—we're not the same race.* But for some reason, we're thought of as extremely different, in a way that can never, ever be adequately accounted for—not because you're male, I'm female, or gay and straight, and all that stuff, but because of the notion of race. Ultimately, you want to have that stuff be invisible; it should be *insubstantial.* There are differences that make little difference, *should* make little difference. I think race might be one of those. But somehow it's not.

There's an overemphasis on cause and effect in criticism, but we don't really live in a cause-and-effect universe. It's not like, *Oh, this happened to me—I'll go home and write a poem.* You might act like that's what it's about, but it's not. There's always so much else going on.

John Yau (b. 1950) is a poet and critic, by turns lyrical and polemic, who has been writing in New York since the mid-1970s. He began reviewing for *Art in America* (1977–1982) and *Arts* (1979–1991), and started writing for *Artforum* in the eighties (1982–1997). From 2007 to 2011 he was the art editor of *The Brooklyn Rail,* leaving to join *Hyperallergic* in 2012. Alongside his many books of poetry, his writing on art includes the volumes *In the Realm of Appearances: The Art of Andy Warhol* (1993); *The Passionate Spectator: Essays on Art and Poetry* (2006); *A Thing Among Things: The Art of Jasper Johns* (2008); and *The Wild Children of William Blake* (2017). Yau has also written monographs on artists such as Catherine Murphy, Thomas Nozkowski, Philip Taaffe, and William Tillyer, along with numerous others. He is an associate professor of critical studies at the Mason Gross School of the Arts at Rutgers University.

John Yau

What was your childhood relationship to language—when did you first experience language as a special thing you could do stuff with?

My parents spoke two languages in our house—a dialect of Chinese spoken around Shanghai to each other, and English to me. My mother studied English in China, so she was fluent. My father's mother was English, and he went to Catholic missionary schools in Shanghai, so he spoke English well. My parents would switch to Chinese when they wanted to speak to each other about their ill-behaved son or some other subject they wanted to keep private, but I slowly realized that if I paid close attention to it, I could understand what they were saying, even if I couldn't speak it. This is a most extreme example of my comprehension: my mother and father knew a woman who was often delusional, and who also spoke this Chinese dialect; she came to the house one day for lunch and said to my mother something in Chinese that I interpreted as, *Is it all right if I park my helicopter on the roof?* After she left, I asked my mother, *Did she really say this?* My mother embarrassedly said yes. At that point, she realized I could understand what was going on. I was ten or eleven.

The cat was out of the bag!

Yes, exactly. My mother had studied French in Shanghai, so she gave me little French lessons as a kid; I learned how to count and say simple things. More importantly, I had a sense that there were *all these languages* in the world. She often told me that her father, my grandfather, who had been a diplomat in Sun Yat-sen's government, spoke four or five languages.

When did you start writing? Did poems come first?

I began writing poems at the end of my freshman year in high
school. I was thirteen. There was a literary magazine at the school.
A teacher said to the class, *You can submit poems or a story*, and a friend and
I decided we would do that. I wrote some poems and submitted them.
I think one, maybe two, were accepted. I was hooked. Around this time,
I also started not going to school—I'd go to the bookstore and sit there
all day. Actually, the people who worked there often let me sit in the
back so I wouldn't be taken in as a truant. I just read a lot of poetry, with
no idea what it meant, except that somehow I was hooked on it. I also
was on the hunt for books by Asian writers and discovered the novels of
Yukio Mishima, Yasunari Kawabata, and Kobo Abe. Then I discovered
the Grolier Poetry Book Shop in Cambridge, Massachusetts—I think I
was fifteen. I'd go there every weekend to find and buy books.

What was the first poem that really spoke to you?

I suppose it would be Robert Lowell's "For the Union Dead" [1960],
which I read when I was fifteen. It was the first poem in which I knew
the references—I knew every landmark he talked about in the poem
because I grew up on Charles Street in Boston, not far from where he
lived. Everything he mentioned I had seen as a child and had strong
memories of—like that photograph of a Mosler safe that survived the
atom bomb dropped on Hiroshima; I remember going past it every
day on Boylston Street on my way to third grade. I knew there was
something creepy about the photograph and its caption, "Rock of
Ages." When I read the poem, I realized that I was not wrong to think
that the ad was creepy. Also, there is the sense of history, of being in
Boston and seeing the different sites he mentions. I read Lowell first,
and then I began reading everyone around him, like Anne Sexton and
Sylvia Plath.

The other big moment happened when I was seventeen and
discovered an anthology by William Pratt, *The Imagist Poem: Modern
Poetry in Miniature* [1963]. It was full of poems by poets connected with
imagism, which is the beginning of modernist poetry. I read the poems
of T. E. Hulme, F. S. Flint, William Carlos Williams, H. D., and Ezra

Pound. The poems were short and simple. I used that to teach myself how to write—I had not taken a class on writing at that point and would not for a few more years. Through that anthology I discovered Ezra Pound and his whole thing about Chinese poetry, which I was completely fascinated with. I read him closely too—with mixed feelings, because you find out about his personal history. The early poems, in *Cathay* [1915], I just read over and over.

I read a lot of anthologies at this time. I thought, *Anthologies are big gatherings; I'll just go through them and find out what I like. If I discover a poet whose work I like, I will go buy a book by that person.* This is how I learned about Robert Kelly, who coedited the anthology *A Controversy of Poets* [1965]. That's where I first discovered the poems of John Ashbery, Frank O'Hara, Robert Kelly, Gerrit Lansing, and Jack Spicer. I bought the anthology partly because somebody in Grolier said that he had been in Cambridge a year or two earlier. Then I found out that he taught at Bard, so I transferred there, from Boston University.

Before we talk about college—what aesthetic experiences were important early on?

My mother took me to the Museum of Fine Arts, Boston, starting at the age of six. The first painting I fell in love with was Monet's painting of his wife wearing a Japanese kimono—*La Japonaise* [1876]. I believe it is Monet's largest figure painting. I was in a weekend class that my mother brought me to; we were all sitting on the floor in front of that painting. The woman asked a question, and I answered it—*There are multiple focuses in the painting, because of the faces on the robe.* That must have been the first time I spoke to strangers about what I saw. She said, *You're right!* I thought, *Okay, that was easy.* [Laughter.]

How old were you?

Probably seven. I've never forgotten it. In fact, for years after I'd left Boston, whenever I went back there, I would go to the museum to look at that painting. There's a Rogier van der Weyden painting in the Museum of Fine Arts—*Saint Luke Drawing the Virgin* [ca. 1435–1440]— that also completely fascinated me; the detailing and woodcarving on the chair Mary's sitting in tell a story. Also a Renoir painting of a man dancing with a young woman, and you don't see the man's face, only the woman's face. Those are the three that really stuck in my head.

None of the Asian art in the museum spoke to you?

It did and it didn't. I think early on I was more fascinated with Egyptian art—especially the mummies—which is pretty typical of children at that age. We had Chinese paintings in my house because my grandfather painted. The other important thing from this period is that my closest friend as a kid was Douglas Way. His father, John Way, was an abstract painter, and he painted in the living room of their apartment in Beacon Hill. So at seven, eight, nine, I see a man making abstract paintings in his living room, like it is a normal activity. He talked about Robert Motherwell and Franz Kline and the influence of calligraphy on abstract expressionism. His son could draw beautifully. I remember being jealous that he could draw a dog better than I could, so I knew I was not an artist pretty early on.

How do you understand that relationship between painting and writing?

I was always more comfortable with writing: it was something that I did and couldn't stop doing. At some point, in addition to writing poems, I knew that I wanted to write about art and began keeping a notebook. The big moment was coming to New York in '74 or '75 and going to the Jasper Johns retrospective at the Whitney. I had never seen anything by him at that point, and I was fascinated by what I saw— I began reading everything I could about his paintings, and none of it made sense of what I experienced. I kept thinking, *There's more to it than what they're saying. I have no idea what it is—I just know there's more.* This happened with other artists—Richard Tuttle, for example.

When I was at Bard, a sculptor named Jake Grossberg said, *You're a poet—you should write about art, because you don't really want to be a professor of English literature, do you?* I was like, *No, I don't!* [Laughter.] Then he said, *All these poets write about art*—and that was when I discovered that Ashbery and O'Hara wrote about art. I had been reading their work, but I had never connected them to art. I liked the idea of living in New York. I also liked that they knew each other but that their writing wasn't

514

similar, and that they didn't seem to fit into the poetry lineages I was learning about. I bought O'Hara's *Collected Poems*, which came out in 1971, while I was still in college. I remember reading it over and over.

In 1974, after I had recovered from a car accident that I had gotten into in my junior year of college, and could finally walk without aid, I moved to New York. Soon after, I heard John Ashbery read at Columbia. I did something I'd never done before, which was I put every book of his I had in a shopping bag—I had ten books of his—and brought them up and asked him to sign them—all of them—which is outrageous. He spelled my name wrong. He wrote "Yao," and I was so uptight I couldn't correct him.

At that point I had no intention of going back to college or getting an MFA, but at the reading he said that he was teaching creative writing at Brooklyn College, and I applied to study with him. A few months later, my girlfriend and I are sitting around our grubby little loft in Lower Manhattan, and the phone rings—it's John Ashbery. He said, *You've been accepted. Would you like to come to Brooklyn College?* That was the beginning.

What was studying with him like?

The first class we had, he talked about translating from languages you don't know, how you could translate by sound—homophonically. I knew that Louis Zukofsky had done that with Catullus, so I thought, *Okay, I'm ready for this*. Then he pulls out pages of Egyptian hieroglyphics for us to translate—*Whoa!* He mentioned people no one in the class had read: Fulke Greville and John Wheelwright. As with Robert Kelly, who was always mentioning someone I had never read, I would write down the names and go to the library to see what they had by them.

Along with reading all over the place, I was regularly going to galleries. At one point, I said to John, *I'd like to learn how to write about art*. He said, *I can't teach you anything. You should just send something to Betsy Baker at* Art in America. I figured it was his way of putting me off, and I dropped it. A week later, he asks, *Have you sent anything to Betsy Baker yet?* Which, of course, I hadn't. He just said, *Well, I think you should*. I got myself together and wrote something—it was probably really an embarrassment, I hope there's no record of its existence—and I sent it to her and didn't hear anything for nearly a year. Then one day, out of the blue, she called and asked me to come to the office. Now, my feeling, and John never said a word about this, is that he pressured Betsy into giving me a chance, because I did not know how to write a review. It's a form, and I didn't know the form.

The first review I wrote was on Alan Cote, an abstract painter who taught at Bard College. A friend of mine read it and said, *You're like an ant crawling over the entire painting because you can't think of anything to say*—it was pure description. Basically, I wrote about whatever they *let* me write about. It was never top-tier artists, it was whatever nobody else wanted to write about. But I thought, *I don't care. This is how I'll learn how to write about art. I will deal with whatever I am allowed to write about.* That's what I did, and at some point I started writing for *Arts Magazine*, where Richard Martin never corrected anything.

I started writing for *Art in America* in '78 or '77. In 1981 or '82, I met Amy Baker, and she said, Artforum *just got this young, new editor, Ingrid Sischy—you should send her something.* I talked to somebody who knew Ingrid and they said, *Forget it—hundreds of people are trying to write for her. You'll never stand a chance.* Then I thought, *Why not?* So I sent her some stuff.

What do you have to lose?

Exactly. I sent her something, and she called me up and said, *Let's have lunch.* I remember she was in sweatpants—the total opposite of Betsy Baker, and she even made a point of saying, *I don't dress like Betsy.*

That is so funny.

I know! Ingrid shows up in sweatpants and a sweatshirt. She said, *I know you know how to describe something because you've been writing for* Art in America, *and that's what they're about. But I'm not interested in description. I'm interested in judgment. I'm interested in what you think, and why you think it.*

The next time we met, we choose three articles that I would write: David True was the first. I think the second was on Hiroshi Sugimoto. The third was on Eric Fischl, Ed Paschke, and Robert Birmelin. I remember Eric Fishl being really annoyed that I wrote about Paschke

516

and Birmelin. He made it clear that I should have written about him alongside David Salle and Julian Schnabel. He was mad at me, and I was like, *Huh?* I was naive then. I thought, *Just write about who you want to write about and they'll like it.* That's proved not to be true. [Laughter.]

I wrote for Ingrid for years, and I really liked her. I remember at that point I lived in Catskill, New York. One time I was was driving back from Boston and she said, *Call me every forty minutes while you're driving so we can go over this article,* something that I had written about Jasper Johns. And every forty minutes I'd stop and find a phone booth, and we'd go over my writing sentence by sentence. *Why did you say this?* I think she did that with all the writers. You felt special and completely nutty. I realized, *This is where I wanted to have landed all along.*

Once a year, Ingrid would have these dinners where all the New York writers showed up—Edit deAk, Rene Ricard, Donald Kuspit, Thomas Lawson—a really motley crew, but all of them really smart and opinionated. I remember the first time, we had dinner together in a Vietnamese restaurant in Chinatown, and she brought two cases of wine—there were around ten New York writers. I was like, *God, that's a lot of wine—that seems unnecessary.* By the end of the night we had finished the wine and were all disagreeing with each other, which was marvelous and probably what Ingrid wanted. I remember Edit deAk throwing wet napkins at Donald Kuspit—like we were high school kids.

When you were learning how to write about art, what were you trying to figure out?

I was trying to figure out what happened. I knew that the official history—the one in books and presented by museums—was wrong. That's something I learned from my father, who told me that America was founded by settlers who destroyed the people who were here, people, as he put it, who crossed the Bering Strait and were descendants of the Chinese. He had an interesting worldview for a man who was Chinese and English—a product of miscegenation. He kept telling me that American history books were full of lies. He was quite adamant about this. The first book he bought me was *Crazy Horse: The Strange Man of the Oglalas* [1942], by Mari Sandoz. I was seven or eight.

I think the other thing was learning to see for myself. I was driven by curiosity rather than by an aesthetic bias. I remember going to meetings of the Alliance of Figurative Artists—this must have been in the late 1970s—and hearing Paul Georges and Aristodimos Kaldis speak. I kept finding out about artists who no one was showing. At one point, I started hanging out at Phyllis Kind Gallery, and I was looking at all the Chicago artists, and people were saying, *How can you even look at that stuff?* I felt I had to learn these different histories—that became a big thing for me.

For one thing, I was always trying to find out about Asian artists— from Wifredo Lam to Martin Wong, both of whom I wrote about in the 1980s. If you have been left out or marginalized, I think you either become sympathetic to people who are left out or you try to assimilate. I was neither Chinese nor white: I did not belong to any group. At the same time, you have to check, *Are you just being sympathetic, or is it really good?* That is something I have to keep learning and thinking about. But I always tell myself, *The worst thing you can do is be wrong. It's not a sin. It's not a crime.* Baudelaire wrote beautifully about Constantin Guys. Today, Guys's work doesn't hold up, but the writing does. If you're a writer, that's your hope—you want to write the best thing you can so that people want to read it, even if it's not about someone they think is important. James Agee's film reviews are an example of what I am talking about.

How did you meet Jasper Johns?

I sent him a letter with three poems. I had written a series of poems called "Corpse and Mirror" [1983], and I wanted to use that as a title of a forthcoming book. I asked him if I could reproduce one of his paintings on the book cover. He wrote back and then we met. My girlfriend also helped too; she was the daughter of Frank Stella and Barbara Rose— Rachel Stella.

Did that connect you to that lineage of critics such as Barbara Rose and Michael Fried?

No.

You weren't sympathetic to your girlfriend's mother?

No.

Did you interact with her at all?

I interacted with Barbara a lot. We agreed to disagree on many things. She did say one very smart thing to me: I was writing about Forrest Bess, and she said, *You can't only write about people who are left out. You have to write about someone who's in the mainstream as well. If you only write about people who are left out, that's how you'll be seen.* That is not a dumb remark. It was like, *Okay, I get it. There's a big picture. You don't want to put yourself in this little outsider ghetto. You want to figure out if you can deal with the whole picture.* That's basically what she said.

Did John Ashbery introduce you to that scene of the New York School poet art world?

Yes, he brought me to openings where I met Alex Katz, Jane Freilicher, Larry Rivers, and Rackstraw Downes. I remember he brought me to an opening and introduced me to David Hockney. I was, like, twenty-seven and meeting all these people. If I had changed my attitude and the way I looked, I suppose I could have slid right into that scene, but I thought, *I have to figure out my own way.* There was a moment where I actually told John, *I can't write about any of the people you've written about. I have to find out everything on my own.*

At the same time, I did meet people by chance—I met Simon Gouverneur after a talk I gave in Baltimore. I believe that I met Calvert Coggeshall, who was friends with Walker Evans, at Betty Parsons, where he showed; we would take long walks in Manhattan whenever he came down from Maine, where he lived. I remember hanging out with Carol Haerer whenever she was in New York. Each one told me a different story. I listened to them all as best I could.

Around 1980 or '81, I met Norman Bluhm through John Bernard Myers, who, at one point, ran Tibor de Nagy Gallery. I was working at Books & Co., and John lived around the corner in a garden apartment. He came in one day, flamboyant and outrageous, and asked what novels of E. F. Benson we had. I knew who he was, and we started talking. He said, *You should come over to my apartment.* He had this amazing art collection, and I recognized all but one of the artists. *Who did that painting?* John was like, *You don't know Norman Bluhm? Well, you should meet him!* I, of course, knew about Norman from O'Hara's poems, as well as from the famous Fred McDarrah photograph of Norman standing on a stepladder, one foot in the air, painting, which was on the cover of *The Artist's World in Pictures* [1961]. Myers showed me *Fragments from Cold* [1977], a book by Paul Auster that he was publishing; it had a work by Bluhm on the cover. I knew Paul and had written to him in Paris when I was at Bard, because his sister Janet went to Bard, and she connected us. He took a bunch of my poems for his magazine, *Living Hand*, but years went by and he never published them. I called Paul and asked him if he would introduce me to Bluhm, and that was how we met. Bluhm came to a party at Books & Co., and Paul introduced us. I invited myself to his studio—I said, *I'd like to see your art.* He was really gruff, you know, but by that point in my life, I was used to that—you just put up with it if you want to meet someone. What's going to happen? They're probably not going to poison you. I took a bus or something out to East Hampton, Long Island, where he and his wife, Cary, lived in a big house with cathedral ceilings that he had designed. There was also a little ranch house on the property. He said I could stay there and not to bother him before noon; he stocked the refrigerators with eggs and coffee, other stuff.

I went to his studio, which was attached to his house, and was knocked out—I saw thirty-five years of work in a three-day period, starting with the late 1940s. In my head I was trying to figure out, *How come Joan Mitchell and Al Held and Grace Hartigan are so famous, and this guy is practically invisible? That makes no sense!* When I met him, he had not had a show in New York in years. It took years before he got a show. I talked to people over and over about him. They all said the same thing—*He's such a hard-ass*, as if somehow the personality was the problem. What does being a "difficult person" mean in the art world anyway? I didn't see Norman act badly—gruff, but not badly. He and Frank O'Hara got along great. I thought, *Okay. What's wrong with this picture?*

At that point, I had real physical issues with my teeth, the after-

520

effects of going through a windshield in that car accident I mentioned earlier. One day, Norman noticed and asked if I had a dentist. I didn't and had not been to one in years. He said, *I've got a dentist for you.* I said, *I can't afford it.* He said, *I'll trade a painting. It will be fine.*

That's so *sweet*!

That's what he did. It's the same spirit as John Ashbery taking this young guy around to all these galleries. Or Jasper Johns writing back, or Joan Mitchell saying I should meet her at her hotel so we can talk, or Jim Nutt and Gladys Nilsson inviting me to their house for dinner and introducing me to Ray Yoshida and Barbara Rossi, or Ed Paschke saying that I could stay at his house when I came to Chicago. A lot of people were very nice to me when I was young.

You started to say you saw the Johns retrospective when you came to New York. You've written on him a number of times, including two book-length studies; you also became friends with him. I want to know the entire storyline.

I wrote him a letter, and I slowly got to know him. At one point, I was having lunch with him every Friday because I have a shrink I see on the Upper East Side, and I'd call him from a phone booth afterward and go see him. At one point, I said that I wanted to write a book on him. He said, *I'm going to tell you everything,* and then laughed. I said, *You're not going to tell me anything, are you?* He said, *That's right!* I was actually glad about that, so that I could figure out what I thought for myself. At the same time, he explained every single technical thing he did in a painting, sculpture, or drawing, and that was great. I also realized that you have to pay attention to what he says—you couldn't go in with an agenda. For instance, I figured out this whole thing about how *Flag* [1954–1955] came from a dream and was painted on a bedsheet, and I asked, *Who else have you told about the bedsheet?* He said, *Oh, I told lots of people; no one ever listened.*

At one point, he told me that he was never going to read anything I wrote about him. I think he has read what I've written, but I don't think he's going to say much—that's fine. We have pretty straightforward conversations, but it's never about his art. That was the same with John

Ashbery—we almost never talked about his poems. I seemed to have picked these two men who don't want to talk about their own work. There's an overemphasis on cause and effect in criticism, but we don't really live in a cause-and-effect universe. It's not like, *Oh, this happened to me—I'll go home and write a poem.* You might act like that's what it's about, but it's not. There's always so much else going on.

It seems like the "judgments" in your criticism have become more important and pronounced recently. I don't know if you've experienced it like that.

Yes, I think that's true.

What do you think that's about?

Getting older—just years of looking. I also wake up and think, *I could be wrong.* And if you think you're wrong, then are you going to change your mind? *Yeah, why not?* That isn't the worst thing. These days, if I feel critical of something, I want to find a way to say what that criticism is and why. I don't think you can be certain of a lot right now, because we live in such a relative situation—anything is "good," everything is "good." Robert Hughes would always say, *Oh, that person can't paint.* Well, when did that become important? What does it mean that anything can be art? I think we're in a bind and have been for many years.

What does "art"—the experience of art and writing about art—mean to you? What have you come to regard it as?

It keeps me alive. I think it's really, *How do you deal with your mortality? What is our time here? What do we do with it? How do we pass the day? How do we use the hours? How do we defer the inevitable?* It's about how you shape the way you pass time. Because there are lots of people whose whole lives are taken up with things they have to do and cannot make decisions about; they are stuck in their lives. I get to pretty much decide how my day is going to be spent and what I'm going to do. Yeah, I go and teach. I do these things. But I spend quite a lot of time deciding what to do with my time. I just finished this new book on Philip Taaffe, and people ask, *When do you sleep?* I think, *It's just about how I use my time.* I had a certain amount of time to do this book, and I did it. I like that

522

immersion where you're just fully taken up with something. It's like going to a movie, except the movie lasts a month instead of three hours. You go to the movie and you enter this world. I'm going to enter Philip Taaffe's world. I just wrote twenty thousand words on him, and it's like, *I could write another twenty thousand from a different point of view, from a slightly different angle—just move the camera two feet to the right.*

I read a bio from the 1990s that said you were working on a book on Anna May Wong, but I never found the book.

I never finished it. I could not find the right form for it. But it led to two books that I am working on. One is about every movie John Ashbery and I ever saw together or talked about. Long before I met him, I read his books, and in *The Vermont Notebook* [1975], he has all these wacky lists. One is a list of names that includes "Rex Reed." I did not know anyone else on the list, but I had read Rex Reed, who is a campy film reviewer for trashy newspapers. With Robert Lowell I recognized everything in his poems, but with Ashbery I didn't recognize *anything*, and "Rex Reed" was the first moment of recognition—*Oh, I know who that is, and I also have some glimmer of what it means.* Later, when I met John, we started talking about Rex Reed and the outrageous and offensive things he said. One of them, he's talking about a movie by the Korean filmmaker Chan-wook Park, and he says like, *Only a culture that buries their eggs for a thousand years and eats rotten cabbage could have made a movie like this.* It's horribly wrong, racist, and funny, and you know that Rex Reed knows that he is doing that.

He's *in* on it.

Yeah, he's in on it. That's the whole thing that John and I got into: *Can you be in on being awful? Are you conscious of the levels of what you're saying?* The book begins with that memory, and it just goes through every movie—we saw Joseph Cornell's movies together in a tiny little temporary theater in SoHo. We went to the Lincoln Film Festival. We watched them at his house on TV. We exchanged VHSs. He was on the lookout for rare Ed Wood films. When he found one, he would make a copy and send it to me. One had a note that said, *This is in pristine condition.* When he found out that I loved Anna May Wong, he sent me videocassettes of her movies that he came across.

What in particular fixated you on Anna May Wong?

At sixteen, I saw her in *Shanghai Express* [1932].

One of the most gorgeous movies ever made—I *love* Marlene.

I'm living in Brookline, Massachusetts. I see an ad for a movie in Cambridge called *Shanghai Express*. I know my mother grew up in Shanghai, and I go only for that reason, naively thinking I would get to see the city my parents lived in. I see Anna May Wong and I'm lost— I've never seen such a beautiful Chinese woman on the screen, with this amazing voice, upstaging Marlene Dietrich. I became completely fascinated with her. To the point that I have a signed postcard by her that a friend of mine bought for me in Germany; I have stationery of hers. I met these people in the eighties, when I was writing the Warhol book, who were film freaks. I met the man who did the Anna May Wong filmography—he was working in a leather goods store on Bleecker Street, and he lived by Tompkins Square Park in this tiny apartment; he was also obsessed with Anna May Wong. I met one guy who published a monthly newsletter about silent film, which I got Ashbery to subscribe to—he loved it. I think knowing John gave me permission to be obsessed with different things that no one else might care about.

One thing that interests me about Ashbery is his book of lectures, *Other Traditions* [2000]. The poets he's writing about are pretty minor, willfully minor in most cases. There are some dimensions of that to your book *The Wild Children of William Blake*, and in your concern for other forgotten art histories. Do you see that as related to Ashbery's influence, or do you think that it's about "outsiderness" more broadly?

"Influence" is a weird word: it makes him sound like a drug or alcohol. *I am under the influence,* so to speak. Really, it is what I took from John, but also from other poets who I read or studied with, such as Robert Kelly.

Once I was teaching Asian American students in UC Berkeley—a writing class. I read this passage from Frank O'Hara where he says, "it's the night like I love it all cruisy and nelly"—I was talking about ways that language could be political without having to announce itself as such. Afterward, these three Chinese kids come up to me and say, *We're staying in this class because we're gay and we want to be able to write the way we want, and you seem cool with that.* I remember some poet saying to me, *John, you're a straight guy, and all you like are gay poets!* I thought, *Maybe we all feel like outsiders, and that's what I'm identifying with.* Like when O'Hara writes, "I . . . cried out 'I am an orphan.'" And he's in on it, right? He's laughing at himself, even as he's dealing with this clearly painful thing. That speaks to me.

Acknowledgments

Foremost, I'd like to thank Laila Pedro, who helped frame this project from its inception and edited every text along the way in its earliest stages. A big thanks is also due to Phong Bui, publisher of *The Brooklyn Rail*, who gave me the space to do anything I wanted over the years, along with the sense that it was all worth doing.

The most important people in my life are artists, who've spent countless hours talking with me in ways that have profoundly shaped my life and thought. For that I want to express special gratitude to Anna Betbeze, Seth Cameron, Candystore, Gaby Collins-Fernandez, Stephen Ellis, Christy Gast, Nancy Goldring, Josephine Halvorson, Nate Heiges, Abby Leigh, Matvey Levenstein, Leigha Mason, Ann McCoy, Genesis Breyer P-Orridge, Nathlie Provosty, Joan Waltemath, Nicole Wittenberg, and Lisa Yuskavage. Additionally, I've learned so much about the art world and its histories from sprawling discussions with Carol Lees and Julia Joern, whom I count on for their unbelievably good advice. Anne Trueblood Brodzky's friendship has been a great gift, bringing so much wisdom, gentleness, and light.

I want to acknowledge the exceptional generosity of all of the writers included here: Hilton Als, John Ashbery, Bill Berkson, Yve-Alain Bois, Huey Copeland, Holland Cotter, Douglas Crimp, Darby English, Hal Foster, Michael Fried, Thyrza Nichols Goodeve, Dave Hickey, Siri Hustvedt, Kellie Jones, Chris Kraus, Rosalind Krauss, Lucy Lippard, Fred Moten, Eileen Myles, Molly Nesbit, Jed Perl, Barbara Rose, Jerry Saltz, Peter Schjeldahl, Barry Schwabsky, Paul Chaat

Smith, Roberta Smith, Lynne Tillman, Michelle Wallace, and John Yau. And, of course, Betsy Baker, to whom this book is dedicated, who's done more for American art criticism than anyone else—our weekly afternoon conversations are a recurring joy of New York life. I'm also grateful to the memory of Bill Berkson, without whose early and tireless encouragement I wouldn't be writing at all.

I'm thankful to the Robert Rauschenberg Foundation and the director of its Rauschenberg Residency, Ann Brady; I met and interviewed Dave Hickey at the residency in 2014, essentially beginning this project. I'd like to extend further gratitude to Arlo Haskell, director of the Key West Literary Seminar, where I worked on parts of these interviews in the summer of 2017.

No one could have asked for a more thoughtful and diligent team for bringing this book to life, especially Doro Globus for her leadership, Mark Thomson for creating the design of my dreams, Clare Fentress for her eagle eye, and Mary Huber for her tireless attention to every single thing. My greatest admiration is reserved for Lucas Zwirner, without whose enthusiasm, intelligence, and vision this book simply wouldn't exist.

*　*　*

Some of these interviews have been published before, though often in very different forms, and appear here with permission:

"In Conversation: Hilton Als with Jarrett Earnest," *The Brooklyn Rail* (April 2016); "In Conversation: John Ashbery with Jarrett Earnest," *The Brooklyn Rail* (May 2016); "In Conversation: Bill Berkson with Jarrett Earnest," *The Brooklyn Rail* (June 2016); "Close Encounters: Douglas Crimp with Jarrett Earnest," *The Brooklyn Rail* (October 2016); "Dave Hickey: In Conversation With Jarrett Earnest (Part One)," *SFAQ* 19 (2015); "Dave Hickey: In Conversation With Jarrett Earnest (Part Two)," *AQ* 1 (2015); "Dave Hickey: In Conversation

With Jarrett Earnest (Part Three)," *AQ* 2 (2015); "Close Encounters: Siri Hustvedt with Jarrett Earnest," *The Brooklyn Rail* (May 2017); "Close Encounters: Chris Kraus with Jarrett Earnest," *The Brooklyn Rail* (September 2017); "Close Encounters: Lucy Lippard with Jarrett Earnest," *The Brooklyn Rail* (December 2017/January 2018); "Close Encounters: Fred Moten with Jarrett Earnest," *The Brooklyn Rail* (November 2017); "Close Encounters: Molly Nesbit with Jarrett Earnest," *The Brooklyn Rail* (July/August 2017); "Close Encounters: Jed Perl with Jarrett Earnest," *The Brooklyn Rail* (February 2018); "Close Encounters: Jerry Saltz with Jarrett Earnest," *The Brooklyn Rail* (June 2017); "Close Encounters: Barry Schwabsky with Jarrett Earnest," *The Brooklyn Rail* (April 2017); "Close Encounters: Roberta Smith with Jarrett Earnest," *The Brooklyn Rail* (March 2017); "Close Encounters: Lynne Tillman with Jarrett Earnest," *The Brooklyn Rail* (November 2016).

**Works by Writers Interviewed
in This Book**

Hilton Als

*Our Town: Images and Stories from the Museum
of the City of New York.* New York: Harry N.
Abrams, 1997.

The Women. New York: Farrar, Straus and
Giroux, 1998.

Foreword to *Drawing Us In: How We Experience
Visual Art.* Edited by Deborah Chasman
and Edna Chiang, pp. vii–xi. Boston:
Beacon Press, 2001.

White Noise: The Eminem Collection. Edited by
Hilton Als and Darryl A. Turner. Boston:
Da Capo Press, 2003.

"Miss Hattie." In *Kara Walker: Dust Jackets for
the Niggerati,* pp. 70–79. Exh. cat. New
York: Gregory R. Miller & Co., 2013.

"Shadows." In *Lorna Simpson: Works on Paper,*
pp. 70–77. Exh. cat. Aspen, CO: Aspen Art
Press, 2013.

Robert Gober: The Heart Is Not a Metaphor.
Edited by Ann Temkin. Exh. cat. New
York: The Museum of Modern Art, 2014.

White Girls. San Francisco: McSweeney's,
2014.

Alice Neel, Uptown. Exh. cat. New York: David
Zwirner Books, 2017.

John Ashbery

Ashbery, John, and James Schuyler. *A Nest of
Ninnies.* Champaign, IL: Dalkey Archive
Press, [1969] 2008.

Reported Sightings: Art Chronicles, 1957–1987.
Edited by David Bergman. Cambridge,
MA: Harvard University Press, 1991.

Other Traditions. Cambridge, MA: Harvard
University Press, 2000.

Selected Prose 1953–2003. Edited by Eugene
Richie. Manchester, UK: Carcanet, 2004.

Collected Poems 1956–1987. Edited by Mark
Ford. New York: Library of America,
2008.

Notes from the Air: Selected Later Poems. New
York: Ecco, 2008.

Rimbaud, Arthur. *Illuminations.* Translated
by John Ashbery. New York: W. W. Norton
& Company, 2012.

Collected French Translations: Poetry. Edited by
Rosanne Wasserman and Eugene Richie.
New York: Farrar, Straus and Giroux,
2014.

Collected French Translations: Prose. Edited by
Rosanne Wasserman and Eugene Richie.
New York: Farrar, Straus and Giroux,
2014.

Collected Poems 1991–2000. Edited by Mark
Ford. New York: Library of America, 2017.

Bill Berkson

O'Hara, Frank. *In Memory of My Feelings.*
Edited by Bill Berkson. New York: The
Museum of Modern Art, [1967] 2005.

Homage to Frank O'Hara. Edited by Bill
Berkson and Joe LeSueur. Billings, MT:
Big Sky Books, 1988.

Berkson, Bill, and Anne Waldman. *Young
Manhattan.* Boulder, CO: Smokeproof
Press / Erudite Fangs Editions, 1999.

Berkson, Bill, and Frank O'Hara. *Hymns of
St. Bridget & Other Writings.* Berkeley: Owl
Press, 2001.

*The Sweet Singer of Modernism & Other Art
Writings 1985–2003.* Jamestown, RI: Qua
Books, 2004.

Berkson, Bill, and Bernadette Mayer. *What's
Your Idea of a Good Time? Letters & Interviews
1977–1985.* Berkeley: Tuumba Press, 2006.

Sudden Address: Selected Lectures 1981–2006.
Austin, TX: Cuneiform Press, 2007.

Portrait and Dream: New and Selected Poems.
Minneapolis: Coffee House Press, 2009.

*For the Ordinary Artist: Short Reviews, Occasional
Pieces & More.* Buffalo, NY: BlazeVOX
books, 2010.

The Far Flowered Shore: 2006 / 2010. Austin, TX:
Cuneiform Press, 2013.

Expect Delays. Minneapolis: Coffee House

Press, 2014.

Invisible Oligarchs. New York: Ugly Duckling
Presse, 2016.

Since When. Minneapolis: Coffee House
Press, 2018.

Yve-Alain Bois

Painting as Model. Cambridge, MA: The MIT
Press, 1993.

Foster, Hal, Rosalind Krauss, Yve-Alain
Bois, and Benjamin H. D. Buchloh. *Art
Since 1900: Modernism, Antimodernism,
Postmodernism.* London: Thames &
Hudson, [1994] 2005.

Bois, Yve-Alain, Joop Joosten, Angelica
Zander Rudenstine, and Hans Janssen.
Piet Mondrian: 1872–1944. Exh. cat. Boston:
Little, Brown and Company, 1994.

Bois, Yve-Alain, and Rosalind Krauss.
Formless: A User's Guide. New York: Zone
Books, 1997.

*Rendezvous: Masterpieces from the Centre Georges
Pompidou and the Guggenheim Museums.*
Edited by Bernard Blistène and Lisa
Dennison. Exh. cat. New York:
Guggenheim Museum Publications,
[1998] 2003.

Matisse and Picasso. Exh. cat. Paris:
Flammarion, 2001.

*Edward Ruscha: Catalogue Raisonné of the
Paintings; Volume One: 1958–1970.*
Göttingen, Germany: Steidl, 2004.

*Ellsworth Kelly: Catalogue Raisonné of Paintings,
Reliefs, and Sculpture, Volume One, 1940–1953.*
Paris: Cahiers d'Art, 2015.

Matisse in the Barnes Foundation. 3 vols. Edited
by Yve-Alain Bois. London: Thames &
Hudson, 2016.

Huey Copeland

Black Is, Black Ain't. Exh. cat. Chicago: The
Renaissance Society, 2013.

*Bound to Appear: Art, Slavery, and the Site of
Blackness in Multicultural America.* Chicago:
University of Chicago Press, 2013.

Douglas Crimp

AIDS: Cultural Analysis/Cultural Activism.
Edited by Douglas Crimp. Cambridge,
MA: The MIT Press, 1988.

AIDS Demo Graphics. Seattle: Bay Press, 1990.

On the Museum's Ruins. Cambridge, MA: The
MIT Press, 1993.

*Melancholia and Moralism: Essays on AIDS and
Queer Politics.* Cambridge, MA: The MIT
Press, 2002.

"Our Kind of Movie": The Films of Andy Warhol.
Cambridge, MA: The MIT Press, 2012.

Before Pictures. Chicago: University of
Chicago Press, 2016.

Darby English

Kara Walker: Narratives of a Negress. Edited by
Ian Berry, Darby English, Vivian
Patterson, and Mark Reinhardt. Exh. cat.
Cambridge, MA: The MIT Press, 2003.

How to See a Work of Art in Total Darkness.
Cambridge, MA: The MIT Press, 2007.

1971: A Year in the Life of Color. Chicago:
University of Chicago Press, 2016.

Hal Foster

*The Anti-Aesthetic: Essays on Postmodern
Culture.* Edited by Hal Foster. New York:
The New Press, [1983] 2002.

Recodings: Art, Spectacle, Cultural Politics. New
York: The New Press, [1985] 1998.

Compulsive Beauty. Cambridge, MA: The MIT
Press, 1993.

Foster, Hal, Rosalind Krauss, Yve-Alain
Bois, and Benjamin H. D. Buchloh.
*Art Since 1900: Modernism, Antimodernism,
Postmodernism.* London: Thames &
Hudson, [1994] 2005.

*The Return of the Real: Art and Theory at the End
of the Century.* Cambridge, MA: The MIT
Press, 1996.

Design and Crime (And Other Diatribes). New
York: Verso, 2002.

Prosthetic Gods. Cambridge, MA: The MIT
Press, 2004.

Pop. Edited by Mark Francis. New York:
Phaidon, 2005.

The Art-Architecture Complex. New York: Verso, 2011.

The First Pop Age. Princeton, NJ: Princeton University Press, 2012.

Bad New Days: Art, Criticism, Emergency. New York: Verso, 2017.

Michael Fried

Powers. Worthing, UK: Littlehampton Book Services, 1971.

Absorption and Theatricality: Painting and Beholder in the Age of Diderot. Berkeley: University of California Press, 1980.

Realism, Writing, Disfiguration: On Thomas Eakins and Stephen Crane. Chicago: University of Chicago Press, 1987.

Courbet's Realism. Chicago: University of Chicago Press, 1990.

To the Center of the Earth. New York: Farrar, Straus and Giroux, 1994.

Manet's Modernism: or, The Face of Painting in the 1860s. Chicago: University of Chicago Press, 1996.

Art and Objecthood: Essays and Reviews. Chicago: University of Chicago Press, 1998.

Menzel's Realism: Art and Embodiment in Nineteenth-Century Berlin. New Haven, CT: Yale University Press, 2002.

The Next Bend in the Road. Chicago: University of Chicago Press, 2004.

Why Photography Matters as Art as Never Before. New Haven, CT: Yale University Press, 2008.

The Moment of Caravaggio. Princeton, NJ: Princeton University Press, 2010.

Four Honest Outlaws: Sala, Ray, Marioni, Gordon. New Haven, CT: Yale University Press, 2011.

Flaubert's "Gueuloir." New Haven, CT: Yale University Press, 2012.

Another Light: Jacques-Louis David to Thomas Demand. New Haven, CT: Yale University Press, 2015.

After Caravaggio. New Haven, CT: Yale University Press, 2016.

Promesse du Bonheur. Photographs by James Welling. New York: David Zwirner Books, 2016.

Thyrza Nichols Goodeve

"You Sober People." In *When Pain Strikes.* Edited by Bill Burns, Cathy Busby, and Kim Sawchuk, pp. 228–246. Minneapolis: University of Minnesota Press, 1998.

Haraway, Donna. *How Like a Leaf: An Interview with Thyrza Nichols Goodeve.* New York: Routledge, 1999.

Ellen Gallagher. Exh. cat. London: Anthony d'Offay Gallery, 2001.

Dave Hickey

Prior Convictions. Dallas: Southern Methodist University Press, 1989.

The Invisible Dragon: Four Essays on Beauty. Los Angeles: Art Issues Press, 1993.

Robert Gober. Edited by Karen Marta. Exh. cat. New York: Dia Art Foundation, 1993.

Air Guitar: Essays on Art & Democracy. Los Angeles: Art Issues Press, 1997.

Stardumb. Edited by Michael Mack. San Francisco: Artspace Books, 2000.

Josiah McElheny: A Prism. Edited by Josiah McElheny and Louise Neri. New York: Skira Rizzoli, 2010.

Pirates and Farmers: Essays on Taste. Santa Monica, CA: RAM Publications, 2013.

25 Women: Essays on Their Art. Chicago: University of Chicago Press, 2016.

Dust Bunnies: Dave Hickey's Online Aphorisms; June 2014–March 2015. Edited by Julia Friedman. Los Angeles: PCP Press, 2016.

Wasted Words: The Essential Dave Hickey Online Collection. Edited by Julia Friedman. Los Angeles: PCP Press, 2016.

Perfect Wave: More Essays on Art and Democracy. Chicago: University of Chicago Press, 2017.

Siri Hustvedt

Reading to You. Barrytown, NY: Station Hill Press, 1983.

The Enchantment of Lily Dahl. New York: Henry Holt & Company, 1996.

Yonder. New York: Henry Holt & Company, 1998.

The Blindfold. New York: Poseidon Press, 2002.

What I Loved. New York: Picador, 2003.

Mysteries of the Rectangle: Essays on Painting. Hudson, NY: Princeton Architectural Press, 2005.

A Plea for Eros. New York: Picador, 2005.

The Sorrows of an American. New York: Picador, 2008.

The Shaking Woman: Or, A History of My Nerves. New York: Picador, 2010.

The Summer Without Men. New York: Picador, 2011.

Living, Thinking, Looking. New York: Picador, 2012.

The Blazing World. New York: Simon & Schuster, 2014.

A Woman Looking at Men Looking at Women: Essays on Art, Sex, and the Mind. New York: Simon & Schuster, 2016.

Kellie Jones

Lorna Simpson. London: Phaidon, 2002.

Hoffman, Fred, Kellie Jones, Marc Mayer, and Franklin Sirmans. *Basquiat.* Exh. cat. London: Merrell Publishers, 2005.

EyeMinded: Living and Writing Contemporary Art. Durham, NC: Duke University Press, 2011.

Now Dig This! Art and Black Los Angeles 1960–1980. Exh. cat. New York: Prestel, 2011.

Witness: Art and Civil Rights in the Sixties. Edited by Kellie Jones and Teresa A. Carbone. Exh. cat. New York: The Monacelli Press, 2014.

South of Pico: African American Artists in Los Angeles in the 1960s and 1970s. Durham, NC: Duke University Press, 2017.

"Swimming with E.C." In *We Wanted a Revolution: Black Radical Women, 1965–85: New Perspectives.* Edited by Catherine Morris and Rujeko Hockley, pp. 49–72. Durham, NC: Duke University Press, 2018.

Chris Kraus

I Love Dick. New York: Semiotext(e), 1997.

Aliens & Anorexia. New York: Semiotext(e), 2000.

Hatred of Capitalism: A Semiotext(e) Reader. Edited by Chris Kraus and Sylvère Lotringer. Los Angeles: Semiotext(e), 2001.

Video Green: Los Angeles Art and the Triumph of Nothingness. Los Angeles: Semiotext(e), 2004.

Kraus, Chris, Jan Tumlir, and Jane McFadden. *LA Artland: Contemporary Art from Los Angeles.* London: Black Dog Publishing, 2005.

Torpor. Los Angeles: Semiotext(e), 2006.

Where Art Belongs. Los Angeles: Semiotext(e), 2011.

Summer of Hate. Los Angeles: Semiotext(e), 2012.

After Kathy Acker: A Biography. Los Angeles: Semiotext(e), 2017.

Rosalind Krauss

Terminal Iron Works: The Sculpture of David Smith. Cambridge, MA: The MIT Press, 1971.

Passages in Modern Sculpture. Cambridge, MA: The MIT Press, [1977] 1981.

The Sculpture of David Smith: A Catalogue Raisonné. New York: Garland Publishing, 1977.

Krauss, Rosalind, Jane Livingston, and Dawn Ades. *L'Amour fou: Photography & Surrealism.* Exh. cat. New York: Abbeville Press, 1985.

The Originality of the Avant-Garde and Other Modernist Myths. Cambridge, MA: The MIT Press, 1985.

The Optical Unconscious. Cambridge, MA: The MIT Press, 1993.

Foster, Hal, Rosalind Krauss, Yve-Alain Bois, and Benjamin H. D. Buchloh. *Art Since 1900: Modernism, Antimodernism, Postmodernism.* London: Thames & Hudson, [1994] 2005.

Bois, Yves-Alain, and Rosalind Krauss.

Formless: A User's Guide. New York: Zone Books, 1997.

Bachelors. Cambridge, MA: The MIT Press, 1999.

The Picasso Papers. Cambridge, MA: The MIT Press, 1999.

"A Voyage on the North Sea": Art in the Age of the Post-Medium Condition. New York: Thames & Hudson, 2000.

Perpetual Inventory. Cambridge, MA: The MIT Press, 2010.

Under Blue Cup. Cambridge, MA: The MIT Press, 2011.

Willem de Kooning Nonstop: Cherchez la femme. Chicago: University of Chicago Press, 2015.

Lucy Lippard

Pop Art. New York: Frederick A. Praeger, 1966.

Ad Reinhardt: Paintings. Exh. cat. New York: Jewish Museum, 1967.

Information. Edited by Kynaston L. McShine. Exh. cat. New York: The Museum of Modern Art, 1970.

Changing: Essays in Art Criticism. New York: Dutton, 1971.

Eva Hesse. Cambridge, MA: Da Capo Press, [1976] 1992.

From the Center: Feminist Essays on Women's Art. New York: Plume, 1976.

Overlay: Contemporary Art and the Art of Prehistory. New York: The New Press, [1983] 1995.

Get the Message? A Decade of Art for Social Change. New York: E. P. Dutton, 1984.

Mixed Blessings: New Art in a Multicultural America. New York: The New Press, [1990] 2000.

Six Years: The Dematerialization of the Art Object from 1966 to 1972. Berkeley: University of California Press, [1993] 1997.

The Lure of the Local: Senses of Place in a Multicentered Society. New York: The New Press, 1998.

On the Beaten Track: Tourism, Art, and Place. New York: The New Press, 1999.

Down Country: The Tano of the Galisteo Basin, 1250–1782. Albuquerque, NM: Museum of New Mexico Press, 2010.

Fred Moten

Arkansas. Boston: Pressed Wafer Books, 2000.

In the Break: The Aesthetics of the Black Radical Tradition. Minneapolis: University of Minnesota Press, 2003.

B Jenkins. Durham, NC: Duke University Press, 2010.

Harney, Stefano, and Fred Moten. *The Undercommons: Fugitive Planning & Black Study*. London: Minor Compositions, 2013.

The Feel Trio. Tucson, AZ: Letter Machine Editions, 2014.

The Little Edges. Middletown, CT: Wesleyan University Press, 2016.

The Service Porch. Tucson, AZ: Letter Machine Editions, 2016.

Black and Blur. Vol. 1 of *consent not to be a single being*. Durham, NC: Duke University Press, 2017.

Stolen Life. Vol. 2 of *consent not to be a single being*. Durham, NC: Duke University Press, 2018.

The Universal Machine. Vol. 3 of *consent not to be a single being*. Durham, NC: Duke University Press, 2018.

Eileen Myles

A Fresh Young Voice from the Plains. New York: Power Mad Press, 1981.

Bread and Water. New York: Hanuman Books, 1988.

1969. New York: Hanuman Books, 1989.

Not Me. New York: Semiotext(e), 1991.

Chelsea Girls. New York: HarperCollins, [1994] 2015.

The New Fuck You: Adventures in Lesbian Reading. Edited by Eileen Myles and Liz Kotz. New York: Semiotext(e), 1995.

Cool for You. New York: Soft Skull Press, [2000] 2008.

The Importance of Being Iceland: Travel Essays in Art. Los Angeles: Semiotext(e), 2009.

Inferno (a poet's novel). New York: OR Books,
2010.

Snowflake / different streets. Seattle: Wave
Books, 2012.

*I Must Be Living Twice: New and Selected Poems
1975–2014*. New York: Ecco Press, 2015.

Molly Nesbit

Atget's Seven Albums. New Haven, CT: Yale
University Press, 1992.

Their Common Sense. London: Black Dog
Publishing, 2000.

*The Pragmatism in the History of Art:
Pre-Occupations 1*. Reading, UK: Periscope,
2013.

*Midnight: The Tempest Essays: Pre-Occupations
2*. Los Angeles: Inventory Press, 2017.

Jed Perl

*Paris Without End: On French Art Since World
War I*. New York: North Point Press, 1988.

Gallery Going: Four Seasons in the Art World.
New York: Harcourt, 1991.

Eyewitness: Reports from an Art World in Crisis.
New York: Basic Books, 2000.

New Art City: Manhattan at Mid-Century. New
York: Vintage Books, [2005] 2007.

Antoine's Alphabet: Watteau and His World.
New York: Vintage Books, [2008] 2009.

*Magicians & Charlatans: Essays on Art and
Culture*. New York: Eakins Press
Foundation, 2012.

*Art in America 1945–1970: Writings from the Age
of Abstract Expressionism, Pop Art, and
Minimalism*. Edited by Jed Perl. New
York: Library of America, 2014.

*Calder: The Conquest of Time: The Early Years:
1898–1940*. New York: Knopf, 2017.

Barbara Rose

American Art Since 1900: A Critical History. New
York: F. A. Praeger, 1967.

Helen Frankenthaler. New York: Harry N.
Abrams, 1970.

Art-as-Art: The Selected Writings of Ad Reinhardt.
Edited by Barbara Rose. Berkeley:
University of California Press, [1975] 1991.

*Agee, William C., and Barbara Rose. Patrick
Henry Bruce: Catalogue Raisonné*. New York:
The Museum of Modern Art, 1979.

Miró in America. Exh. cat. Houston: Museum
of Fine Arts, Houston, 1982.

Lee Krasner. Exh. cat. New York: The
Museum of Modern Art, 1983.

*Autocritique: Essays on Art and Anti-Art,
1963–1987*. New York: Weidenfeld &
Nicolson, 1988.

Magdalena Abakanowicz. New York: Harry N.
Abrams, 1994.

Painting After Postmodernism: Belgium – USA.
Exh. cat. Tielt, Belgium: Lannoo
Publishers, 2016.

Jerry Saltz

*Fischl, Eric, and Jerry Saltz. Sketchbook with
Voices*. New York: Alfred van der Marck
Editions, 1986.

Beyond Boundaries: New York's New Art. New
York: Alfred van der Marck Editions,
1986.

*An Ideal Syllabus: Artists, Critics and Curators
Choose the Books We Need to Read*. Edited by
Jerry Saltz. New York: Frieze, 1998.

*Seeing Out Loud: Village Voice Art Columns Fall
1998–Winter 2003*. Berkeley: The Figures,
2003.

Seeing Out Louder: Art Criticism 2003-2009.
Manchester, VT: Hudson Hills Press,
2009.

Peter Schjeldahl

White Country. New York: Corinth, 1968.

An Adventure of the Thought Police. London:
Ferry Press, 1971.

Dreams. New York: Angel Hair, 1973.

Since 1964: New and Selected Poems. New York:
Sun, 1978.

The Brute. Los Angeles: Little Caesar Press,
1981.

The 7 Days Art Columns: 1988–1990. New York:
The Figures, 1991.

*The Hydrogen Jukebox: Selected Writings of Peter
Schjeldahl, 1978–1990*. Edited by MaLin
Wilson. Berkeley: University of

California Press, 1991.

Columns & Catalogues. New York: The Figures, 1994.

Let's See: Writings on Art from The New Yorker. London: Thames & Hudson, 2008.

Barry Schwabsky

The Widening Circle: Consequences of Modernism in Contemporary Art. New York: Cambridge University Press, 1997.

Vitamin P: New Perspectives in Painting. Edited by Barry Schwabsky. New York: Phaidon, 2002.

Book Left Open in the Rain. New York: Black Square Editions, 2008.

Vitamin P2. Edited by Barry Schwabsky. New York: Phaidon, 2011.

Words for Art: Criticism, History, Theory, Practice. Berlin: Sternberg Press, 2013.

Tightrope Walk: Painted Images After Abstraction. Exh. cat. London: White Cube, 2015.

Trembling Hand Equilibrium. New York: Black Square Editions, 2015.

The Perpetual Guest: Art in the Unfinished Present. New York: Verso, 2016.

Heretics of Language. New York: Black Square Editions, 2018.

Paul Chaat Smith

Bates, Sara, Jolene Rickard, and Paul Chaat Smith. *Indian Humor*. Exh. cat. San Francisco: American Indian Contemporary Arts, 1995.

Smith, Paul Chaat, and Robert Warrior. *Like a Hurricane: The Indian Movement from Alcatraz to Wounded Knee*. New York: The New Press, 1996.

James Luna: Emendatio. Edited by Truman Lowe and Paul Chaat Smith. Exh. cat. Washington, DC: National Museum of the American Indian, 2006.

Fritz Scholder: Indian/Not Indian. Edited by Lowery Stokes Sims. Exh. cat. New York: Prestel, 2008.

Everything You Know about Indians Is Wrong. Minneapolis: University of Minnesota Press, 2009.

Smith, Paul Chaat, and Candice Hopkins. *Brian Jungen: Strange Comfort*. Exh. cat. Washington, DC: National Museum of the American Indian, 2010.

Ratcliff, Carter, and Paul Chaat Smith. *Kindred Spirits: Native American Influences on 20th Century Art*. Exh. cat. New York: Peter Blum Edition, 2011.

Afterword to *Officially Indian: Symbols That Define the United States*. By Cécile Ganteaume. Foreword by Colin G. Calloway. Minneapolis: University of Minnesota Press, 2017.

Smith, Paul Chaat. "Radio Free Europe." In *Jimmie Durham: At the Center of the World*. Edited by Anne Ellegood, pp. 135–137. Exh. cat. New York: Prestel, 2017.

Lynne Tillman

Haunted Houses. New York: Poseidon Press, 1987.

Absence Makes the Heart. London: Serpent's Tail, 1990.

Motion Sickness. London: Serpent's Tail, 1991.

Cast in Doubt. New York: Poseidon Press, 1992.

The Madame Realism Complex. New York: Semiotext(e), 1992.

The Velvet Years: Warhol's Factory 1965–1967. New York: Thunder's Mouth Press, 1995.

The Broad Picture: Essays 1987-1996. London: Serpent's Tail, 1997.

No Lease on Life. New York: Harcourt, 1998.

Bookstore: The Life and Times of Jeannette Watson and Books & Co. New York: Harcourt, 1999.

This Is Not It. New York: Distributed Art Publishers, 2002.

American Genius, A Comedy. New York: Soft Skull Press, 2006.

Someday This Will Be Funny. New York: Red Lemonade, 2011.

What Would Lynne Tillman Do? New York: Red Lemonade, 2014.

The Complete Madame Realism and Other Stories. Los Angeles: Semiotext(e), 2016.

Men and Apparitions. New York: Soft Skull Press, 2018.

Michele Wallace

Black Macho and the Myth of the Superwoman. New York: Verso, [1978] 2015.

Faith Ringgold: Twenty Years of Painting, Sculpture and Performance (1963–1983). Edited by Michele Wallace. Exh. cat. New York: Studio Museum in Harlem, 1984.

Invisibility Blues: From Pop to Theory. New York: Verso, [1990] 2016.

Black Popular Culture. Edited by Gina Dent. New York: The New Press, [1992] 1998.

"The Search for the 'Good Enough' Mammy: Multiculturalism, Popular Culture, and Psychoanalysis." In *Multiculturalism: A Critical Reader.* Edited by David Theo Goldberg, pp. 259–268. Hoboken, NJ: Wiley, 1994.

"Anger in Isolation: A Black Feminist's Search for Sisterhood." In *Words of Fire: An Anthology of African-American Feminist Thought.* Edited by Beverly Guy-Sheftall, pp. 220–228. New York: The New Press, 1995.

"Passing, Lynching, and Jim Crow: A Genealogy of Race and Gender in U.S. Visual Culture, 1895–1929." PhD diss., New York University, 1999.

Dark Designs and Visual Culture. Durham, NC: Duke University Press, 2004.

American People, Black Light: Faith Ringgold's Paintings of the 1960s. Exh. cat. Purchase, NY: Neuberger Museum of Art, 2010.

John Yau

Corpse and Mirror. New York: Henry Holt & Company, 1983.

Radiant Silhouette: New and Selected Work, 1974–1988. Boston: Black Sparrow Press, 1989.

In the Realm of Appearances: The Art of Andy Warhol. New York: Ecco Press, 1993.

Hawaiian Cowboys. Boston: Black Sparrow Press, 1995.

The United States of Jasper Johns. Cambridge, MA: Zoland Books, 1996.

Borrowed Love Poems. New York: Penguin Books, 2002.

Ing Grish. Illustrated by Thomas Nozkowski. Philadelphia: Saturnalia Books, 2005.

Paradiso Diaspora. New York: Penguin Books, 2006.

A Thing Among Things: The Art of Jasper Johns. New York: Distributed Art Publishers, 2008.

Further Adventures in Monochrome. Port Townsend, WA: Copper Canyon Press, 2012.

"All the World's a Stage: The Art of Martin Wong." In *Martin Wong: Human Instamatic.* Edited by Antonio Sergio Bessa, pp. 37–62. Exh. cat. London: Black Dog Publishing, 2016.

Catherine Murphy. Foreword by Sveltlana Alpers. New York: Skira Rizzoli, 2016.

Al Taylor: Early Paintings. Exh. cat. New York: David Zwirner Books, 2017.

Thomas Nozkowski. London: Lund Humphries, 2017.

The Wild Children of William Blake. New York: Autonomedia, 2017.

Further Reading

Works by Writers Not Interviewed in This Book

Kathy Acker
Bodies of Work: Essays. London: Serpent's Tail, 1997.

Svetlana Alpers
The Art of Describing: Dutch Art in the Seventeenth Century. Chicago: University of Chicago Press, 1983.

Dore Ashton
Out of the Whirlwind: Three Decades of Arts Commentary. Ann Arbor, MI: UMI Research Press, 1987.

W. H. Auden
The Dyer's Hand and Other Essays. New York: Random House, 1962.

Mikhail Bakhtin
Rabelais and His World. Translated by Hélène Iswolsky. Bloomington, IN: Indiana University Press, [1965] 1984.

James Baldwin
The Fire Next Time. New York: Vintage, [1963] 1992.

Amiri Baraka
Blues People: Negro Music in White America. New York: Harper Perennial, [1963] 1999.

Roland Barthes
The Responsibility of Forms: Critical Essays on Music, Art, and Representation. Translated by Richard Howard. New York: Hill & Wang, 1985.

Georges Bataille
Visions of Excess: Selected Writings, 1927-1939. Edited by Allan Stoekl. Translated by Allan Stoekl, Carl R. Lovitt, and Donald M. Leslie Jr. Minneapolis: University of Minnesota Press, 1985.

Charles Baudelaire
The Painter of Modern Life and Other Essays. Translated and edited by Jonathan Mayne. New York: Phaidon, 1964.

Michael Baxandall
Painting and Experience in Fifteenth-Century Italy: A Primer in the Social History of Pictorial Style. 2nd ed. New York: Oxford University Press, [1972] 1988.

Walter Benjamin
Illuminations: Essays and Reflections. Edited and with an introduction by Hannah Arendt. Translated by Harry Zohn. New York: Schocken Books, [1955] 1969.

John Berger
Ways of Seeing. New York: Penguin Books, [1972] 2008.

Benjamin H. D. Buchloh
Formalism and Historicity: Models and Methods in Twentieth-Century Art. Cambridge, MA: The MIT Press, 2015.

Scott Burton
Scott Burton: Collected Writings on Art and Performance 1965–1975. Edited by David J. Getsy. Chicago: Soberscove Press, 2012.

T. J. Clark
Farewell to an Idea: Episodes from a History of Modernism. New Haven, CT: Yale University Press, 1999.

Thomas Crow
The Rise of the Sixties: American and European Art in the Era of Dissent. New Haven, CT: Yale University Press, [1996] 2005.

Hubert Damisch
The Origin of Perspective. Translated by John Goodman. Cambridge, MA: The MIT Press, [1987] 1994.

Elaine de Kooning
The Spirit of Abstract Expressionism: Selected Writings. New York: Braziller, 1994.

Teresa de Lauretis
Alice Doesn't: Feminism, Semiotics, Cinema. Bloomington, IN: Indiana University Press, 1984.

Samuel R. Delany
The Motion of Light in Water: Sex and Science Fiction Writing in the East Village. Minneapolis: University of Minnesota Press, [1988] 2004.

Gilles Deleuze
The Logic of Sense. Edited by Constantin V. Boundas. Translated by Mark Lester with Charles Stivale. New York: Columbia University Press, [1969] 1990.

Edwin Denby
Dance Writings and Poetry. Edited by Robert Cornfield. New Haven, CT: Yale University Press, 1998.

Jacques Derrida
The Truth in Painting. Translated by Geoffrey Bennington and Ian McLeod. Chicago: University of Chicago Press, [1978] 1987.

Denis Diderot
Diderot on Art, Volume I: The Salon of 1765 and Notes on Painting. Translated by John Goodman. Introduction by Thomas Crow. New Haven, CT: Yale University Press, 1995.
Diderot on Art, Volume II: The Salon of 1767. Translated by John Goodman. Introduction by Thomas Crow. New Haven, CT: Yale University Press, 1995.

David C. Driskell
Two Centuries of Black American Art. Exh. cat. New York: Knopf, 1976.

Umberto Eco
The Open Work. Translated by Anna Cancogni. Cambridge, MA: Harvard University Press, [1962] 1989.

James Elkins
Why Art Cannot Be Taught. Champaign, IL: University of Illinois Press, 2001.

Vilém Flusser
Artforum // Essays. Edited by Martha Schwendener. Berlin: Metaflux, 2017.

Henri Focillon
The Life of Forms in Art. Translated by George Kubler. New York: Zone Books, [1942] 1989.

E. M. Forster
Aspects of the Novel. New York: Penguin Books, [1927] 2005.

Michel Foucault
Manet and the Object of Painting. Translated by Matthew Barr. London: Tate Publishing, [1971] 2009.

Amy Goldin
Art in a Hairshirt: Art Criticism 1964-1978. Edited by Robert Kushner. Stockbridge, MA: Hard Press Editions, 2012.

E. H. Gombrich
Art and Illusion: A Study in the Psychology of Pictorial Representation. New York: Phaidon, [1960] 2002.

Jennifer A. González
Subject to Display: Reframing Race in Contemporary Installation Art. Cambridge, MA: The MIT Press, 2008.

Lawrence Gowing
Selected Writings on Art. Edited by Sarah Whitfield. London: Ridinghouse, 2015.

Renée Green
Other Planes of There: Selected Writings.
Durham, NC: Duke University Press,
2014.

Clement Greenberg
Art and Culture: Critical Essays. Boston:
Beacon Press, [1961] 1965.
The Collected Essays and Criticism. Edited by
John O'Brian. 4 vols. Chicago: University
of Chicago Press, 1986–1993.

Saidiya Hartman
*Scenes of Subjection: Terror, Slavery, and
Self-Making in Nineteenth-Century Africa.*
New York: Oxford University Press, 1997.

Eleanor Heartney
*Postmodern Heretics: The Catholic Imagination in
Contemporary Art.* New York: Midmarch
Arts Press, 2004.

Thomas B. Hess
Willem de Kooning. Exh. cat. New York: The
Museum of Modern Art, 1968.

Denis Hollier
*Against Architecture: The Writings of Georges
Bataille.* Translated by Betsy Wing.
Cambridge, MA: The MIT Press, [1974]
1990.

bell hooks
Art on My Mind: Visual Politics. New York: The
New Press, 1995.

Robert Hughes
*Nothing If Not Critical: Selected Essays on Art and
Artists.* New York: Knopf, 1990.

Gary Indiana
Let It Bleed: Essays 1985–1995. London:
Serpent's Tail, 1996.

Jill Johnston
*Secret Lives in Art: Essays on Art, Literature,
Performance.* Chicago: Chicago Review
Press, 1994.

Donald Judd
Donald Judd Writings. New York: Judd
Foundation/David Zwirner Books, 2016.

Michael Kimmelman
*Portraits: Talking with Artists at the Met, the
Modern, the Louvre and Elsewhere.* New
York: Random House, 1998.

Wayne Koestenbaum
My 1980s & Other Essays. New York: Farrar,
Straus and Giroux, 2013.

Max Kozloff
The Privileged Eye: Essays on Photography.
Albuquerque, NM: University of New
Mexico Press, 1987.

Siegfried Kracauer
*From Caligari to Hitler: A Psychological History of
the German Film.* Revised and expanded
edition. Princeton, NJ: Princeton
University Press, [1947] 2004.
History: The Last Things Before the Last. New
York: Oxford University Press, 1969.

Hilton Kramer
The Age of the Avant-Garde: 1956–1972. New
York: Farrar, Straus and Giroux, 1973.

George Kubler
*The Shape of Time: Remarks on the History of
Things.* New Haven, CT: Yale University
Press, [1962] 2008.

Jean-Claude Lebensztejn
Pissing Figures 1280–2014. New York: David
Zwirner Books, [2016] 2017.

Claude Lévi-Strauss
The Way of the Masks. Translated by Sylvia
Moldeski. Seattle: University of
Washington Press, [1982] 1988.

Samella Lewis
African American Art and Artists. 3rd ed.
Berkeley: University of California Press,
[1978] 2003.

Jacqueline Lichtenstein
*The Eloquence of Color: Rhetoric and Painting in
the French Classical Age.* Translated by
Emily McVarish. Berkeley: University of
California Press, [1989] 1993.

Glenn Ligon
*Yourself in the World: Selected Writings and
Interviews.* Edited by Scott Rothkopf. New
Haven, CT: Yale University Press, 2011.

Janet Malcolm
*Forty-One False Starts: Essays on Artists and
Writers.* New York: Farrar, Straus and
Giroux, 2013.

Thomas McEvilley
Art & Discontent: Theory at the Millennium.
Kingston, NY: McPherson, 1991.

Kobena Mercer
*Welcome to the Jungle: New Positions In Black
Cultural Studies.* New York: Routledge,
1994.

Maurice Merleau-Ponty
*The Merleau-Ponty Aesthetics Reader: Philosophy
and Painting.* Edited by Galen A. Johnson.
Translated by Michael B. Smith.
Evanston, IL: Northwestern University
Press, 1993.

Leonard B. Meyer
*Music, the Arts, and Ideas: Patterns and
Predictions in Twentieth-Century Culture.*
Chicago: University of Chicago Press,
[1967] 1994.

Richard Meyer
*Outlaw Representation: Censorship and
Homosexuality in Twentieth-Century
American Art.* Oxford, UK: Oxford
University Press, 2002.

Annette Michelson
*On the Eve of the Future: Selected Writings on
Film.* Cambridge, MA: The MIT Press,
2017.

Cookie Mueller
*Walking Through Clear Water in a Pool Painted
Black.* New York: Semiotext(e), 1990.

Amy Newman
Challenging Art: Artforum 1962–1974. New
York: Soho Press, 2000.

Bob Nickas
*The Dept. of Corrections: Collected Writings
2007–2015.* New York: Karma, 2015.

Linda Nochlin
Women Artists: The Linda Nochlin Reader.
Edited by Maura Reilly. New York:
Thames & Hudson, 2015.

Brian O'Doherty
Collected Essays. Berkeley: University of
California Press, 2018.

Frank O'Hara
Art Chronicles: 1954–1966. New York: Braziller,
[1975] 1991.

Craig Owens
*Beyond Recognition: Representation, Power, and
Culture.* Edited by Scott Bryson, Barbara
Kruger, Lynne Tillman, and Jane
Weinstock. Berkeley: University of
California Press, 1992.

Erwin Panofsky
Perspective as Symbolic Form. Translated by
Christopher S. Wood. New York: Zone
Books, [1927] 1991.

Robert Pincus-Witten
Eye to Eye: Twenty Years of Art Criticism. Ann Arbor, MI: UMI Research Press, 1984.

Marcel Proust
Proust, Marcel, and John Ruskin. *On Reading.* Translated by Damion Searls. London: Hesperus Press, 2011.

Arlene Raven
Feminist Art Criticism: An Anthology. Edited by Arlene Raven, Cassandra L. Langer, and Joanna Frueh. New York: Routledge, [1988] 2018.

Lane Relyea
Your Everyday Art World. Cambridge, MA: The MIT Press, 2013.

Alois Riegl
Historical Grammar of the Visual Arts. Translated by Jacqueline E. Jung. New York: Zone Books, [1966] 2004.

Cedric Robinson
Black Marxism: The Making of the Black Radical Tradition. Chapel Hill, NC: University of North Carolina Press, [1983] 2000.

Avital Ronell
The Telephone Book: Technology, Schizophrenia, Electric Speech. Lincoln, NE: University of Nebraska Press, 1989.

Jacqueline Rose
The Jacqueline Rose Reader. Edited by Justin Clemens and Ben Naparstek. Durham, NC: Duke University Press, 2011.

Harold Rosenberg
The Tradition of the New. Boston: Da Capo Press, [1959] 1994.

Robert Rosenblum
On Modern American Art: Selected Essays by Robert Rosenblum. New York: Abrams, 1999.

Raymond Roussel
Impressions of Africa. Translated by Rayner Heppenstall and Lindy Foord. London: Calder Publications, [1910] 1988.

John Ruskin
Modern Painters. Abridged and edited by David Barrie. New York: Knopf, [1843–1860] 1988.

Edward Said
On Late Style: Music and Literature Against the Grain. New York: Pantheon, 2006.

David Salle
How to See: Looking, Talking, and Thinking About Art. New York: W. W. Norton & Company, 2016.

Irving Sandler
A Sweeper-Up After Artists: A Memoir. New York: Thames & Hudson, 2003.

Meyer Schapiro
Modern Art: 19th and 20th Centuries: Selected Papers. New York: Braziller, [1978] 2011.

James Schuyler
Selected Art Writing of James Schuyler. Edited by Simon Pettet. Boston: Black Sparrow Press, 1999.

Sanford Schwartz
The Art Presence. New York: Horizon Press, 1982.

Kenneth Silver
Esprit de Corps: The Art of the Parisian Avant-Garde and the First World War, 1914–1925. Princeton, NJ: Princeton University Press, [1989] 1992.

Rebecca Solnit
As Eve Said to the Serpent: On Landscape, Gender, and Art. Athens, GA: University of Georgia Press, 2001.

Abigail Solomon-Godeau
Photography at the Dock: Essays on Photographic History, Institutions, and Practices. Minneapolis: University of Minnesota Press, 1994.

Susan Sontag
Against Interpretation. New York: Picador, [1966] 2001.

Gayatri Chakravorty Spivak
An Aesthetic Education in the Era of Globalization. Cambridge, MA: Harvard University Press, 2012.

Leo Steinberg
Other Criteria: Confrontations with Twentieth-Century Art. Chicago: University of Chicago Press, [1972] 2007.

Adrian Stokes
The Image in Form: Selected Writings of Adrian Stokes. Edited by Richard Wollheim. New York: Penguin Books, 1972.

David Levi Strauss
From Head to Hand: Art and the Manual. Oxford, UK: Oxford University Press, 2010.

David Sylvester
Interviews with American Artists. New Haven, CT: Yale University Press, 2001.

Michael Taussig
What Color Is the Sacred? Chicago: University of Chicago Press, 2009.

Robert Farris Thompson
Flash of the Spirit: African & Afro-American Art & Philosophy. New York: Vintage, 1984.

Anne M. Wagner
Three Artists (Three Women): Modernism and the Art of Hesse, Krasner, and O'Keeffe. Berkeley: University of California Press, 1996.

Simone Weil
Gravity and Grace. New York: Routledge, [1947] 2002.

Lawrence Weschler
Seeing Is Forgetting the Name of the Thing One Sees: Over Thirty Years of Conversations with Robert Irwin. Expanded edition. Berkeley: University of California Press, [1982] 2009.

Alfred North Whitehead
Modes of Thought. New York: Free Press, [1938] 1968.

Oscar Wilde
The Complete Works of Oscar Wilde: Stories, Plays, Poems and Essays. New York: Harper Perennial, [1989] 2008.

Ellen Willis
The Essential Ellen Willis. Edited by Nona Willis Aronowitz. Minneapolis: University of Minnesota Press, 2014.

Names of people, artworks, books, magazines, and institutions have been indexed. Underlined page spans indicate an interview.

400 Blows, The (film) 324

Abbott, Steve 331–2
Abelove, Henry 114–15
Acconci, Vito 8, 404
Acker, Kathy 259–61, 263, 264–5, 267–8
Acosta, Oscar Zeta 451
AIM (American Indian Movement) 444–52
Als, Hilton 16–27; and *Artforum* 20; and Barnard College 19; and *The City Sun* 20; and Nesbit, Molly 339, 343–4, 348, 351; and The New School 19; and Turner, Darryl 19–20; and *The Village Voice* 20; *Alice Neel, Uptown* 24–5; *I Only Want You to Love Me* (artwork) 20; *Life Is Beautiful Now* (exhibition) 20; "The Only One" 26; "Tristes Tropiques" 22; *White Girls* 21–2, 24; *The Women* 21–2, 23, 25, 26, 27
American Indian Movement (AIM) 444–52
Americans (exhibition) 456–8
Andre, Carl 378
Antioch College 444
Aranke, Sampada 80
Arbus, Diane 384
Arneson, Robert 39
Arnett, Bill 320
Art in America (journal): and Bois, Yve-Alain 59–60; and Cotter, Holland 93, 96–7, 99; and Foster, Hal 149–50, 156; and Hickey, Dave 209; and Krauss, Rosalind 276; and Myles, Eileen 327, 330; and Rose, Barbara 382; and Saltz, Jerry 396, 397, 399; and Schjeldahl, Peter 418–19, 419–20; and Smith, Roberta 461–2; and Yau, John 516
Art Institute of Chicago 391
Art International (journal) 112, 168, 274, 287, 379

Art Journal (journal) 287
Artforum (journal) 8, 9, 112, 148–9, 384–5, 397; and Als, Hilton 20; and Fried, Michael 175; and Goodeve, Thyrza Nichols 192–3, 196; and Krauss, Rosalind 273, 277–8; and Nesbit, Molly 343; and Rose, Barbara 379–80, 386; and Smith, Roberta 462; and Yau, John 516
ARTnews (journal) 166, 169, 372, 377–8; and Ashbery, John 30, 115; and Berkson, Bill 41, 44; and Crimp, Douglas 111–12, 114, 115; and Schjeldahl, Peter 419
Arts Magazine (journal): and Cotter, Holland 92–3; and Fried, Michael 167–8; and Judd, Donald 364; and Lippard, Lucy 286–7; and Perl, Jed 358; and Saltz, Jerry 395; and Schwabsky, Barry 434, 435; and Yau, John 516
Artscribe (journal) 435
Ashbery, John 11, 28–37; and *ARTnews* 30, 115; and Berkson, Bill 43, 47; and Cotter, Holland 91–2; and Crimp, Douglas 115; and Harvard University 37; and Hess, Thomas B. 30; and New York University 30; and Schjeldahl, Peter 414, 418; and Schuyler, James (Jimmy) 30; and Yau, John 515–16, 518, 521–2, 523, 524; *Hebdomeros* 33–4; *Illuminations* 34; *John Ashbery: Collages* (exhibition) 33; *Other Traditions* 37, 524; *Some Trees* 36; *The Tennis Court Oath* 36
Ash-Milby, Kathleen 452
Ashton, Dore 288
Assis, Machado de 21
Associated Press 45–6
Augustine, Saint 47
Auster, Paul 520
Austin, J. L. 208, 313
Avant-Garde (journal) 416

Bacharach, Burt 17–18
Baker, Betsy 149, 276; and Cotter, Holland 93, 96–7; and Crimp, Douglas 111–12; and Myles, Eileen 331; and Saltz, Jerry 396; and Smith, Roberta 461–2; and Yau, John 515–16
Bakhtin, Mikhail 239

Baldwin, James 88, 124, 136, 503–5
Balken, Debra Bricker 127
Balthus (Balthasar Klossowski de Rola) 358,
    373
Bankowsky, Jack 339, 343
Banks, Dennis 445
Bannard, Darby 166, 167
Barad, Karen 75–6
Baraka, Amiri 12, 132, 247, 308–10, 319, 417
Bard College 514
Barnard College 19, 342, 375
Barney, Matthew 12, 193–6, 198, 202, 399
Barthes, Roland 61, 154, 156; and Bois,
    Yve-Alain 52–4, 62–3; and Krauss,
    Rosalind 279–80; *A Lover's Discourse* 19,
    53; *Roland Barthes par Roland Barthes* 53;
    Writing Degree Zero 280
Bataille, Georges 65, 67, 156–7, 278–9
Bates, Ulku 94
Beatles, the 324
Bellini, Giovanni 9
Benglis, Lynda 223, 384
Benjamin, Walter 349, 350–1
Benzi, Roberto 50
Bergman, Ingmar 324
Berkeley (University of California) 70, 80,
    342
Berkson, Bill 9, 38–47; and *ARTnews* 41, 44;
    and Ashbery, John 43, 47; and Goodeve,
    Thyrza Nichols 200–1; and San Francisco
    Art Institute 45; *Sudden Address* 45
Berrigan, Ted 326
Blackmur, R. P. 164
Blackwood, Michael 386
Bladen, Ronald 466
Blair, Dorothy 285
Blinman, Eric 301
Bloom, Harold 147
Blues for Smoke (exhibition) 429–30
Bluhm, Norman 518–20
Bogan, Louise 163
Bois, Yve-Alain 48–67; and *Art in America*
    59–60; and Barthes, Roland 52–4, 62–3;
    and Fried, Michael 59; and Greenberg,
    Clement 57; and Krauss, Rosalind 57–8,
    59, 278; and *October* 157; *Art Since 1900* 64;
    Formless: A User's Guide 64–5; *Painting as*

Model 57, 59, 60–1, 64; *Rendezvous:
    Masterpieces from the Centre Georges
    Pompidou and the Guggenheim Museums*
    (exhibition) 49
Bonnefoi, Christian 56
Bourdon, David 418
Bowles, Paul 187–8
Brancusi, Constantin 50
Brant, Peter 387
Brooklyn College 362, 515
Brooklyn Rail, The (journal) 9–10
Brothers Quay, the 196, 197
Brown, Henry "Box" 128
Bryant, William Cullen 324
Buchloh, Benjamin 157, 345
Bui, Phong 9
Burden, Chris 256
Burton, Scott 462, 465

Cage, John 383
Calder, Alexander 360–1, 372
Canaday, John 288
Cannon, Virginia 412
Caravaggio, Michelangelo Merisi da 172,
    179–81, 425
Carlin, Deborah 307
Caro, Anthony 164, 168, 170, 173, 177, 183
Castelli, Leo 378–9
Catlett, Elizabeth 255, 257
Catullus 264
Centre Georges Pompidou (Paris) 49, 56
Cézanne, Paul 232
Chandler, John 297
Chapman, Marshall 215
Chastel, André 55
Chomsky, Noam 207–8
City Sun, The (newspaper) 20
City University of New York (CUNY) 60, 90,
    94
Clark, Lygia 51–2
Clark, Ron 188–9, 196
Clark, T. J. 70, 151
Clay, Jean 51, 56, 292
Cleveland Museum of Art 121
Clifford, James 190–1
Cohen, George 286
Collège de France 54, 55

Columbia University 94–5, 149–52, 343–4,
    356–7, 375–6
*Coming Attractions: An Anthology of American
    Poets in Their Twenties* (book) 325
Cone, James 317
Cook, Walter W. S. 376
Cooke, Lynne, *Mixed Use, Manhattan*
    (exhibition) 109
Coolidge, John 274
Cooper, Dennis 325, 331–2
Copeland, Huey 12, 68–82; and Moten, Fred
    75; and Simpson, Lorna 76; and Wallace,
    Michele 74–5; *Bound to Appear* 70, 71–3,
    76–8, 79, 80–1; *In the Shadow of the Negress*
    80–1; "Outtakes" 76; *Touched by the Mother*
    76
Coplans, John 277–8, 384–5
Copley, John Singleton 86–7
Corbett, William 307–8
Cote, Alan 516
Cotter, Holland 84–100; and *Art in America*
    93, 96–7, 99; and *Arts Magazine* 92–3; and
    Ashbery, John 91–2; and Baker, Betsy 93,
    96–7; and Columbia University 94–5;
    and CUNY 90, 94; and Hunter College
    94; and *The New York Times* 96–7
Cowley, Malcolm 360
Crary, Jonathan 156
Crashaw, Richard 414
Creeley, Robert 309
Cremaster film cycle 12, 193–6, 198, 202, 399
Crimp, Douglas 102–18; and *Art International*
    112; and *ARTnews* 111–12, 114, 115; and
    Baker, Betsy 111–12; and English, Darby
    128; and Greenberg, Clement 109–10;
    and Krauss, Rosalind 112, 113; and *October*
    113–14, 157; *AIDS Demo Graphics* 114, 127;
    Before Pictures 105–7, 110, 112, 114–15;
    "Getting the Warhol We Deserve" 116–17;
    Greater New York (exhibition) 109;
    Melancholia and Moralism 114, 117; *Mixed
    Use, Manhattan* (exhibition) 109; *On the
    Museum's Ruins* 112–13, 127, 132; "Our Kind
    of Movie": The Films of Andy Warhol 110;
    "Pictures" 110
Croce, Arlene 357
Crow, Tom 341

CUNY (City University of New York) 60, 90,
    94
Curtis, Jackie 43

Damisch, Hubert 54, 56, 60, 67
David, Jacques-Louis, *The Oath of the Horatii*
    175–6, 179
Davis, Asa J. 250
de Chirico, Giorgio, *Hebdomeros* 33–4
de Kooning, Willem 45, 281, 360
De Quincey, Thomas 212–13
DeAk, Edit 295
Delaney, Beauford 311–12
Deleuze, Gilles 213
Denby, Edwin 91, 357, 365
De-Pixelation (exhibition) 133–4
Derrida, Jacques 56, 58, 61, 156, 313, 316
Dewhurst, Robert 263
di Paolo, Giovanni 392
Dia Center for the Arts 506–8
Dial, Thornton 320
Dickens, Charles 233
Dickinson, Emily 85, 86
Diderot, Denis 174, 175, 176, 194
Didi-Huberman, Georges 65
Dlugos, Tim 325
Documenta X (exhibition) 344
Douglass, Frederick 79
Droll, Donald 293
Duchamp, Alexina (Teeny) 340
Duchamp, Marcel 208, 282, 339, 343
Duncan, David Douglas 356
Dunham, Carroll 463–4, 485–6
Durham, Jimmie 445–6, 447, 450
Duve, Thierry de 282

Eco, Umberto 52–3
École Pratique des Hautes Études 52–3
Edel, Leon 361–2
Edwards, Brent 319
El Greco 163
El Kholti, Hedi 262
Eleey, Peter 109
Eliot, George 266–7
Eliot, T. S. 169
Ellison, Ralph 508
Ellmann, Richard 361

English, Darby 12, <u>120–43</u>; and Crimp,
    Douglas 128; and Moten, Fred 132–3;
    and University of Rochester 128; *1971: A
    Year in the Life of Color* 125, 130, 134–5; *To
    Describe a Life* 124, 135, 136–7, 140
Erlich, Victor 65
Ernst, Max 287–8

Fagin, Larry 39–40
Fassbinder, Rainer Werner 324
Fast Forward: Paintings from the 1980s
    (exhibition) 473–4
Faulkner, William 22
Feature Gallery (New York) 20
Feher, Michel 156
Fénéon, Félix 57
Fiedler, Leslie 164
Fischbach Gallery (New York) 293
Fischl, Eric 394–5
Fitzgerald, Frances 449–50
Fitzsimmons, Jim 274, 287, 379
FlashArt (journal) 435
Focillon, Henri 346, 347, 349; *The Life of
    Forms in Art* 124, 140
Fogg Museum of Art (Harvard) 170, 310–11
Forster, E.M. 218
Foster, Hal 7, <u>144–59</u>; and *Art in America*
    149–50, 156; and Columbia University
    149–52; and Fried, Michael 151; and
    Krauss, Rosalind 146–7, 150–1; and
    October 156–8; *The Anti-Aesthetic* 156; *Art
    Since 1900* 158–9; *Bad New Days* 152; *Design
    and Crime* 152–3; *The Return of the Real* 116
Foucault, Michel 58, 213, 278, 342
Francis, Robert 34
Franco, James 403–4
Frankenthaler, Helen 365
Freedberg, David 344
Freedberg, Sydney 274
Freud, Sigmund 53
Fried, Michael 12, 130, 149, <u>160–85</u>, 315, 467;
    and *Art International* 168; and *Artforum*
    175; and *Arts Magazine* 167–8; and Bois,
    Yve-Alain 59; and Foster, Hal 151; and
    Greenberg, Clement 166–7, 169–70; and
    Krauss, Rosalind 173; and Perl, Jed 358;
    and Rose, Barbara 377, 379, 380;

Absorption and Theatricality 174, 175, 176,
    215; "Art and Objecthood" 172, 173–4,
    360; *Four Honest Outlaws* 181; *The Moment
    of Caravaggio* 172, 179; *Why Photography
    Matters as Art as Never Before* 181

Galerie Denise René (Paris) 51
Gallagher, Ellen 201
Gallup, Dick 417
Geldzahler, Henry 382
Giacometti, Alberto 278–9
Ginzburg, Ralph 416
Giorgione 238
Gladstone Gallery (New York) 133–4
Glier, Mike 126
Gober, Robert 211, 223
Goin, Peter 302
Goldin, Leon 356
Goodeve, Thyrza Nichols 12, <u>186–204</u>; and
    Artforum 192–3, 196; and Berkson, Bill
    200–1; and New York University 188–9;
    and Whitney Museum of American Art
    372–3; *How Like a Leaf* 196–8; "Twilight of
    the Art World: From Representation to On-
    tology" 202; "You Sober People" 199, 200
Goodman, Marian 412
Gorchov, Ron 481–2
Gould, Stephen Jay 317
Goya (journal) 377
Goya, Francisco 236
Greater New York (exhibition) 109
Green, Renée 71–2, 80
Greenberg, Clement 64, 130, 315, 365, 432;
    and Bois, Yve-Alain 57; and Crimp,
    Douglas 109–10; and Fried, Michael
    166–7, 169–70; and Krauss, Rosalind
    274–5, 276–7; and Lippard, Lucy 293–4;
    and Rose, Barbara 380–1; and Smith,
    Roberta 472, 475; *Art and Culture* 281;
    "Collage" 59, 170
Griffin, Farah Jasmine 253
Grigsby, Darcy Grimaldo 70
Grossman, Allen 165
Guattari, Félix 342
Guggenheim Museum, Solomon R.
    (New York) 49, 111
Gundaker, Grey 253

Guston, Philip 45, 46, 463
Gutiérrez, Gustavo 317

Haacke, Hans 57
Hall, Stuart 506–7
Hals, Frans 121
Hamilton, Ann 196
Hammer Museum (UCLA) 253, 254
Hammond, Harmony 91, 296, 297, 301
Hammons, David 256
Hansa Gallery (New York) 377
Haraway, Donna 191, 192, 196–9, 200
Harlem on My Mind (exhibition) 248
Harney, Stefano 307, 308, 318
Harper, Phillip Brian 74–5
Harrison, Rachel 412
Hartman, Saidiya 79
Harvard University 60, 87, 88; and Ashbery,
    John 31, 37; and Krauss, Rosalind 274;
    and Moten, Fred 306–7, 309
Heilmann, Mary 226
Hemingway, Ernest 217, 218
Herbert, Robert (Bob) 60, 342, 351
Heresies (journal) 295–6, 297
Herrnstein, Richard 316
Hess, Thomas B. 30, 368–9, 378
Hesse, Eva 290–1
Hickey, Dave 7, 10, 206–28, 369, 403; *Air
    Guitar* 213; and *Art in America* 209; *The
    Invisible Dragon: Four Essays on Beauty* 212,
    213–14; *Obit: The Musical* 212; *Pirates and
    Farmers* 212; *Prior Convictions* 227
Hirschhorn, Thomas 133–4, 135
Hirst, Damien 211–12, 219–20
Hofstra, David 488
Holiday, Billie 505
Hollier, Denis 278–9
Howard, Richard 61
Howard University 497
Hughes, Chris 362
Hunter College (New York) 94, 481–2
Hurston, Zora Neale 71, 128–9
Hustvedt, Siri 230–43; "Becoming Others"
    231; *The Blindfold* 235; "The Delusions of
    Certainty" 239; "Embodied Visions:
    What Does It Mean to Look at a Work of
    Art?" 237; *Living, Thinking, Looking* 237;

Mysteries of the Rectangle 234, 237; *What I
Loved* 234; *A Woman Looking at Men Looking
at Women* 231

Incomplete History of Protest, An (exhibition)
    498–9
Information (exhibition) 291–2
Institute of American Indian Arts (Santa Fe)
    453
Institute of Fine Arts (New York University)
    110
International News Service 46
Isabella Stewart Gardner Museum (Boston)
    86

Jakobson, Roman 65, 320
James, Henry 221
Jameson, Fredric 59, 64
Janeway, Carol Brown 363–4
Janson, H. W. 249
Jefferson, Margo 507
Jersey Journal, The (newspaper) 415–16
Jewish Museum (New York) 289
Johns, Jasper 137, 224, 379, 380–1, 514, 518,
    521–2
Johns Hopkins University 58–9
Johnson, Barbara 309
Johnson, Joyce 500–1
Johnson, Ray 90
Johnston, Jill 91, 333–5
Jokel, Lana 386
Jones, Elvin 311–12
Jones, Hettie 256
Jones, Kellie 11–12, 244–57; *Deja Vu*
    (exhibition) 250; *Energy/Experimentation*
    (exhibition) 245; *EyeMinded: Living and
    Writing Contemporary Art* 245; *Now Dig
    This!* 253, 254; *South of Pico* 253, 256
Jones, Lisa 248–9
Jones, Willi Posey 495
Journal of Art, The (journal) 385, 387
Journeys from Berlin/1971 (film) 189–90
Joyce, James 361
Judd, Donald 128, 364, 468; and Krauss,
    Rosalind 274; and Rose, Barbara 377,
    380; and Smith, Roberta 461, 467, 469,
    470–1, 473

Kael, Pauline 357
Karp, Ivan 379
Kelly, Ellsworth 115–16
Kelly, Robert 513
Kermani, David 36–7, 115
Kierkegaard, Søren 238–9, 242
Kimmelman, Michael 137
Kirby, Michael 104
Kitaj, R.B. 263
Knight, Christopher 216
Koch, Kenneth 31, 41, 416
Koolhaas, Rem 344
Koons, Jeff 118, 211, 223, 372–3, 489
Kozloff, Joyce 295, 296
Kozloff, Max 287, 290, 379–80, 432, 461
Kramer, Hilton 167–8, 286, 294, 362, 364–5, 366, 382
Kramer, Peter 200
Kraus, Chris 11, 258–70; and Myles, Eileen 327–8; *After Kathy Acker* 259–61; *Aliens & Anorexia* 263; "Emotional Technologies" 270; *How to Shoot a Crime* 269; *I Love Dick* 261, 267; "Shit on My Sleepmask" 259; *Torpor* 261, 270; *Video Green* 259, 261, 262–3; *Where Art Belongs* 264; "You Are Invited to Be the Last Tiny Creature" 264
Kraus, Karl 265
Krauss, Rosalind 7, 60, 111, 149, 272–82, 315, 341; and *Art in America* 276; and *Art International* 274; and *Artforum* 273, 277–8; and Bois, Yve-Alain 57–8, 59, 278; and Crimp, Douglas 112, 113; and Foster, Hal 146–7, 150–1; and Fried, Michael 173; and Greenberg, Clement 274–5, 276–7; and Harvard University 274; and Judd, Donald 274; and Nesbit, Molly 343, 348; and *October* 157, 277–8, 384–5; *L'Amour fou* 358; *Formless: A User's Guide* 64–5; "Grids" 275; "Notes on the Index" 57; *The Optical Unconscious* 279, 352; "Sculpture in the Expanded Field" 275; *Under Blue Cup* 280, 282; "Video: The Aesthetics of Narcissism" 278
Kropotkin, Pyotr 316
Kruger, Barbara 148
Kubler, George 124, 250; *The Shape of Time* 218, 220, 346–7

Kwinter, Sanford 156

La Rocco, Claudia 45–6
Lamont, Buddy 448
Lauretis, Teresa de 191–2
Lawrence, D.H. 207
Lebensztejn, Jean-Claude 60
Leider, Philip 149, 274, 293, 378
Leonard, Zoe 107, 136
Leonardo, Boff 317
Levinthal, David 225
Lewis, Norman 248
Lewis, Samella 255
LeWitt, Sol 295
Leys, Ruth 167, 171
Leyshon, Cressida 412
Liberman, Alexander 362
Lichtenstein, Jacqueline 214
Life (journal) 29
Life Is Beautiful Now (exhibition) 20
Ligon, Glenn 12, 80, 128–9, 136–7; *To Disembark* 71–2, 76–7; *Narratives* 71; *Runaways* series 128; *Untitled (I Feel Most Colored When I Am Thrown Against a Sharp White Background)* 128; *Untitled (I Remember the Very Day That I Became Colored)* 128
Lipman, Jean 382
Lippard, Lucy 11, 284–303, 498, 501–2; and *Art International* 287; and *Art Journal* 287; and *Arts Magazine* 286–7; and Greenberg, Clement 293–4; and Rose, Barbara 384; *From the Center* 297; "Change and Criticism: Consistency and Small Minds" 302; *Changing* 288; *Cracking* 293; *Down Country* 301–2; *Eva Hesse* 290; *The First Stone* 292–3; *I See/You Mean* 292; *Information* (exhibition) 291–2; *The Lure of the Local* 300; *Mixed Blessings* 297–8; *Overlay* 298–9, 300; *Undermining* 301
Longfellow, Henry Wadsworth 85
Lorde, Audre 132
Los Angeles (University of California) 60
Lotringer, Sylvère 259, 261, 262, 269
Louis, Morris 162, 170
Loving, Al 245
Lowell, Robert 87, 512
Luna, James 452, 453

Macula (journal) 55, 56, 57
Madame Realism (Lynne Tillman) 479–80, 482
Maleczech, Ruth 266
Man Who Envied Women, The (film) 191
Manet, Édouard 174–5, 427
Mangold, Sylvia Plimack 330
Mapplethorpe, Robert 214–15, 365
Marian Goodman Gallery (New York) 181–2
Marker, Chris 345
Marnie (film) 189
Marshall, Kerry James, *Untitled (Policeman)* (artwork) 137, 138–9
Martin, Agnes 106, 177
Martin, Richard 93, 395, 434, 516
Marx, Karl 313
Matisse, Henri 56, 100
Mattoon, Danielle 462
Maupin, David 344
Mauss, Marcel 67
McQueen, Steve 454
McShine, Kynaston 291, 292
Means, Russell 445–6
Mendelsohn, Everett 316
Merleau-Ponty, Maurice 172–3
Merrill, James 124
Metropolitan Museum of Art, The (New York) 98, 163, 248
Meyer, Richard 137
Michelson, Annette 113, 149, 190, 277–8, 385
Michigan, University of 71
Millet, Jean-François 176
Minneapolis Institute of Art 232
Misfits, The (film) 24
Miss, Mary 296
Mixed Use, Manhattan (exhibition) 109
Mnuchin, Robert 387
MoMA PS1 (New York) 109, 253, 254
Mondrian, Piet 50, 63–4, 232
Monet, Claude 513
Monroe, Marilyn 24
Montano, Linda 8–9
Morellet, François 51
Morris, Robert 145
Morrison, Toni 500
Moten, Fred 12, 304–21; and Copeland, Huey 75; and English, Darby 132–3; and

Harvard University 306–7, 309; *Black and Blur* 310–11; "The Case of Blackness" 81; *In the Break* 80, 308–9, 310, 314; *The Undercommons* 317
Motherwell, Robert 276
Mrabet, Mohammed 187–8
Munch, Edvard 232, 426–7
Murray, Elizabeth (Liz) 226, 245–6, 257
Musée National d'Art Moderne (Paris) 49, 50
Museo Reina Sofía (Madrid) 53, 109
Museum of Art and Design (New York) 33
Museum of Fine Arts (Boston) 86, 87, 513
Museum of Modern Art, The (New York) 18, 29, 98, 281, 291–2, 372, 495–6; MoMA PS1 109, 253, 254
Myers, John Bernard 518–19
Myles, Eileen 11, 262, 322–36; and *Art in America* 327, 330; and Kraus, Chris 327–8; and *The Village Voice* 329, 334; *Chelsea Girls* 324, 328, 329, 330; *The New Fuck You* 335; *Not Me* 328

Nation, The (journal) 438
National Gallery of Art (Washington, DC) 281
National Museum of the American Indian (Washington, DC) 456–8
Neel, Alice 24–5
Nesbit, Molly 194, 338–53; and Als, Hilton 339, 343–4, 348, 351; and *Artforum* 343; and Barnard College 342; and Krauss, Rosalind 343, 348; *Atget's Seven Albums* 342, 343, 352; "The Copy" 339–41; *Midnight: The Tempest Essays* 347–8; *The Pragmatism in the History of Art* 343, 346; *Their Common Sense* 343, 348, 352
New Criterion, The (journal) 358, 362, 364
New Museum (New York) 20
New Republic, The (journal) 358, 363, 366
New School, The (New York) 19, 42
New York (journal) 91, 403–4
New York Arts Journal (journal) 90, 91
New York Review of Books, The (journal) 363, 372–3
New York Times, The (newspaper) 96–7, 462, 464, 465

New York University 30, 110, 188–9
New Yorker, The (journal) 92, 216, 412
Newman, Amy 9
Newsweek (journal) 46
Nochlin, Linda 126
Noland, Kenneth 12, 170, 177, 183, 294
Notley, Alice 325–6
Now Dig This! Art and Black Los Angeles 1960–1980 (exhibition) 253, 254

Obrist, Hans Ulrich 345
Ochs, Phil 417
O'Connor, Flannery 22
October (journal) 108, 116, 149, 159, 281; and Crimp, Douglas 113, 114, 157; and Foster, Hal 156–8; and Krauss, Rosalind 157, 277–8, 384–5
Ofili, Chris 313
O'Hara, Frank 41, 42, 43, 44, 308, 515, 524–5
Ohlson, Doug 481–2
O'Keeffe, Georgia 115
Olitski, Jules 170, 288
Oppositions (journal) 278
Orozco, Gabriel 345, 351
Owens, Craig 59–60, 148, 149, 479, 483
Owens, Laura 412

Padgett, Ron 326
Page, Evelyn 285–6
Panicelli, Ida 192–3
Panofsky, Erwin 55
Park, Chan-wook 523
Parkett (journal) 195, 196
Passion of Anna, The (film) 324
Paternosto, César 302
Paula Cooper Gallery (New York) 469–70
Pearson, Hank 288–9
Pedro, Laila 10
Pemberton, John 249
Perl, Jed 354–73; and *Arts Magazine* 358; and Columbia University 356–7; and Fried, Michael 358; *Antoine's Alphabet* 364, 369, 370; *Art in America 1945–1970* 357; *Calder: The Conquest of Time* 360, 364; "The Life of the Object" 358; *New Art City* 359, 363, 370; *Paris Without End* 358, 363
Perrone, Jeff 461

Phillips Collection, The (Washington, DC) 273
Phyllis Kind Gallery (New York) 518
Picasso, Pablo 356
Pindell, Howardena 298
Pink Flamingos (film) 324
Piper, Adrian 314
Pollock, Jackson 57, 379
Pope, Alexander 397–8
Pope.L 135
Popper, Karl 317
Pound, Ezra 512–13
Prélude à la gloire (film) 50
Presley, Elvis 324
Prince, Richard 152
Princeton University 146, 164, 165–6
Proust, Marcel 21
Pryor, Richard 22–3
Purifoy, Noah 254

Rainer, Yvonne 107, 189–92, 202
Rancière, Jacques 342
Ranney, Ed 301–2
Rauschenberg, Robert 18, 320, 379
Réalités (journal) 51
Recherches (journal) 342
Reed, Rex 523
Reese Palley (New York) 209
Réforme (journal) 50
Reinhardt, Ad 289; *Art-as-Art* 383
Rembrandt 426
Rendezvous: Masterpieces from the Centre Georges Pompidou and the Guggenheim Museums (exhibition) 49
René, Denise 51
Renoir, Pierre-Auguste 310–11, 479, 513–14
Ricard, René 327
Richter, Gerhard 45, 366
Riding, Laura 37
Riefenstahl, Leni 425
Rietman, Jaap 277
Rifkin, Adrian 342
Riley, Bridget 474
Rimbaud, Arthur 34, 35
Ringgold, Faith 493, 494–5, 496–7, 501
Riopelle, Jean-Paul 50
Rivers, Eugene 316

Robho (journal) 51
Robinson, Marilynne 104
Rochester, University of 107, 114, 128
Ronell, Avital 196, 199–200
Rosand, David 357
Rose, Barbara 275, 287, 374–88; and *Art in America* 382; and *Art International* 379; and *Artforum* 379–80, 386; and Fried, Michael 377, 379, 380; and Greenberg, Clement 380–1; and Judd, Donald 377, 380; and Lippard, Lucy 384; and Smith College 375; and Yau, John 518–19; "ABC Art" 382–3; *Autocritique* 375, 387; "Diane Arbus: The Art of Extreme Situations" 384; "Pop in Perspective" 381
Rose, Jacqueline 138
Rosenberg, Harold 166, 169
Rosenblum, Robert 420
Rosenquist, James 145, 419
Rosenthal, Deborah 356–7
Roszak, Theodore 167
Roussel, Raymond 35
Rubin, Jerry 417
Rubin, Larry 294
Ruscha, Ed 212, 281
Rushing, Andrea Benton 250
Ruskin, John 221
Ryan, Kay 140, 141–3
Ryman, Robert (Bob) 55, 64, 297

Saar, Betye 257
Said, Edward 149
Saint-Gaudens, Augustus 422
Sala, Anri 181–2
Saltz, Jerry 12, 215, 390–406, 464–5, 475; and *Art in America* 396, 397, 399; and *Arts Magazine* 395; and Baker, Betsy 396; and *The Village Voice* 401–2; *Beyond Boundaries* 394, 395; "May Day" 397; "Our Bodies, Our Selves, You Asshole" 397; *Sketchbook with Voices* 394; "A Year in the Life: Tropic of Painting" 397, 398
San Francisco Art Institute 45, 201
Sans Soleil (film) 345
Santa Cruz (University of California) 188
Sarah Lawrence College 107, 114, 188
Satie, Erik 361

Saussure, Ferdinand de 313
Scarlett, Roger (Evelyn Page and Dorothy Blair) 285
Schapiro, Meyer 342, 357, 376, 377
Schapiro, Miriam 295–6
Schechner, Richard 104
Schjeldahl, Peter 7, 11, 216, 326–7, 366, 399, 408–27; *The 7 Days Art Columns* 467; and *Art in America* 418–19, 419–20; and *ARTnews* 419; and Schwabsky, Barry 439; "Édouard Manet" 427; "Edvard Munch: The Missing Master" 426; *The Hydrogen Jukebox* 123, 124–5; *Let's See: Writings on Art from* The New Yorker 433
Schnabel, Julian 220–1, 222, 223
Scholder, Fritz 453–4
Schuyler, James (Jimmy) 30
Schwabsky, Barry 428–40; and *Arts Magazine* 434, 435; and *The Nation* 438; and Schjeldahl, Peter 439; and Yale University 434–5; *The Perpetual Guest* 429–30; *Words for Art* 435
Screen (journal) 148
Scully, Vincent 351
Seattle Art Museum 145
Sebastian, Mihail 261
Sellers, Terence 269
Serra, Richard 153–4, 156, 275–6, 422, 423
Seuphor, Michel 50
Sheridan, Philip 414
Sherman, Cindy 148
Shiff, Richard 215–16
Shoemaker, Jack 363
Shoes of the Fisherman, The (film) 318–19
Siegelaub, Seth 295, 297
Silver, Kenneth 19, 344
Silvers, Bob 363
Simon Watson Gallery (New York) 20
Simonds, Charles 293, 297, 298–9
Simone, Nina 9
Simpson, Lorna 71–2, 76, 80, 81
Singier, Gustave 49
Sischy, Ingrid 516–17
Skelton, John 414
Slive, Seymour 274
Smith, Clodus R. 443–4
Smith, David 276

Smith, Kiki 479

Smith, Paul Chaat 442–58; and American Indian Movement (AIM) 444–52; and Durham, Jimmie 445–6; *Americans* (exhibition) 456–8; "The Big Movie" 454; *Everything You Know about Indians Is Wrong* 451; *Like a Hurricane* 446–9, 452, 455; "Radio Free Europe" 447

Smith, Roberta 11, 215, 396, 403–4, 460–76; and *Art in America* 461–2; and *Artforum* 462; and Greenberg, Clement 472; and Judd, Donald 461, 467, 469, 470–1, 473; and *The New York Times* 462, 464, 465; and Whitney Museum of American Art 466; "Scott Burton: Designs on Minimalism" 462, 465

Smith College 285–6, 375

Smithson, Robert 275, 289–90

Solomon R. Guggenheim Museum (New York) 49, 111

Solomon-Godeau, Abigail 126–7

Sondheim, Alan 267

Sontag, Susan 146, 480

Spillers, Hortense 74–5

Spivak, Gayatri Chakravorty 61, 153

Steinberg, Leo 60, 125, 277, 280

Stella, Frank 165–6, 167, 168, 380; *Irregular Polygons* 170, 171

Stella, Rachel 518

Sterne, Laurence 212

Stevens, Wallace 178–9

Stewart, Ellen 104

Studio International (journal) 300

Studio Museum in Harlem 506–8

Taaffe, Philip 473–4, 522–3

Talley, André Leon 26

Tanya Bonakdar Gallery (New York) 404

TDR/The Drama Review (*Tulane Drama Review*) (journal) 104

Tea, Michelle 262

Tel Quel (journal) 385

Texas, University of 207

Thandeka, Reverend Dr. 132

Thek, Paul 91, 263

Thomas, Hank Willis 256

Thomas, Roy 320

Thompson, Robert Farris 11–12, 250–2, 253

Thomson, Virgil 361

Thuillier, Jacques 55

Tibor de Nagy Gallery (New York) 33

Tillim, Sidney 368

Tillman, Lynne 326, 478–91; and Hunter College 481–2; *Cast in Doubt* 483–4, 485; *Haunted Houses* 484, 490; *Madame Realism* 479–80, 482; *What Would Lynne Tillman Do?* 484–5

Tiravanija, Rirkrit 345

Tomlin, Bradley Walker 30

Truffaut, François 324

Tulane Drama Review (TDR/The Drama Review) (journal) 104

Tulane University 103–4

Turner, Darryl 19–20

Turner, J. M. W. 232–3

Tuttle, Richard 9

Tynianov, Yuri 65

University of California: Berkeley 70, 80, 342; Los Angeles (UCLA) 60; Santa Cruz 188, 190–2

University of Michigan 71

University of Rochester 107, 114, 128

University of Texas 207

Utopia Station (artwork) 345–6

van der Weyden, Rogier 99, 513

van Gogh, Vincent 100

Vassar College 340, 341

Vendler, Helen 307

Vermeer, Johannes 235–6

Vignelli, Massimo 278

Village Voice, The (newspaper) 253, 451, 463; and Als, Hilton 20; and Myles, Eileen 329, 334; and Saltz, Jerry 401–2

Vogue (journal) 362

Wagner, Anne M. 70

Wakefield, Neville 195

Waldman, Diane 111

Walker, Alice 499–500

Walker, Hamza 140

Walker Art Center (Minneapolis) 232

Wall, Jeff 181

Wallace, Michele 11, _492–508_; and Copeland, Huey 74–5; and Howard University 497; and The Museum of Modern Art 495–6; and Ringgold, Faith 493, 494–5, 496–7; and Walker, Alice 499–500; and WSABAL (Women Students and Artists for Black Art Liberation) 496, 498–9; *Black Macho and the Myth of the Superwoman* 500–1, 502–3; "Black Popular Culture" (conference) 506–8; "Black Women and White Women" 500–1; *Invisibility Blues* 506–8
Walter, Franz Erhard 53
Warhol, Andy 19, 42, 209–10; *a: A novel* 487
Warrior, Robert 447, 449
Warwick, Dionne 17–18
Waters, John 324
Watteau, Jean-Antoine 176, 364, 369, 370
Way, John 514
Weil, Simone 137–8, 139
Wellesley College 273
Westfall, Stephen 93
Weyden, Rogier van der 99, 513
Wheelock, Arthur 236, 237
White, Hayden 190, 191
Whiteread, Rachel 351
Whitman, Walt 89
Whitney Museum of American Art 98, 188, 196; and Goodeve, Thyrza Nichols 372–3; and Smith, Roberta 466; *Blues for Smoke* (exhibition) 429–30; *Fast Forward: Paintings from the 1980s* (exhibition) 473–4; *An Incomplete History of Protest* (exhibition) 498–9
Whitten, Jack 255, 432
Wieners, John 263
Wieseltier, Leon 362–3, 366
Wilde, Oscar 361; "The Critic as Artist" 13, 397, 424; *De Profundis* 424
Williams, Tennessee 21
Williams, William Carlos 429
Williams, William T. 249
Williams College 125, 131–2
Wilson, E.O. 316
Wilson, Edmund 357
Wilson, Fred 71–3, 80
Wilson, James Q. 316

Wilson, Judith 507
Wilson, Robert 90
Wittgenstein, Ludwig 312
Women Students and Artists for Black Art Liberation (WSABAL) 496, 498–9
Wong, Anna May 523–4
Wright, Bagley 145
Wright, Charles B. 145
Wright, Frank Lloyd 401
Wright, Karen 235
Wright, Virginia 145
WSABAL (Women Students and Artists for Black Art Liberation) 496, 498–9

Yale University 60, 341–2, 351, 378, 434–5
Yau, John 11, 434, _510–25_; and *Art in America* 516; and *Artforum* 516; and *Arts Magazine* 516; and Ashbery, John 515–16, 518, 521–2, 523, 524; and Brooklyn College 515; and Johns, Jasper 521–2; and Rose, Barbara 518–19; *The Wild Children of William Blake* 524
Yuskavage, Lisa 9

Zone Books 156–7
Zwirner, Lucas 10–11

What it Means to Write About Art
Interviews with art critics

Published by
David Zwirner Books
529 West 20th Street, 2nd Floor
New York, New York 10011
+1 212 727 2070
davidzwirnerbooks.com

Managing Director: Doro Globus
Editorial Director: Lucas Zwirner

Editor: Jarrett Earnest
Project Manager: Mary Huber
Copy Editor: Clare Fentress
Indexer: Tanya Izzard

Designed by Mark Thomson

Distributed in the United States
    and Canada by
ARTBOOK | D.A.P.
75 Broad Street, Suite 630
New York, New York 10004
artbook.com

Distributed outside the United States
    and Canada by
Thames & Hudson, Ltd.
181A High Holborn
London WC1V 7QX
thamesandhudson.com

ISBN 978–1–941701–89–8
LCCN 2018906606

Printed in Estonia by Tallinna
    Raamatutrükikoja OÜ